The Masting and Rigging of English Ships of War

1625-1860

The Masting and Rigging of English Ships of War

1625-1860

James Lees

CONWAY

© JAMES LEES 1979, 1984

First published in Great Britain in 1979 by Conway Maritime Press, a division of Chrysalis Books Plc
9 Blenheim Court
Brewery Road
London N7 9NY

www.conwaymaritime.com
Revised edition 1984
Reprinted 1990, 1995, 2001

ISBN 85177 290 0

A member of the Chrysalis Group plc

Printed and bound in Spain by Bookprint, S.L., Barcelona

Contents

Foreword

This is a most useful book for the sailing ship modelmaker and for all students of such ships and their rigging. Mr Lees is a master craftsman himself, employed as a full-time expert at the National Maritime Museum at Greenwich where, under the former Keeper and Head of the Department of Ships, Mr George P B Naish, VRD, BA, FSA, his work for many years has been the care and maintenance of one of the most valuable, extensive, and accurately made collections of ship models in the world. He led the museum's small team which built the superb detailed models of Captain Cook's *Endeavour*, the former Whitby collier-bark which Cook used on his first great voyage, which were presented by the British Government to the Governments of Australia and New Zealand, during the Bicentenary celebrations of Cook's discoveries.

In preparing this work now presented, he has had the great assets of twenty-five years personal and active work with the finest models, access to contemporary drafts, drawings, paintings, builders' models, and books in the unrivalled storehouse of the National Maritime Museum, and his own energy, application and skill. Both the Director, Mr Basil Greenhill, CMG, and the Keeper have been most helpful. A book of this detailed accuracy and stature has long been wanted in the modelmakers' and students' world, and I am delighted that Mr Lees has found time to prepare a work so worthy of the subject

Alan Villiers
Oxford, 1975

Illustrations

Introduction

Knowledge of rigging and the dimensions of masts and yards has been handed down to us through the years by numerous books and manuscripts. Samuel Pepys was instrumental in this by starting to collect books, manuscripts and models, and the preservation of nautical material has been continued up to the present day.

The period after the deposition of King Charles I is one of the finest from the student's point of view but prior to that time and as far back as 1625, a fair amount of information is available. However, 1625, is the earliest date that one can really hope to obtain accurate information. I have therefore taken that date as the starting point of this thesis, finishing about 1860 when sail became of secondary importance to steam.

I have no doubt that some readers will disagree with me over some of the conjectural dates given, but where no definite information has been available I have tried to keep to the nearest feasible establishment date. With regard to the leads of various ropes, especially of those appertaining to the early stunsails, I have looked at these from the rigger's point of view and put down the most likely lead to have been used.

I have been very fortunate in having access to the books, manuscripts and draughts in the National Maritime Museum, and in my position at the museum I have been able to study models much more intensively than the ordinary visitor. I should like to acknowledge the assistance given to me by the staff of the various departments concerned and to thank the Trustees of the National Maritime Museum for permission to make use of the photographs of the models reproduced in this book. The following are the books, manuscripts and other sources that I have drawn upon for information.

The earliest is Manwaring's *Sea Dictionary* written about 1623 though not published until 1644. This is a very interesting book and while only giving a few proportionate sizes of masts and yards and no rope sizes, a very clear description is given of the various ropes, blocks and yards used on board

ship during the early part of the seventeenth century. A manuscript called *A Treatise on Rigging* dated 1625 and reprinted in the *Mariner's Mirror* proved a fount of knowledge. Another book of this period is Smith's *A Sea Grammar* published in 1627 and reprinted a number of times. The reprint dated 1692 has a drawing and numerical guide of a rigged ship of the seventeenth century. This book is another dictionary very similar to Manwaring's. Henry Bond, a teacher of mathematics, wrote a book published in 1642 called *The Boatswain's Art* but the proportionate dimensions of masts and yards given by him do not conform to other books or manuscripts of the period; the lengths given for the masts are about 12 feet longer than those on the Admiralty list of 1640 and the sizes of the spars vary accordingly, as do the sizes of cordage. Some of the details are of use, however, and it has been a case of sorting the good from the bad.

The Science Museum has a manuscript list, written in 1640 for the Lord High Admiral, in which are given the names of ships in the Royal Navy at that time, and the size of masts and spars for each individual ship. This list is of particular interest with regard to the *Sovereign of the Seas* for, with Payne's engraving of the ship, the size of masts and spars given in the list and the rigging details given in Haywood's *The Sizes and Lengths of Rigging* of 1654, a really complete picture is obtainable. This book of rigging by Haywood gives all the sizes of cordage used on the individual ships of that period and names the ships in their different rates. Haywood also had another edition of this book published after the restoration of King Charles II in which he gives the changes in ships' names after the restoration.

Anthony Deane's manuscript, *A Doctrine of Naval Architecture*, preserved in the Pepysian library at Cambridge, was written about 1670. In it are given the sizes of ropes for six rates of ships and a drawing of each rate with a numerical guide for the First Rate. Another manuscript, written by Battine in 1684, explains how to find the dimensions of masts and yards and the breadth of the tops for six rates. He also gives the dimensions of masts, yards, caps and trestletrees for twelve named ships. In 1685 a manuscript was written by an unknown author in which are given the mast and spar dimensions of ships of that year. This manuscript is in the Admiralty Library. The final work of reference for the seventeenth century is another anonymous manuscript which gives the dimensions of the masts and yards for a Sixth Rate ship and also the size of the sails for the same ship. This manuscript is in the National Maritime Museum's collection.

The eighteenth century is covered by a number of books and manuscripts. The first, by Sutherland and published in the year 1711 is called the *Ship Builder's Assistant*. This work shows the proportions of all masts, spars and cordage as worked out from the dimensions of the vessel; it also lists the blocks and deadeyes used on a ship of 600 tons. In 1719 we have the *Establishment Book* which sets down among other things the size of masts, spars, tops and so forth, for ships of that establishment. It also describes the alterations to be carried out to ships built prior to that date to bring them up to the standard set in 1719. Another book by Sutherland, called *Shipbuilding Unveiled* was published in 1729. This book is more for the mathematician than for the rigger as, for example, the proportionate dimensions of masts and spars are given in relation to the square root of tunnage. However in this work are included the dimensions for a ship of 46 feet beam, gun deck length 170 feet, and there are also the dimensions for a ship of a slightly smaller size. The next *Establishment Book*, dated 1745, gives the same sort of information as in that of 1719 but covers the 1745 Establishment. A manuscript written by William Wilkins in 1754 also covers the Establishment of 1745 and includes the number of deadeyes required for eight rates of ships. A dictionary called *A Naval Expositor* was written by Blankley and published in 1750.

In 1765 Murray's *Treatise on Shipbuilding* was published. Giving the dimensions of masts and spars for an East Indiaman, a merchant snow and a merchant sloop, it also describes the method of obtaining the lengths of masts and spars from the length and breadth of the ship for seven rates of naval ships and the proportions of the tops, caps, trestletrees etc. Falconer's *Marine Dictionary* was published in 1769. This very well known work, revised and reprinted several times, has a number of useful plates in the 1769 edition. Among other items the proportions of masts and yards and the dimensions of tops for Royal Navy ships are given. Between the years 1780) and 1795 Admiral Penrose wrote a manuscript giving the mast and spar dimensions according to the Establishment of 1773. This manuscript also gives some of the standing rigging sizes and these and the mast and spar dimensions are for a variety of different rates. A Captain E Rotherham wrote a manuscript between 1787 and 1830 giving not only mast and yard dimensions but also the sizes of the lower and upper trestletrees and crosstrees of the 1773 Establishment. The final book of the eighteenth century, and the most useful, is Steel's *Seamanship and Sail-making* which is a very complete book full of information on seamanship, rigging, sailmaking, mast and spar making, and too well known to require further introduction.

So on to the last century of sail, a century of change and experiment. Seemingly all ideas that looked promising were tried out in the Royal Navy, some of which proved a success and others a failure. Consequently these last years of sail are perhaps the hardest to understand. Very few books of rigging were written in the nineteenth century but fortunately a large number of contemporary rigged models are in existence which helps to cover that deficiency.

In 1815 another edition of Falconer's *Dictionary* was published. This edition was revised by Burney and gives a very full description of blocks and tackles and the dimensions of masts and yards both for Royal and merchant ships. It contains also, as in the previous editions of Falconer, abundant illustrations. Fincham's *Treatise on Masting Ships*, dated 1829, is a book written by a professional mast maker. He goes fully into details and problems of mast and spar making and gives tables for finding the right proportions of all types of ships' masts and spars from the cutter to the First Rate. A book by John Edye called *Equipment and Displacements of Naval Ships* was published in 1832 and gives the dimensions of masts and spars. These dimensions are also to be found in Kipping's *Rudimentary Treatise on Masting, Mast Making and Rigging of Ships* of 1853. About twenty editions of this book have been published but the rigging tables and descriptions are applicable only to merchant ships except for mast and spar dimensions in the appendix which describes Royal Navy practice. Finally, a very useful book called *Naval Cadets Guide* was published in 1860. This was written for the guidance of the trainee cadets by Lieutenant G S Nares, who was at that time an instructor in HMS *Britannia*. The guide is mostly in the form of questions and answers, and gives a very clear picture of the rigging to be found on a First Rate ship at the close of the sail era.

Because very little information is available concerning the pre-clipper ship era I have not attempted to cover the masting or rigging of merchant ships which in many cases depended solely upon the master or owner of the ship, unlike the Royal Navy where set rules were laid down.

While it is not my intention to teach people how to rig a model, I hope that this book will prove of great assistance to those who, having a rudimentary knowledge of the art of rigging, have not had the opportunity to browse through the literature and other material in the National Maritime Museum.

I have set out the information regarding the masts, spars and rigging in what I consider to be the clearest way, and the reader should be able to find any information quickly and easily without hunting through the book. For this reason I have not separated standing and running rigging as I know from experience that this often necessitates turning from one part of a book to another in a most annoying fashion. Also, as I consider that illustrations show much more clearly than words how various items are fitted or rigged, I hope the reader will find those in this book helpful.

With regard to masts and spars, the methods of mast construction are not dealt with in great detail here as I do not consider this to be of any use to the modelmaker but should he want to study this aspect I would refer him to Fincham's book on mast making and Steel's *Masting and Mastmaking* where he will find it very clearly explained. Where possible, as in the case of my description of the taper of masts and spars, I have used manuscripts and books of the period, but where no definite information was available I have based my notes on contemporary models or pictures. I think that the drawings will show more clearly than words the various furnishings on the masts or spars, and by means of both drawings and notes a complete picture can be drawn up. I must, however emphasize that a lot of the following work is based on an average as shown in various sources and models and exceptions will be found, for example, in the number of wooldings on the masts. There were also a small number of ships that varied from the general rule, but in order to give a clear picture, I have thought it best to ignore these exceptions.

Although the majority of the information and photographs are from the archives of the National Maritime Museum, I must acknowledge the permission given to me to reproduce the illustration from Anthony Deane's manuscript in the possession of the Pepysian Library, Magdalene College, Cambridge, and also to the Brethren of Trinity House for their permission to reproduce the photographs of the model *Breda.*

Masting I

1 Masts, bowsprit and jibboom

The first two chapters should be read in conjunction with the mast and spar proportion tables which are to be found in the Appendix.

FORE AND MAIN MASTS

Taper Ratio to the diameter of the mast at the partners:

	To 1719	1719 to 1800	After 1800
Heel	5/6	5/6	5/6
First quarter	42/43	60/61	60/61
Second quarter	14/15	14/15	14/15
Third quarter	5/6	6/7	6/7
Hounds	9/13	3/4	4/5
Head	4/7	5/8	3/4

Cheeks length Up to 1640/60 the cheeks were very short, only covering the hound's length. After this period they were extended to reach two fifths of the distance between the mast cap and the partners at the upper deck; bibs were also introduced, jointed and bolted to the cheeks. The · length held good until 1745 when they were increased to reach a point half-way between the stop at the hounds and the partners. After 1773 they came two thirds of the way down the mast between the hounds and the partners. The width tapered and diminished at the lower end, finishing up a half diameter of the mast wide.

Hounds length In all periods these were two thirds of the length of the mast head. Up to 1640/60 each hound had a sheave set in it to take the lower yard tie. Hounds were, in effect, the part of the cheek that was left flat under the trestletree position. It is quite possible that the name *cheek* was taken to mean, in the first place, the outer shell of the sheaves in the hounds, and when sheaves were no longer required *cheek* was retained.

Bibs came into being a few years after ties were no longer used on the lower yards. They were at all periods four fifths the length of the hounds long, and the breadth was two fifths the bib's length. The thickness at the upper end was half the thickness of the trestletrees.

The front fish was a strengthening piece of wood sometimes fastened on the fore side of the mast. It was from about 1773 that masts were built with a front fish called a *rubbing paunch.* Prior to that date a fish was usually only used for repairing a sprung or damaged mast. Some models do show a front fish prior to 1773, but these are the exceptions rather than the rule and I do not advise fitting them on a model earlier than 1773. The length of the fish was generally the same throughout all periods, coming from the stop at the hounds to within a foot or two from the upper deck. They were made to fit between the cheeks and sometimes a filling piece was fitted between the edge of the cheeks and fish; the depth was usually the same as the cheeks. There were variations, but I have based the above on an average as shown on contemporary models.

The rubbing paunch took the place of the front fish when iron hoops were introduced. It was fitted and made in much the same manner as the fish although it was narrower, being about one third of the diameter of the mast in width, with the depth about one third of the width. Its purpose was to prevent the chafing of the yard against the iron hoops.

Iron hoops were used to bind the masts together, and were put on round the mast under the cheeks and rubbing paunch. Except on the mast head, I have not come across any models fitted with iron hoops prior to the introdection of the iron bands which replaced the rope wooldings in 1800; on the mast head they are shown as early as 1733. I would certainly advise modellers to fit them on the mast head from 1773, and would estimate the date of their introduction as about 1719, but this is only conjectural. On average five hoops, each about 3 inches wide, were put on the mast head – the upper one just below the cap, and the lower one just above the stop at the hounds. When iron bands were fitted, the iron hoops were placed between the bands. Hoops were also put on between the partners and the heel and were spaced the same distance apart as the bands and hoops combined on the upper part of the mast.

Rope wooldings were in use up to 1800. The average number on the main mast varied between nine on large ships and six on small ships; the fore mast had generally one less than the main. The width of the wooldings was 12 inches. Wooden hoops were nailed to the mast at the top and the bottom of each woolding to serve as a protection and to help keep the wooldings in position on the mast. These hoops were about 1 1/2 inches wide.

Iron bands superseded the rope wooldings in 1800. They were 3 inches wide, and the same number were fitted as with rope wooldings. They encircled the mast and lay over the cheeks and under the rubbing paunch.

Mast head battens of wood, eight to each mast, were put on the mast head to protect the rigging from touching the iron hoops or chafing the mast head. The length of these battens was from the stop of the hounds to a point three fifths up the head, the breadth was one eighth of the given diameter of the mast and the thickness was one half of the breadth. The upper ends of the battens were snaped sharply off to the mast.

Mast head length for both main and fore masts, in inches per yard length of the respective mast, was as follows: up to 1670, 3¾ inches; 1670 to 1700, 4½ inches; 1700 to 1719, 4 inches. From 1719 to 1773 it was 5 inches on the main and 4¾ inches on the fore. Thereafter the ratios for both masts became the same once more, which from 1773 to 1850 was 5 inches, and from 1850 onwards 6 inches per yard length of the respective mast.

MIZEN MAST

Taper was of the same ratio as on the main and fore masts.
Cheeks Used only after about 1790 (large ships) and 1805 (all ships): the same proportions as on the main and fore.
Hounds were the same proportionate length as on the main and fore masts.
Bibs were the same proportionate size as on the main and fore masts.

A front fish was not fitted as a permanent furnishing.
A rubbing paunch was fitted in the same way as on the main and fore masts, and was the same proportionate length and width.
Iron hoops are not shown on the mizen mast of any contemporary model in the National Maritime Museum, except on the head. I would, however, advise readers to fit them on large ships after 1773 on the mast head, and on the rest of the mast after 1800. They were fitted in the same way as on the main and fore masts, and were the same width.
Rope wooldings were introduced on

the mizen in about 1733. There were generally two less wooldings on the mizen mast than on the fore mast and these were fitted in the same way as those on the fore and main masts.
Iron bands superseded the rope wooldings in 1800, and were fitted in the same manner as those on the fore and main masts.
Mast head battens were fitted in the same way as the main and fore mast battens.
Mast head length in inches per yard of the mizen mast, was as follows: up to about 1780, 3¾ inches; 1780 to 1805, 4 inches; 1805 to 1850, 4½ inches; from 1850 onwards, 5 inches.

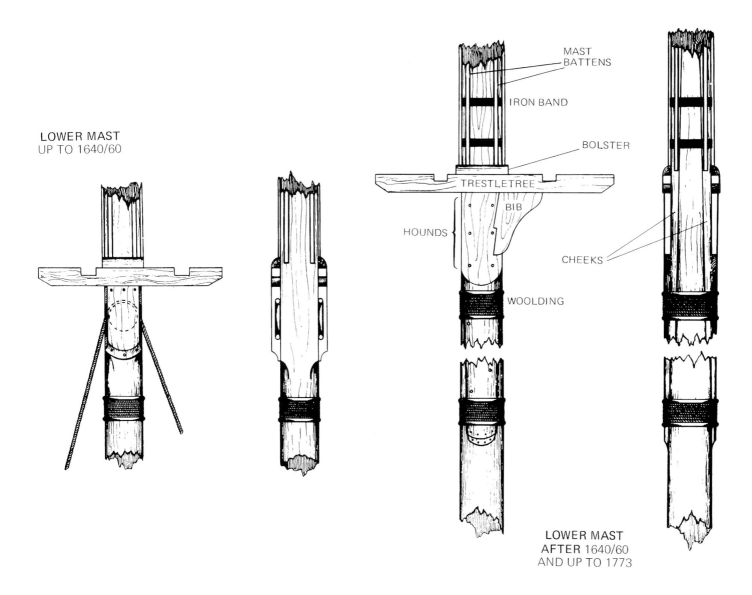

LOWER MAST
UP TO 1640/60

MAST BATTENS

IRON BAND

BOLSTER

TRESTLETREE

BIB

HOUNDS

CHEEKS

WOOLDING

LOWER MAST
AFTER 1640/60
AND UP TO 1773

I MASTING
Fore and main topmasts

FORE AND MAIN TOPMASTS

Taper during all periods, for the lower part of the head was seven tenths, and for the upper part of the head was eleven twentieths, of the diameter of the mast at the lower cap. Up to 1773 from the lower cap to the heel the mast was round, and the same diameter as at the lower cap. After 1773 the mast was octagonal between the heel and the lower cap.

Hounds were octagonal and were half the length of the mast head until 1700, two thirds the length from 1700 to 1773 and from 1773 on they were four fifths the length of the head. The hounds tapered slightly, as will be seen in the illustrations.

The head was left square and was one tenth of the mast in length.

The heeling was the part of the mast which fitted between the lower trestle-trees. It was made square to fit between the crosstrees and the trestle-trees. Up to 1675 the heeling terminated the lower end of the mast; after that date an additional piece was cut on the lower end and was called the *Block*. Up to 1675 the heeling was about 4 feet long; after 1675 the heeling was twice the length of the block.

The block from 1675 to 1745 was left square and was of the same diameter as the octagonal part of the mast. The edges of the block were slightly rounded. From 1745 to 1815 the block was made octagonal. The length of the block up to 1815 was one seventh of the length of the lower mast head. After 1815 the block was made round, and was very short, being only about 6 inches long; it was iron bound.

Top rope sheaves Up to 1657 only one sheave was let into the mast and it ran athwartships. The lower part of the sheave was about one foot from the end of the mast, and a groove was cut in the heel on either side of the mast above the sheave so that the top rope had a clear run round the sheave. After 1675 two sheaves were let in: the lower sheave on the block, running diagonally from the forward port face to the after starboard face; the upper sheave was let in above the heeling on the opposing diagonal plane to the lower one. The lower part of the upper sheave was about 6 inches up from the

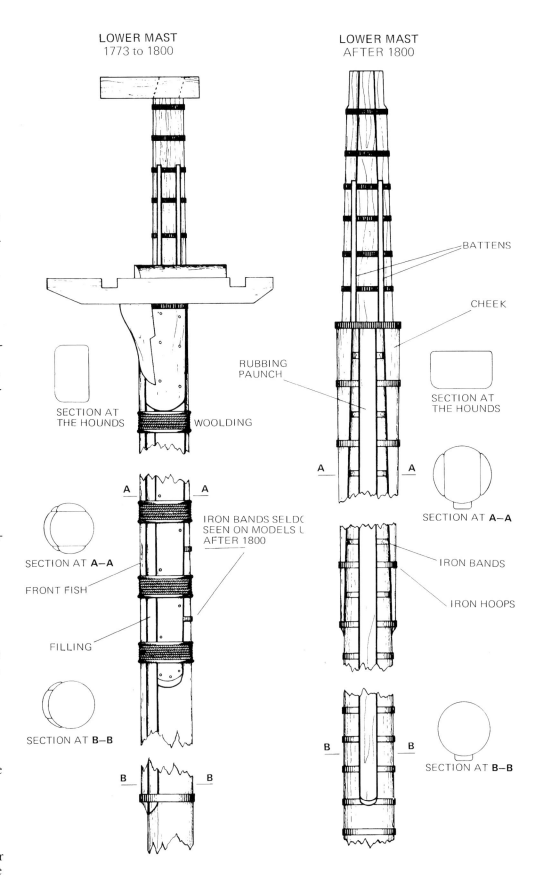

LOWER MAST
1773 to 1800

LOWER MAST
AFTER 1800

BATTENS

CHEEK

RUBBING
PAUNCH

SECTION AT
THE HOUNDS

WOOLDING

SECTION AT
THE HOUNDS

A   A

SECTION AT **A–A**

IRON BANDS SELDO
SEEN ON MODELS L
AFTER 1800

SECTION AT **A–A**

IRON BANDS

SECTION AT **A–A**

FRONT FISH

IRON HOOPS

FILLING

SECTION AT **B–B**

B   B

B   B

SECTION AT **B–B**

upper end of the heeling. Grooves were cut in the heeling for a lead to the lower sheave; it was not necessary for grooves to be cut for the lead to the upper sheave. The length of the sheaves was one and one sixth the diameter of the mast. After 1815 the lower sheave was cut in the heeling just below the fid hole.

The fid hole was cut through the heeling athwartships, halfway up the heeling. The height of the hole was about one third of the given diameter of the topmast, and about one quarter of the given diameter wide.

Cheek blocks from 1745 to 1815, were bolted to the topmast head just below the cap. Two bolts were used, going through one block, through the mast head and through the block on the other side. These bolts acted as pins for the sheaves of the blocks. The length of the cheek blocks was two and a half times the width of the topmast head; the width was seven eighths the width of the topmast head and the thickness half the width of the topmast head. There were two sheaves, one above the other; each sheave was one quarter the thickness of the block wide, and the diameter of the sheaves was the same as the width of the block. The sheave holes were the thickness of the sheave longer than the sheave. The remainder of the cheek was equally divided on the top, middle and lower sections. Tenons were cut out 2 inches square on the top, middle and lower sections; in length these tenons were three eighths the thickness of the block. Mortices were cut into the masthead to take these tenons and the sheave holes were coppered.

MIZEN TOPMAST

Taper was of the same proportions as on the fore and main topmasts.

Hounds were the same proportionate length and diameter as those on the fore and main topmasts. Hounds were not fitted on the mizen topmast until about 1745/50; before that date the upper part of the mizen topmast was finished in exactly the same way as the fore and main topgallant masts. The date of 1745/50 is conjectural and based on models and paintings. Sutherland first mentions mizen topgallant

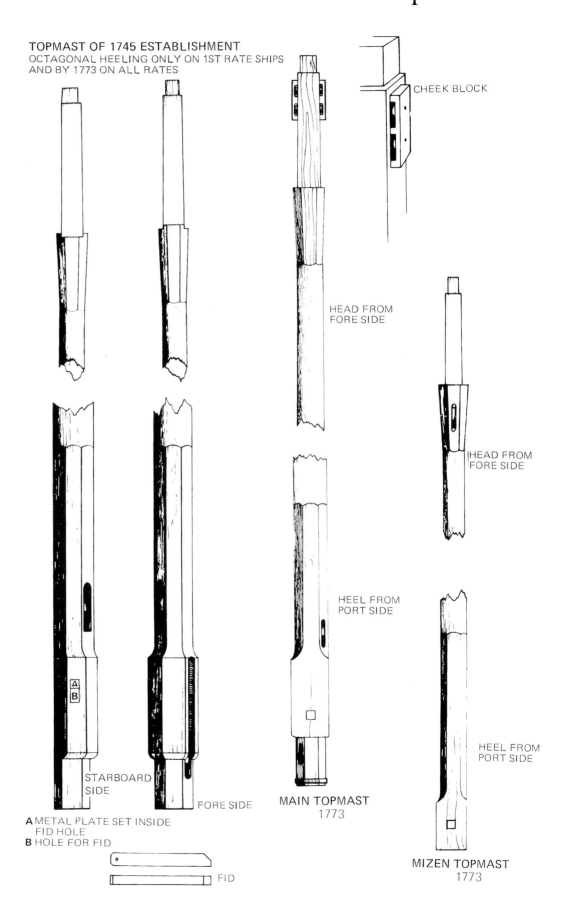

TOPMAST OF 1745 ESTABLISHMENT
OCTAGONAL HEELING ONLY ON 1ST RATE SHIPS AND BY 1773 ON ALL RATES

CHEEK BLOCK

HEAD FROM FORE SIDE

HEAD FROM FORE SIDE

HEEL FROM PORT SIDE

HEEL FROM PORT SIDE

STARBOARD SIDE

FORE SIDE

A METAL PLATE SET INSIDE FID HOLE
B HOLE FOR FID

FID

MAIN TOPMAST 1773

MIZEN TOPMAST 1773

masts in 1729, but only as additional to the topmasts and I think therefore that one must consider the introduction on all ships as about 1745 to 1750. Large ships probably first carried topgallants but they were found on all rates by 1750.

The Head was the same as the fore and main topmast heads from 1810: before that, it was the same as the fore and main topgallant mastheads.

The Heel of the mizen topmast was made like that of the fore and main topgallant masts up to 1745/50; after that date the heeling was the same as the fore and main topmast heeling.

The block was found only on the mizen topmast after 1810 and was then made the same as the fore and main topmast blocks.

Top Rope Sheaves Only one sheave was let into the mast. The sheave ran athwartships in the manner described for the fore and main topmasts prior to 1675, and it ran in the same plane as the upper sheave in the main topmast after that date.

The Fid Hole was cut in the same fashion as those of the fore and main topmasts.

Cheek Blocks were not fitted on the mizen topmast.

FORE AND MAIN TOPGALLANT MASTS

Taper During all periods the hounds and stop were ten thirteenths, and the pole or royal mast one half, of the diameter of the mast at the topmast cap. Up to 1810 the lower part of the mast between the heeling and the topmast cap was left round; after that date it was made octagonal from the heeling to two diameters below the topmast cap.

Hounds were similar to those on the topmasts and were about half the length of the topmast hounds; the upper part was of such a diameter as to just clear the topmast cap. From about 1815 the hounds were round and the rigging stop was a shoulder. In 1834 a funnel to prevent the rigging from chafing the mast was proposed and was adopted shortly afterwards.

The Head of the topgallant mast was made square as on the topmast, and was of the same proportional length

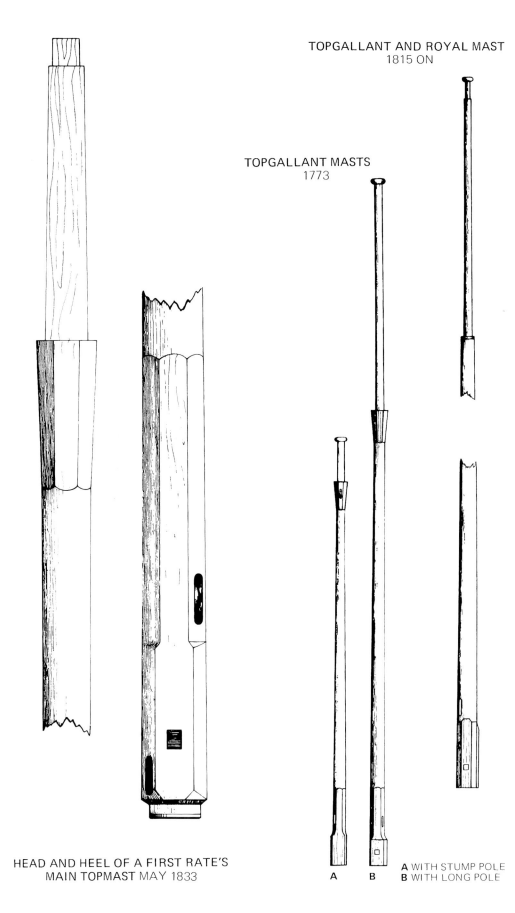

HEAD AND HEEL OF A FIRST RATE'S
MAIN TOPMAST MAY 1833

TOPGALLANT AND ROYAL MAST
1815 ON

TOPGALLANT MASTS
1773

A WITH STUMP POLE
B WITH LONG POLE

A   B

as the topmast head when the flag pole was fitted by trestletrees, crosstrees and a cap. At other times the head, comprising the stump or pole and later the royal mast, was made round. Trestletrees and crosstrees, fitted to the topgallant mast on the hounds on large ships to enable shrouds to be fitted to the long flag pole, were only used up to 1719. On small ships, and after 1719 on all ships, the flag pole was a continuation of the topgallant mast and therefore the mast was round all the way up from the hounds. Just above the stop, for a distance of one diameter of the mast at the stop, the pole or royal mast was left square.

The Heeling terminated the lower end of the topgallant mast, no block being fitted. The heel was square.
The length of the heeling was two and a half times the diameter of the topgallant mast.

Top rope sheave Up to 1745 a sheave, its lower edge just above the heeling, was cut athwartships. After 1745 the sheave was set diagonally from the starboard forward face to the after port face. The length of the sheave was one and one sixth of the diameter of the mast.
Sheave for topgallant yard tie Set fore and aft, the upper edge of the sheave was half the diameter of the mast below the hounds and was in length one and one sixth the diameter of the mast at the stop.
The Fid Hole was cut athwartships half way up the heeling, the proportions being height one third, and width one quarter of the diameter of the topgallant mast.
The Fid of the topgallant masts, from about 1860, differed from the topmast fids, being put in from both sides in the form of wedges. They were secured together with a strop of iron and the reason for this was that rolling and pitching had a tendency to work loose the normal type of fid on the topgallant masts.
Preventer Fid After about 1865 a short piece of iron was put through a hole in the mast two feet above the fid hole as a preventer, should the normal fid work loose.

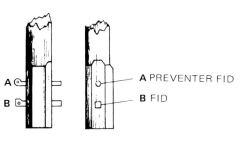

A PREVENTER FID
B FID

TOPGALLANT FID MENTIONED IN ALSTON'S SEAMANSHIP BOOK OF 1860 (THE FID WAS DESIGNED BY SIR ROBERT SEPPINGS)

A ROPE STROP FOR A TACKLE WHEN UNFIDDING
B FID SHOE
C IRON BAND WITH A PIN HOLDING THE SHOE IN POSITION
D FID

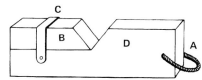

Sheave for staysail halliard From 1709 a sheave was let into the main topgallant mast just above the rigging stop. This sheave was the same size as the tie sheave and ran fore and aft.

MIZEN TOPGALLANT MAST
Taper The mizen topgallant mast was of the same proportionate taper as that of the fore and main topgallant masts; the lower part of the mast was also the same.
The hounds were of the same proportions as those on the fore and main topgallant masts.
The head was the same as on the fore and main topgallant masts.
The heeling was the same as on the fore and main topgallant masts.
The top rope sheave was the same as on the fore and main topgallant masts.
The sheave for topgallant yard tie was the same as on the fore and main topgallant masts.
The fid hole was the same as on the fore and main topgallant masts.
The fid and preventer fid was the same as on the fore and main topgallant masts.

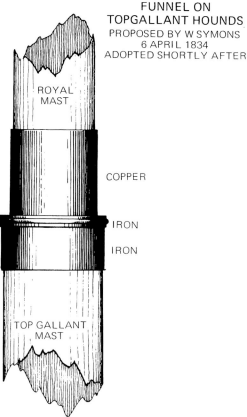

FUNNEL ON TOPGALLANT HOUNDS
PROPOSED BY W SYMONS
6 APRIL 1834
ADOPTED SHORTLY AFTER

ROYAL MAST

COPPER

IRON

IRON

TOP GALLANT MAST

ROYAL MASTS OR POLES
The heel was square halfway up to the topgallant cap, when the topgallant masts carried crosstrees and trestletrees and also a cap. At all other times the royal mast or pole was the continuation of the topgallant mast.
The fid hole was cut athwartships, two diameters above the lower end of the mast.
Taper The ratio of the taper to the diameter of the mast at the topgallant mast cap or rigging stop was six sevenths at the heel, three quarters at the head and five eighths at the upper head at the truck.
Royal rigging stop A shoulder was cut at the head of the royal mast to form a stop seven thirty-thirds of the length of the royal mast below the truck.
The truck generally had two sheaves set in it, one either side. The truck was tenoned onto the head of the mast; the size of the truck was about twice the diameter of the mast at the upper head.
A sheave for the royal yard tie was cut in the royal mast just below the rigging stop and was one and one sixth

I MASTING
Royal masts or poles

BOWSPRIT 1773

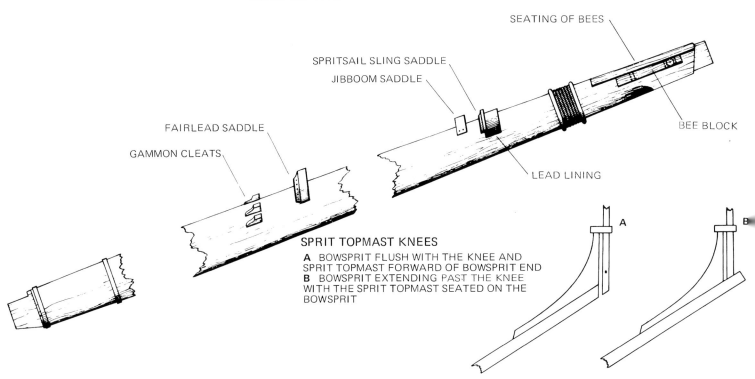

SEATING OF BEES

SPRITSAIL SLING SADDLE

JIBBOOM SADDLE

BEE BLOCK

FAIRLEAD SADDLE

GAMMON CLEATS

LEAD LINING

SPRIT TOPMAST KNEES

A BOWSPRIT FLUSH WITH THE KNEE AND
SPRIT TOPMAST FORWARD OF BOWSPRIT END
B BOWSPRIT EXTENDING PAST THE KNEE
WITH THE SPRIT TOPMAST SEATED ON THE
BOWSPRIT

of the royal mast's diameter in length.
A sheave for the flying jib was let into
the fore royal mast just above the topgallant rigging stop, on some ships. This
was for the flying jib halliard and was
only fitted after 1800.

BOWSPRIT

Taper The ratio of the taper to the
diameter at the bed (the bed being
three tenths of the length of the bowsprit from the heel or butt) was:

	To 1719	1719 to 1800	After 1800
Heel or butt	3/4	6/7	5/6
First quarter	30/31	60/61	99/100
Cap	1/2	5/9	2/3

It should be noted that the size given
as the cap is not to be confused with
the actual bowsprit cap but applies to
the outer end of the bowsprit before
the tenon is cut for the cap to sit on.
Rope wooldings were introduced
about 1670 on large ships, and by 1710
all ships were so fitted. They were put
on in exactly the same way as on the
lower masts, with an average of five on
large ships descending to three on the
smallest ships.

Iron bands superseded rope wooldings
in 1800 and were also fitted as on the
lower masts; approximately eleven
were fitted on large ships decreasing to
eight on small ships.
Sprit topmast knee Before the complete transition of sprit topmast to
flying jibboom, the end of the bowsprit was fitted with a long knee to
support the sprit topmast. The vertical
part of the knee was tenoned into and
supported the sprit cap; the length of
the lower part of the knee was the
same as that of the fore mast head; the
upper part of the knee was two thirds
of the length of the lower part; the
thickness was half of the diameter of
the outer end of the bowsprit and the
edges were chamfered off. Up to 1675
the knee was placed so that the sprit
topmast came to within a foot of the
outer end of the bowsprit but after
1675 the sprit topmast was butted
onto the end of the bowsprit. The
knee allowed the sprit topmast to be
at 90 degrees to the waterline or sloping just slightly forward of this angle.
The outboard end of the bowsprit was
flattened to provide a good seating for
the knee.

Bees appear about 1700 when, for the
first time, jibsails were fitted without a
sprit topmast. The length of the bees
was the same as the length of the bowsprit cap, the width was half the great-
est diameter of the bowsprit, and the
thickness was one quarter of the width
at the edge next to the bowsprit but
thinning to three quarters of this
thickness at the outer edge. The bees
stood up from the level at the outer
edge by the thickness of the inner
edge plus 1 inch. When first fitted, two
holes were made on each bee to take
the strops or collars of the fore topmast stay and preventer stay and after
1745 the foremost hole in the starboard bee and the aftermost hole in
the port bee were made large enough
to take the fore topmast stay and preventer stay; these holes were also
lengthened slightly for a good lead to
the bee blocks and the other hole in
each bee was only used in an emerg-
ency. Until 1745 the outer edge of
each bee was shaped like the letter B
but after this date the edge was
straight. On most ships from 1850
small sheaves were let into the bees on
the outer edge set at a slight angle and

were for the fore topsail bowlines. The outer end of the bowsprit was left square once bees were introduced, to allow them a good seating, and edges underneath the square portion were chamfered off.

Bee blocks were seven ninths the length of the bees, half the width, and 2 inches per foot length in depth, when first introduced. The fore topmast stay and preventer stay were taken through sheaves let into the bee block under the appropriate holes in the bees. A hole was also cut through the bee blocks under the other holes in the bees. The bee blocks were bolted on through the bowsprit, the bolts acting as pins for the sheaves. By about 1815 the bee blocks were three quarters of the length of the bees, and only the sheaves were cut in the blocks, the bee blocks not covering the other holes in the bees. The starboard block was put on with its foremost edge butting up to the bowsprit cap; the port block was placed with its after edge just in from the after edge of the bees. The width and the depth of the blocks were the same as when they were first introduced, but by 1850 these blocks were only half as long as the bees and fitted in the same way as before.

Jibboom saddle When jibbooms were carried without a sprit topmast, a saddle was required to let the jibboom lie parallel with the bowsprit. This saddle, in length half the diameter of the bowsprit and in width half the diameter of the jibboom, was nailed on the bowsprit one third of the length of the jibboom from the cap. On large ships after 1733, when the jibboom was carried in conjunction with the sprit topmast, two figure of eight irons were put on the bowsprit on the starboard side: one, a foot in from the forward end of the bowsprit; the other, one third of the length of the jibboom from the end of the bowsprit. Before 1733 the jibboom, when carried with the sprit top, was secured by two lashings in the same position as the figure of eight irons.

The spritsail yard saddle was put on the bowsprit just forward of the jibboom saddle. It differed in shape from the jibboom saddle in that it was a thickening on the upper side of the bowsprit with the after end of the saddle raised to act as a cleat: this was to prevent the spritsail yard slings from slipping down the bowsprit. This saddle was not used before 1773. Lead was used as a pad under the slings to stop them galling the bowsprit. The saddle was put on one fifth of the length of the bowsprit in from the outer end.

A gammoning fish was an additional fitting on the bowsprit from about 1801, on top of the bowsprit, running from the knightheads to about one foot forward of the foremost gammon lashing. This was only found on large ships where two gammon lashings were fitted and grooves were cut into the fish to keep the gammoning in position.

Thumb cleats Five cleats were nailed on top of the bowsprit to stop the gammon lashing from sliding down the bowsprit. Also three cleats were used, one on top and one on either side of the bowsprit to keep the bowsprit shrouds, bobstays and so forth, in position. Apart from those on the gammoning, these cleats were used wherever there was a possibility of rigging sliding down the bowsprit.

Fairlead saddle Between 1719 and 1805, a saddle with holes in was nailed on top of the bowsprit just forward of the gammon lashing and was used for additional leads to those of the gammon lashing blocks. After 1805, it was sometimes the practice to put a strop, with four thimbles seized on it, round the bowsprit; these thimbles acting as leads in lieu of the saddle. The gammon lashing block went out of use about 1780 and the saddle only was used as a lead.

SPRIT TOPMAST

Taper at the hounds was two thirds, and at the head five ninths, of the diameter of the mast at the sprit cap.

The heel was square to a distance of halfway to the cap. The lower end was shaped either to fit on top of the bowsprit or, when carried at the end of the

BEES

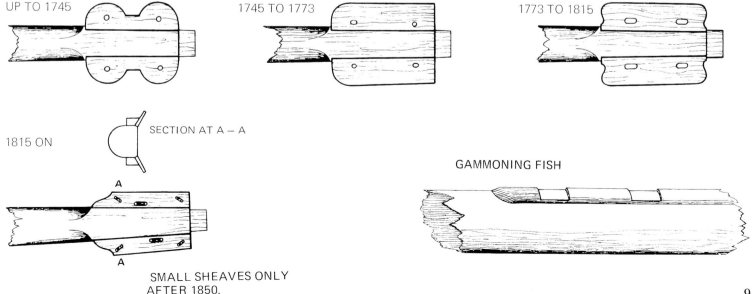

UP TO 1745

1745 TO 1773

1773 TO 1815

1815 ON

SECTION AT A — A

A
A

SMALL SHEAVES ONLY
AFTER 1850.

GAMMONING FISH

I |MASTING
Sprit topmast

BOWSPRIT CARRYING A JIBBOOM
AND A SPRIT TOP

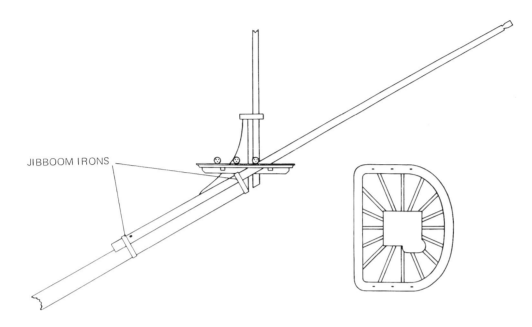

JIBBOOM IRONS

JIBBOOM INNER END
STARBOARD SIDE

 UP TO 1735

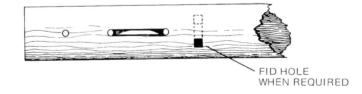

FID HOLE
WHEN REQUIRED

 1735 TO 1815

END SECTIONS

 1815 ON

bowsprit, to conform to the under part of the bowsprit head; in the latter case, a fid was required, and the fid hole was cut so that the lower end of the topmast was flush with the under side of the bowsprit. The fid rested across the sprit trestletrees, and the heel of the sprit topmast was taken through a hole cut in the sprit top.
The head of the sprit topmast was similar to the fore topgallant mast head when fitted with a doubling. The hounds were octagonal and wide enough to come half way across each of the upper trestletrees; they were the same length as the fore topgallant hounds.
A sheave for the sprit topsail yard tie was cut fore and aft, just below the hounds, and was the same proportionate length as the fore topgallant yard tie sheave.

SPRIT TOPMAST FLAG POLE
Taper in a ratio to the diameter of the sprit topmast at the topmast cap, was six sevenths at the heel and the head at the truck was three quarters.
The heel was made in the same way as the fore topgallant flag pole when carried with a doubling. In length it was the same as the fore topgallant flag pole heel.
Head No sheaves were put into the flag pole, the flag either being laced on to the pole or flown from sheaves on the truck which was tenoned onto the head.

JIBBOOM
Taper of the outer end was two thirds of the diameter of the jibboom at a point one third of its length from the inner end. This inner end was the same as the given diameter of the jibboom. Up to 1735 the whole length of the jibboom was round. After this date the inner end was made octagonal for a distance of three and a half diameters from the extreme inner end and, finally, from 1815 the heel was always made square. When the jibboom was carried with a sprit top by means of irons a fid was required and the hole cut diagonally from the port upper side to the starboard lower side at a 45 degree angle, 3 inches forward of the heel rope sheave. A hole for the heel lashing was drilled through the jib-

10

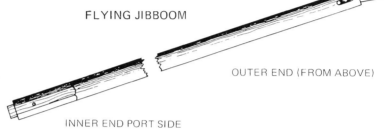

JIBBOOM OUTER END
(AS SEEN FROM ABOVE)

UP TO 1773

1773 to 1794

AFTER 1794

FLYING JIBBOOM

OUTER END (FROM ABOVE)

INNER END PORT SIDE

boom in line with the heel rope sheave. This hole was placed half way between the heel and the sheave. After about 1815 a groove was cut on top of the heel to take the heel lashing and the hole was no longer required.

Outer end Up to about 1773 a shoulder was formed for the rigging stop one and a half diameters from the end; this shoulder was superseded by a necking. When flying jibboom irons were fitted, the necking was formed two diameters in from the outer end and the outer half of the necking was made octagonal to allow the flying jibboom iron a good seating. Prior to the fitting of this iron the necking or shoulder was made round.

Flying jibboom irons were placed at 45 degrees on the octagonal section at the outer end of the jibboom between the necking and the half sheave and the shape was as is shown in the illustrations. The first issue of flying jibbooms was in 1794.

Sheaves A sheave for the heel rope was cut athwartships in the heel one and a half diameters from the inner end and was one and one sixth diameters in length. A sheave for the outhauler was

METHOD OF SECURING A TRYSAIL MAST
TO THE FORE AND MAIN MASTS
NAVY OFFICE 20 NOVEMBER 1818 SIGNED BY R SEPPINGS

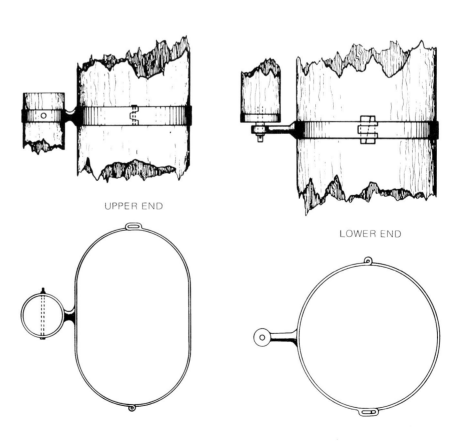

UPPER END

LOWER END

cut up and down a few inches abaft the rigging stop, and after 1815 a half sheave was cut at the very end of the jibboom for the topgallant stay.

FLYING JIBBOOM

Taper at the inner end was three quarters, and at the outer end was two thirds, of the diameter at a point level with the outer end of the jibboom. The flying jibboom was stepped on the bowsprit cap 45 degrees on the starboard side of the jibboom and the inner end was left octagonal for a distance of three diameters. A hole was bored horizontally one diameter's length from the after end and a necking was formed one diameter in length from the outer end for a rigging stop. A sheave was let in vertically 1 1/2 inches aft of the rigging stop and an open sheave cut in vertically at the extreme outer end. Usually the after end had a square tenon cut on to step into the bowsprit cap.

TRYSAIL MASTS

General remarks The masts were the same diameter all the way down; there seems to be no set rule for the diameter, except that it was not more than one half of the diameter of the mizen mast. There were various recognised methods of stepping the masts: one method was to step it into an eye in a clasp hoop a few feet from the deck but the most popular way was to step it into a chock of wood at the partners of the mast. The upper end of the mast was either set into a cap between the trestletrees or was held in position with a fid passing through the upper part and resting on the trestletrees. On the mizen trysail mast a chock of wood was set for a saddle for the boom and a clasp hoop was put round the saddle and the mizen mast.

METHOD OF SECURING A TRYSAIL MAST
TO A MIZEN MAST

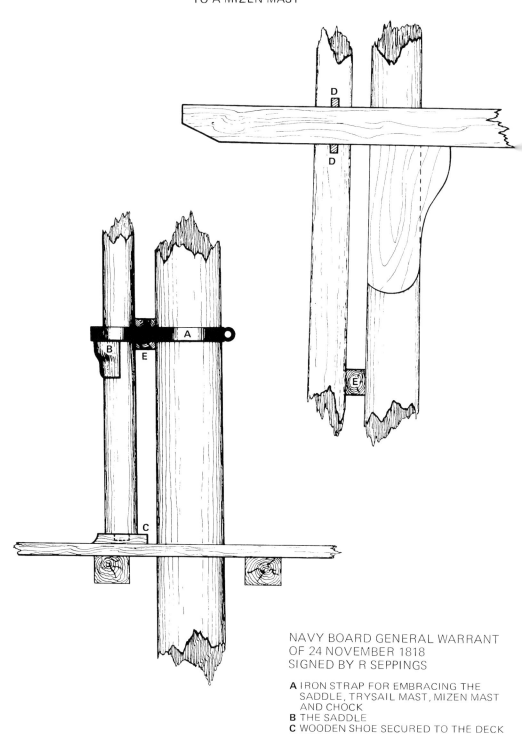

NAVY BOARD GENERAL WARRANT
OF 24 NOVEMBER 1818
SIGNED BY R SEPPINGS

A IRON STRAP FOR EMBRACING THE
   SADDLE, TRYSAIL MAST, MIZEN MAST
   AND CHOCK
B THE SADDLE
C WOODEN SHOE SECURED TO THE DECK
D FIDS
E SPACING CHOCKS

2 Yards, gaffs and booms

FORE AND MAIN YARDS

Taper of the yard arms in a ratio to the diameter of the yard at the slings was one third up to 1719, three sevenths between 1719 and 1805 and one half after 1805.

The yard arm during all periods was one twenty-fourth of the length of the yard.

Yard arm cleats were one half of the given diameter of the yard in length, one quarter of the length in breadth and two thirds of the breadth in thickness. The date for the introduction of these cleats is not known, but my personal view is that until between 1640 and 1660 the yard arm had two pairs of cleats, one to stop the rigging sliding off the yard when it was lowered and the other to keep the rigging in position when the yard was set. These cleats were nailed on the fore and after sides of the yard arms. After 1640/60 only the cleats to stop the rigging from moving in on the yard were required.

Sling cleats Up to 1763 the length of each cleat was one twentieth the length of the yard, but from 1763 to 1815 the length of each cleat was one twenty-fifth the length of the yard. They each had a shoulder one third of the length and during all periods the breadth was one quarter of the length and in depth,

two thirds of the breadth. These were nailed on to the fore side of the yard each side of the centre. The gap between the inner ends of the cleats was one quarter of the diameter of the yard up to 1745 and from 1745 to 1763, one half of the diameter; from 1763 to 1815 this gap was the same as the diameter. After 1815 sling cleats were no longer fitted; instead, stop cleats were often nailed on top of the yard the same distance apart as the sling cleats would have been. These cleats were one thirtieth of the length of the yard.

Roband strip During the seventeenth century strips of wood with holes in them were nailed under the yard on either side of the centre to stop the robands from chafing against the mast, the robands in the centre of the sail being taken through the holes in the strip instead of round the yard. The length of the strips was one eighth of the length of the yard and the gap between the strips was half the length of one strip.

General remarks Up to about 1690 the yards were round for their whole length. After about 1690 the centre was left octagonal for about a quarter of the length of the yard. From 1815 the after face of the eight square was made half the length of the yard, but the other seven faces were still one quarter the length. From 1773 the practice on large ships was to make the yards of two pieces scarfed together and, in this case, instead of eight squaring, battens of the same length as the eight squaring would have been, were nailed on. This practice was normal on most ships after 1805 except for small vessels. When jackstays were carried it was usual to omit the batten on the fore face of the yard to allow

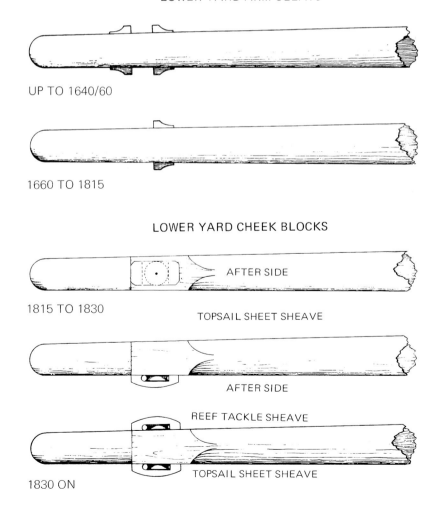

LOWER YARD ARM CLEATS

UP TO 1640/60

1660 TO 1815

LOWER YARD CHEEK BLOCKS

AFTER SIDE

1815 TO 1830

TOPSAIL SHEET SHEAVE

AFTER SIDE

REEF TACKLE SHEAVE

TOPSAIL SHEET SHEAVE

1830 ON

the sail to be carried without fear of chafing. From 1815 sheaves, bolted through the yard with a shell nailed over the sheave to form a block, were set on the after side of the yards for the topsail sheet. From 1830 a similar sheave for the reef tackle was bolted onto the fore side of the yard. The use of these cheek blocks obviated the need for yard arm cleats.

Stunsail boom irons Four irons were required, one on each end of the yard arm and the others one third of the length of the stunsail booms in from the ends. The inner ones after 1773 were made so that the part to take the boom was able to be opened. The outer irons were fitted on the yard ends with straps and bolts. The irons were set at a 45 degree angle between the top of the yard and the fore side of the yard. After 1773 the outer irons often had a roller under them to help in hoisting out the boom. Also after about 1850 the boom irons were set at a 22 1/2 degree angle from the horizontal.

Jackstay bolts After 1811 eyebolts were hammered along the top of the yard to take the jackstay, the inner one about 3 feet from the slings, the outer one just in from the yard arm cleats and the rest spaced along the yard about 2 feet 6 inches from each other.

THE CROSSJACK YARD

Taper was of the same proportions as the fore and main yards.

Yard arms were one twenty-fourth of the length of the yard. Note that sometime in the seventeenth century, the arms were a little longer—as much as one twentieth. I have also seen contemporary models of the early eighteenth century with much shorter arms; the proportion of one twenty-fourth seems, however, to have been the general rule.

Yard arm cleats were fitted in the same way as those on the fore and main yards, and were of the same proportionate dimensions.

Sling cleats were in the form of stop cleats, the distance apart being the same proportionately as those of the fore and main. Sling cleats ceased to be used after 1815 though sometimes

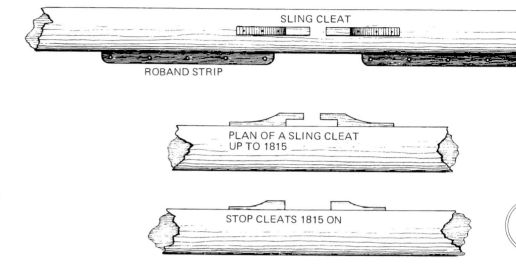

UPPER SIDE OF YARD

SLING CLEAT

ROBAND STRIP

PLAN OF A SLING CLEAT
UP TO 1815

STOP CLEATS 1815 ON

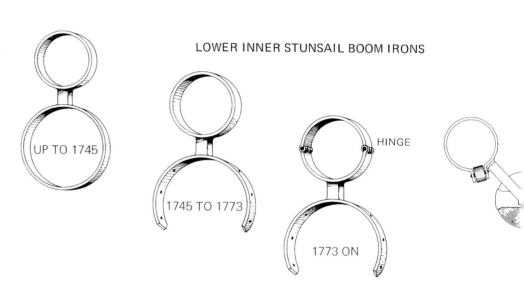

LOWER INNER STUNSAIL BOOM IRONS

UP TO 1745

1745 TO 1773

1773 ON

HINGE

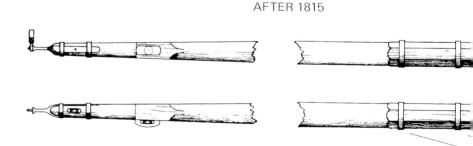

TOPSAIL YARD
AFTER 1815

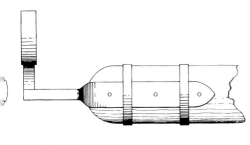

WER OUTER STUNSAIL BOOM IRON

UP TO 1773

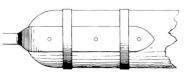

1773 ON

EYEBOLTS FOR THE TYE BLOCKS
AFTER 1840

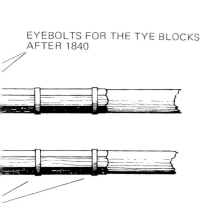

IRON HOOPS WERE USED WHEN THE
WAS MADE OF TWO PIECES AND HAD BATTENS
AD OF EIGHT SQUARING

after that date stop cleats were put on top of the yard, as on the fore and main yards.

General remarks Up to about 1745 the yard was made round for its whole length. From 1745 to 1830, the centre of the yard was sixteen squared for a quarter of the length of the yard. After 1830 the yard was made with the after side eight squared for half the yard, and the other faces sixteen squared and gave in effect fifteen faces. Another way to arrive at this shape was to sixteen square the centre quarter and nail on a batten covering the after two faces for half of the yard.

No cheek blocks were put on the yard as on the fore and main yards; instead, in about 1815, a sheave running up and down was let in the yard just inboard from each arm. This sheave was for the mizen topsail sheet.

No boom irons were fitted, but a ferrule was driven on the ends of the yard arms. When chain slings were used, it was sometimes the practice to fit a band in the centre of the yard with an eyebolt set in it. This obviated the use of the usual thimble strapped there. Though introduced in 1810, this band was not in general use until about 1850.

Jackstay bolts were never required on the crossjack yard.

THE FORE, MAIN AND MIZEN TOPSAIL YARDS

Taper of the yard arms in a ratio to the diameter of the yard at the slings was one half before 1706 and three sevenths after that date.

Fore and main yard arm length, in a ratio to the total length of the yard was as follows: up to about 1655, one twenty-fourth; 1655 to about 1680, one twentieth; 1680 to about 1719, one eighteenth; 1719 onwards one twelfth. These lengths up to 1719 are conjectural but should allow for the various reefs introduced in the seventeenth century.

Mizen yard arm length, in a ratio to the total length of the yard was as follows: up to about 1700, one twenty-fourth; 1700 to 1710, one twentieth; 1710 to 1788, one eighteenth; 1788 to 1815, one sixteenth; 1815 onwards, five seventy-seconds.

Yard arm cleats were three quarters of the diameter of the yard at the slings in length. In width, they were a quarter of their length, and in depth, three quarters of their width. These cleats were not required after cheek blocks were fitted on the yard arms.

Sling cleats were made like the lower yard sling cleats until about 1773 after which date they took the form of stop cleats which were set one diameter apart at each side of the slings. When made like the lower yard cleats they were of the same proportional dimensions, but when in the form of stop cleats the length was one inch per yard length of the yard; the width was one quarter of the length and the depth was three quarters of the width.

Up to about 1680/1700 the yards were round for the whole length but after this the centres of the yards were eight squared; this octagonal section was one quarter of the length of the yard up to 1810 and after then one eighth of the length. On the fore and main topsail yard a sheave was let into each arm about one foot from the end; the mizen topsail yard was not fitted with these sheaves until 1700. After 1815 cheek blocks were fitted to the after side of the yard arms to take the topgallant sheets.

Stunsail boom irons Up to 1810, both inner and outer irons took the form of figure of eight irons driven onto the yard, the inner ones one third of the length of the stunsail from the end of the yard, the outer one driven on close to the end. After 1810, the outer irons, set at an angle of 45 degrees, were set into the end of the arms like the irons on the lower yards. The mizen topsail yard did not carry irons but instead had a ferrule set on the end of the yard. No rollers were used on the irons. The inner irons after 1773 were made to open to let the boom in. From 1834 the outer irons were detachable. Also after 1850 the irons were set at an angle of 22 1/2 degrees from the horizontal.

Jackstay bolts These were fitted like those on the lower yards.

FORE, MAIN AND MIZEN TOPGALLANT YARDS

Taper was the same as on the topsail yards.

I MASTING
Fore, main and mizen topgallant yards

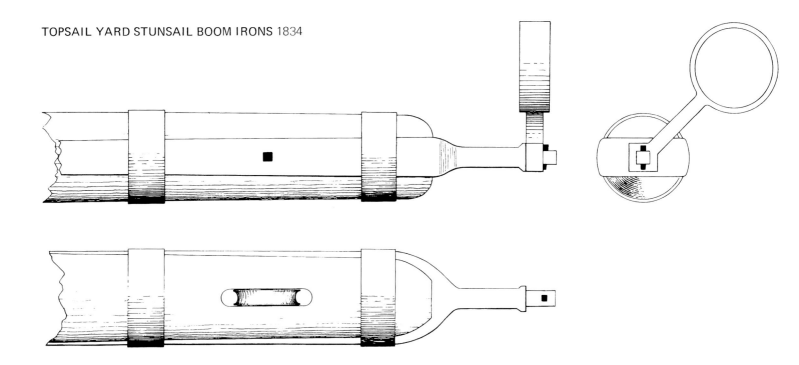

Length of yard arms was one twenty-fourth of the length of the yard.
Yard arm cleats were of the same proportions as those on the topsail yards.
Sling cleats were in the form of stop cleats and were each at one diameter's distance from each side of the slings. The length of each cleat was one inch per yard length of the yard, width one quarter of the length and depth three quarters of the width.
General remarks A ferrule and an eyebolt were put on the extreme ends of the yards for the stunsail halliard jewel block. The method of making the topgallant yards followed the same pattern as the topsail yards. Jackstay bolts were fitted as on the lower yards.

FORE, MAIN AND MIZEN ROYAL YARDS

Taper of the yard arm in a ratio to the diameter of the yard at the slings was five twelfths.
Yard arms were of the same proportionate length as the topgallant yards.
Yard arm cleats were of the same proportionate dimensions as the topgallant yards.
Sling cleats were of the same proportionate dimensions as the topgallant yards.

General remarks These yards were made sixteen square for one quarter of the length of the yard at the centre while the remainder of the yard was round. Jackstay bolts were fitted as on the lower yards.

THE MIZEN YARD

Taper in a ratio to the diameter at the slings, was as follows: the lower arm was one half up to 1745 and two thirds after that date; the upper arm was two thirds up to 1745 and two fifths from then on. The slings were one twenty-second of the length of the yard forward of the centre.
Length of yard arms The lower arm was one sixty-sixth and the upper arm was one seventy-second of the length of the yard. Note that the length of the lower arm only applied when the sail was carried the whole length of the yard.
Yard arm cleats were of the same proportionate dimensions as the topsail yard cleats and were fitted on the port and starboard side of the yard. Lower cleats were only fitted when the sail stretched the whole length of the yard.
Sling cleats were stop cleats of the same proportionate dimensions as the crossjack stop cleats and were nailed

on the starboard side of the yard one diameter of the yard apart.
General remarks At all times the yard was round for its whole length. The lower end had a ferrule round it and from 1650 an eyebolt was let into the lower end. Another eye, introduced in about 1719, and a smaller eye than that on the lower end, was also let into the upper end to take a halliard block. A ferrule was put round the upper end also when this eyebolt was fitted.

THE SPANKER GAFF

Taper of the outer end was one half of the inner end.
Outer end After about 1818, 3 feet extra above the given length was allowed and an eyebolt was set in the end of this extra length: this was for flying signals clear of the sails. Before then an eyebolt was set in the outer end and in both cases a ferrule was put on.
Inner end In all periods a jaw was made at the inner end. The inside of the jaws was usually covered with leather and shaped to fit the mast or trysail mast. There was a hole in each side of the jaw to take the parrel rope. When the gaff went straight on the mast, the jaws had to encompass the cheeks. The length of the scarf of the

jaws was between 4 and 5 feet, and the inside of the jaws made at an angle of 45 degrees. Three iron bands were put on to bind the scarf together.
General remarks A shoulder was sometimes set on the outer end of the gaff as a rigging stop and was placed one fifteenth of the length of the gaff from the outer end.

TRYSAIL GAFF
The taper was the same as the spanker gaff. No extra length was allowed for the signals as on the spanker gaff, but a ferrule and eye were put on the end. The jaws were the same as the spanker gaff.

THE DRIVER BOOM
Taper of the outer end was three quarters and of the inner end two thirds of the given diameter, which was one third from the outer end.
Jaws The length of the jaws was between 4 and 5 feet. The width of the jaws was sufficient to encompass the mast or trysail mast, enabling the inside of the jaws to be leathered. The edges of the jaws outside were rounded off and a hole made in each side of the jaws for the parrel rope. Three hoops were put on the jaws, one over the after end of the tongue, one about 6 inches from the throat of the jaws and the third equally spaced between.
General remarks An eyebolt was let into the top of the boom by the throat of the jaws. A sheave was cut in vertically about 6 inches from the outer end, and an eye and ferrule put on the outer end. The forward end of the boom where the jaws were scarfed was left square, the tongues of the jaws being rounded off to fair in with the rest of the boom. After 1818 two eyebolts each side were driven into the boom where the boom passed over the taffrail, the bolts each side being about a foot apart. Two snatch sheaves, one each side, were bolted on two thirds in from the outer end. Two cleats were also nailed on, one each side, a couple of feet forward of the jaws. Another cleat was put on under the boom by the other cleats, and eyebolts set in just aft of these three cleats. After about 1840 a spider band was put on the after end of the boom with an

SPANKER GAFF

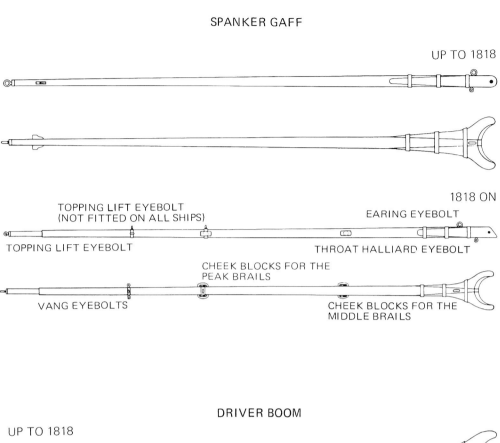

UP TO 1818

1818 ON

TOPPING LIFT EYEBOLT
(NOT FITTED ON ALL SHIPS)

EARING EYEBOLT

TOPPING LIFT EYEBOLT

THROAT HALLIARD EYEBOLT

CHEEK BLOCKS FOR THE
PEAK BRAILS

VANG EYEBOLTS

CHEEK BLOCKS FOR THE
MIDDLE BRAILS

DRIVER BOOM

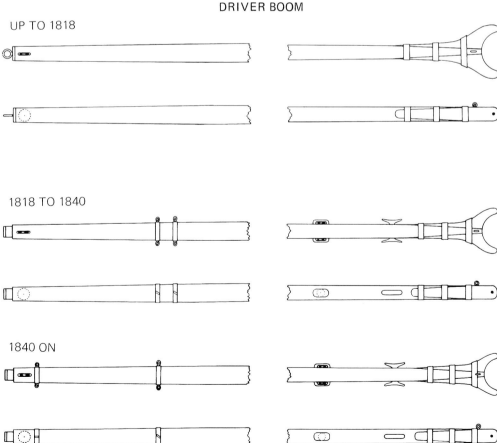

UP TO 1818

1818 TO 1840

1840 ON

17

eyebolt on either side. Up to 1818 an eyebolt was set in the after end of the boom. After 1818 the after end was cut with a shoulder.

THE DRIVER YARD
Taper was the same as on the fore topgallant yard.
General remarks The driver yard was made round for its entire length and had no cleats fitted.

THE SPRITSAIL YARD
Taper in a ratio to the diameter at the slings, was in the same proportions as the topgallant yards.
Yard arms were of the same proportions as the topgallant yards in length.
Yard arm cleats were of the same proportions as the topgallant yards.
Sling cleats were of the same propor-

tions as the topgallant yards.
General remarks The eight squaring and so forth followed the same pattern as the topgallant yards but no eyebolts were fitted to the ends.

THE SPRIT TOPSAIL YARD
Taper in a ratio to the diameter at the slings, was in the same proportions as the topgallant yards.
Yard arms were of the same proportions as the topgallant yards in length.
Yard arm cleats were of the same proportions as the topgallant yards.
Sling cleats were of the same proportions as the topgallant yards.
General remarks This yard was made in the same way as the topgallant yards; no eyebolts, ferrules or stunsail booms were fitted.

LOWER STUNSAIL BOOMS
Taper of these booms started one third out from the inboard end, and the outer end was two thirds of the given diameter.
General remarks During all periods a ferrule and a hook were driven onto the inboard end. Up to about 1810 a hole for the lashing of the tack block was bored through the boom one diameter in from the outer end in a fore and aft line. After 1810 a necking was left on the boom. On some ships after 1810 a spider band was put on the boom midway along the boom with three eyebolts on the band—one on the upper side and the others on the fore and after sides. The boom was made round for the whole length.

THE UPPER STUNSAIL BOOMS
These were round for their whole length and were parallel one third from the inboard tapering to two thirds at the outer end. Up to about 1810 a hole was bored through the inboard end one diameter in from the end. After then ferrules and eyes were set in each end of the boom, the hole no longer being required. On some ships the inboard end was left octagonal for a distance of about one foot but this was not the general practice.

THE STUNSAIL YARDS
Taper The same proportionate taper as the topgallant yards.
General remarks These yards were made round for their whole length and yard arm cleats were fitted as on the topgallant yards. There were two positions for the placing of the sling cleats: until about 1816 they were one third from the inboard end and after this date the cleats were placed in the centre of the yards. The older method was still favoured by some ships, however, and I have seen a print of 1850 showing this method; indeed the mast and spar list of 1845 gives two lengths of stunsail yards and I have no doubt that the shorter yard was carried one third out, and the longer yard one half the way out.

LOWER STUNSAIL BOOM

UP TO 1810

LOOKING FROM AFT

1810 ON

LOOKING FROM AFT

ALTERNATIVE 1810 ON

LOOKING FROM AFT

STUNSAIL YARD

UP TO 1816

LOOKING FROM ABOVE

1816 ON

LOOKING FROM ABOVE

UPPER STUNSAIL BOOM

UP TO 1810

LOOKING FROM AFT

1810 ON

LOOKING FROM AFT

PLAN OF MAIN TOP UP TO 1650

A HOLES FOR FUTTOCK PLATES
B UPPER CAPPING
C LOWER CAPPING
D RIBS
E TOP RIM

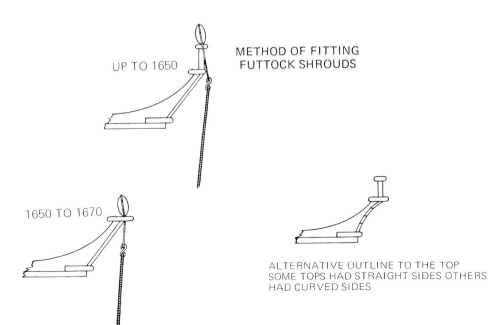

SECTION AT X–X

3 Tops, caps and trucks

THE TOPS

The method of constructing the tops in the seventeenth century is unknown and it is only possible to give a conjectural idea. However by reversing the law of evolution I believe it is possible to arrive at a satisfactory conclusion. We know the size of the tops from 1640 and also the length of the crosstrees for most periods, which gives us a good start. By scrutiny of engravings and paintings it is clear that the sides of the tops were planked up. To secure these sides, ribs or knees must have been required. Payne's engraving of the *Sovereign of the Seas* shows that these knees were visible from the outside of the top, therefore the most obvious way to secure the side planking would have been to nail them to rebates in the knees. Half way up the sides was a capping piece through which, after 1650, the futtock deadeye plates were taken. The lower half of the sides came out at an angle and that was the only part to be planked up; the upper half of the sides was an extension of the knees with another lighter capping or rail on top. Mizen and sprit tops only had the lower half, the futtock capping being also the upper capping. On most ships the upper half was at right angles to the base of the top though other ships had the upper half

UP TO 1650

1650 TO 1670

METHOD OF FITTING FUTTOCK SHROUDS

ALTERNATIVE OUTLINE TO THE TOP SOME TOPS HAD STRAIGHT SIDES OTHERS HAD CURVED SIDES sloping slightly outwards. That gives a broad outline of the early tops—now to break it down even further.

All through the known history of the tops the same method of planking the bottom was used, and I see no reason why this method should have been different in the seventeenth century. First planks were laid fore and aft either side of the square hole and then athwartships on the fore and after sides of the square hole. Where the two series of planks met they were half lapped into each other. These planks would be about 2 1/2 to 3 inches thick and probably about 6 inches wide. They were then nailed together, the nails being clenched over rooves on the under side.

Round the outside and flush with the outer edge of the top a rim was nailed, about 6 inches wide by 1 inch deep, made, I should imagine, in eight segments. On the bottom were nailed the knees, radiating from the edge of the square hole and overlapping the rim of the top. The distance apart at the outer edge was about 18 inches. These knees were probably made in three sections, the first section running from the square hole to about a couple of feet from the outer edge. The second section must have been grown timber to form the angle between the bottom and the sides; it would be scarfed onto the first section and would come about a foot up the side; onto the end of this section the first capping rail was ten-

METHOD OF HALF LAPPING THE FLOOR AT THE TOP

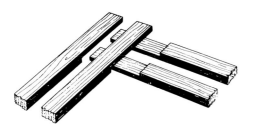

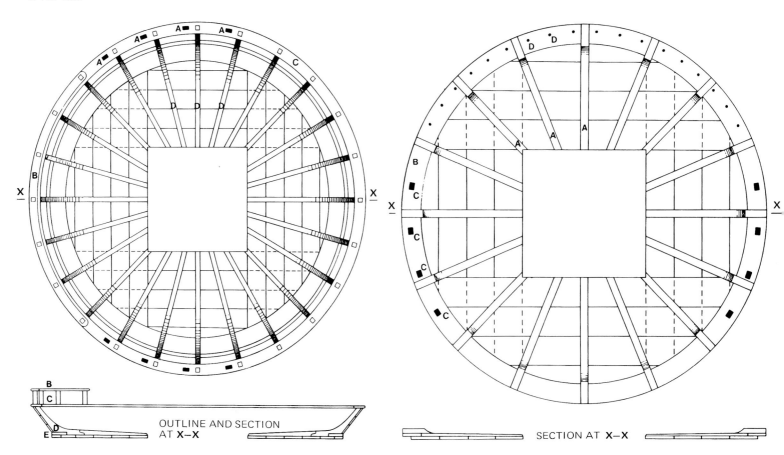

PLAN OF A MAIN TOP 1650 TO 1670

A HOLES FOR FUTTOCK PLATES
B UPPER CAPPING
C LOWER CAPPING
D RIBS
E TOP RIM

OUTLINE AND SECTION AT X–X

PLAN OF A MAIN TOP 1670 TO 1700

A BATTENS
B TOP RIM
C MORTICE FOR FUTTOCK PLATES
D HOLES FOR CROWSFEET

SECTION AT X–X

oned. The third section was scarfed onto the second section to form the upper half of the side, with the top rail tenoned onto the end. The planking nailed onto the sides was probably 3/4 inch thick and, I should imagine, slightly curved to give the round form—not a very difficult operation when one considers the number of knees and consequently how short the planks would have to be.

The knees would have been about 4 inches wide where the planks were nailed thus allowing about 1 inch rebate either side leaving a 2 inch section visible on the outer side. The top section of the knees was 2 inches square, and the section of the knees on the base of the top was probably 2

inches wide and tapering from about 4 inches thick at the join of the centre section to about 1 inch thick at the edge of the square hole. The holes for the deadeye plates in the capping were in all probability faced with iron to prevent the plates from cutting into the capping, as indeed they were in later periods.

The first alteration to the tops in making them flatter was to do away with the top section (about 1650) making all tops as described for the mizen and sprit tops with the exception of the retention of part of the top section on the after end of the tops of the main and fore masts. Also during this period, no planking is shown up the sides and the ribs or knees are narrower in

consequence. By 1670 the tops, though still round, were completely flat, made as previously except that instead of the knees, battens were nailed across the base of the top. The number of battens varied but were placed radially round the bottom, not more than sixteen battens being required; certainly less battens were used than knees. On the outside edge of the top a capping piece or rim was nailed, overlapping the edge slightly and through this rim the futtock plates were placed. Not all tops were made with the capping piece overlapping the side—some were made with flush sides.

At the beginning of the eighteenth century the tops lost their round form. A few years earlier, about 1695, the

PLAN OF MIZEN TOP UP TO 1670 — SECTION AT A–A — GUNWALE KNEE BATTEN — HOLE FOR FUTTOCK PLATE

PLAN OF A MIZEN TOP 1670 TO 1695 — SECTION AT A–A

PLAN OF A SPRIT TOP FROM 1670 TO WHEN JIBBOOMS WERE CARRIED — SECTION AT A–A

PLAN OF A SPRIT TOP UP TO 1670

PLAN OF A MIZEN TOP 1695 TO 1700

PLAN OF A SPRIT TOP WHEN JIBBOOMS WERE CARRIED

MASTING
Tops

mizen top had the after end squared off, then by about 1700 the fore and main followed suit, as did the sprit top. It was not just a matter of cutting off the curvature; the tops first had rounded corners then finally the square corners. Up to about 1719 the corners of the tops were rounded while the forward edge was gradually changed from a semi-circle to an elliptical form. Battens were nailed on the bottom as in previous years. The rim of the top was about 6 inches wide and overlapped the edge by a couple of inches; up to 1719 the rim was about 4 inches deep and sloped inwards as shown in the illustration, the battens resting on top of the rim. The rim on the after edge of the top was flat and had holes cut in it for the stanchions of the rail; there were usually four stanchions on

the main and fore tops and three on the mizen, only large ships carrying a rail on the sprit top fitted as on the mizen. The futtock plates were placed through holes in the side rim and top; the first deadeye was placed level with the after side of the topmast, the after one about 6 inches from the after end of the top with the others equally spaced between.

The top at this time was fitted so that both crosstrees were visible inside the edges of the square hole. The visible section of the crosstree was called the 'lubbers wood'—see the description of the crosstrees. Holes were drilled through the fore rim of the top for the crowsfeet. The number of battens varied from ship to ship, but were usually spaced about a foot apart at the outer edges with one more batten put on the

after end than on one side, and one less on the fore end than on one side. As I mentioned before there seems to be such a variation between different ships that I have had to base the number on the average as shown on contemporary models.

I think the illustrations show how the tops were planked, or at least how I think they must have been; suffice to say that they probably followed the usual method of fore and aft, and athwartship planking, scarfed together. After about 1719, the corners of the tops were relatively square, and about this time another method of finishing off the outer edge of the tops was tried out: the rim around the edge of the top was flush with the edge, the battens lay on top of the rim with their ends squared off and a thin up-

PLAN OF A TOP 1700 TO 1719
TAKEN FROM A CONTEMPORARY MODEL OF A 20 GUN SHIP
OF ABOUT 1710

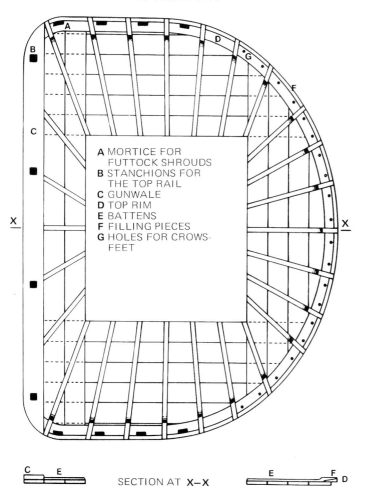

A MORTICE FOR FUTTOCK SHROUDS
B STANCHIONS FOR THE TOP RAIL
C GUNWALE
D TOP RIM
E BATTENS
F FILLING PIECES
G HOLES FOR CROWS-FEET

SECTION AT X–X

PLAN OF A TOP 1719 TO 1745
TAKEN FROM A CONTEMPORARY MODEL OF A 100 GUN SHIP
OF ABOUT 1719

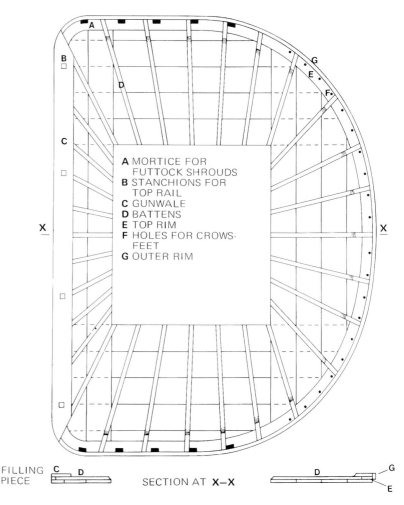

A MORTICE FOR FUTTOCK SHROUDS
B STANCHIONS FOR TOP RAIL
C GUNWALE
D BATTENS
E TOP RIM
F HOLES FOR CROWS-FEET
G OUTER RIM

FILLING PIECE

SECTION AT X–X

right rim was then nailed to the ends of the battens. The rest of the top was made as in previous years but as I have not come across this method of finishing off the top after 1733 I presume it was a trial between 1719 and 1733. The following method of constructing the tops seems to have been used up to the early nineteenth century: The bottom planking was made up of between 2 1/2 and 3 inch thick planks, depending on the size of the ship, scarfed together as before. A board was nailed around the rim overlapping the edge about 4 inches, this board being between 7 and 8 inches wide and about 1 1/4 inches thick. Battens were then nailed on the bottom laying on top of the rim, about five on each side, five on the fore part and six on the after part. These battens were 4

inches thick on the outer edge tapering to 2 inches thick at the square hole. (On the mizen tops the rim was about 6 inches wide.) Between the battens filling pieces were placed, covering the rim at the sides and narrowing to half the rim on the fore part. There were no filling pieces on the after edge; instead, a broad plank called the gunwale was nailed over the after battens, and was about a foot wide on the main and fore and about 9 inches wide on the mizen tops. Through the gunwale and into the top, four mortices were cut (three on the mizen) to take the stanchions for the top rail. Through the filling pieces, rim and top, slots were cut for the futtock plates. On some ships a block of wood was bolted inboard of the filling pieces with grooves so that it set over the battens

and on the base of the top. This block was about 8 inches wide and three times the depth of the battens thick; it had square holes cut in it for the swivel guns, and these holes were further strengthened with an iron plate. The rail in the top was about 3 feet high and in most ships made of wood, though in some small ships both rail and stanchions were made of iron. This rail was usually finished off by having canvas or netting laced to it. Holes for the crowsfeet were made as before through the fore rim. In 1802 two holes were cut through the top on either side of the centre fore side of the topmast to take the slings of the lower yards. Both crosstrees were visible in the square hole during this period.

PLAN OF A CONTEMPORARY MODEL MAIN TOP
1745 ESTABLISHMENT FOR A FIRST RATE SHIP

PLAN OF A MAIN TOP
FROM STEEL'S MAST MAKING 1794 — 36 GUN SHIP
LARGER SHIPS WOULD REQUIRE MORE BATTENS

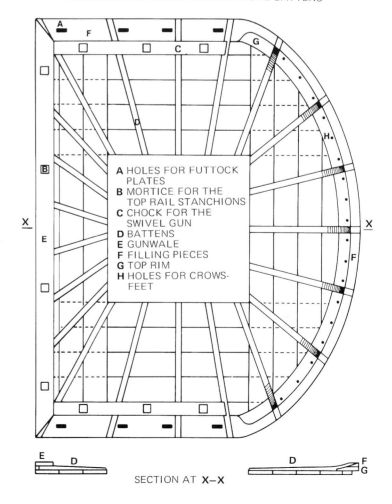

A PLATE FOR FUTTOCK SHROUD
B STANCHIONS OF THE TOP RAIL
C CHOCK FOR SWIVEL GUNS
D BATTENS
E GUNWALE
F FILLING PIECES
G SIDE BATTEN
H TOP RIM
I HOLES FOR CROWS-FEET

A HOLES FOR FUTTOCK PLATES
B MORTICE FOR THE TOP RAIL STANCHIONS
C CHOCK FOR THE SWIVEL GUN
D BATTENS
E GUNWALE
F FILLING PIECES
G TOP RIM
H HOLES FOR CROWS-FEET

SECTION AT X–X

SECTION AT X–X

I MASTING

Tops

Another alteration of the tops took place about 1802; then, by Admiralty order the tops of large ships could be made in two halves. This necessitated the use of additional crosstrees carried on the upper side of the tops; by bolting through these upper crosstrees and the lower crosstrees the two halves were held together. Also about this time the use of crowsfeet was dispensed with so that holes were no longer required in the fore rim. When the tops were made in two halves the battens were nailed on in a different pattern as shown in the illustration.

In 1815 the tops were made 18 inches wider at the after end than at the first deadeye, (12 inches on the mizen). This widening of the tops had been used by some shipwrights a few years previously but was not officially recognised until 1815.

After about 1833 the battens were finally dispensed with and the tops were completely flush decked except for the rim, upper crosstrees and diagonal riders between the two upper crosstrees. A bolster was fitted just aft of the hole for the slings (a single hole by this time). The top was also strengthened by a metal strip bolted into the capping piece at the sides. There were variations to the above, one by Symonds where the fore end of the top was on hinges.

Another innovation of 1815 was to fit an upward-hinging flap over the lubbers hole covering the fore part of the hole, with the after half planked over. The single hole for the slings mentioned above was used when chain slings were fitted.

The square hole mentioned here was not really square but was slightly wider athwartships than fore and aft. The actual size of the square hole before 1769 I cannot give, but a proportion of one third the diameter of the top when round tops were used and two fifths the breadth when squared tops were used should be approximately correct. After 1769 the size is given in the Appendix. The position of the square hole when round tops were

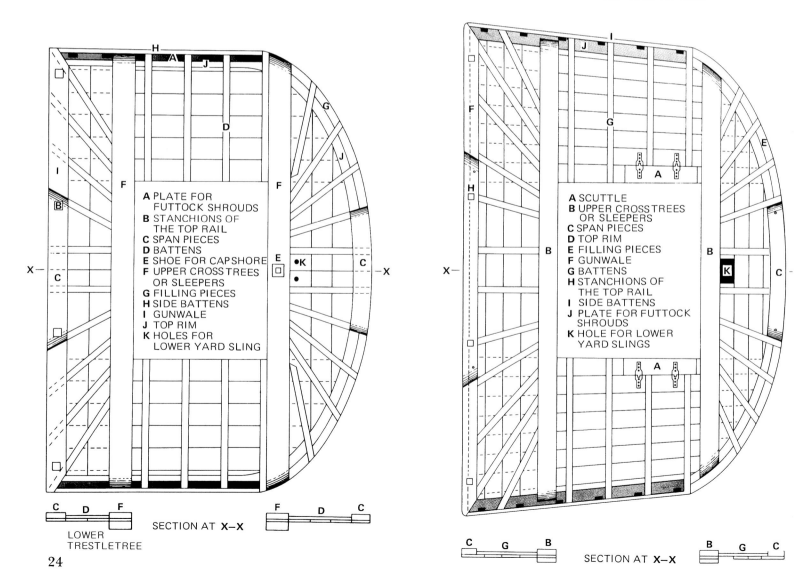

PLAN OF TOP 1802 TO 1815

A PLATE FOR FUTTOCK SHROUDS
B STANCHIONS OF THE TOP RAIL
C SPAN PIECES
D BATTENS
E SHOE FOR CAPSHORE
F UPPER CROSSTREES OR SLEEPERS
G FILLING PIECES
H SIDE BATTENS
I GUNWALE
J TOP RIM
K HOLES FOR LOWER YARD SLING

LOWER TRESTLETREE

SECTION AT X–X

PLAN OF TOP 1815 TO 1833

A SCUTTLE
B UPPER CROSSTREES OR SLEEPERS
C SPAN PIECES
D TOP RIM
E FILLING PIECES
F GUNWALE
G BATTENS
H STANCHIONS OF THE TOP RAIL
I SIDE BATTENS
J PLATE FOR FUTTOCK SHROUDS
K HOLE FOR LOWER YARD SLINGS

SECTION AT X–X

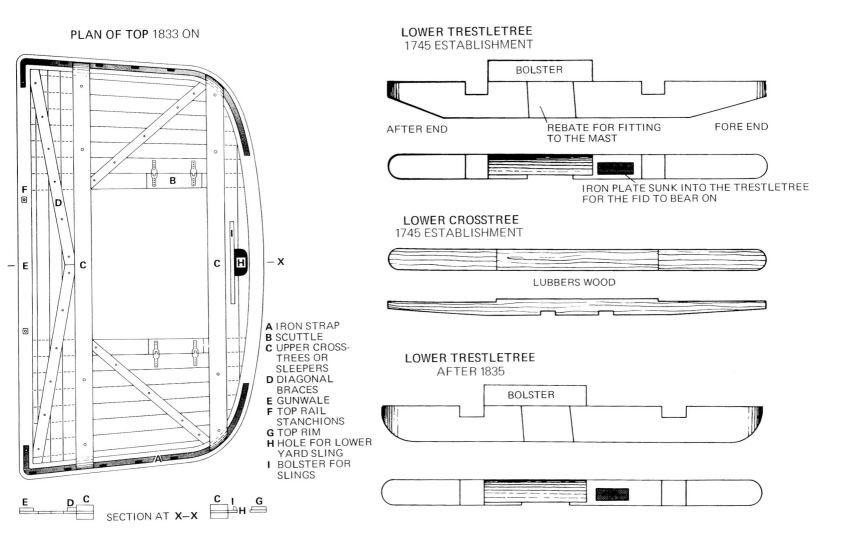

PLAN OF TOP 1833 ON

LOWER TRESTLETREE
1745 ESTABLISHMENT

BOLSTER

AFTER END

REBATE FOR FITTING
TO THE MAST

FORE END

IRON PLATE SUNK INTO THE TRESTLETREE
FOR THE FID TO BEAR ON

LOWER CROSSTREE
1745 ESTABLISHMENT

LUBBERS WOOD

LOWER TRESTLETREE
AFTER 1835

BOLSTER

A IRON STRAP
B SCUTTLE
C UPPER CROSS-
  TREES OR
  SLEEPERS
D DIAGONAL
  BRACES
E GUNWALE
F TOP RAIL
  STANCHIONS
G TOP RIM
H HOLE FOR LOWER
  YARD SLING
I BOLSTER FOR
  SLINGS

SECTION AT X—X

used must have been in the centre of the top to allow both crosstrees to be the same length. When the squared tops were used the after edge of the hole came one fifth the width of the top from the after edge of the top. The sprit top did not have a large square hole. It was only of a sufficient size to fit round the mast and knee with enough room either side of the trestletrees to take the leads of ropes. The hole was large enough for the jibboom to pass through when carried with a sprit top. The jibboom was fitted on the starboard side of the bowsprit.

THE LOWER CROSSTREES AND TRESTLETREES
The crosstrees and trestletrees altered very little over the centuries. The dimensions of them for most periods

are not given in the Appendix; however, when not known they can easily be worked out by reference to the top sizes, both trestle- and crosstrees coming to within an inch or so from the edge of the top.

Only two crosstrees were fitted, set in the trestletrees for their depth less an inch; the crosstrees were slotted down to a depth of an inch. When the crosstrees were set inside the square hole of the tops an additional thickness was left on top of them called the lubbers wood; this stood proud of the upper face of the crosstree a distance of 1 1/2 inches. This extra thickness was not counted as the depth of the crosstrees. It was used from about 1712/19 onwards.

The ends of the trestletrees were snaped, one end from half the depth to one

and a half depths from the end, the other end from half the depth to one depth from the end; the long snape was on the fore end. This snape gave way to rounding in 1835. The ends were also rounded in the vertical plane during all periods.

The trestletrees were set in the mast to a depth of one eighth the trestletrees' width, a groove being taken out of them for this purpose. The edges of the trestletrees were chamfered except for the upper edges and the inside edge between the crosstrees. An iron plate three quarters of an inch thick, two fifths of the trestletrees wide and three quarters the length of the square hole was nailed to the top of the trestletree in the way of the fid.

The ends of the crosstrees were rounded in the vertical plane, the under sides

MASTING
Lower crosstrees and trestletrees

SLEEPER

FOR A PLAN VIEW OF THE SLEEPERS
REFER TO THE DIAGRAM OF THE TOPS

tapered from half their thickness to a distance of a quarter the length from each end, up to 1815, and after then to one crosstree's breadth from the square hole; the edges of the taper were chamfered off.

As mentioned in the section devoted to the tops, at one period additional crosstrees called sleepers were carried on the upper side of the tops; these sleepers were the same width but only half the thickness of the lower crosstrees, and tapered on their upper surface like the lower surface of the lower crosstrees, the ends being rounded in the horizontal plane. A chock was required to keep the topmast spaced from the lower mast. This chock was the same depth as the trestletrees and the same width as the crosstrees and was nailed to the fore side of the mast, fitting snugly between the trestletrees. A bolster was nailed on top of the trestletrees. In length, it just cleared the fid hole to the after edge of the after crosstree, was 1 1/2 inches wider than the trestletrees, and as deep as it was wide; the outer edge was rounded to a quarter circle. Sometimes the outer surface of the bolster was coppered.

Sprit crosstrees and trestletrees were made in a similar manner to the lower mast crosstrees and trestletrees but bolsters were not required and no lubbers wood was left on the crosstrees. Eyebolts were put in the after end underside of the fore and main trestletrees in 1810 for the truss pendants, and in the fore end in 1815 for the jibsail and main staysail.

When round tops were used, the centre of the trestletrees was level with the fore side of the lower mast; after the round tops went out of fashion it was the general rule to place the after crosstree one fifth the length of the

trestletree from the after end, this measurement reading to the after edge of the crosstree.

THE TOPMAST TRESTLETREES AND CROSSTREES

The trestletrees and crosstrees altered very little up to the early nineteenth century, the main difference being the number of crosstrees carried. Up to about 1706 there were two long and one short; from 1706 to 1719 three long, but only the two after ones were used for shrouds, the fore one being empty. From 1719 to the early nineteenth century three crosstrees were still carried but they all carried a shroud. When two long crosstrees were fitted, the after one butted against the after side of the topmast, the fore one against the fore side of the topgallant mast, while in between the masts a short crosstree was fitted overlapping the outer edge of the trestletrees a few inches each side. The outer one third of each crosstree curved aft so that the foremost one came level with the centre of the topgallant mast. When three long crosstrees were used the centre one took the place of the short centre one.

The crosstrees were set in the trestletrees so they stood proud about 1/2 inch, half the depth being cut out of the crosstree less 1/2 inch, and the rest out of the trestletrees. The ends of the crosstrees were rounded and had a hole 4 inches in from each end for the topgallant shrouds. Crosstrees tapered on the under side from half their depth at the outer end to a distance of one third from the outer end.

The trestletrees were snaped similarly at both ends which was from half the depth to the depth's distance from the ends. The ends were rounded on the vertical plane like the lower trestle-

trees. The position of the trestletrees was such that the centre was level with the fore side of the topmast. From about 1790, sheaves for the main topgallant bowlines were put in the after ends of the fore topmast trestletrees angled slightly outwards.

From 1815 until 1835 it was the practice to carry either three long and one short crosstree or two long and two short crosstrees. They were made in the same way as before but a short one was fitted on the fore side of the topgallant mast, with one long crosstree carried in between the masts; one was abaft the topmast and the other one as far aft of the topmast as the distance between the first and second long crosstrees. This was to enable the topgallant mast to be struck abaft the topmast when necessary. When two long and two short crosstrees were fitted, the second short one replaced the long one abaft the topmast making, from forward, a short, long, short, long sequence. These short crosstrees were the same width and depth as the long ones but only extended a trestletree's width outboard of each trestletree; the ends were rounded in the vertical plane.

Holes were made in the long crosstrees as before for the topgallant shrouds, though at this period it was sometimes the practice to slot the ends and fit rollers instead of the holes. The after crosstree was usually made a foot longer than the others at this time, and when three long crosstrees and one short crosstree were carried, the foremost one was a foot shorter than the centre one with the after crosstree one foot longer than the centre one. The lengths given to the crosstrees in the tables apply in the first instance to the shortest of the two long crosstrees and in the second instance to the centre long crosstree. This method of carrying an extra crosstree required longer trestletrees than before 1815 though the snape and so forth was the same. The positioning of these longer trestletrees was such that the centre of the trestletrees was level with the centre of the topmast.

In 1833 a new, entirely different pattern of crosstrees called framed crosstrees was authorised.

The after one was slightly curved aft and longer than the forward one; a slot was cut in each end and a roller fitted and about 6 inches in from these slots another roller was let in. A short crosstree was fitted between the masts as in previous years except that the ends were not rounded. The foremost crosstree curved the same as the after one but was 2 feet shorter and a roller was let in 6 inches from each end. Two

iron stays were used to join these crosstrees together, one each side. The end made fast to the after crosstree was made to slide onto the crosstree; the other end had a fork and was bolted to the foremost crosstree. This end came about one foot in from the end of the crosstree.

Hinged to the ends of the fore crosstree were two curved pieces of wood joined together in the centre by means

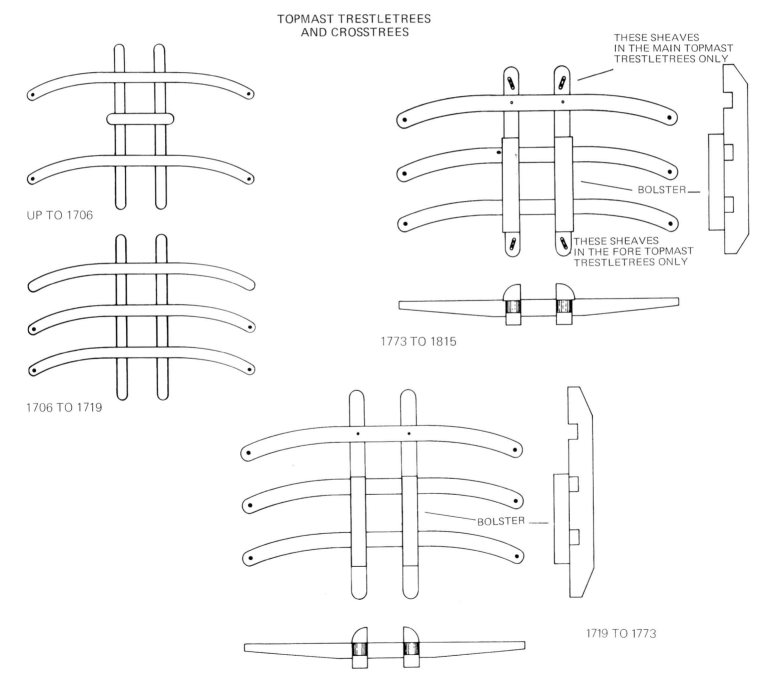

TOPMAST TRESTLETREES
AND CROSSTREES

UP TO 1706

1706 TO 1719

THESE SHEAVES IN THE MAIN TOPMAST TRESTLETREES ONLY

BOLSTER

THESE SHEAVES IN THE FORE TOPMAST TRESTLETREES ONLY

1773 TO 1815

BOLSTER

1719 TO 1773

MASTING
Topmast trestletrees and crosstrees

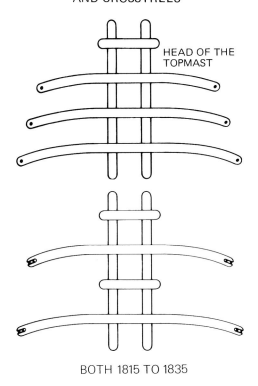

TOPMAST TRESTLETREES
AND CROSSTREES

HEAD OF THE
TOPMAST

BOTH 1815 TO 1835

of another piece of curved wood with two bolts and two iron hoops, the whole forming a curved extension to the foremost crosstree and the fore ends of the trestletrees. The crosstrees were let in to the trestletrees as in previous years. The fore part of the crosstrees was leathered. The above sounds complicated but reference to the illustration should make it abundantly clear.

During all periods a chock was required between the trestletrees under the crosstree forward of the topmast; after 1815 an additional chock was required abaft the topmast. These chocks were the same width as the crosstrees and came down level with the lower edge of the trestletrees. They were nailed to the topmast.

When the framed pattern of crosstrees was used, an iron plate was bolted under the trestletrees and chocks forming a square frame round the topmast which helped to hold everything together. Also at this period the crosstrees were no longer tapered on the under side and the ends of the trestletrees were not snaped but were rounded as those of the lower trestletrees. Bolsters were required, nailed onto the trestletrees with grooves cut in them to fit over the crosstrees. They came from just forward of the crosstree on the fore side of the topmast to a few inches aft of the after edge of the crosstree abaft the topmast. They were one inch wider than the trestletrees with a depth of six sevenths the width and the outer edge cut in a quarter circle.

It should be noted that before the mizen was fitted with a topgallant mast, the crosstrees and trestletrees were the same as those described for the topgallant masts. The following should be a guide to the dimensions when no definite information is available.

Trestletrees	Length	Depth	Breadth
Up to 1719	Three sevenths of the length of the lower trestletree.	1 1/8 inches to every foot of the length.	Three quarters of the depth.
1719 to 1773	One fifth of the length of the topgallant mast.	25/26 of an inch to 1 foot of the length.	Three quarters of the depth.
1773 to 1815	3 3/4 inches to every 3 feet of the topmast length.	1 inch to 1 foot of the length.	Two thirds of the depth.
1815 to 1835	Two ninths of the length of the topgallant mast.	Five forty-fourths of the length.	Five ninths of the depth.
1835 onwards	Three sevenths of the foremost crosstree.	1 7/8 inches to every foot of the length.	Five ninths of the depth.
1719 mizen	A half of the main top trestletree.	1 inch to 1 foot of the length.	Ten thirteenths of the depth.

Crosstrees	Length	Depth	Breadth
Up to 1719	Half a diameter of the masthead longer than the trestletrees.	Half of the depth of the trestletrees.	As the trestletrees.
1719 to 1773	Four fifteenths of the length of the topgallant mast.	Half of the depth of the trestletrees.	As the trestletrees.
1773 to 1815	One and two thirds the length of the trestletrees.	Seven eighths of the depth of the trestletrees.	As the trestletrees.
1815 to 1835	Twice the length of the trestletrees.	Eight ninths of the depth of the trestletrees.	As the trestletrees.
1835 onwards	After crosstree, five ninths the length of the topgallant mast to the stops. The fore crosstree was 2 feet shorter than the after one.	Five sixths of the depth of the trestletrees.	As the trestletrees.

MAIN TOPMAST TRESTLETREES AND CROSSTREES
NAVY BOARD WARRANT 1833, GIVES INSTRUCTION
THAT THE FORE PART OF THE CROSSTREES TO
BE LEATHERED

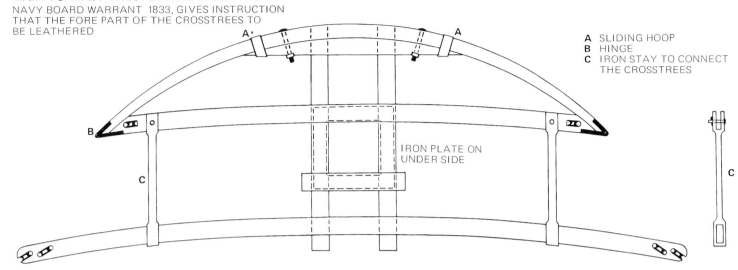

A SLIDING HOOP
B HINGE
C IRON STAY TO CONNECT
   THE CROSSTREES

IRON PLATE ON
UNDER SIDE

THE TOPGALLANT TRESTLE- AND CROSSTREES

The topgallant trestletrees and cross-trees were used during the seventeenth century on the fore and main topgal-lant masts and on the mizen and sprit topmasts. They were used for keeping the flag staffs in position. The trestle-trees were made in the same way as those for the topmasts but the cross-trees differed in that the after one curved aft while the forward one curv-ed forwards. Shrouds were seldom fitted, though I should imagine that with large ships it was sometimes nec-essary to rig shrouds, especially when a strong breeze was blowing, and that consequently the curvature of the crosstrees enabled the flag pole to be stayed all round. Holes would be re-quired in the ends of the crosstrees to lead the shrouds through so that they could be seized to the topgallant rigging.

The length of the trestletrees should be about half the length of those on the mast below and the proportions of width and depth the same as the pro-portions for the trestletrees on the mast below. The crosstrees were usual-ly just slightly shorter than the trestle-trees and were the same width and depth; they were set on the trestletrees by having half their depth cut out in the way of the trestletrees while a similar amount was cut out of the trestletrees.

THE MAST CAPS

Up to 1820 the length of the caps was four times the diameter of the round holes, the breadth twice the diameter of the round hole and the depth up to 1745 half the breadth and after 1745 two fifths the breadth. From 1820 the length was twice the breadth, the breadth one and three quarters the diameter of the round hole and the depth two thirds of the breadth. Up to about 1820 the fore and after ends of the caps were squared with the cor-ners slightly rounded; after that date the ends were rounded and were bound with iron which was between 3/8 and 5/8 inch thick, and one third the depth of the cap wide.

The cap was leathered inside the round hole, the hole being made 3/4 inch wider to allow room for this leather-ing. The fore part of the round hole up to 1820 was the depth of the cap from the end and after 1820 it was two thirds the depth from the end. The space between the after edge of the round hole and the fore edge of the square hole was the width of the cross-trees plus half the taper of the mast-head, and the amount allowed for the fore shoulder of the mast tenon. The square hole was nine tenths fore and aft and four fifths athwartships the size of the upper mast head.

Lower cap eyebolts Four eyebolts were put under the caps one either

SEVENTEENTH CENTURY
SPRIT TOPMAST
AND FORE AND MAIN
TOPGALLANT CROSSTREES

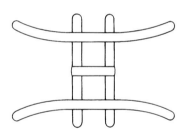

LOWER CAP

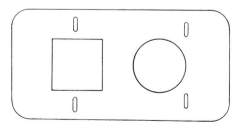

Mast caps

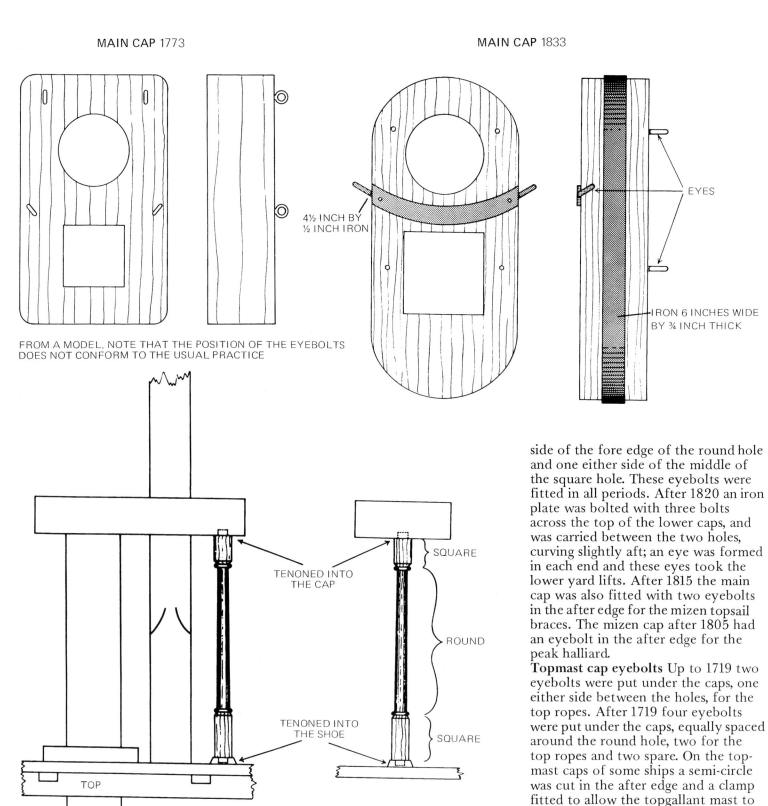

MAIN CAP 1773

FROM A MODEL. NOTE THAT THE POSITION OF THE EYEBOLTS
DOES NOT CONFORM TO THE USUAL PRACTICE

MAIN CAP 1833

4½ INCH BY
½ INCH IRON

EYES

IRON 6 INCHES WIDE
BY ¾ INCH THICK

TENONED INTO
THE CAP

SQUARE

ROUND

TENONED INTO
THE SHOE

SQUARE

TOP

CAP SHORE

side of the fore edge of the round hole
and one either side of the middle of
the square hole. These eyebolts were
fitted in all periods. After 1820 an iron
plate was bolted with three bolts
across the top of the lower caps, and
was carried between the two holes,
curving slightly aft; an eye was formed
in each end and these eyes took the
lower yard lifts. After 1815 the main
cap was also fitted with two eyebolts
in the after edge for the mizen topsail
braces. The mizen cap after 1805 had
an eyebolt in the after edge for the
peak halliard.

Topmast cap eyebolts Up to 1719 two
eyebolts were put under the caps, one
either side between the holes, for the
top ropes. After 1719 four eyebolts
were put under the caps, equally spaced
around the round hole, two for the
top ropes and two spare. On the topmast caps of some ships a semi-circle
was cut in the after edge and a clamp
fitted to allow the topgallant mast to
be carried abaft the topmast when
chasing. Caps were made this way from
1815 to 1835.

Cap shores On some ships, especially
large ones, it was the practice to fit a

TOPMAST CAPS

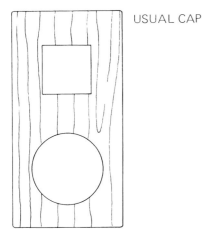

USUAL CAP

SOME SHIPS 1815 TO 1835

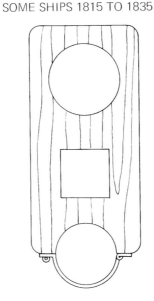

1745 ESTABLISHMENT

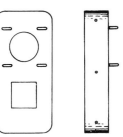

shore under the fore end of the lower caps, tenoned into the underside of the cap and the top. Its purpose was to take the strain of the weight of the fore overhang of the cap from the shoulders of the mast tenon. I have seen a contemporary model dated 1720 so fitted and this was only a 50 gun ship, but it was usually only the First and Second rates that carried them. Between 1810 and 1850 the main lower cap had a hole through the after edge for the mizen topgallant stay.

THE BOWSPRIT CAP

The bowsprit cap differed from the mast caps in that the top and bottom edges were cut at an angle to the fore and aft faces, allowing the cap to be carried at a 90 degree angle to the waterline. The angle of the top and bottom edges followed the steeve of the bowsprit.

The round hole for the jibboom was leathered and the amount left round the hole was half its diameter. The distance between the lower edge of the round hole and the upper edge of the square was two sevenths the diameter of the bowsprit. The square hole was three quarters the diameter of the outer end of the bowsprit across, and seven eighths down.

A groove was cut in the after face of the cap on the starboard side of the holes, coming down as far as level with the centre of the square hole. This

BOWSPRIT CAPS

BEFORE 1805 CAPS WERE THE SAME BUT WITH SQUARE CORNERS

1805 TO 1820

AFTER 1820

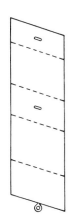

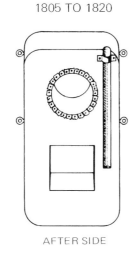

AFTER SIDE

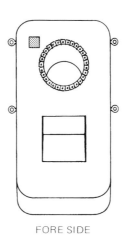

FORE SIDE

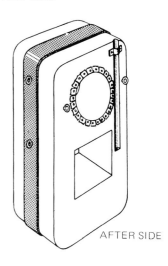

AFTER SIDE

groove was to take the jack staff. It was as wide as the jack staff and half as deep and a clasp on the upper part of the cap and a hole in the bees held the staff in position. The corners of the cap, up to about 1805, were squared off; after then they were rounded. After about 1820 the cap was iron bound like the mast caps.

When flying jibbooms were fitted, a socket was cut in the fore face of the cap at a 45 degree angle to the centre of the round hole so that the flying jibboom was carried on the starboard upper side of the jibboom. This socket was usually square and was cut half way between the round hole and the edge of the cap.

Up to 1820 the length of the cap was five times the diameter of the jibboom, the breadth was twice the diameter of the jibboom plus half the diameter of the jack staff (this additional amount was usually carried on the starboard side to allow extra room for the staff) and the thickness was four ninths of the breadth. After 1820, when iron bound caps were used, the length was five times the diameter of the jibboom, the breadth twice the diameter of the jibboom and the thickness 1 inch less than the jibboom's diameter.

Four eyebolts were driven into the side of the cap, two on each side, the upper one for the man-ropes, between the upper part of the round hole and the top of the cap, the lower one for the spritsail lift and the jibboom foot-ropes between the round hole and the square hole. After 1773 an additional eye was put in the bottom of the cap on the edge for the spritsail halliards. Eyebolts were also required after 1830 for the jibboom heel lashing; they were let in the after face of the cap on either side of the round hole and this necessitated cutting the groove for the jack staff closer to the bowsprit.

4 Ancillary spars and equipment

MARTINGALE BOOM OR DOLPHIN STRIKER

When first introduced in 1794, the striker was a piece of wood nailed on the fore side of the bowsprit cap. Its sole use was to take the martingale stay, for which purpose a score was cut on the outer end of the striker. By 1800 the stay was taken through a sheave in the striker. By 1805 the following ropes, from the lowest one up, were led through sheaves: fore royal stay, flying jibboom martingale, flying jib stay and fore topgallant stay. The martingale stay was by this time spliced round the striker above the fore topgallant stay sheave. In 1815 a further sheave or hole was put in the striker, close to the jaws, for the jib stay. This being a period of evolution, it is impossible to be any closer with the date, but by 1840, chain had replaced the ropes for the martingale stay and a spider band was put on the striker with one eyebolt for the stay and two more for the back ropes.

Some ships experimented with double strikers, but this does not seem to have been a general practice; it only meant doubling up of stays and was used about 1813 for only a few years. The upper end of the striker was fitted with jaws in 1815 and carried abaft the bowsprit cap. The illustrations will show the various changes on the striker. Its length was approximately half the length of the spritsail yard, or, when spreaders were used, the same length as one spreader.

THE SPREADERS OR SPRITSAIL GAFF

These replaced the spritsail yard during the period 1811/30 onwards; they were fitted with jaws and the whole length, was round, tapering slightly to the outer end. The spreader yard arm was made similar to the spritsail yard arm and in fact the spreaders were like half a spritsail yard with jaws on the inner end. A hole for the flying jibboom guys was drilled through the outer end of the spreader, just outboard of the rigging stop, in a fore and aft line.

DOLPHIN STRIKERS

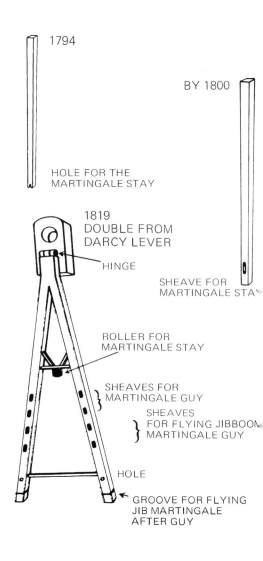

1794

BY 1800

HOLE FOR THE MARTINGALE STAY

1819 DOUBLE FROM DARCY LEVER

HINGE

SHEAVE FOR MARTINGALE STAY

ROLLER FOR MARTINGALE STAY

SHEAVES FOR MARTINGALE GUY

SHEAVES FOR FLYING JIBBOOM MARTINGALE GUY

HOLE

GROOVE FOR FLYING JIB MARTINGALE AFTER GUY

THE ENSIGN STAFF AND JACK STAFF

Both of these staffs were round the whole length and tapered slightly towards the truck. They were sometimes fitted with cleats for the flag halliards.

QUARTER DAVITS

Quarter davits came into general use about 1810. They were lengths of timber 8 to 10 inches square in section.. The length of the davits depended upon the build of the ship but they had to be long enough to allow the boats to be lowered clear of the ship's side when they were topped at an angle of about 40 degrees above the horizontal position.

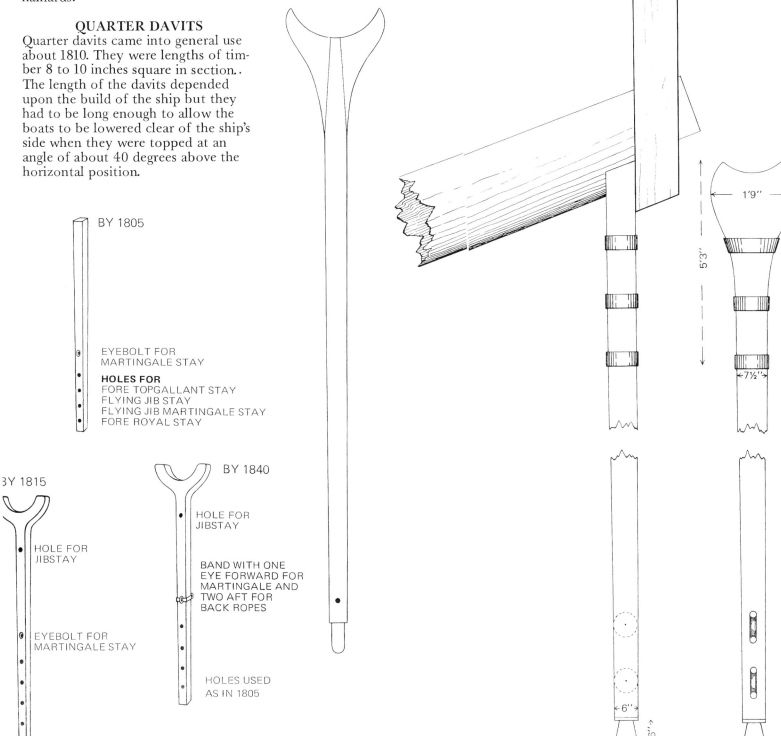

SPREADER OR SPRITSAIL GAFF

METHOD OF FITTING A DOLPHIN STRIKER WITH JAWS ON A 74 GUN SHIP
NAVY BOARD WARRANT
2 MAY 1815

BY 1805

EYEBOLT FOR MARTINGALE STAY

HOLES FOR
FORE TOPGALLANT STAY
FLYING JIB STAY
FLYING JIB MARTINGALE STAY
FORE ROYAL STAY

BY 1815

HOLE FOR JIBSTAY

EYEBOLT FOR MARTINGALE STAY

BY 1840

HOLE FOR JIBSTAY

BAND WITH ONE EYE FORWARD FOR MARTINGALE AND TWO AFT FOR BACK ROPES

HOLES USED AS IN 1805

1'9''

5'3''

7½''

6''

6''

I MASTING
Quarter davits

There were two sheaves in the head of each davit for the boat's fall, set so that a length of solid wood, equivalent to half the diameter of the sheaves was left at the end of the davit. The heel of the davit was rounded and secured to the ship's side by a bolt running through lugs set in the ship's side just above the mizen channels.

Where possible, and this was only when both davits could be carried above the mizen channels, iron crutches were bolted to the channels and supported the davits. The davits rested in the crutches and were held in place with a fore lock bolt. When crutches were fitted the davits were only about 8 inches square. When only one davit a side could be carried above the channels, crutches could not be used and the davits were supported solely by the topping lift; consequently they were made stouter and the 10 inch size was used.

QUARTER DAVIT FITTED TO HMS DRYAD
7 JUNE 1811

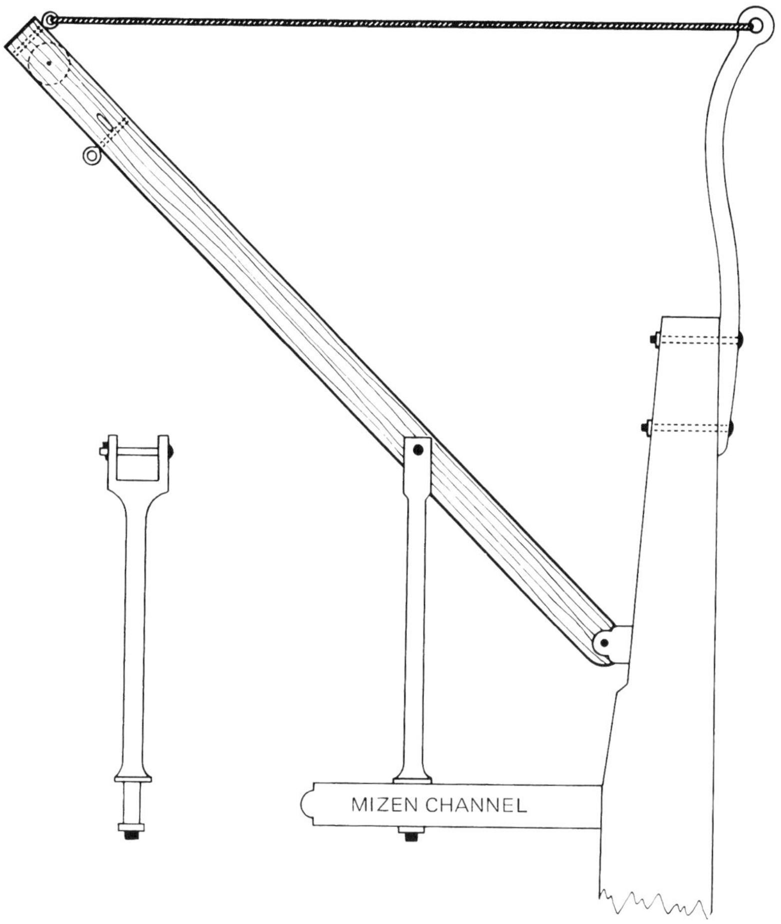

MIZEN CHANNEL

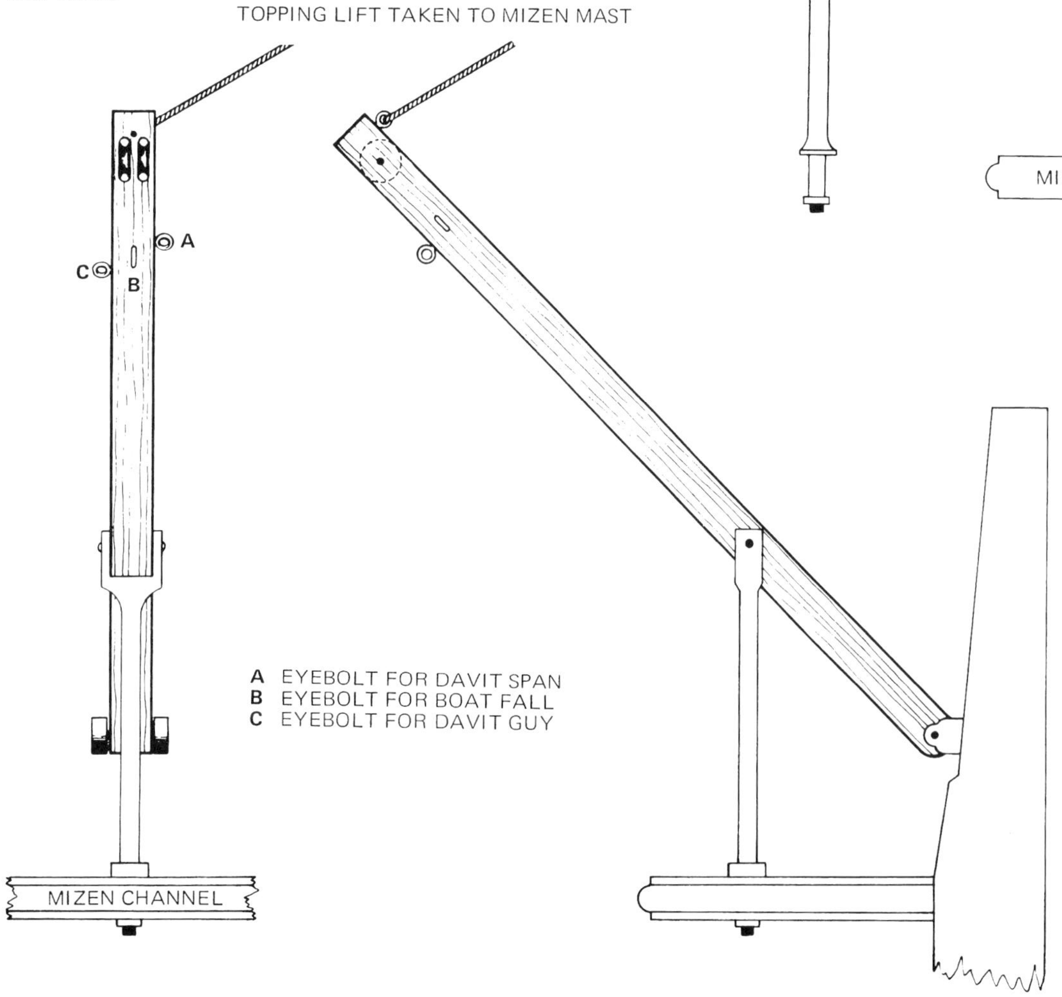

TOPPING LIFT TAKEN TO MIZEN MAST

A EYEBOLT FOR DAVIT SPAN
B EYEBOLT FOR BOAT FALL
C EYEBOLT FOR DAVIT GUY

QUARTER DAVITS DESIGNED BY
SIR ROBERT SEPPINGS

MIZEN CHANNEL

When davits were first used, guys and jackstays were secured to the davits by seizing them to thimbles stropped to the head of the davits just below the sheave, while the topping lift was secured at the davit head by a running eye in the end of the lift. Thumb cleats held the rigging in place on the davits. A few years after the introduction of the davits, eyebolts were used instead of the thimbles, the position of these eyebolts being as follows: the jackstay eyebolt was put in about 1 foot 9 inches from the head, the guy eyebolt about 2 feet from the head, the topping lift bolt about 3 inches from the head, and an eyebolt for the standing part of the boat's fall under the davit, 1 foot 6 inches from the head, all eyebolts being on the centre-line of the davits.

When no crutches were used, pieces of wood were nailed along the upper face of the davit for the foot treads. Some davits were also fitted with a cleat for turning up the boat's fall; the cleat was bolted on the upper side close to the davit's heel. Most times, however, the fall belayed inboard of the ship.

On HMS *Dryad* in 1811 an idea was tried whereby the topping lift ran from the head of the davits to iron stanchions bolted on the inside of the bulwarks in line with the davits. I believe that this was only an isolated experiment.

THE FISH DAVIT
Up to 1773 the fish davit was carried across the forecastle; its length was 7/9ths the breadth of the ship. It was square in section, the dimensions at the centre being 1 1/2 inches per yard in length. The davit tapered towards both ends, the ends being four fifths the size of the centre. Each end was made the same way with a necking formed about a foot from the ends. About 6 feet in from each end a hole was drilled from the fore to after faces; these holes were for a hand rope which ran continuously with overhand knots worked in it. Just inboard from these holes, but on the upper face, an eyebolt was set for the use of a topping lift tackle.

After 1773 the davit was made shorter and was used from the fore channels.

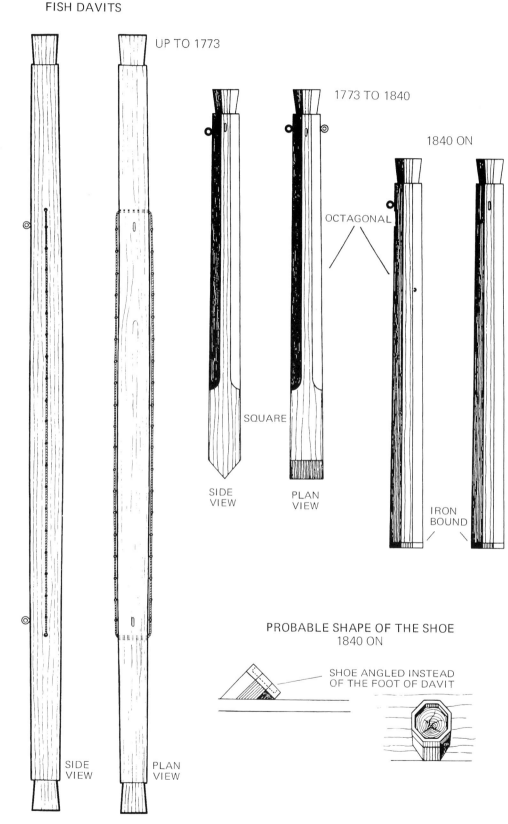

FISH DAVITS

UP TO 1773

1773 TO 1840

1840 ON

OCTAGONAL

SQUARE

SIDE VIEW

PLAN VIEW

IRON BOUND

SIDE VIEW

PLAN VIEW

PROBABLE SHAPE OF THE SHOE
1840 ON

SHOE ANGLED INSTEAD OF THE FOOT OF DAVIT

BOOMKINS

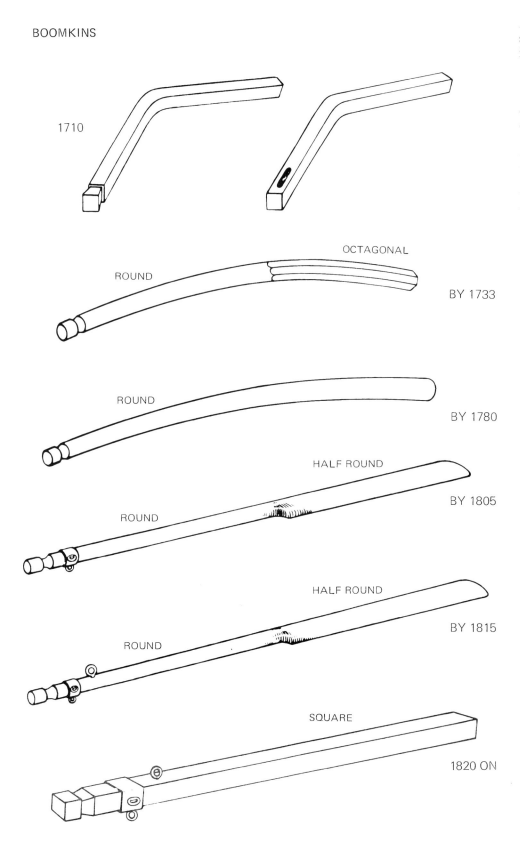

1710

OCTAGONAL

ROUND

BY 1733

ROUND

BY 1780

HALF ROUND

ROUND

BY 1805

HALF ROUND

ROUND

BY 1815

SQUARE

1820 ON

Its length was three tenths of the ship's breadth and its dimensions 1 inch per foot length. The inboard end was made square for a distance of three fourteenths of the length and the rest of the length was octagonal. The outer end was slightly smaller than the inner end (about 1 inch). A necking was formed one diameter in from the outer end and just inboard from this necking, on the upper face, an eyebolt was set for the topping lift; two other eyebolts for the guys were let in just outboard from the upper eyebolt but in the fore and after faces. The inboard end was shaped to fit against the ship's side and the channel. The shoe to stop the davit from slipping was only a flat wooden or iron batten bolted to the channel and shaped to fit the heel of the davit. After about 1840, the davit was used on the bill board as well as on the channels. It was made as in previous years but its heel was set in a step on the bill board or channels. It was usually octagonal all the way down. Though a shoe for stepping the davit is mentioned in many seamanship books of this period, I can find no description of them. I presume that the shoe was made either of iron or wood, probably the latter, in the shape of the heel of the davit. Its purpose was to stop the davit from slipping. Also at this time, the fore and after guys were spliced round the necking of the davit, and the eyebolts on the fore and after sides were not fitted; only the eyebolt for the topping lift was required.

THE BOOMKINS OR BUMKINS
Boomkins were generally introduced about 1710, though as early as 1680 there is evidence that some ships were fitted with them. When first used they were quite short, only protruding outboard for 6 feet or so. They were also curved sharply downwards, were square in section and about an inch wide to every foot in length. A necking was formed on the outer end for the strop of the tack block. However, I have seen an early example with a sheave in the end instead of the necking but this seems to have been the exception rather than the rule. The early boomkin did not taper.

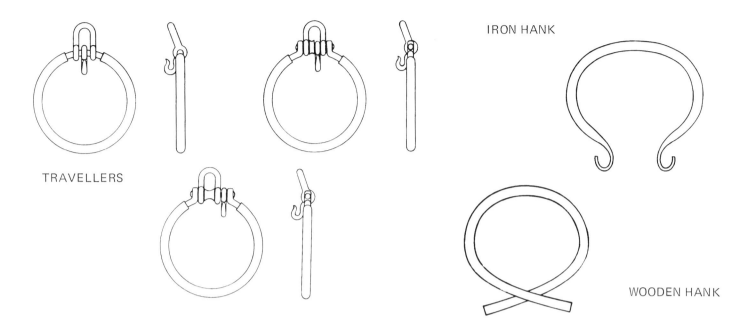

IRON HANK

TRAVELLERS

WOODEN HANK

By 1733 the boomkins were longer and though they still curved downwards, the curve was much less severe. Generally, the inboard section was half round or octagonal, while the outboard section was round. The boomkins tapered towards the outboard end, being about one quarter narrower there than at the heel. Their length varied with the individual ship, but they had to be long enough so that when the fore yard was braced sharply, the yard arm and the boomkin were in a straight line. Usually the boomkins butted against the beakhead though sometimes they butted or were bolted against knightheads on either side of the bowsprit, this latter method being used mainly after 1800. A necking was formed on the outer end until the close of the era of sail.

By about 1780 the boomkins had almost lost the downward curve, being either straight or only very slightly curved. They were made to the same proportions as in previous years.

In 1805 or thereabouts, as well as the necking, a spider band with three eyebolts was fitted just inboard of the necking; these eyebolts were for the boomkin shrouds. The boomkins were made straight and were half-round inboard and round on the outboard section.

From about 1815 an additional eye-

bolt, to take the slip securing the standing part of the tack, was fitted above the boomkin just abaft of the shroud eyes.

From about 1820, the boomkins, though fitted with eyes and so forth as previously, differed in that they were made almost square, 1 inch deeper than the width, the width being 3/4 inch to every foot in length. This was the final alteration.

THE TRAVELLERS AND HANKS

Travellers were used on the jibboom and flying jibboom. There were two types used. One consisted of a large ring carrying a shackle and hook sometimes with a thimble alongside the hook. The ring was made of iron between about 5/8 and 1 1/4 inches thick, the thickness dependent upon the size of the ship; the diameter of the ring was one and a quarter times the diameter of the jibboom. To prevent the ring from chafing the boom, it was covered in leather. The hook, shackle and thimble were a loose fit on the ring; the thimble was only required when the jibstay was made fast to the traveller, the stay being seized round the thimble. The other type of traveller was only used on the flying jibboom. It comprised an iron ring, split in the middle with the ends turned up, flattened out and held together with a

span bolt. On this span bolt a shackle, roller and hook were placed. The proportions of this traveller were the same as the jibboom traveller and it was also covered in leather. The illustrations should show clearly the differences between the two types used.

Hanks were required for some of the staysails and were made slightly larger than the appropriate stay. They were usually made of iron, bent round to a bow shackle shape with an eye in each end and were about 1 inch thick. Steel, in his book on masting and sailmaking, describes some made of wood notched together, but I have seen no model with wooden hanks and recommend the modeller to use the metal type.

SPANKER AND TRYSAIL HOOPS

As I mention in the rigging section, the spanker and trysails required hoops on the mast or trysail masts. These hoops were made of wood, usually ash, bent round and fastened together with a long scarf joint. They were about 2 inches thick and of such a diameter as to slide easily on the widest part of the masts. I have seen some really exquisite hoops on ship models and a good modelmaker should find it relatively easy to make them.

1 *Breda* fore mast, 1692.
Note the cheeks and
woodings.

2 *Breda*, 1692. Foot of
main mast.

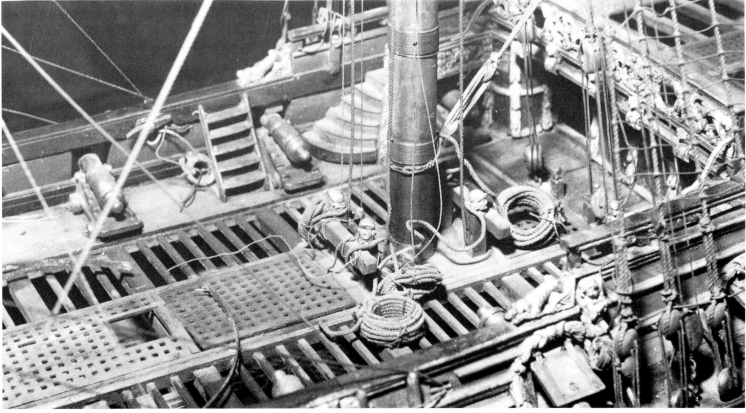

I MASTING
Masting on models

3 Fore mast of the *Medway*, 1742. Note the dolphin round the mast.

4 Head of the fore mast of the *Medway*, 1742.

5 Mizen mast head of the *Endeavour* model, 1768. (Not contemporary)

6 *Breda*, 1692. Sprit top from forward.

7 *Breda*, 1692. Sprit top showing futtock shrouds.

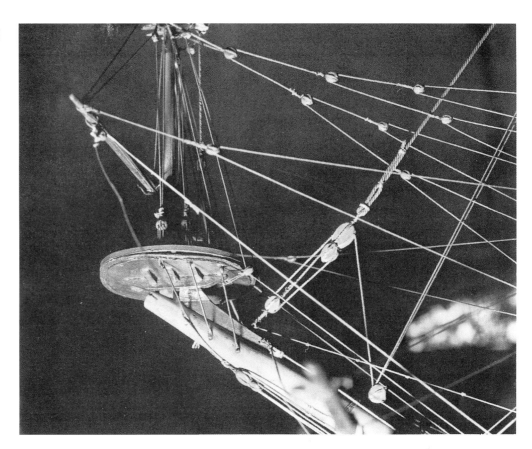

8 *Breda*, 1692. Fore top from the bows.

9 *Breda*, 1692. Main top from the bows.

10 Mizen top of a 20 gun ship of about 1710. Note the futtock shrouds.

11 Mizen top of a 20 gun ship of about 1710.

12 Fore top of the *Medway*, 1742, from below. Note the lead blocks under the top.

I MASTING
Masting on models

13 Main top of the *Medway,* 1742, from aft.

14 The main top of the *Medway,* 1742.

15 Mizen top of the *Medway*, 1742.

I MASTING
Masting on models

16 Mizen top of the *Medway,* 1742

17 Mizen top of the *Medway,* 1742.

18 Looking up at the fore top of the *Endeavour* model.

19 Fore topmast head of the *Medway*, 1742.

20 Draught of main topmast crosstrees and main top by Symonds.

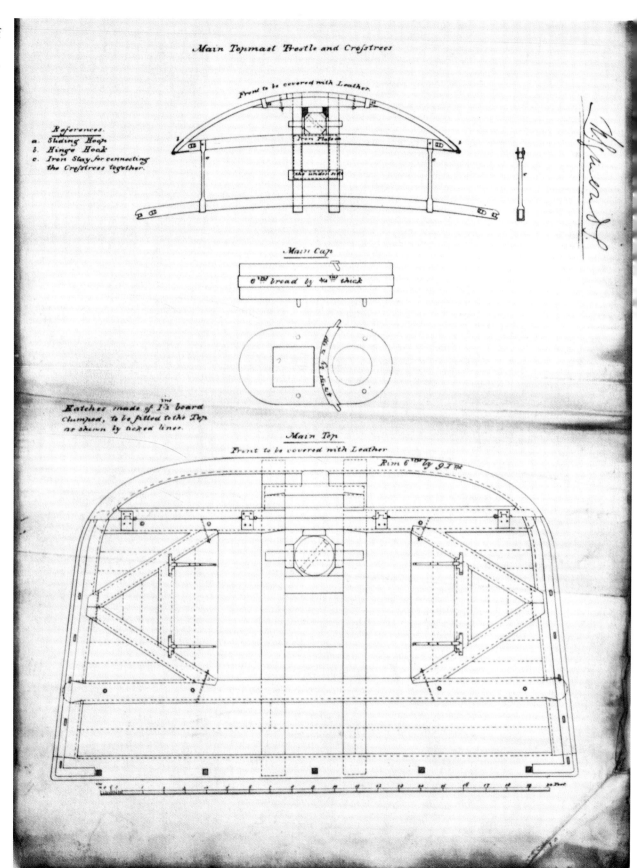

21 Draught of 1745 establishment (for 44 gun ships).

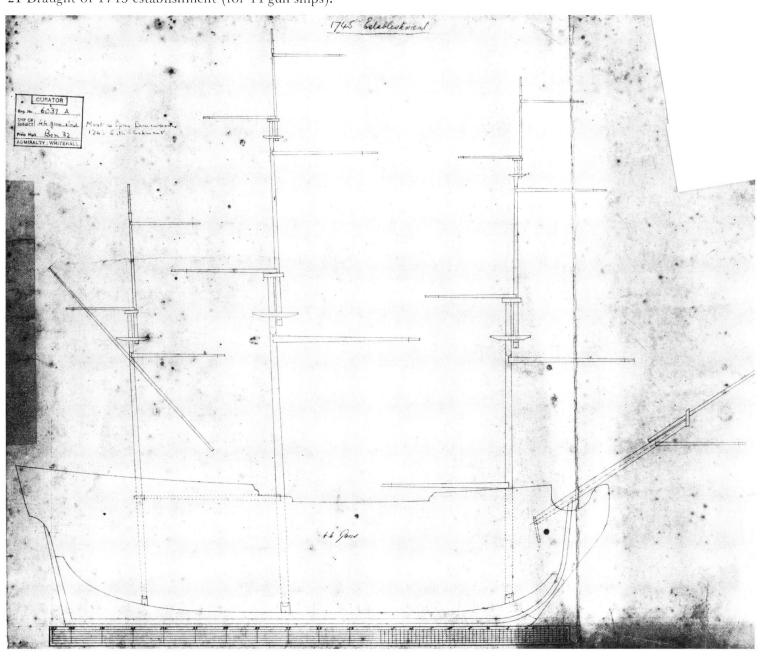

model of the *Victory* of 1737. Note the sprit topmast with the jibboom.

23 Main topmast head of the *Medway*, 1742.

24 Bowsprit cap, bees and so forth, of the *Medway*, 1742. Note the rather peculiar method of stepping the jack staff.

25 Draught of masts and spars of a 60 gun ship.

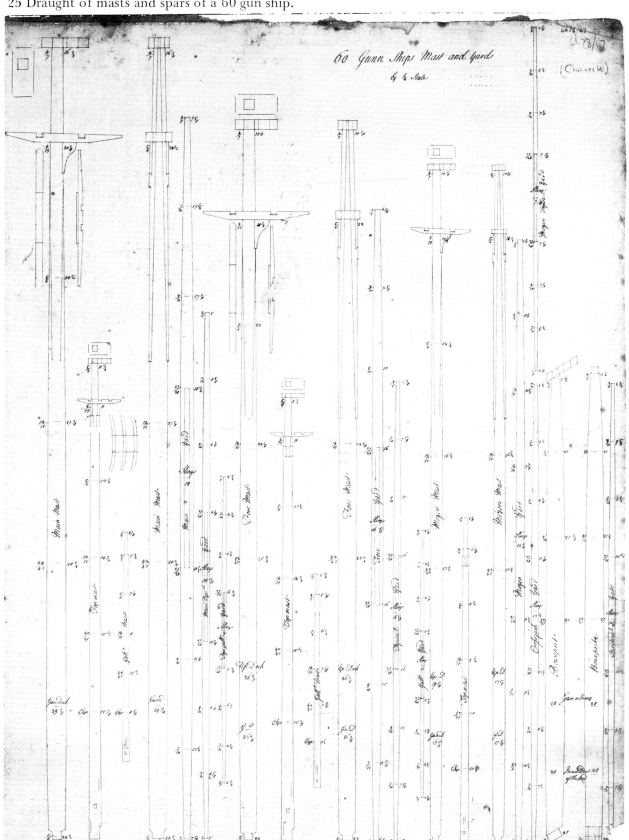

Rigging II

5 Lower masts, bowsprit and jibbooms

RIGGING TO THE FORE MAST
The stay was usually cable laid. Up to 1815 it was secured at the mast head by a small splice butting against a mouse raised on the stay. After 1815 a leg was spliced into the stay and an eye spliced into the end of both leg and stay; they were then seized together abaft the mast head with a rose lashing. During all periods they were served round the upper part to a distance of about 6 feet below the mouse or throat of the legs. The stay was usually wormed for the whole length. Up to 1690 the lower end had a deadeye seized into it; after that date a heart was used. On some ships after about 1840, iron thimbles were used instead of hearts.
The collar was fitted round the bowsprit with a deadeye or heart seized in the bight. It was held in place on the bowsprit by thumb cleats and the collar was spliced to form a strop. A round seizing was used to tighten the collar round the bowsprit and heart or deadeye, hearts being used after 1690. From about 1733, the collar was put on double, being made like a large strop. It was taken under the bowsprit and both parts of the collar were laid in the scores of the heart, two scores being made in the heart for this purpose. The two ends of the collar were

then seized together under the bowsprit with a rose lashing. The shape of the heart was altered in about 1773 and an open heart introduced. The collar was seized to the heart by two seizings laid in scores cut in the heart for this purpose. From about 1840 some ships used iron thimbles instead of hearts, but this was not a general rule.
A lanyard was used to haul taut the stay to the collar. When deadeyes were used, a stopper knot was made in the end of the lanyard; the other end was rove through alternate eyes, starting with the upper deadeye. The end, after hauling taut, was taken through the throat between the deadeye and the stay, led under itself to form a half-hitch, then wound round the stay and stopped to it. When hearts were used, the lanyard was spliced into the upper heart, then rove through alternate hearts, using as many turns as the

heart would allow or until the lanyard was used up. The end of the lanyard was seized to the turn of the lanyard adjacent to itself with a couple of seizings.
A preventer stay was fitted in the same way as the stay, and was introduced in about 1700. Usually the preventer was carried above the stay, but on small ships it was sometimes carried under it. Both the stay and preventer stay were sometimes turned in cutter-stay fashion, especially after about 1840. During wartime in the eighteenth century up to about 1810, the stay and preventer stay were often snaked together, the snaking being seized alternately to the preventer stay and stay and finishing up close to the hearts. I have not seen any evidence of snaking before the eighteenth century.
A collar was fitted in the same way as the stay collar. The collars of both

TURNING IN OF THE LOWER STAYS

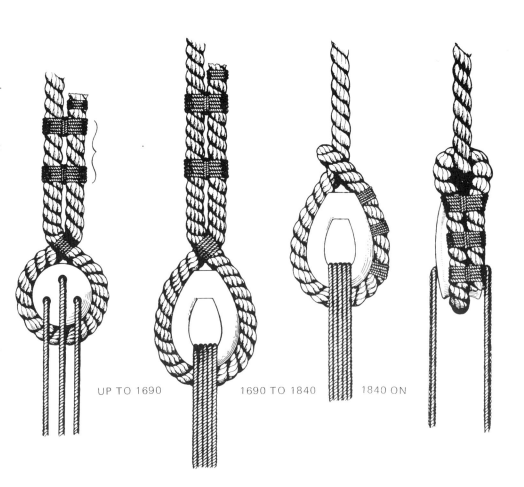

UP TO 1690   1690 TO 1840   1840 ON

stay and preventer stay on some ships were made long enough to allow the jibboom to be taken through them; this was not the general practice, however, until about 1773 when open hearts were introduced. Hearts were not used on the preventer stay until 1719, deadeyes being used prior to that date. When iron thimbles were used, the collars were seized so that the thimbles lay to the side of the jibboom, the preventer on the starboard side and the stay on the port side. From 1733 the collar was double as described for the forestay collar.

A lanyard was fitted in the same way as the stay lanyard.

Shrouds were mostly made of shroud laid rope, though sometimes cable laid rope was used. Shrouds were put on the masthead in pairs, the first pair being the forward starboard one, the next the forward port one, then starboard and port alternately, seized together allowing the bight round the mast to be between one and a quarter and one

STAY AND PREVENTER STAY
WORMED AND SNAKED

FORE STAY COLLARS

A UP TO 1690
B 1690 TO 1733
C 1733 TO 1773
D 1773 ON
E 1840 ON

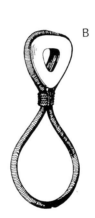

A   B   C

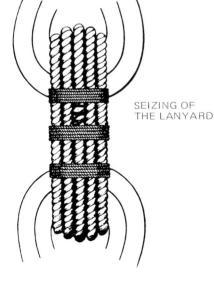

SEIZING OF
THE LANYARD

D

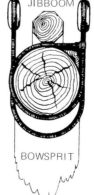

JIBBOOM

E

THE CHOCK IS WEDGE SHAPED AND ITS PURPOSE
IS TO HOLD THE STROP TO THE SIDE OF THE BOWSPRIT

BOWSPRIT

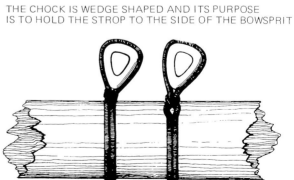

FORE STAY
COLLAR

PREVENTER
STAY COLLAR

II RIGGING
Rigging to the fore mast

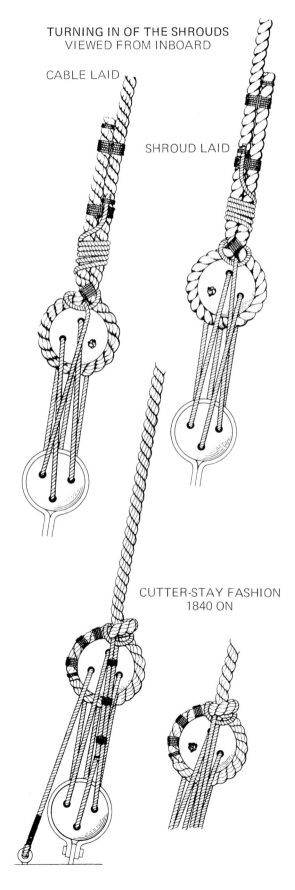

TURNING IN OF THE SHROUDS
VIEWED FROM INBOARD

CABLE LAID

SHROUD LAID

CUTTER-STAY FASHION
1840 ON

and a sixth the circumference of the mast head.

The bight was served to a distance of about 8 feet either side of the middle. The foremost shroud was wormed and served right down; the others were usually wormed, but not served below the served part round the mast head. A deadeye was turned in the end, left handed if shroud laid rope was used, right handed if cable laid. The end of the shroud was crossed at the deadeye and a throat seizing put on; two round seizings were put on round both parts of the shroud, the end of the shroud being capped with canvas. From about 1840, the deadeyes were turned in cutter-stay fashion. To turn in a deadeye in this way, the shroud was taken down the fore side of the deadeye, round the deadeye and its end taken round the standing part of the shroud from out to in, then laid alongside the part of the shroud round the deadeye. A throat and two round seizings were put on the two parts. Wider scores were made in the deadeyes when cutter-stay fashion was used. After 1805 the shrouds were always made of cable laid rope. To prevent the shrouds from twisting it was the practice, especially in the nineteenth century, to lash an iron bar across the shrouds just above the upper deadeye; this was known as the sheer pole. It was carried on the outboard side of the shrouds and was about 2 inches in diameter.

The Lanyard, up to the time of the introduction of turning the deadeyes in cutter-stay fashion, had a stopper knot made in one end; the other end rove either through the right hand hole of the upper deadeye when shrouds were made of right handed rope, or left hand hole in the case of cable laid rope; then, through alternate holes between the upper and lower deadeyes, the end finishing up by reeving through the throat above the upper deadeye, half-hitching round itself and wound spirally round the shroud, the extreme end being seized to the shroud. With turning in cutter-stay fashion, however, a different method of fitting the lanyards was introduced. First the end of the lanyard was spliced into eyebolts set in the channels abaft and a little inboard of the deadeyes;

the other end rove through the after hole in the upper deadeye, through alternate holes, through the throat, forward round the shroud and a clove-hitch was formed on the shroud inside the throat, finishing up by being seized to the last part of the lanyard with three seizings. Some ships used a stopper knot on the lanyard for a few years after the cutter-stay fashion was introduced.

A swifter was not always rigged and usually refers instead to the after shroud; if there was an odd number of shrouds, the after one was called the swifter. There was nothing unusual in this shroud except that the upper end was fitted at the mast head by means of an eye splice, the lower being secured exactly the same as other shrouds.

Pendants of tackles were fitted each side of the mast. In large ships there were two a side and in ships of 50 guns and below, only one. When two pairs were fitted, they were rigged like the shrouds, that is, the pendants were made from one length of rope seized to form a bight round the mast. When only one pair was rigged, they were fitted individually with eye-splices. In all cases, the pendants were served for their whole length. In the seventeenth century the foremost pendant came a little under half way down the mast but in the eighteenth and nineteenth centuries they came level with the upper catharpins. Up to 1780, a single block was spliced into the end; after that date a thimble was used. When two pendants were fitted on each side, the after ones were 1 foot longer than the forward ones. In First and Second Rate ships between 1733 and 1773, the aftermost pendant had a long-tackle block spliced in the end; it had no runner, the fall reeving straight through this block. The foremost pendant was, however, fitted in the usual way with a single block.

Runners of tackles are very seldom seen rigged in models. They were about four times the length of the pendant and had a double block spliced in one end. This block made up one part of the tackle falls; the other end either rove through the block in the pendant or rove through a block hooked into the thimble of the pen-

UPPER CATHARPINS

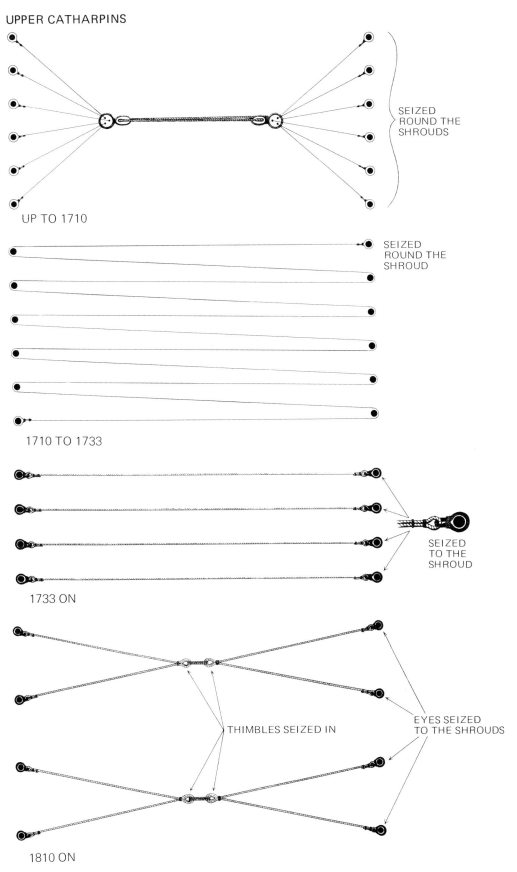

SEIZED
ROUND THE
SHROUDS

UP TO 1710

SEIZED
ROUND THE
SHROUD

1710 TO 1733

SEIZED
TO THE
SHROUD

1733 ON

THIMBLES SEIZED IN

EYES SEIZED
TO THE SHROUDS

1810 ON

dant, whichever was applicable. The end was seized or hitched to any object to be hoisted. On models showing the runner, the end is usually seized to a deadeye on the fore channels. In small ships the runner was often dispensed with, and the falls rove through the pendant block or block hooked into the pendant thimble.

Falls of tackles consisted of a single block used in conjunction with the double block on the runner, the lower block being hooked, or in later years shackled, to an eyebolt in the deck close to the bulwarks. The standing part of the falls was spliced to the lower block strop, the running part leading from the upper block.

Upper catharpins were used to bowse in the shrouds in the way of the futtock staves. There were many ways of rigging the catharpins, the most general being as follows: during the seventeenth century the legs rove through a deadeye on either side, making six legs in all. Each leg was seized to a shroud and the two deadeyes were hove taut by a fall rove through single blocks stropped to them; the fall was then made fast round itself. From about 1700 to about 1733, a single line was used, running from port to starboard round each shroud and futtock stave, the ends being seized to a shroud; the parts were then bowsed in by frapping them in two or three bundles. After about 1733, the legs were short lengths of rope running from one shroud on the port side to its opposite shroud on the starboard, being seized to the shrouds and the futtock staves. There were four in number, except for the period between 1733 and 1750, when they numbered the same as the futtock shrouds, and they were served all over. An alternative method of fitting the upper catharpins, from about 1810 on, was to have the legs only coming half way between the shrouds, and then seizing the two opposite sides together in the centre. The legs comprised two pieces of ropes on each side; each end had an eye spliced in it and was seized to the shrouds. A thimble was seized in the bight of each leg and were connected to their opposite number with a lashing.

43

II | RIGGING
Rigging to the fore mast

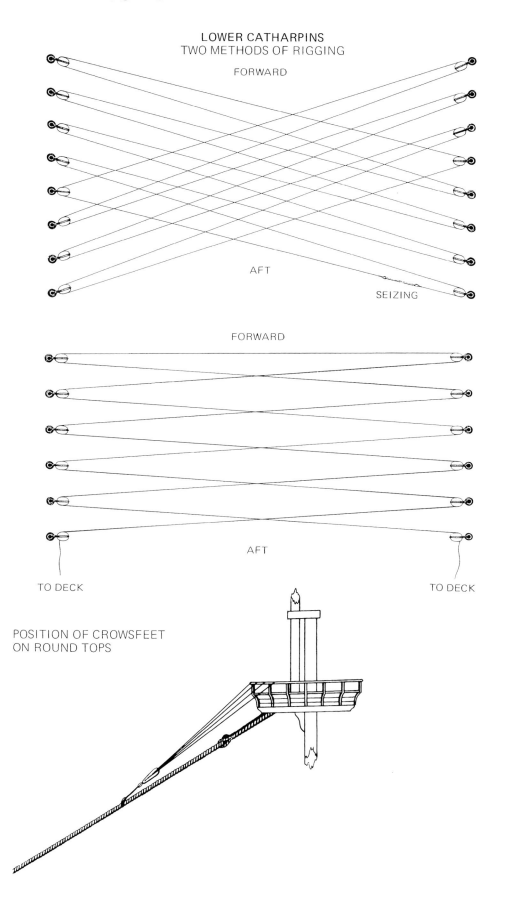

LOWER CATHARPINS
TWO METHODS OF RIGGING

FORWARD

AFT

SEIZING

FORWARD

AFT

TO DECK

TO DECK

POSITION OF CROWSFEET
ON ROUND TOPS

Lower catharpins were used to bowse in the lower part of the shrouds; they were only in use up to about 1730 at the latest. They were continuous lengths of rope rove through small blocks seized to the lower shrouds about one third up the shrouds, and they ran from side to side in a diagonal pattern. The ends were either secured to the shrouds, brought down to deck and hitched to a timber head, or seized together.

Ratlines were spaced 13 to 15 inches apart and had an eye spliced in one end through which they were seized to the fore shroud. The other end was clove-hitched round each shroud in turn and had an eye spliced in the end which was seized to the second shroud from aft, counting the swifter as a shroud. About every sixth ratline was taken to the swifter or aftermost shroud on some ships. On some ships between 1733 and 1773 the first six ratlines started from the second shroud from forward, the rest of the ratlines being rigged as before. After 1773 the first six ratlines and the upper six ratlines started from the second shroud from forward and finished at the second shroud from aft: the remainder covered all shrouds.

Wooldings of rope were used up to 1800, when iron bands took their place. The number varied, but on an average eight or nine were put on the mast. They consisted of turns of rope bound tightly round the mast at an equal distance from each other. About ten turns of rope were taken for each woolding. On either side of each, a piece of wood was nailed to keep the woolding (which was also nailed to the mast) in place. When a front fish was fitted to the mast, the woolding encircled both mast and fish, while an iron hoop was put on round the mast but under the front fish between each woolding. For a description of the iron bands which superseded the woolldings, reference should be made to the section devoted to mast furnishings.

Crowsfeet were probably introduced in the middle of the seventeenth century, and comprised a rope spliced round the strop of the euphroe block, its other end reeving through the centre hole in the rim of the top from

CROWSFEET OF THE TOP

MAIN STAY COLLAR
1690 TO 1810

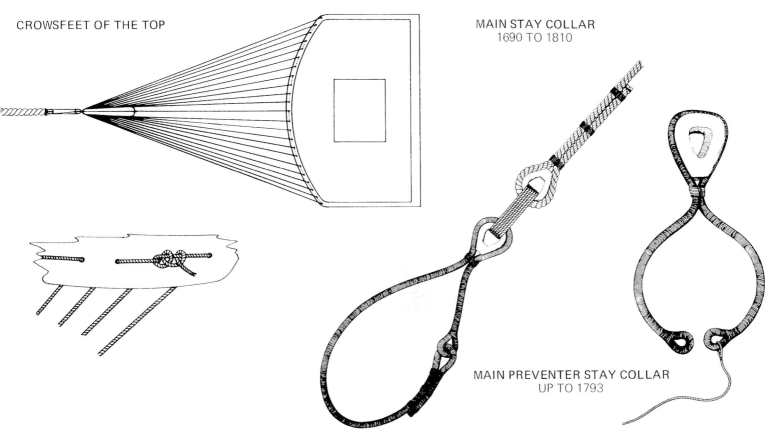

MAIN PREVENTER STAY COLLAR
UP TO 1793

above, up through the next hole to port, through the upper hole of the euphroe block, up through the inner starboard hole in the top and so on until the end finally came out of the outer hole on the starboard side of the top. There it was hitched to the under part of the previous lead through the top. It ceased to be generally used by the end of the eighteenth century.

Euphroe tackle comprised a single block stropped to the euphroe block and another block seized to the stay. The standing part of the fall was made fast to the upper block. The running part, after reeving through both blocks was either hitched to the stay below the lower block or was made fast round the tackle.

Standing backstay sizes are given in rigging dimensions of the seventeenth century, but I doubt very much if they were ever fitted. In all probability the after shroud or swifter was called the standing backstay in this period, and I would advise anyone to consider it as incorporated with the shrouds. I have

only come across one model (dated 1740) which shows a standing backstay, and this was fitted in the same way as the shrouds.

RIGGING TO THE MAINMAST
The stay was secured in the same way as the fore stay. In the seventeenth century the deadeye or heart in the lower end usually came level or just forward of the fore mast. In some ships, especially in the early seventeenth century, it came a little abaft the fore mast. In the eighteenth and nineteenth centuries the heart came just abaft the forecastle head. The stay led to the starboard side of the fore mast. The shape of the heart varied little over the years, the only difference being after about 1810 when the stay led to the inside of the fore bulwarks and a slightly different shape of heart was introduced. From about 1840 on some ships iron thimbles were used instead of hearts; this was only an experiment, however.

The collar, up to about 1690, comprised a long strop with a deadeye seized in the bight, the rope leading through a hole in the beak below the bowsprit before being spliced together. The collar came between the forecastle rails and the deck. After 1690 a heart was used, the rope leading as before but instead of being spliced together to from a strop, one end had a small eye spliced in it and the other end rove through this eye and was then hitched or seized to its own part; the end with the eye-splice always lay on the port side of the bowsprit. During all periods the collar was served all over. The collar ceased to be used about 1810 when the heart was shackled directly to an eyebolt either set into the inside of the bulwarks on the starboard side of the bowsprit or set in the deck on the starboard side of the fore mast.

A lanyard was fitted in the same way as the fore stay lanyard.

A preventer stay was fitted at the upper end in the same way as on the fore mast. The lower end had the usual

II RIGGING
Rigging to the mainmast

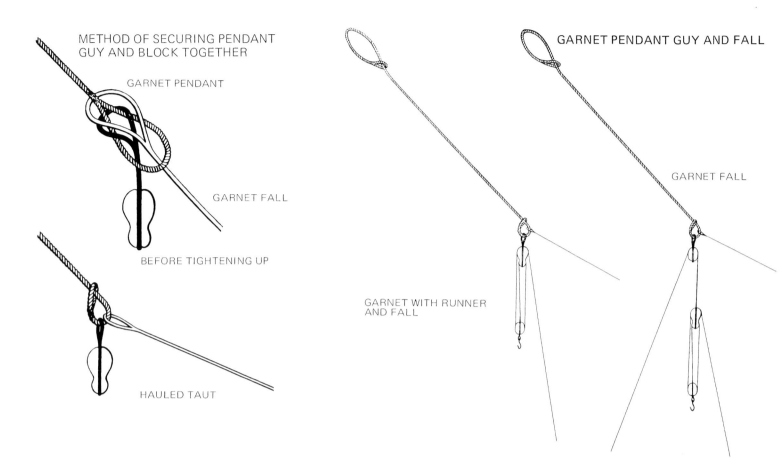

METHOD OF SECURING PENDANT
GUY AND BLOCK TOGETHER

GARNET PENDANT

GARNET FALL

BEFORE TIGHTENING UP

HAULED TAUT

GARNET WITH RUNNER
AND FALL

GARNET PENDANT GUY AND FALL

GARNET FALL

heart seized in it but only came abaft the fore mast until 1793 when, by Admiralty order, it led, like the main stay, to the bowsprit. After 1810 it led either to the bulwarks or to the deck on the opposite side to the main stay. The preventer stay was introduced in about 1700. When taken to the bowsprit, the preventer stay led to the same side of the mast as the mainstay.

The collar was formed of a length of rope with an eye in each end and was seized with a throat lashing round the heart. It was served all over and was of such a length that the two ends could be lashed together on the fore side of the fore mast with a rose lashing. When carried on the mast, the collar was usually placed so that there was a gap of about 2 feet between the stays at the fore mast. From 1793 the collar was put round the bowsprit below the gammon lashing in a similar way to the main stay collar. After 1810 the collar was dispensed with and the heart was shackled to an eyebolt in the deck at the foot of the fore mast,

and on the other side of the mast to that taking the main stay heart. Neither the stay nor the preventer stay collars were ever fitted with open hearts.

The lanyard was fitted in the same way as the stay lanyard.

Shrouds, swifters and their lanyards were fitted as on the fore shrouds. Usually one or two more shrouds were fitted each side than on the fore mast; swifters were fitted as on the fore mast.

Pendants, runners and falls of tackles were fitted the same as the fore mast pendants, runners and falls of tackles.

Girtlines were used to hoist jeer blocks, caps, and so forth up the mast and unrove when not in use. They are not expected to be seen on models.

Upper and lower catharpins were fitted in the same way as the fore mast catharpins, the lower ones being only used up to 1733.

Ratlines were fitted in the same way as the fore mast ratlines.

Wooldings were fitted in the same way

as the fore mast wooldings. Usually one more woolding was carried on the main mast than on the fore mast.

The pendant of the garnet consisted of an eye spliced in each end with the lower end reeving through the eye in the upper end thus forming a noose round the main mast head. The pendant led forward from the mast head between the trestletrees and was hauled forward over the main hatch by the garnet guy. The eye in the other end was a long eye. The pendant of the garnet was replaced by the stay tackle pendant about 1730.

The guy of the garnet was connected to the pendant as illustrated, its purpose being to keep the garnet in position over the hatch; it led to the fore jeer bitts where it was belayed.

A runner of the garnet was sometimes used in large ships to give added power to the falls. It was rigged in a similar way to the runners of the tackles. A long-tackle block was spliced in one end and the other end rove through a

MAIN STAY TACKLES

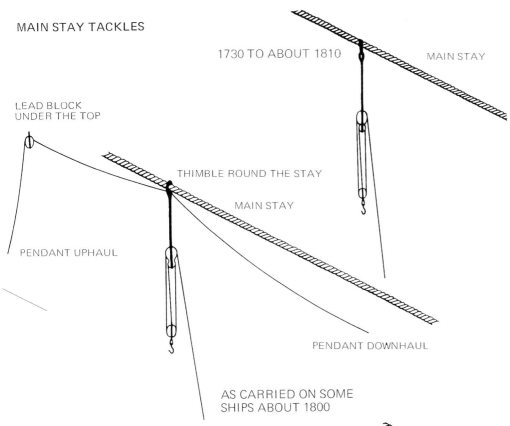

1730 TO ABOUT 1810

MAIN STAY

LEAD BLOCK
UNDER THE TOP

THIMBLE ROUND THE STAY

MAIN STAY

PENDANT UPHAUL

PENDANT DOWNHAUL

AS CARRIED ON SOME
SHIPS ABOUT 1800

used (between the years 1733 and 1745) was a short pendant seized to the main stay over the fore hatch in a similar manner to the stay tackle pendant. The fall was similar to the stay tackle fall. About 1773 or a little after, the pendant was dispensed with and a double block was seized to the stay in its place, the fall reeving between this block and a single hook block.

The winding tackle was a rope, onto which a double block was seized, fastened between the main and fore mast heads with a single hook block connected by a fall to this double block. This winding tackle was used to get guns, and so forth on board and was taken down when finished with. From about 1773 the winding tackle comprised a pendant secured to the main mast head, with a four-fold block toggled to the end; a guy was hitched to the pendant and rove through a block lashed to the fore yard outboard of the ship's side and the guy made fast on deck. A fall was rove between the four-fold block and a treble hook block.

single block in the end of the garnet pendant.

Falls of the garnet comprised a long-tackle block seized to the pendant or spliced into the runner whichever was applicable, and a single hook block. The running part rove from the long-tackle block down to deck.

A stay tackle pendant took the place of the garnet pendant and was seized to the main stay over the main hatch, a small eye being spliced into the upper end to take this seizing; a double block was spliced into the lower end. At the end of the eighteenth century a thimble was spliced into the upper end of the pendant to enable the pendant to slide up and down the stay, the thimble being around the stay; this system did not last long because of the wear on the stay. The stay tackle was in use from 1730 to about 1810.

The stay tackle fall consisted of the same type of blocks and rove in the same way as the garnet falls. A runner was never rigged with the stay tackle.

The fore hatch stay tackle, when first

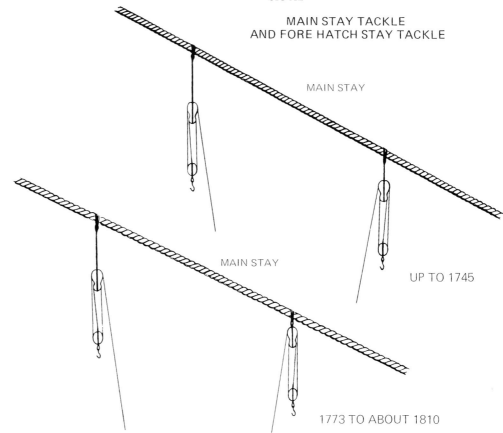

MAIN STAY TACKLE
AND FORE HATCH STAY TACKLE

MAIN STAY

MAIN STAY

UP TO 1745

1773 TO ABOUT 1810

SETTING UP THE MIZEN STAY

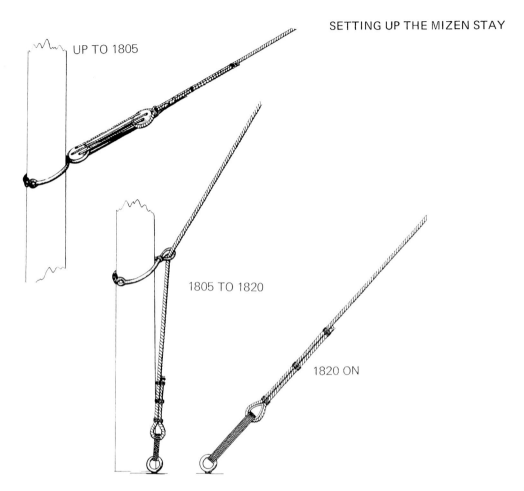

UP TO 1805

1805 TO 1820

1820 ON

RIGGING TO THE MIZEN MAST

The mizen stay upper end was fitted in the same way as the fore stay. Up to 1805 the lower end had a deadeye seized into it and was connected by a lanyard to a deadeye stropped about 6 feet up the main mast from the upper deck. From 1805 to about 1820 the stay led through a bullseye or thimble stropped in the same position as the deadeye in previous years to the main mast, and was secured to an eyebolt in the deck abaft the mast by means of a lanyard and thimble in the end of the stay. From 1820 on, the stay, wormed in the same way as the fore and main stays, led directly to the deck on the port side of the main mast and was secured there to an eyebolt by means of a lanyard and thimble. The collar was made from a piece of rope with an eye spliced in each end. The deadeye, bullseye or thimble was seized in the bight and the ends taken on either side of the mast where they were secured together with a rose lashing. The collar was served all over.

A preventer stay was in general use from 1820. The upper end was fitted in the same way as the mizen stay. The lower end was set up on the starboard side of the mast similar to the mizen stay. An Admiralty order of 1793 allowed the use of a preventer stay when required, in which case it would be taken to the main mast in a similar way to the mizen stay.

Shrouds were rigged in the same way as the fore shrouds.

Burton pendants were fitted in the same way as the fore topmast burton pendants, these being the equivalent of the pendants of tackles on the fore and main masts. During the seventeenth century there was a period of about twenty years, 1650 to 1670, when only the largest ships carried them and even then not all were so fitted. However, when they were fitted the lower end had a single block spliced into it; this single block was superseded by a long-tackle block about 1700 and remained like that until 1770. Then, first an eye was spliced into the pendant end, followed a few years later by a thimble. Up to about 1770 the burton pendants were led aft of the mast and the falls made fast to an eyebolt abaft the mizen channels where they were set up to act as a shifting backstay. The pendants were the same proportionate length as the fore tackle pendants.

Falls, up to 1700, comprised two single blocks, one in the pendant, the other a hook block which was set up where required. After 1700 the falls comprised a long-tackle block in the pendant and a single hook block. In both cases the running part rove from the upper block. When thimbles or eyes were spliced into the ends of the pendants the falls comprised either two single hook blocks or one single and one double hook block, but these were only rigged when required and usually the pendants were seized to the after mizen shroud by the futtock stave. From 1733 the running part of the fall rove through a sheave or hole in a timber head just forward of the mizen topmast backstay and was belayed round the timber head.

Upper catharpins were rigged in the same way as the fore and main catharpins.

Ratlines were rigged in the same way as those on the fore and main masts but were taken across all shrouds.

Wooldings were not used on the mizen until about the middle of the eighteenth century. Fewer wooldings were fitted on the mizen than on the other masts, the average number being three on small ships to seven on large. Like the other masts, iron bands superseded the rope wooldings in 1800.

Crowsfeet were rigged in the same way as the fore and main crowsfeet.

RIGGING TO THE BOWSPRIT

Gammoning was used in all periods and usually only one was fitted, though large ships were sometimes fitted with two. One end was made fast round the bowsprit with a round turn and was then clenched to the bowsprit. The other end rove through the hole in the stem and up to the bowsprit. About ten turns were taken, keeping the gammoning turns forward on the bowsprit and aft in the hole, thus giving the appearance of a twist. The turns were frapped together in the middle by as many turns as there were over the bowsprit, the end being seized to an adjacent turn.

Shrouds were an innovation of 1706, one shroud a side being carried until 1810. Fitted with a deadeye or heart in the forward end, the after end had a hook which hooked into an eyebolt in the bows. After 1810 two shrouds a side were carried, fitted in the same way. In about 1850 the innermost ones were made of chain and were fitted with lanyards forward and aft. Hearts were usually used in preference to deadeyes from about 1773.

Collars were made either by splicing the ends together and seizing a deadeye or heart in the bight, or by splicing a small eye in each end and seizing a deadeye or heart in the bight. In the first case, the collar was made of such a length as to fit round the bowsprit and deadeye, the seizing holding it tight round the bowsprit. In the second case, the strop was long enough to fit round the deadeye or heart with the two ends almost meeting round the bowsprit; the ends were then lashed together with a lanyard. Very often the collars on the bowsprit were covered with leather, which applied to all collars.

Lanyards were fitted in the usual way.

Bobstays were introduced in about 1685 when one was fitted and quite a thin one at that. This single bobstay held good until about 1719 when two were fitted. Two were used up to 1800 when, on 14 May, three were authorised. In about 1850 chain bobstays shackled to the stem superseded the rope bobstays. Bobstays of rope were made by reeving the rope through a hole in the stem and splicing both

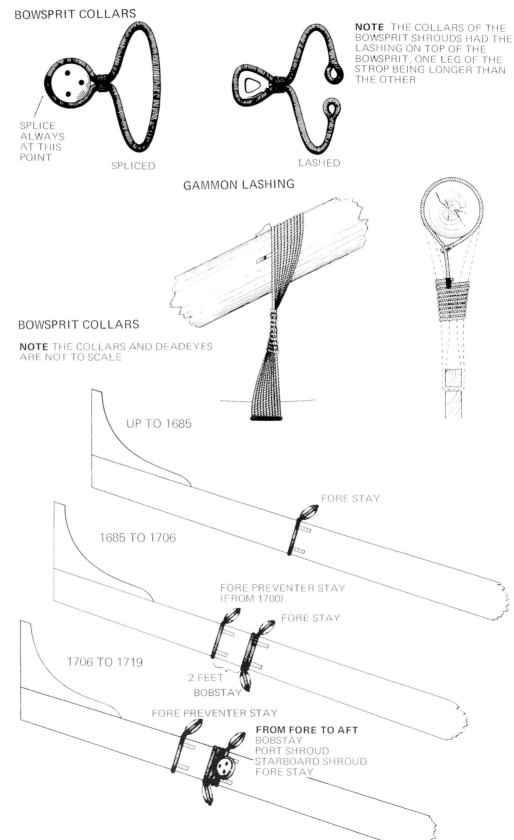

BOWSPRIT COLLARS

SPLICE ALWAYS AT THIS POINT

SPLICED

LASHED

NOTE THE COLLARS OF THE BOWSPRIT SHROUDS HAD THE LASHING ON TOP OF THE BOWSPRIT, ONE LEG OF THE STROP BEING LONGER THAN THE OTHER

GAMMON LASHING

BOWSPRIT COLLARS

NOTE THE COLLARS AND DEADEYES ARE NOT TO SCALE

UP TO 1685

1685 TO 1706

FORE STAY

1706 TO 1719

FORE PREVENTER STAY (FROM 1700)

FORE STAY

2 FEET

BOBSTAY

FORE PREVENTER STAY

FROM FORE TO AFT
BOBSTAY
PORT SHROUD
STARBOARD SHROUD
FORE STAY

II RIGGING
Rigging to the bowsprit

BOWSPRIT COLLARS

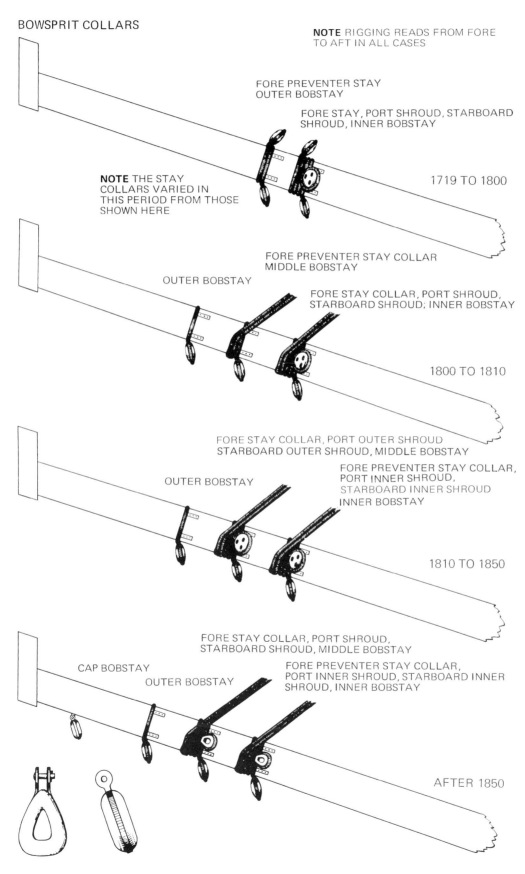

NOTE RIGGING READS FROM FORE TO AFT IN ALL CASES

FORE PREVENTER STAY
OUTER BOBSTAY

FORE STAY, PORT SHROUD, STARBOARD SHROUD, INNER BOBSTAY

NOTE THE STAY COLLARS VARIED IN THIS PERIOD FROM THOSE SHOWN HERE

1719 TO 1800

FORE PREVENTER STAY COLLAR
MIDDLE BOBSTAY

OUTER BOBSTAY

FORE STAY COLLAR, PORT SHROUD, STARBOARD SHROUD; INNER BOBSTAY

1800 TO 1810

FORE STAY COLLAR, PORT OUTER SHROUD
STARBOARD OUTER SHROUD, MIDDLE BOBSTAY

FORE PREVENTER STAY COLLAR, PORT INNER SHROUD, STARBOARD INNER SHROUD INNER BOBSTAY

OUTER BOBSTAY

1810 TO 1850

FORE STAY COLLAR, PORT SHROUD, STARBOARD SHROUD, MIDDLE BOBSTAY

CAP BOBSTAY

FORE PREVENTER STAY COLLAR, PORT INNER SHROUD, STARBOARD INNER SHROUD, INNER BOBSTAY

OUTER BOBSTAY

AFTER 1850

ends together. The splice lay in the groove of a deadeye or heart that was seized in the bobstay; this deadeye or heart in turn connected with a deadeye or heart in the collar by means of a lanyard. At all times rope bobstays were served all over. When chains were used, the lower end was shackled to the stem with a long shackle and the upper end was secured by a lanyard to a thimble on the bowsprit. Hearts were usually used in preference to deadeyes from about 1840.

Cap bobstays were introduced about 1850. The forward heart was bolted to an eyebolt under the bowsprit just aft of the dolphin striker jaws. The heart had a metal strap instead of a collar. The bobstay was fitted in a similar fashion to the other bobstays. The date 1850 is from when most ships in prints and illustrations are shown as carrying a cap bobstay.

Collars were made in a similar way to shroud collars. The order for putting these collars on the bowsprit is given in that section devoted to the furnishings and order of dressing masts and spars.

Lanyards were fitted in the usual way.
Horses, or manropes, up to 1740 the forward ends were seized to eyebolts on either side of the sprit topmast knee or bowsprit cap; the after ends were seized to eyes set in the timber heads on either side of the bowsprit. A pair of short legs were seized to the fore stay above the heart and were used to trice up the horses. Similar legs, to bowse down the horses abaft of the beakhead, were fitted round the bowsprit. Both these pairs of legs were made of a length of rope with a small eye spliced in the ends, the horses reeving through these eyes before being made fast. After 1740 the horses, though fitted in the same manner, did not require tricing up, and by 1765 both tricing up and bowsing down were dispensed with. During the nineteenth century stanchions were used to take the inner end of the horses and were fitted where timber heads were shown previously. Until the early eighteenth century deadeyes were used to secure the horses; this practice ceased in about 1706 except on large ships where they were used well into

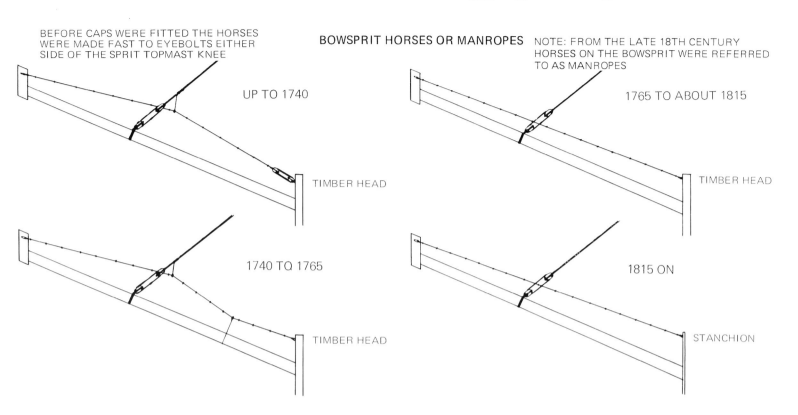

BEFORE CAPS WERE FITTED THE HORSES
WERE MADE FAST TO EYEBOLTS EITHER
SIDE OF THE SPRIT TOPMAST KNEE

BOWSPRIT HORSES OR MANROPES

NOTE: FROM THE LATE 18TH CENTURY
HORSES ON THE BOWSPRIT WERE REFERRED
TO AS MANROPES

UP TO 1740

1765 TO ABOUT 1815

TIMBER HEAD

TIMBER HEAD

1740 TO 1765

1815 ON

TIMBER HEAD

STANCHION

the eighteenth century and in some cases as late as 1740.

Wooldings were fitted in the same way as main and fore mast wooldings, and only from the end of the seventeenth century until 1800 when iron bands superseded the rope wooldings. The number of wooldings varied between two and six, depending on the size of the ship.

RIGGING TO THE JIBBOOM

Guy pendants, from 1710 to 1773, were made of one length of rope hitched in the centre round the end of the jibboom. The ends came halfway between the jibboom end and the spritsail yard. From 1773 to 1810 the pendants were fitted in the same way but were much longer, reeving through a thimble strapped to the top of the spritsail yard a quarter way in from each of the yard arms, or through a hole bored through the yard, as from 1810 to 1850. In all cases a single block was spliced into the end of each pendant. From 1773 to 1810 the length of the pendants each side was about one and a half times the length of the jibboom. Up to 1810 only one pendant each side was carried. From 1810 to 1840, two

pendants a side were fitted; they were put on the jibboom end in pairs, seized together in a similar manner to the shrouds on the mast, those on the starboard being fitted first. The other ends ran through holes in the spritsail yard. The outer one had a block spliced into the end. The inner pendant rove through a block stropped to an eyebolt in the bows, up through the block in the outer pendant, back through a hole in the bow and made fast to the inside of the forecastle bulwark. From 1840 on, a single pendant was carried each side and only came as far as the spritsail yard or spreader, whichever was carried, where it was spliced round the yard arm. In small ships, tackles were dispensed with and instead of having single blocks spliced into the pendants, a thimble was used, lanyards taking the place of the falls. From 1840 on, the pendants were cut spliced round the jibboom end.

Guy pendant falls When a short pendant was fitted, a runner was spliced round the spritsail yard arm, then rove through the pendant block, back through another block stropped to the top of the spritsail yard at the quarters and led to the forecastle head where it

was made fast. After 1773 and up to 1810, a single block was stropped or hooked to an eyebolt on the fore side of the cathead. A fall was rove between this block and the block in the pendant, the hauling part leading in on the forecastle.

Horses or footropes were fitted, one on each side of the jibboom, hanging in the centre about 2 feet from the boom; the forward ends were either spliced separately round the jibboom end or cut-spliced together to fit the jibboom end, and the inner end was seized to an eye set either side of the bowsprit cap on the forward face. Figure of eight or overhand knots were made about 2 feet apart along each horse.

Dolphin striker jaw ropes When spreaders took the place of spritsail yards, it was a practice in some ships to fit the dolphin striker in place by means of a rope reeving through holes in the jaw of the dolphin striker and taken round the bowsprit just aft of the cap, reeving through the hole in the opposite side of the jaws. A stopper knot was made in each end, close to the jaws.

A martingale stay was used from the innovation of the dolphin striker to the end of the sail era, the martingale stay consisting of a length of rope spliced round the jibboom end and spliced round the dolphin striker. About 1840 chain replaced the rope; it was shackled to an eye on the striker and lashed to the jibboom.

The martingale back stay consisted of a length of rope seized in the bight round the dolphin striker or, as after 1840, shackled to eyes on the striker and secured to eyebolts in the fore sides of the catheads with a lanyard running between the eyebolts and thimbles spliced in the backstay. When first introduced, the martingale stay was combined with the backstay and led through the striker, being set up with a fall (comprising a double and single block) to an eyebolt in the head, port side of the bowsprit. By about 1805 the stay and backstay were separated and fitted as above.

Lanyards were fitted in the usual way.

The crupper was a lashing of rope which was taken about seven turns, with cross turns between the bowsprit and jibboom, round the heel of the jibboom and bowsprit. From about 1850 chain replaced the rope.

A heel lashing was fitted during the last twenty or so years of the sail era. A chain came from an eyebolt in the bowsprit cap and was taken round the jibboom heel and back up to an eyebolt in the opposite side of the bowsprit cap. Both ends of the chain being seized or shackled to the eyebolts.

JIBBOOM LASHING AND CRUPPER

RIGGING TO THE FLYING JIBBOOM

Flying jibboom guys, one on each side, were either cut spliced together to fit round the outer end of the flying jibboom or eye-spliced separately to fit the flying jibboom. The flying jibboom guys ran to eye-bolts either in the catheads themselves, or in the bows near to the catheads.

On large ships a tackle, consisting of a single block spliced in each guy, and a single block stropped or hooked to each eyebolt, with the fall leading in through the forecastle bulwarks and belayed there, was used to tighten up the flying jibboom guys. Smaller ships made do with thimbles and lanyards made fast outboard; the guys ran through a hole in the outer ends of the spritsail yard or spreaders before being made fast.

A flying martingale stay was spliced round the flying jibboom outer end, rove through the second hole from the lower end of the striker and was usually hitched to an eyebolt in the bows close to the bowsprit, starboard side.

Horses or footropes were carried, one a side hanging in the centre about 2 feet from the flying jibboom, the forward ends either cut-spliced or eye-spliced to fit round the flying jibboom. The after ends were seized and hitched to the jibboom guys close to the jibboom head, and figure of eight or overhand knots were made in the horses about 2 feet apart.

6 Topmasts

RIGGING TO THE FORE TOPMAST

The stay had an upper end fitted like the lower mast stay. There were a number of ways of setting up the lower end, the most usual being as follows: up to 1670, a single block was spliced in the end; from 1670 to 1680, a three hole deadeye was used; after 1680 and until bees were fitted with sheaves (in about 1745), a fiddle block was used. When bees were first introduced on the bowsprit, (about 1700 in small ships to about 1719 in large ships), they had two holes on either side, the strop of a single block going through the two forward holes and round the bowsprit leaving enough room for the jibboom to pass between. In about 1745 these holes were superseded by sheaves underneath the bees with the lead to the sheaves running through the bees. The stay first of all rove through the single block stropped to the bowsprit, and then a long-tackle block was seized in the end; When bees had sheaves, the stay rove through the fore starboard sheave, a heart was turned in the end, superseded by the end of the eighteenth century by a thimble. On some large ships however a long-tackle block was used instead of a heart or thimble.

A collar was required to secure the lower deadeye between 1670 and 1680. It was put on around the bowsprit just below the sprit topmast knee, and

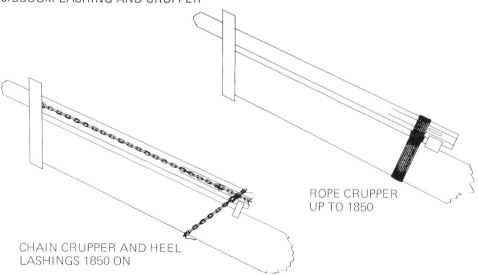

CHAIN CRUPPER AND HEEL
LASHINGS 1850 ON

ROPE CRUPPER
UP TO 1850

had a deadeye seized in it. The collar was served all over and connected up with a lanyard to the deadeye in the stay.

A stay tackle was required to set up the stay before 1670, from 1680 to 1745, and on some large ships right up to the end of the said era. Actually, in the early periods the tackle was really a simple whip with one end of it seized to an eyebolt about half way up the after side of the sprit topmast knee; the other end was taken through the block in the end of the stay, through another block stropped to the bowsprit about half way down to the lower part of the sprit topmast knee (sometimes an eyebolt was put in the knee and the block seized to this eyebolt) and finally the whip was led into the forecastle. There were other variations for the lead of this whip but the method I have described was the most widely used.

From 1680 to 1745 when a long-tackle block was turned in the stay, a single block was seized to an eyebolt half way down the lower part of the sprit topmast knee, the standing part of the tackle was made fast to the strop of this block; the hauling part rove through the long-tackle block, through the single block, back through the long-tackle block, then through the centre sheave of a treble block strapped to the bowsprit about 1 foot below the sprit topmast knee, and was made fast on the forecastle. The outer sheaves of this treble block were for the fore topsail bowlines. The only other time when a tackle was used was when a block was turned in the stay after reeving the stay through the bees. In this case the other block required to make up the fall was hooked to an eyebolt in the bows close to and on the starboard side of the bowsprit; this hook block was always a single block.

A lanyard was required when hearts or thimbles were used, apart from when the stay was fitted with deadeyes. The lanyard was spliced through the heart or thimble on the stay; the heart or thimble through which the lanyard then rove was secured to an eyebolt in the bows close to, and on the starboard side of the bowsprit, the heart or thim-

METHODS OF SETTING
UP THE FORE TOPMAST STAY

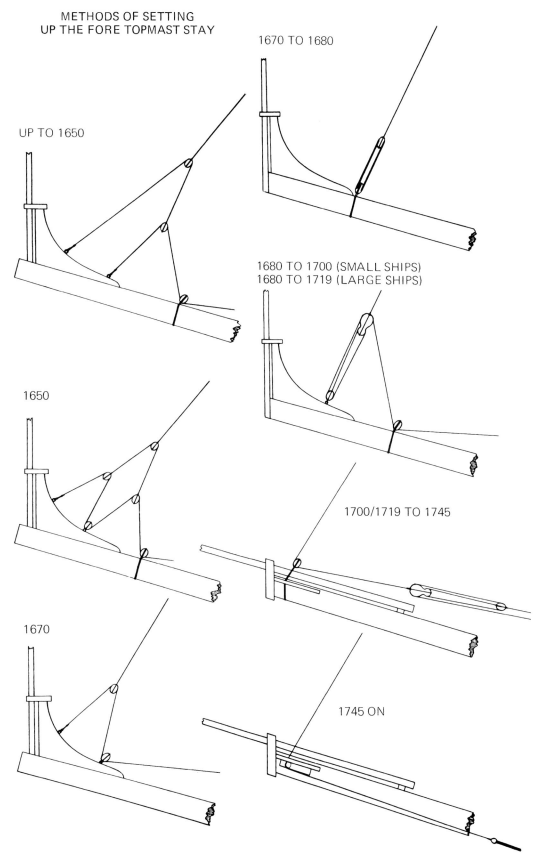

UP TO 1650

1650

1670

1670 TO 1680

1680 TO 1700 (SMALL SHIPS)
1680 TO 1719 (LARGE SHIPS)

1700/1719 TO 1745

1745 ON

ble being seized into a strop which was set round a small thimble on the eyebolt. In the last days of sail, a shackle was sometimes used, in which case the large thimble to take the lanyard was seized into a strop together with a smaller thimble; this small thimble was then shackled directly to the eyebolt. In all cases, the lanyard, after reeving through the hearts or thimbles about ten times, was secured by being frapped round itself.

A preventer stay was introduced about 1700. The upper end was fitted in the same way as the stay. The lower end, up to the introduction of the jibboom – that was about 1705 in small ships, by 1712 in ships of 60 guns and under and by 1719 in all rates – was secured by deadeyes and a lanyard. The collar for the lower deadeye was put on the bowsprit just below the topmast stay. When bees were fitted without sheaves, a single block was seized in a strop taken through the after holes in the bees. This strop was made long enough to allow the jibboom to pass through

and a long-tackle block was seized in the end of the preventer stay. There were exceptions to this: on some small ships up to 1745, deadeyes were retained, the lower deadeyes being seized in a strop through the bees as described. When sheaves were fitted under the bees, the preventer stay rove through the after port sheave and was set up like the stay.

A collar was made and fitted like the stay collar.

The tackle, before the preventer stay was taken through the bees, rove from the single block on the bowsprit to the long-tackle block on the preventer stay. The standing part spliced into the strop of the single block; the hauling part, after coming from the long-tackle block, rove through a single block stropped to the bowsprit just abaft of the preventer stay; thence it led to the forecastle where it was belayed.

The lanyard was fitted in the same way as the stay lanyard, but on the port side.

Shrouds were fitted in the same way as the lower shrouds, and set up with deadeyes and lanyards in the fore top.

Ratlines were fitted in the same way as the lower ratlines and taken across all shrouds.

Futtock shrouds, before about 1820, were hooked into the topmast deadeye plates which protruded just below the top; the lower end was taken round the futtock stave, then seized to the lower shrouds. After 1820, the lower end was secured to a necklace round the lower mast which was about the length of the head below the top. The upper end of the futtock shrouds were fitted as in previous years.

Ratlines were fitted in the same way as other ratlines.

Burton pendants were used in all periods, cut-spliced together, put over the mast head before anything else and fitted one on each side of the mast. A single block was spliced in the end up to 1780; after then a thimble was used. They were about the same length as

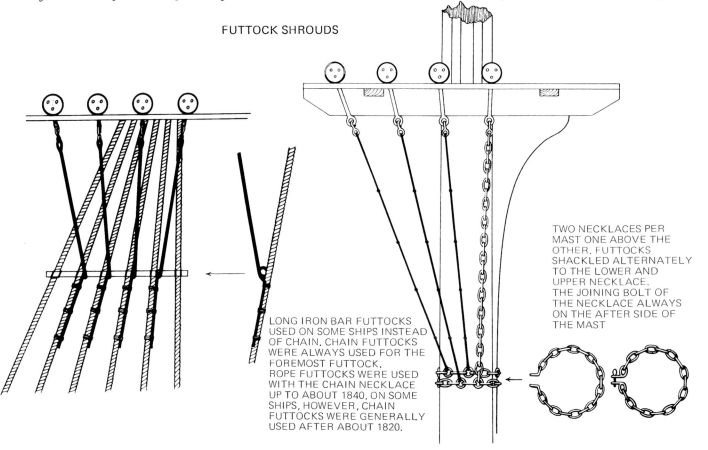

FUTTOCK SHROUDS

LONG IRON BAR FUTTOCKS USED ON SOME SHIPS INSTEAD OF CHAIN. CHAIN FUTTOCKS WERE ALWAYS USED FOR THE FOREMOST FUTTOCK. ROPE FUTTOCKS WERE USED WITH THE CHAIN NECKLACE UP TO ABOUT 1840, ON SOME SHIPS, HOWEVER, CHAIN FUTTOCKS WERE GENERALLY USED AFTER ABOUT 1820.

TWO NECKLACES PER MAST ONE ABOVE THE OTHER. FUTTOCKS SHACKLED ALTERNATELY TO THE LOWER AND UPPER NECKLACE. THE JOINING BOLT OF THE NECKLACE ALWAYS ON THE AFTER SIDE OF THE MAST

the pendants on the lower mast and were served all over.

Burton falls, prior to 1780, had the standing part spliced round the pendant at the head of the pendant block. The hauling part rove through a single hook block and back through the pendant block; it was usually made fast to a deadeye or shroud in the top when not in use, the fall being made up in the top, with the end coiled and lashed to the fall. When a thimble was used on the pendant, the fall was only hooked to the pendant when required; at other times the pendant was seized to the shrouds. Both upper and lower block were hook blocks when thimbles were used.

Standing backstays had the upper ends set up the same as the shrouds but the lower ends with deadeyes and lanyards. The backstay was in use from about the middle of the seventeenth century. Two pairs were fitted up to 1670, then three pairs were fitted on First Rates, followed a few years later by three pairs on large two-deckers, other ships still retaining two pairs. Steel gives three pairs for First Rates down to 60 gun ships and this number remained consistent to the end of the sail era. When first fitted, the lower deadeyes were carried on stools abaft the channels; later the foremost stay came to the channel about halfway along, and the other or others to a stool. About 1719 only the aftermost backstay came to a stool, the other being rigged to the channel. Sometimes, instead of a stool, the deadeyes were fixed to an eyebolt in the ship's side, especially in small ships. By about 1800, all the backstays came to the channels.

Breast backstays had the upper and lower ends set up in the usual fashion, but according to models in the National Maritime Museum, very few English ships were fitted with them. The standing backstay seems to have served the same purpose by having the foremost backstay well forward along the channels. I have seen comtemporary models - one of the 1719 Establishment and one of the 1733 Establishment - carrying a breast backstay, and then not found any again until 1839. When fitted, they ran abreast of the mast. Personally, I would not fit them unless

they were shown on a painting or print of a model I intended to make, and then would only fit them after 1719.

Running breast backstay had the upper end fitted like the other backstays. The lower end had a single block spliced in the end and came down level with the top of the bulwarks. As a conjectural date for their introduction, I would give 1733 at the earliest, though it is possible that large ships only carried them that early and smaller ships not until 1763; I cannot get any nearer than that, however.

Running breast backstay falls A whip was formed by leading a rope through the block in the running breast backstay and making one end fast to an eyebolt in the channels abreast of the mast; the other end had a double block spliced in it which connected by the fall to another double block hooked to an eyebolt in the channels about 2 feet aft from the standing part of the whip. On small ships, a single block was hooked in the channels instead of

the double block. In both cases the hauling part of the fall led from the upper block down to the timber heads or pin rail of the bulwarks.

Shifting backstay size is given in the rigging tables, but this would not be seen generally as it was only used to give additional stay to the mast when sailing, and would be unrove in port or whenever it was thought fit. A pendant, half as long again as the burton pendant, was fitted however. A thimble was spliced in the lower end, while the upper end fitted the same as the burton pendant.

Shifting backstay falls consisted of a long-tackle block hooked in the thimble of the pendant, and a single block hooked in the fore channels or to an eyebolt in the deck.

Toprope pendants Until 1640, the toprope was seized to an eyebolt beneath the lower mast cap, rove through the sheave in the topmast, up through a block seized to another eyebolt in the cap on the other side and led down to deck, where it rove through a sheave

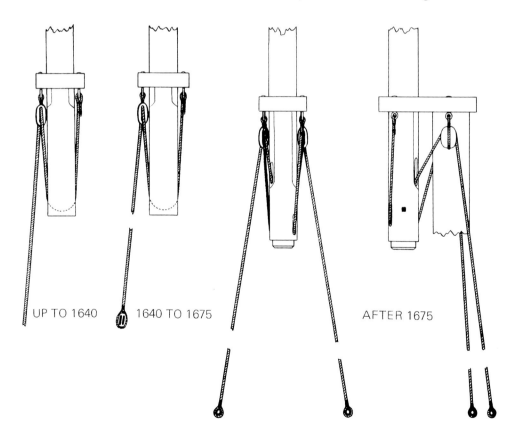

UP TO 1640   1640 TO 1675   AFTER 1675

TOP ROPE PENDANTS

II RIGGING
Rigging to the main topmast

in the knighthead abaft the mast, and was then belayed to the knighthead. After 1640 and up to about 1675, the toprope rove as before, but instead of reeving through the knighthead, a double block was seized in the end and a tackle formed with this block and one abaft the mast on deck. From 1675 to about 1800, two topropes were used, and two sheaves were fitted in the heel of the topmast; each toprope then rove through a sheave and through a block hooked to an eyebolt under the cap on each side of the mast. The standing part was made fast, as before, to eyebolts under the cap. There were thimbles seized in the lower ends of each pendant. After 1800, the topropes were unrove after the mast was topped. When two pendants were carried, the one made fast to the port side of the cap rove through the lower sheave of the topmast. On large ships it was sometimes the practice to hook treble blocks in the pendants instead of double ones.

Toprope falls were introduced in about 1640 and consisted of two double blocks, one seized in the end of the pendant and the other seized to an eyebolt in the deck abaft the mast. The standing part of the fall was made fast to the upper block and the hauling part was belayed to the bitts. After 1675, two falls were required, one for each toprope. They rove as before, but the lower block was made fast to the main deck on either side of the main hatch, the falls leading to either side of the belfry. When treble blocks were used in the pendants, the standing part was made fast to the lower block.

Crowsfeet were seldom fitted, and only when round tops were carried; the *Sovereign of the Seas* is an example.

Upper catharpins The earliest contemporary model in the National Maritime Museum showing catharpins on the topmasts is one dated 1805, and this is an isolated example. It seems to me that their use was optional, that they were probably added in wartime and only fitted at the end of the eighteenth and early nineteenth centuries. When fitted, they comprised lengths of rope the same size as the topgallant shrouds with an eye spliced in each end. They were served all over. There

were as many as topgallant shrouds and they were seized to the futtock staves between the topmast shrouds; there was no need of them when the topgallant shrouds no longer led to the topmast shrouds.

RIGGING TO THE MAIN TOPMAST

The stay had the upper end fitted in the same way as the fore topmast stay. Up to about 1805, the lower end was taken through a single block stropped to the after side of the fore mast head just above the fore stay; the main topmast stay was then led down abaft the fore mast and a long-tackle block was seized in the end; the stay was then set up with the stay tackle fall. After 1805 a bullseye or thimble was stropped to the fore mast head instead of the single block used in previous years. The lower end of the stay led down abaft the mast as before but instead of seizing a block in the end, a heart or a thimble was used; the stay

was set up by means of a lanyard reeving between the heart or thimble in the stay and an eyebolt in the deck abaft the fore mast.

During the nineteenth century prior to 1840, the stay was sometimes set up in the fore top with thimbles and a lanyard. From about 1840 the stay rove through a clump block stropped to the fore mast head just above the preventer stay clump block and was taken down to the deck and made fast with thimbles and a lanyard.

The collar was made from a length of rope with a small eye spliced in one end. The block, heart, bullseye, or thimble through which the stay was to reeve, was seized in the bight of this rope so that the eye-splice was in a short leg, the end without the splice forming a long leg. To fit the collar on the mast head the long leg was taken round the mast then rove through the eye in the short leg, taken back and hitched and seized to its own part.

The tackle fall comprised a long-tackle

MAIN TOP MAST STAY
AND PREVENTER STAY

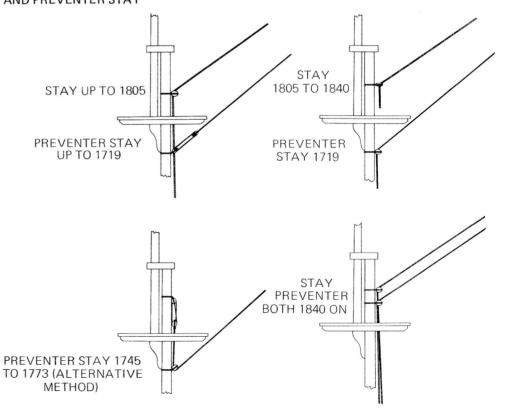

STAY UP TO 1805

PREVENTER STAY
UP TO 1719

STAY
1805 TO 1840

PREVENTER
STAY 1719

PREVENTER STAY 1745
TO 1773 (ALTERNATIVE
METHOD)

STAY
PREVENTER
BOTH 1840 ON

block seized in the end of the stay and a single block hooked to an eyebolt abaft the foot of the mast on the upper deck. The standing part spliced into the strop of the lower block, the running part leading down abaft the mast.

The lanyard was rigged in the same way as the other lanyards; it was only used after 1805 when the stay was set up with hearts or thimbles.

A preventer stay was in use after 1700. The upper end was fitted in the same way as the stay and the preventer lay below the stay. Up to 1719 the lower end had a deadeye seized in it and was set up with a lanyard to a deadeye stropped to the fore mast at the bibs. After 1719 a block was stropped to the mast at the bibs instead of a deadeye; the preventer stay rove through this block down to deck, being made fast in the same way as the stay. Like the stay, after about 1840 the preventer rove through a clump block stropped to the fore mast head and made fast like the stay. It was sometimes the practice between 1745 and 1773 to lead the preventer up through the block at the bibs and make it fast by taking it through the top, splicing a single block in the end which connected up to another single block stropped half way up the mast head by means of a fall. The standing part made fast to the upper block and the fall made up round itself.

The collar was fitted in the same way as the stay collar.

The tackle fall was fitted in the same way as the stay tackle. The lower block hooked to an eyebolt near the stay tackle eyebolt. The stay eyebolt was a little to port and the preventer to starboard of the midship line.

The lanyard was rigged in the same way as the stay lanyard and when deadeyes were used, the same as a shroud lanyard.

Shrouds and lanyards were rigged the same as the fore topmast shrouds and lanyards.

Ratlines were fitted the same as the fore topmast ratlines.

Burton pendant and falls were fitted the same as the fore top mast burton pendants and falls.

Standing back stays and lanyards were

rigged the same way as the fore topmast standing backstays and lanyards. The main topmast sometimes carried one more stay than the fore topmast, especially in the seventeenth century. The main topmast backstay was introduced a few years before those on the fore topmast and was an innovation of about 1640.

Breast backstay The same observations apply here as for the fore topmast breast backstay.

Running breast backstay and falls were rigged the same way as the fore topmast running breast backstay.

Shifting backstay and falls The same observations apply here as for the fore topmast shifting backstay.

Futtock shrouds were rigged the same way as the fore topmast futtock shrouds.

Ratlines were fitted the same way as the fore topmast ratlines.

Toprope pendant and falls rigged in the same way as the fore topmast toprope pendant. The falls led to eyebolts in the deck aft of the main mast. When

the quarterdeck came up to the mainmast the falls led through holes in the deck, the eyebolts always remaining on the main deck.

Catharpins The same observations apply here as for the fore topmast catharpins.

Crowsfeet The same observations apply here as for the fore topmast crowsfeet.

RIGGING TO THE MIZEN TOPMAST

The stay had the upper end fitted like the fore and main topgallant stays. Up to about 1680 the lower end was set up to the aftermost main shrouds with crowsfeet and consequently had a single block spliced in the end. Some ships retained this method of setting up the stay until 1700 but the majority after 1680 had a deadeye spliced in the end of the stay which set up with a lanyard to another deadeye, stropped either to the main mast head or to the mast at the bibs. The deadeyes were fastened at the bibs up to about

SETTING UP THE MIZEN TOPMAST STAY

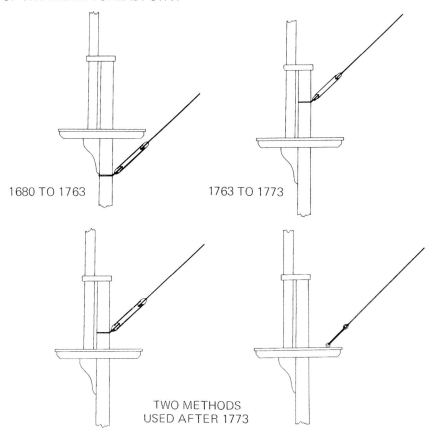

1680 TO 1763

1763 TO 1773

TWO METHODS
USED AFTER 1773

1763, then were shifted to the mast head. About 1773 the deadeyes were replaced by thimbles and two methods were used, one in which the thimble at the mast was stropped half way up the mast head, the other where the stay was set up to an eyebolt in the main top abaft the mast. After 1719 on some large ships, blocks were used instead of deadeyes; also on some ships between 1745 and 1773 a single block was stropped to the mainmast at the bibs, the stay rove upwards through this block and was set up by a tackle rove between a block spliced in the end of the stay and another one stropped half way up the mainmast head, as described for the main topmast preventer stay.

A collar was applicable only when deadeyes, blocks and thimbles were used. The thimble, block, or deadeye was seized in the bight and a small eye was spliced into either end. The ends were then lashed together on the fore side of the main mast through these eyes.

Stay crowsfeet were rigged as shown in the illustrations. Briefly, they comprised seven ropes, one reeving through the block in the stay with a block spliced on each end. One block went to port, the other to starboard. These blocks in turn had a similar rope reeved through them again with a block in each end; a rope was then taken through these blocks and the ends seized to the main shrouds forming a diamond and triangular pattern of rope work. Sometimes these crowsfeet were very elaborate comprising fifteen separate parts, but usually seven parts were sufficient.

Shrouds and ratlines were fitted in the usual way.

Standing backstays were an innovation of about 1670. The upper and lower ends were rigged as other backstays; only one a side was carried up to about 1737 when the large three-deckers then carried two a side. Up to about 1815 the lower deadeyes were either fitted to stools or deadeye plates bolted directly to the ship's side abaft of and slightly higher than the mizen channels. When two backstays were rigged each side, the foremost one often led to the mizen channel, while the aftermost

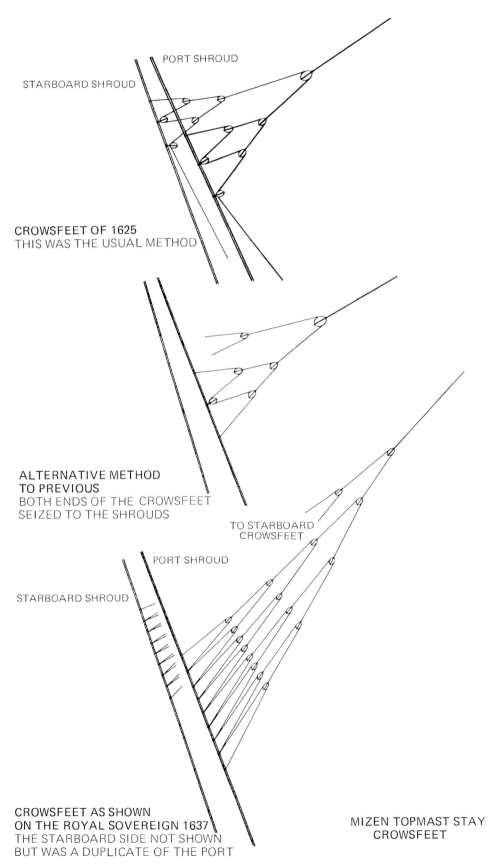

PORT SHROUD

STARBOARD SHROUD

CROWSFEET OF 1625
THIS WAS THE USUAL METHOD

ALTERNATIVE METHOD TO PREVIOUS
BOTH ENDS OF THE CROWSFEET SEIZED TO THE SHROUDS

TO STARBOARD CROWSFEET

PORT SHROUD

STARBOARD SHROUD

CROWSFEET AS SHOWN ON THE ROYAL SOVEREIGN 1637
THE STARBOARD SIDE NOT SHOWN BUT WAS A DUPLICATE OF THE PORT

MIZEN TOPMAST STAY CROWSFEET

one led to a stool or plate. After 1815 backstays led to the mizen channel, the channel being extended for this purpose. This method was often used on large ships at the end of the seventeenth century.

Shifting backstay When the burton pendants were not used as pendants for the shifting backstays, additional pendants were fitted to the mizen topmast with an eye-splice. They were about half as long again as the lower pendants and had a thimble spliced into the lower ends.

The tackle consisted of a long tackle rigged in the usual way, with the upper block hooked into the thimble in the pendant and the lower block hooked to the eyebolt either in the mizen channels, the side of the ship abaft the mizen channels, or to the inside of the bulwarks.

Futtock shrouds and ratlines were fitted in the same way as those on the fore and main topmasts.

The top rope pendant served the same purpose as the fore and main top rope pendants and was fitted in the same way. There was, however, only one top rope rigged, which was unrove after the mast was topped and not left rigged as on the fore and main topmasts.

Top rope falls were fitted the same as those on the fore and main topmasts.

Flagstaff stay Sometimes when topgallant masts were not carried a flagstaff above the mizen topmast was fitted to allow the mizen flags to be flown higher. In large ships a stay was needed, coming from the flagstaff to the main mast head, generally hitched to the main stay or around the mainmast head, though sometimes secured with deadeyes and lanyard in the main top.

Flag halliards before topgallant masts were fitted, came to the sheaves in the mizen topmast truck and, like the fore and main halliards, belayed to any convenient place on deck.

Catharpins were very seldom fitted; it is as well to ignore them altogether.

Burton pendants were carried by a few large ships before about 1650, and were fitted in the same way as on the fore and main topmasts. After that date they ceased to be used. Falls for them were rove in the same way as on the fore and main topmasts.

RIGGING TO THE SPRIT TOPMAST

Shrouds were fitted in the usual way: that is in pairs, starboard first, with the third shroud each side being cut-spliced to its opposite number. Usually three shrouds a side were carried. The lower ends were set up with deadeyes and lanyards in the sprit top. The lower deadeye was generally strapped with iron and connected to a futtock plate which was in turn bolted underneath the bowsprit.

The lanyard was fitted in the usual way.

Crane lines is an early name for the backstay pendants and crowsfeet.

Backstay pendants During the seventeenth century up to about 1680, the backstay was connected to the fore mast forestay by means of a pendant and crowsfeet; sometimes more than one pendant was used. The pendant or

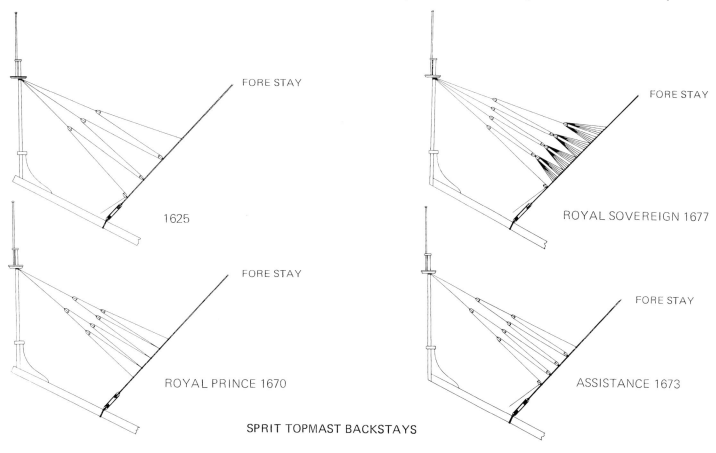

FORE STAY

1625

FORE STAY

ROYAL PRINCE 1670

FORE STAY

ROYAL SOVEREIGN 1677

FORE STAY

ASSISTANCE 1673

SPRIT TOPMAST BACKSTAYS

II RIGGING
Rigging to the sprit topmast

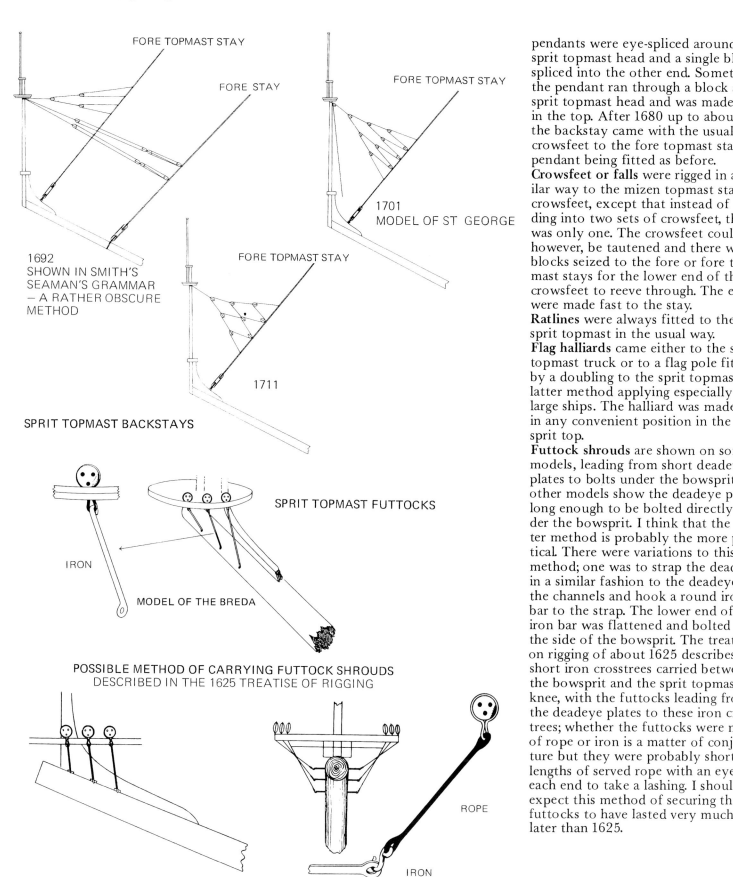

FORE TOPMAST STAY

FORE STAY

1692
SHOWN IN SMITH'S
SEAMAN'S GRAMMAR
— A RATHER OBSCURE
METHOD

FORE TOPMAST STAY

1701
MODEL OF ST GEORGE

FORE TOPMAST STAY

1711

SPRIT TOPMAST BACKSTAYS

IRON

MODEL OF THE BREDA

SPRIT TOPMAST FUTTOCKS

POSSIBLE METHOD OF CARRYING FUTTOCK SHROUDS
DESCRIBED IN THE 1625 TREATISE OF RIGGING

ROPE

IRON

pendants were eye-spliced around the sprit topmast head and a single block spliced into the other end. Sometimes the pendant ran through a block at the sprit topmast head and was made fast in the top. After 1680 up to about 1710 the backstay came with the usual crowsfeet to the fore topmast stay, the pendant being fitted as before.

Crowsfeet or falls were rigged in a similar way to the mizen topmast stay crowsfeet, except that instead of dividing into two sets of crowsfeet, there was only one. The crowsfeet could, however, be tautened and there were blocks seized to the fore or fore topmast stays for the lower end of the crowsfeet to reeve through. The ends were made fast to the stay.

Ratlines were always fitted to the sprit topmast in the usual way.

Flag halliards came either to the sprit topmast truck or to a flag pole fitted by a doubling to the sprit topmast, the latter method applying especially in large ships. The halliard was made fast in any convenient position in the sprit top.

Futtock shrouds are shown on some models, leading from short deadeye plates to bolts under the bowsprit; other models show the deadeye plates long enough to be bolted directly under the bowsprit. I think that the latter method is probably the more practical. There were variations to this method; one was to strap the deadeyes in a similar fashion to the deadeyes on the channels and hook a round iron bar to the strap. The lower end of the iron bar was flattened and bolted to the side of the bowsprit. The treatise on rigging of about 1625 describes short iron crosstrees carried between the bowsprit and the sprit topmast knee, with the futtocks leading from the deadeye plates to these iron crosstrees; whether the futtocks were made of rope or iron is a matter of conjecture but they were probably short lengths of served rope with an eye in each end to take a lashing. I should not expect this method of securing the futtocks to have lasted very much later than 1625.

60

7 Topgallant and royal masts

RIGGING TO THE FORE TOPGALLANT AND ROYAL MASTS

The stay had its upper end fitted snugly over the topgallant mast head with an eye-splice. The lower end, up to the introduction of the jibboom, led through a block stropped to the sprit topmast head and usually had a single block seized in the end. When jibbooms were fitted, the stay led through a block, usually a single one (though sometimes the centre sheave of a treble block was used), seized to the end of the jibboom. The outer sheaves of this treble block were used for the topgallant bowlines. On large ships a single block was seized in the end of the stay. On small ships the stay led straight inboard where it was belayed and in some cases it was hitched round the forestay collar. When taken in to the forecastle it led through the lead block on the gammon lashing. Shortly after the dolphin striker was introduced, the stay led through a sheave in the jibboom end, through a hole in the striker, then to the bows close to the bowsprit — generally on the starboard side. A thimble was seized in the end which set up by a lanyard to an eyebolt in the bows. Some large ships had a single block turned in instead of a thimble.

Stay tackle Up to the early eighteenth century and prior to the introduction of the jibboom, a single whip was rigged through the block in the end of the stay; the standing part made fast to a deadeye plate or eyebolt on the starboard side of the sprit top, the running part coming down to the port side of the sprit top and hitched to either a deadeye plate or eyebolt in the top. An alternative method was to seize a single block to the sprit cap and reeve a fall between this block and the one in the end of the stay (the stay still rove through the block at the sprit topmast head). The standing part of the fall was made fast to the block at the cap and the running part was taken to the forecastle rails via the gammon lashing multiple block; this method was used for the last few years before the introduction of the jibboom. From the time the jibboom was carried until the stay rove through the striker, the stay was taken directly to the forecastle via the gammon lead block, no tackle being required except on large ships. When a block was turned in the stay instead of a thimble, a single block was seized to an eyebolt in the bows close to the bowsprit starboard side. A fall rove between this block and the one in the stay, the standing part made fast to the block in the bows, the hauling part leading in onto the forecastle or made fast round the tackle and expended by frapping turns round the tackle; this latter was the usual practice.

Shrouds, up to about 1719, were fitted in two pairs, the bight being seized round the topgallant mast head and deadeyes seized in the lower end. From then to the early nineteenth century three pairs were fitted; the upper ends fitted as usual, the lower ends, however, ceased to have deadeyes and the shrouds led through the crosstrees and were seized to the futtock staves, thus forming futtock shrouds. From the early nineteenth century until the end of the sail era, two pairs of shrouds were once more rigged: the lower ends rove through the crosstrees, round the futtock staves and led down and made fast with a lashing to the deadeye plates or eyebolts in the lower top. In 1820, when a necklace was fitted round the topmast, the shrouds led through the crosstrees and were either lashed or shackled to the necklace or were led through small sheaves or rollers fitted to the necklace and taken down to the lower top.

Lanyards were only required up to 1719 when the shrouds were set up to the crosstrees with deadeyes; they were fitted in the usual way.

Ratlines were not fitted up to about 1715; from then until 1745 large and sometimes small ships had them fitted all the way up the shrouds. After 1745 very few ships had ratlines and those few that did carry them had the lower section of the shrouds only so fitted, about six ratlines being rigged. This lack of ratlines was one of the noticeable features of ships during the late eighteenth and nineteenth centuries.

Standing backstays were in use from about 1645. Up to the early nineteenth century they came down to a stool — the same stool that the topmast backstays came to — abaft of the fore channels. When no provision was made for a stool, an eyebolt was used instead. Usually only one backstay was used on each side, though in the largest ships sometimes two were rigged. The upper end was spliced to fit the topgallant mast head and the lower end had a deadeye seized in it. From the early nineteenth century to the close of the sail era the backstay, fixed as usual with deadeyes and a lanyard, came to the channels. On small ships, thimbles were often used instead of deadeyes.

A flagstaff stay was sometimes necessary before royal masts were carried, whenever a flagstaff was fitted above the fore topgallant mast especially on large ships. This stay was spliced round the flagstaff head and led through a block stropped to the sprit topmast head to be made fast in the sprit top with deadeyes and a lanyard. When royal masts were introduced, this stay became the royal stay (qv).

Futtock shrouds came from the deadeye plates on the crosstrees up to 1719 and were hitched round the futtock stave. Usually no ratlines were fitted. After 1719 the futtock shrouds were incorporated with the topgallant shrouds.

A top rope was used for topping the

61

II RIGGING
Rigging to the main topgallant and royal masts

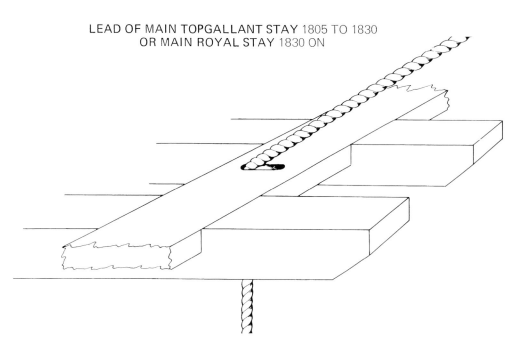

topgallant mast and was unrove once the mast was topped. The top rope was clenched to an eyebolt under the topmast cap, rove through the sheave in the heel of the topgallant mast, through a block seized to an eyebolt on the other side of the cap and led down to deck.

A royal stay was in use after 1719, the upper end being spliced to fit the royal mast head. Up to about 1801, the lower end was spliced round the jibboom end. Shortly after the dolphin striker came into use, the stay was led through a sheave in the end of the flying jibboom, through the striker and was made fast by thimbles and a lanyard to an eyebolt in the bows next to the bowsprit on the opposite side to the topgallant stay.

A royal backstay was in use after 1719, the upper end being spliced to fit the royal mast head. The lower end, until the early nineteenth century, came either to a stool or an eyebolt next to the topgallant backstay, and after that to the channels. Deadeyes were used on the large ships, thimbles on the smaller ones.

Halliards were used for hoisting up the flags. Usually a sheave was fitted on each side of the truck and the halliards hitched to any convenient point on the bulwarks.

The top rope was unrove once the mast was topped, being only required when the mast was fitted with a doubling and was rigged in the same way as the topgallant top rope.

RIGGING TO THE MAIN TOPGALLANT AND ROYAL MASTS

The stay had its upper end fitted in the same way as the fore topgallant stay. Up to 1733, the lower end rove through a block stropped to the fore topmast head above the fore topmast stay; the lower end of the stay was then led down to the fore top where it was made fast with a long-tackle similar to that on the main topmast stay. After 1733 and up to about 1805, the stay rove through a block as before but was hitched to the collar of the main topmast stay lead block, instead of using a tackle. After 1805 until the end of the sail era the stay rove through a sheave in the after fore topmast crosstree between the trestletrees, being made fast in the fore top with a lanyard and thimbles. During the seventeenth century on some ships the tackle was often dispensed with and the stay hitched as from 1733 to 1805. From about 1830 the stay was taken through a hole in the fore mast cap and was made fast in the top. This was only the case in harbour or when staysails were not going to be used. When

it was intended to set staysails, the stay was taken through the sheave in the crosstree and the royal stay taken through the thimble at the topgallant mast head.

Shrouds were rigged in the same way as the fore topgallant shrouds.

Ratlines were fitted in the same way as the fore topgallant ratlines; they were in use from 1715 to 1745.

The standing backstay was rigged in the same way as the fore topgallant backstay.

The flagstaff stay was fitted at the upper end like the fore topgallant flagstaff stay, and the same observations apply. The lower end rove through a block stropped to the fore topgallant mast head and was secured to the trestletree in the fore top with deadeyes and a lanyard. Sometimes a deadeye was stropped to the fore topgallant mast head and the stay made fast there without leading to the fore top.

Futtock shrouds were rigged in the same way as the fore topgallant futtock shrouds.

The royal stay had its upper end rigged in the same way as on the fore royal mast. The lower end from 1719 to 1805 led through a block at the fore topgallant mast head and was made fast to the after crosstree of the fore topmast with a lanyard and thimbles. After 1805 to 1830 a thimble was used instead of the block at the fore topgallant mast head, the stay reeving through this thimble and making fast as before in the fore top. From 1830 on, the stay led through a sheave in the after crosstree of the fore topmast and was made fast in the fore top with a lanyard and thimbles. When staysails were to be flown, the royal stay was taken through the thimble at the topgallant mast head and the main topgallant stay taken through the sheave in the crosstree.

The royal backstay was rigged in the same way as the fore royal backstay.

Halliards were rigged in the same way as the fore royal halliards.

The top rope was rigged in the same way as the fore royal top rope.

RIGGING TO THE MIZEN TOPGALLANT AND ROYAL MASTS

The mizen topgallant stay was introduced in about 1760. The upper end fitted in the same way as the fore and main topgallant stays. The lower end, up to about 1780, rove through either an eyebolt in the after side of the main mast cap or a block stropped to the main mast head close to the cap, and was hitched to the after side of the main stay. From 1780 to 1810, this lower end led through a thimble strapped to the main topmast head and was made fast in the main top with thimbles and a lanyard. From 1810 to 1850, instead of going through the eyebolt or block, a hole was made through the after side of the main cap and the stay rove through this, the lower end being made fast in the main top with thimbles and a lanyard to the main stay or collar of the main yard's sling. After 1850, the stay rove through a sheave in the main topmast crosstrees and was led down to the main top where it was made fast as before.

Shrouds were fitted in the same way as the fore topgallant shrouds. Usually only two shrouds a side were carried, and these only in the nineteenth century.

Ratlines were very seldom fitted.

The backstay was fitted round the mizen topgallant mast head with either a cut-splice or separate eye-splices (from 1810 to 1830 one a side was carried). The lower end of the backstay led to a stool abaft the mizen channels where it was made fast with either deadeyes and a lanyard or with thimbles and lanyard. After about 1830, two stays were fitted each side, first of all both coming to a stool, then, about 1840, one coming to the mizen channels and the other to a stool. being made fast in the usual manner — deadeyes on the large ships, thimbles on smaller vessels.

Futtock shrouds were incorporated with the topgallant shrouds (see the observations regarding the fore topgallant futtocks).

The top rope was rigged in the same way as on the main topgallant mast.

The royal stay was in use after about 1810, and was fitted in the same way as the fore and main royal stays. The lower end of the royal stay rove through the sheave in the after topmast crosstree and was made fast to an eyebolt in the main top with thimbles and a lanyard.

The lanyard was fitted in the usual way.

The royal backstay was introduced about 1810; usually one a side was carried, though large ships sometimes carried two a side. The upper ends of the royal backstay were spliced to fit round the royal mast head, the lower ends coming to stools abaft the mizen channels and made fast with either deadeyes and lanyard or thimbles and lanyard.

The lanyard was fitted in the usual way.

The halliard was fitted in the same way as the fore and main royal halliards.

LOWER TIES

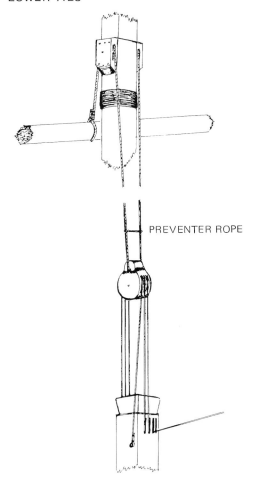

PREVENTER ROPE

8 Lower yards and sails

RIGGING TO THE FORE YARD AND COURSE

The truss, not to be confused with the truss pendant and falls described later, was the name given to a rope secured to the centre of the lower yard with a timber-hitch, and led straight down to the deck. The purpose of this rope was to assist in hauling down the lower yard. It was not used after about 1650 when the yard was no longer lowered to furl the sail.

Ties had one end seized to the yard at the slings; the other end was taken through the sheave in the hounds of the mast from forward to aft, led down abaft the mast, passed through the athwartship hole in the 'ramshead' (a block especially made for this purpose) up through the sheave in the hounds on the other side of the mast and was seized with a round turn to the yard close to the standing part of the tie at the slings. The tie was of such a length as to allow the yard to be lowered to the deck and when the yard was hoisted, the 'ramshead' block cleared the knighthead abaft the mast by a few feet. The tie was usually a four stranded rope. It ceased to be used by about 1640 in small ships and by 1660 in large ships, although no definite date can be given. Between each tie above the 'ramshead' a preven-

II RIGGING
Rigging to the fore yard and course

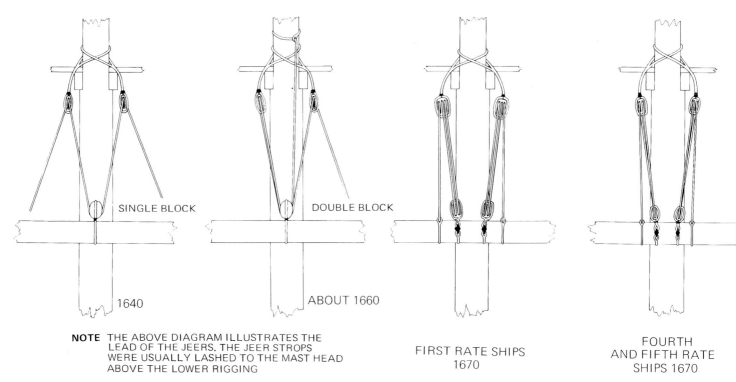

SINGLE BLOCK

DOUBLE BLOCK

1640

ABOUT 1660

NOTE THE ABOVE DIAGRAM ILLUSTRATES THE LEAD OF THE JEERS. THE JEER STROPS WERE USUALLY LASHED TO THE MAST HEAD ABOVE THE LOWER RIGGING

FIRST RATE SHIPS 1670

FOURTH AND FIFTH RATE SHIPS 1670

ter rope was sometimes seized. Its purpose was to prevent the tie from running through the 'ramshead' should the tie carry away.

The halliard rove through the knighthead abaft the mast and through the 'ramshead' alternately, the standing part made fast to an eyebolt in the side of the knighthead, the running part hitched round the knighthead. The 'ramshead' usually had three sheaves for the halliard, the knighthead four, one being used for the fore topmast top rope.

Jeers, when first rigged, were used in conjunction with the ties and consisted of a rope seized to the yard at the slings, rove through a block seized under the top and led down through a block stropped round the mast close to the deck and then belayed to the bitts. Some ships, especially the large ones, had a rope coming either side; the smaller ships however only had the one jeer. The jeer gradually took the place of the ties and consequently had to have more purchase power so that by about 1640 three blocks were used. A single one was strapped to the centre of the yard and two single blocks

were hung by means of a long strop or pendant from the head, just above the forestay, the blocks hanging below the top on either side of the mast outside of the trestletrees but inside the fore stay collar. The usual method was to lash the blocks to the mast head through the bight of the strop, stop cleats being nailed either side of the mast to hold the lashings in position. The jeer, when three single blocks were used, rove through one of the upper blocks from aft to forward, through the block on the yard, up through the other upper block going forward to aft, then down to deck where both ends were belayed to the bitts or where one end seized to an eyebolt, and the other end was only used for hoisting and lowering. In this case it is probable that a tackle would have been used for hoisting. Another form of jeer tackle which may have been used in the second half of the seventeenth century comprised a double block on the yard with two single blocks from the mast head as before, with the jeer reeving thus: the standing part made fast to the mast head led through one sheave of the

double block, up through one single block, back through the second sheave of the double block, up through the other single block then down to deck.

By about 1670 double jeers made up of two separate jeers were used. The upper blocks in First Rate ships were treble sheaved and hung from the mast head as before with a long strop. The yard had two blocks strapped at the slings, a little apart with small double straps, one leg longer than the other so the straps could be seized on the fore side of the yard. These blocks were double ones. The standing part of each jeer was hitched or seized round the yard close to the blocks. The running parts rove between the upper and lower blocks each side and ran down to the bitts, port and starboard, where they were belayed. On Second and Third Rate ships, four double blocks were used, the jeers rigged as before except that the standing part was made fast round the mast head. On Fourth and Fifth Rate ships two double and two single, and on the Sixth Rates and below, two single and one double block were used. The num-

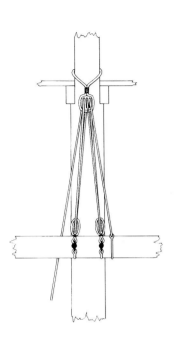

1811 ON

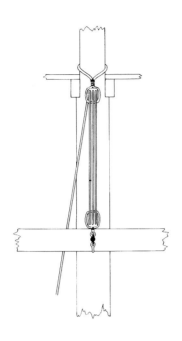

ALTERNATIVE
1830 ON

sling was secured by a lanyard in the case of rope slings, and by a slip when chain was used. This thimble was strapped in the same manner as the jeer blocks except that it was a single strap, not double. The two eyes of the strap were fastened together on the fore side of the yard by a rose lashing.

The rope sling comprised a length of rope with a thimble seized in the bight. One end of the rope had an eye spliced into it and was shorter than the other end. The long end was put through the lubber's hole, round the mast head and down. The short end was put through the lubber's hole on the other side of the mast and the long end was taken through the eye in the short end then backed and secured to its own part with three seizings. The sling was held in position abaft the mast head by a cleat just above the fore stay collar. When chain was used it rove the same way but both ends were secured to the slip either with a split link, shackle or lanyard. The

ber of blocks and the purchase power of the jeers remained about the same until the early nineteenth century. During the latter part of the eighteenth century, about 1773, a tie was reintroduced on small ships of 28 guns and under. The jeer tie, as it was called, consisted of two single upper blocks and one single block on the yard. The jeer rove through the blocks in the same way as that of 1640, but in each end a double block was spliced which connected up by a fall to a treble block hooked to an eyebolt on deck either side of the mast, the hauling part belaying as usual to the bitts. In the nineteenth century, 1811 to be exact, the jeers were unrove after the yard was slung, the weight of the yard being borne by chain slings. The jeers used then were a treble block lashed to the mast head through a hole in the centre of the top and hanging between the trestletrees on the foreside of the foremost crosstree, and two single blocks on the yard. When rigged, the standing part was made fast to the yard, then led through the outside sheave of the treble block, down through the block next to the stand-

ing part, from after to forward, up through the centre sheave, forward to aft, down through the other single block, aft to forward, up through the other sheave in the treble block, forward to aft and down to the bitts, usually on the starboard side. By about 1830 two treble blocks were sometimes used, one from the mast head as before and the other on the yard. The standing part made fast either to the upper block strop or bent to the mast head. Often after 1811 the jeer blocks as well as the jeers were taken down once the yard was hoisted and the slings made fast.

The slings came into use during the last quarter of the eighteenth century, probably in 1773. This date is only conjectural, however. Slings were first used as an addition to jeers. These rope slings were changed to chain slings during wartime and these latter eventually took over the important job of keeping the lower yards slung into position. That was from 1811 onwards. Whether chain or rope, the sling was secured to a thimble strapped to the centre of the yard, or, after about 1840, to chain strops. The

LOWER YARD SLINGS

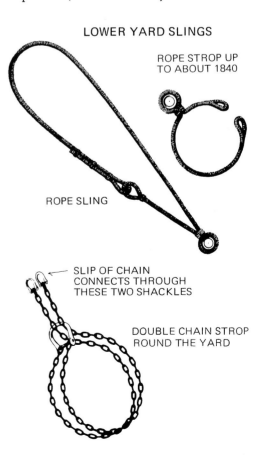

ROPE STROP UP
TO ABOUT 1840

ROPE SLING

SLIP OF CHAIN
CONNECTS THROUGH
THESE TWO SHACKLES

DOUBLE CHAIN STROP
ROUND THE YARD

II RIGGING
Rigging to the fore yard and course

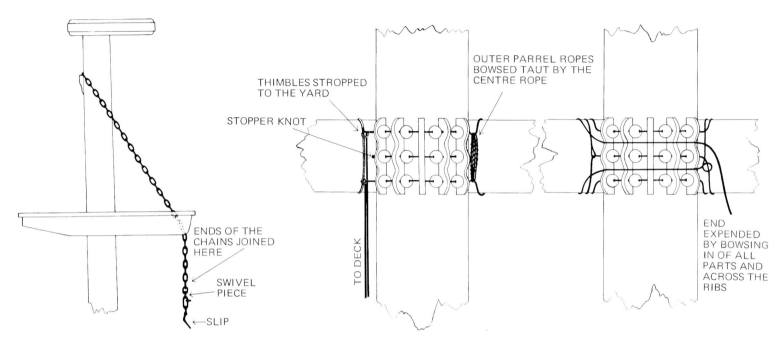

THIMBLES STROPPED
TO THE YARD

OUTER PARREL ROPES
BOWSED TAUT BY THE
CENTRE ROPE

STOPPER KNOT

TO DECK

END
EXPENDED
BY BOWSING
IN OF ALL
PARTS AND
ACROSS THE
RIBS

ENDS OF THE
CHAINS JOINED
HERE

SWIVEL
PIECE

←SLIP

PARREL WITH LEAD TO
DECK (MOST RIBS AND TRUCKS
HAVE BEEN OMITTED FOR CLARITY)

PARREL MADE FAST ON THE
YARD (MOST RIBS AND TRUCKS
HAVE BEEN OMITTED FOR CLARITY)

chain was sometimes taken round the top of the cap instead of to the cleat abaft the mast head. The rope slings should be served for their whole length. From about 1802 there were two holes, one on each side of the centre of the fore part of the top for the slings to reeve through but after 1811 only one hole was fitted. It is likely that chain slings were used from 1793 when, by Admiralty Order, they were allowed on the crossjack.

Parrel rope The method of fitting parrels is not definitely known and the illustration is my own interpretation. The manuscript of 1625 describes one way, though in a rather vague fashion, while other writers just describe the fittings of the parrels and do not state the method used for rigging them. When the yard had to be lowered to furl the sail, quite obviously it was necessary to be able to slack off the parrel from the deck. When the yard was kept hoisted and the sail furled on the yard, there was no necessity to slack off the parrel from the deck. So in the first instance the parrel rope must have led from the deck, round

the yard, through the series of holes in the parrel, and back to the deck; or, one end may have been made fast to the yard. When no lead to the deck was required, the parrel rope was expended by turns round the yard and parrel. (This was superseded by truss pendants by about 1760.) The illustrations show the various methods which could have been used and it is really up to the reader to take his choice. Descriptions of the parts of a parrel are given in the section devoted to blocks.

The breast rope is mentioned as a rope to keep the yard well into the mast and could only have acted as a truss, being made fast to the yard leading round the ribs of the parrel, round the yard and back round the parrel and yard for a couple of times, or until expended. When the yard was lowered, this rope would have to be let go from aloft to enable the parrel to slack off a little, so that the parrel with yard could slide down the mast. The breast rope would not be used until the yard was kept permanently aloft, and was used only on the larger ships, the par-

rel rope being used for this purpose on smaller ships.

The nave line was rove between a small block seized to the middle rib of the parrel, and another one made fast to the mast head. Its purpose was to hoist up the parrel and presumably it helped to stop the parrel from jambing against the wooldings when the yard was hoisted. The nave line is not mentioned in rigging lists until 1684. When truss pendants were fitted, a nave line was also used, being taken through a block secured to the after crosstree or toggled to the top abaft the crosstree; a thimble was spliced into the end and through this thimble a short length of rope was rove. The ends made fast to the truss pendants in the centre abaft the mast, but no block was secured to the centre of the truss pendants abaft the mast.

Truss pendants and falls superseded the parrels in about 1760 and were, in some rigging lists, referred to as truss parrels. There were two pendants on the lower yards, rigged as follows: each pendant had an iron thimble spliced into one end; these ends were

66

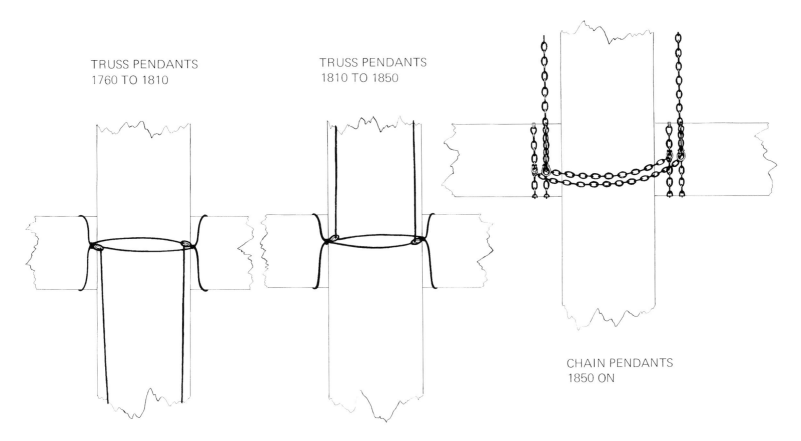

TRUSS PENDANTS
1760 TO 1810

TRUSS PENDANTS
1810 TO 1850

CHAIN PENDANTS
1850 ON

taken round the yard, one to port, the other to starboard of the mast, and were then seized to their own parts tightly round the yard, leaving the thimbles just clear abaft the yard. The other ends were taken behind the mast and passed through the opposing pendant thimbles; they then led down on either side of the mast, and a block was seized (or hooked, in which case the pendant was seized round a small thimble) in the ends; other blocks were hooked into eyebolts in the deck, close to and either side of the mast, and falls were then rove between these blocks and those in the pendant, being made fast to the bitts. Generally, double blocks were used throughout.

From 1810 the pendants were made shorter and instead of leading down to deck, they rove upwards towards the after ends of the trestletrees. A double block was hooked to an eyebolt under the after end of each trestletree, and falls were rove between these blocks and those in the end of the truss pendants and made fast as before to the bitts. After 1815 in some ships, sheaves

were placed on the after ends of the trestletrees to replace the blocks previously hooked there, but not all vessels were rigged in this manner, some retaining the eyebolts and blocks instead of sheaves. In about 1830 some ships had the pendants leading up through the top, and the fall was rove between the truss pendant blocks and other blocks hooked under the lower cap on either side. From about 1840 the pendants were once again made longer and were taken through single blocks hooked under the after ends of the trestletrees; double blocks were seized in the ends, connecting by a fall to single blocks hooked on the channels by the second shroud from aft. The falls belayed to the shroud pin rack.

After 1850 chain trusses were used, rigged as follows: four chain strops were secured to the yard with rose lashings, two on either side of the slings, the lashings laying on top of the yard. A shackle was put on each strop abaft the yard, the two shackles for the starboard truss a little higher than those for the port truss. The shackles

to which the truss pendants were shackled were small ones, while the shackles for reeving the pendants through were larger bow shackles. The small shackle on the starboard side of the slings was on the innermost truss strop, while the small shackle on the port side was on the outer truss strop, thus allowing each pendant to have a clear hauling part. The truss pendants were shackled to the strops, taken round the mast, through the bow shackles, up through iron blocks shackled to eyebolts in the after ends of each trestletree and led down to deck. Double blocks were hooked to the ends, connecting as before to single blocks hooked in the channels by means of a fall.

II RIGGING
Rigging to the fore yard and course

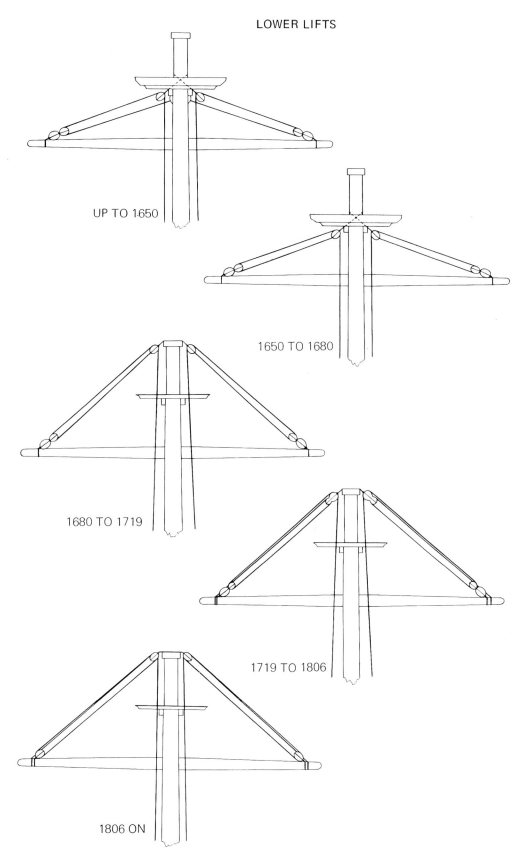

LOWER LIFTS

UP TO 1650

1650 TO 1680

1680 TO 1719

1719 TO 1806

1806 ON

Lifts, until about 1680, led under the top as follows: a block was made fast to the mast head by means of a long strop or pendant; this block hung just below the top and the pendant or strop made fast just above the fore stay collar. Another block was made fast to the yard arm; this block, up to 1680, had its own strop and was seized to the strop of the topsail sheet block. From 1680 until 1806 the block was stropped together with the sheet block by means of a long strop seized together tightly between the two blocks. After 1806 the sheets rove through the yard arm and the lift block was stropped on its own to the yard arm. A single block was used for the upper lift block until 1719, when it was superseded by a long-tackle block. In 1806 this long-tackle block was changed to an ordinary double block. The use of a pendant or long strop for the upper block lasted until 1680. The standing part of the lift was made fast to the forestay collar below the top until 1650, when it was made fast to the pendant or long strop. The running part rove through the yard arm block, up through the upper block and down to deck where it was made fast by the foremost shroud. From 1680 the upper block was fitted to the cap by means of a span; the lift rove as before with the standing part made fast to the span. From 1719, when the long-tackle block or double block was used, the standing part of the lift was made fast to the yard arm close to the lower block, reeving up through the upper block, thence to deck and belayed as before; there were, of course, lifts on either end of the yard. From about 1760 to 1800 the upper block was seized to an eyebolt in the cap instead of being fitted with a span, and from 1806 the upper block was seized to a plate bolted on top of the cap (see the section devoted to furnishings of masts and yards).

During the last few years of sail, from 1850, a tackle comprising a double block spliced into the lifts and a single block, seized or hooked to an eyebolt in the deck alongside the mast was sometimes used on the lower end of the lifts, the fall being belayed to the bitts.

The cap span was a length of rope

8 Lower yards and sails
Rigging to the fore yard and course II

LIFT BLOCKS ON THE YARD ARMS

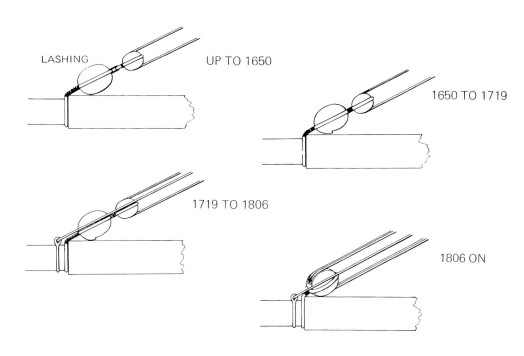

LASHING   UP TO 1650

1650 TO 1719

1719 TO 1806

1806 ON

LIFT BLOCKS ON THE CAPS

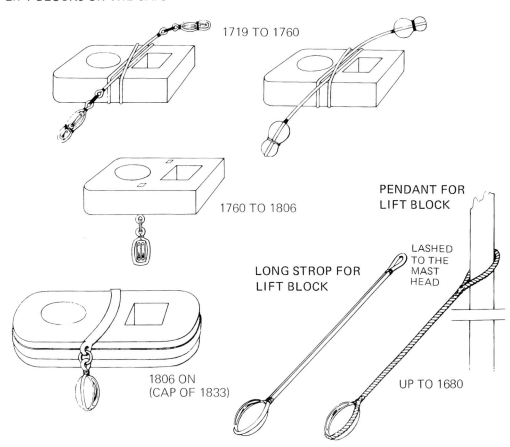

1719 TO 1760

1760 TO 1806

1806 ON
(CAP OF 1833)

LONG STROP FOR
LIFT BLOCK

PENDANT FOR
LIFT BLOCK

LASHED
TO THE
MAST
HEAD

UP TO 1680

with a block spliced into each end and was either clove-hitched round the cap or taken round with a round turn. In both instances a seizing was put on close to the blocks and round both parts of the span, which would have been of such a length as to allow the blocks to be close to the cap after being seized and hitched. An alternative method of making the span was to have a small eye spliced in each end of the span, seizing the lift blocks to these eyes with the lift blocks being stropped with a soft eye.

The **jigger tackle** mentioned in some of the rigging lists, was used to assist the hoisting up of the yard by being seized to the lifts. The tackle consisted of blocks with tails; once the yard was hoisted, the tackles were taken off, the lifts being belayed on their own. Their main purpose was to take the weight of the yard arms while the jeers or halliards took the weight of the yard at the slings.

Footropes or horses were not introduced until about 1675; there were two footropes, one on each side of the yard. The outer ends were always fitted in the same way by being spliced round the yard arm but the method of fitting the inner ends varied a little. Up to about 1706 each inner end had a deadeye seized in it; these connected up with a lanyard to deadeyes strapped to the yard by the slings inside the cleats, the footropes hanging 2 feet under the yard. After 1706 the inner ends still had the deadeyes seized into the ends, but instead of having them on the yard, the two ends were connected by a lanyard, making in effect one footrope. The footropes were secured to the centre of the yard by means of a lashing taken round the lanyard and round the yard, but sometimes, instead of going round the yard, the lashing was taken around another lashing put on between the quarter blocks. After 1760 the footropes crossed each other in the middle of the yard, and the ends were made fast by a lashing, reeving through a thimble in the end of each footrope, and the yard by the sling cleat: that is, port footrope lead to the starboard sling and starboard to port. After 1811 the footropes were seized to the jackstay on the yard.

69

II RIGGING
Rigging to the fore yard and course

Sometimes the footropes at this time were made from one length of rope, but usually two footropes were used and were seized by means of a thimble spliced into the ends. When footropes were first introduced, stirrups were used only on large ships and one, or at the most, two a side were rigged on the yard: during the eighteenth century two and three stirrups each side were carried, depending on the size of the ship, small ships carrying one a side. By the end of the eighteenth century all ships had at least two a side, most ships had three, and this remained to the end of the sail era. The stirrups should allow the footropes to hang 3 feet below the yard; before the introduction of the jackstay they were put on the yard by three round turns and then nailed to it. After jackstays were fitted, the stirrups were seized to the jackstay; the upper ends had thimbles spliced into them while the lower ends had a small eye-splice or, from the latter half of the eighteenth century, a thimble in them. The footrope rove through these eyes or thimbles before being fixed to the yard. All stirrups were served from where they fixed to the yard to the lower end. When thimbles were used on both ends, the serving went the whole length; as a precautionary measure, the lower ends of the stirrups were seized to the footropes to prevent them running through the stirrup should they carry away.

Brace pendants were in use up to about 1815 and always fitted the same way. An eye-splice was formed in one end to fit snugly round the yard arm and the other end had a single block spliced into it. The lengths of the pendants are given in the Appendix. Preventer braces did not have pendants. Between about 1719 and 1773 some ships were fitted with two pendants on either yard arm, the second one slightly longer than the first; these longer pendants acted as preventers in case the brace pendant carried away. When ships were fitted with two pendants the brace blocks were fitted with a strop and thimble; both pendants were spliced in the thimble and the ends of the pendants on the yard were individually spliced

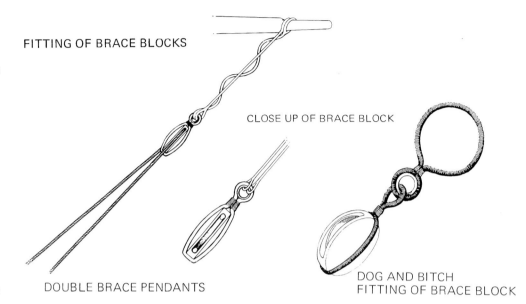

FITTING OF BRACE BLOCKS

CLOSE UP OF BRACE BLOCK

DOUBLE BRACE PENDANTS

DOG AND BITCH
FITTING OF BRACE BLOCK

round the yard arm. These double pendants were used only on the fore and main lower and topsail yards.
Braces, up to 1805, altered very little in the method of rigging, the standing part being always made fast to the stay, the running part reeving through a block either on the stay or stay collar, then down to deck. However there were a few differences, mainly concerning the position to which the standing part was made fast.
During the early seventeenth century the standing part had an eye spliced into the end and this in turn was seized to an eye in a piece of rope about a fathom in length with an eye in each end, which was clove-hitched round the stay, the clove-hitch being made in the centre of the rope, the ends the same length. The braces, after being seized to the rope on the stay, rove through the brace pendant block, led aft through blocks fitted by means of a long strop or pendant hitched round the stay a few feet above the standing part; each of these blocks cleared the stay by about 2 feet. The running part then led to the bulwarks. The position of the standing part was less than half-way up between the two masts but gradually through the seventeenth century the position was moved up the stay until by 1719 (by starting at 0.4 and progressing to 0.55, 1719 should be about the right date), the positon was a little over half way. After 1719 the position remained at about 0.55 between

the masts, until about 1733 when it was 0.66, by 1745 0.75 and finally, by 1765 the standing part was made fast to the mainstay collar by the mouse. The running part, after about 1706, led directly down from the block on the stay to lead blocks seized or hooked to eyebolts in the deck on either side of the main hatch; it is possible that this lead was in use much earlier but models of the period do not show it. The brace should be made fast to the main bitts. The standing part of the brace was sometimes made fast directly to the stay and the short length of rope dispensed with.
In about 1805 the blocks previously carried on the stay were seized to eyebolts at the bibs of the main mast, and in about 1815 the pendants were dispensed with and the blocks were stropped to the yard with dog and bitch strops. This method of fastening the blocks to the yard enabled them to lay flat with their cheeks parallel to the deck. The lead of the brace was the same and the running part led down and through a sheave in the main bitts.
A preventer brace was used only in wartime when a block was seized on each yard arm on the fore side. The standing part was hitched round the bowsprit cap, rove through the blocks on the yard, through blocks on a span round the bowsprit cap and was taken in on the forecastle. Preventer braces are very seldom seen on models and I

YARD TACKLE AND TRICING LINES

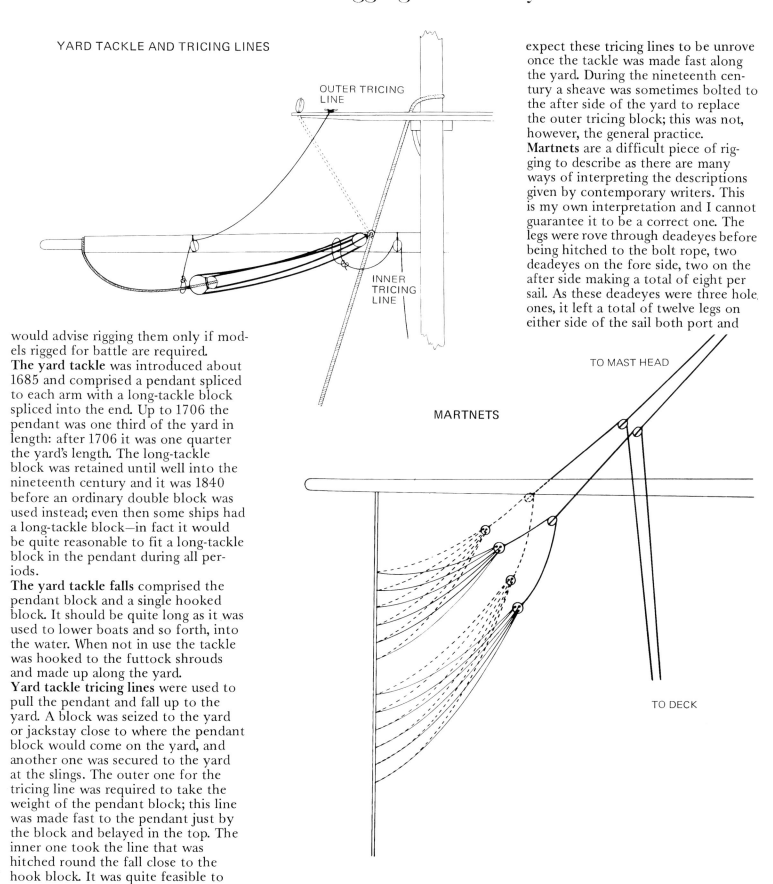

OUTER TRICING LINE

INNER TRICING LINE

MARTNETS

TO MAST HEAD

TO DECK

expect these tricing lines to be unrove once the tackle was made fast along the yard. During the nineteenth century a sheave was sometimes bolted to the after side of the yard to replace the outer tricing block; this was not, however, the general practice.

Martnets are a difficult piece of rigging to describe as there are many ways of interpreting the descriptions given by contemporary writers. This is my own interpretation and I cannot guarantee it to be a correct one. The legs were rove through deadeyes before being hitched to the bolt rope, two deadeyes on the fore side, two on the after side making a total of eight per sail. As these deadeyes were three hole ones, it left a total of twelve legs on either side of the sail both port and

would advise rigging them only if models rigged for battle are required.

The yard tackle was introduced about 1685 and comprised a pendant spliced to each arm with a long-tackle block spliced into the end. Up to 1706 the pendant was one third of the yard in length: after 1706 it was one quarter the yard's length. The long-tackle block was retained until well into the nineteenth century and it was 1840 before an ordinary double block was used instead; even then some ships had a long-tackle block—in fact it would be quite reasonable to fit a long-tackle block in the pendant during all periods.

The yard tackle falls comprised the pendant block and a single hooked block. It should be quite long as it was used to lower boats and so forth, into the water. When not in use the tackle was hooked to the futtock shrouds and made up along the yard.

Yard tackle tricing lines were used to pull the pendant and fall up to the yard. A block was seized to the yard or jackstay close to where the pendant block would come on the yard, and another one was secured to the yard at the slings. The outer one for the tricing line was required to take the weight of the pendant block; this line was made fast to the pendant just by the block and belayed in the top. The inner one took the line that was hitched round the fall close to the hook block. It was quite feasible to

II RIGGING
Rigging to the fore yard and course

starboard. (I have seen a painting depicting hearts instead of deadeyes and a total of forty legs on each side but this is an isolated example.) The pairs of deadeyes were fastened together by a rope which was seized round one of them, rove through a block and was seized to the other. The legs, fastened to the leech, should enable the deadeyes to be about 6 feet from the leech. The leg running through the block should enable the block, when the sail is furled, to come within a few feet below the fore topmast crosstrees. It is easier to sketch martnets than to describe them and the illustration should be referred to.

Martnet falls Blocks were fastened to the fore topmast head by a long strop or pendant. A rope was spliced round the block in the legs, rove through the block on the pendant and led down to deck; it was quite probable that a long-tackle was fastened to the end of this rope in large ships. In small ships a snatch block was probably secured to the foot of the mast and the rope snatched into it, enabling the rope to be manned along the deck when furling the sail. As previously mentioned, this method of rigging the martnet legs and falls is my own idea and readers may prefer to work out their own definitions.

Leechline legs superseded the martnets in about 1650 in small ships and a few years later in large ships. When first introduced, the leechline legs were very simple and comprised a rope made fast to the leech of the sail, the rope leading through a block stropped about a quarter way along the yard from the arms hanging on the fore side up through a block seized to the fore stay collar close up under the top and down to the fore bitts. By 1675 the leechlines were more complicated on large ships and were fitted thus: one end of the leechline was fastened to the leech, the other end rove through a block on the yard, through a block stropped together with another block—head to head—back through another block on the yard and across to the leech. The block stropped head to head was for the leech whip. Small ships had one leech a side; by 1700 all ships had leechlines

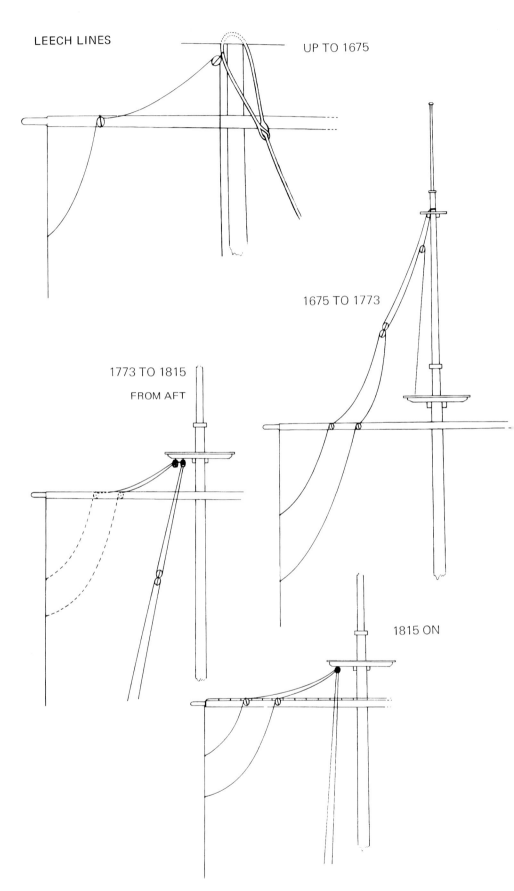

LEECH LINES

UP TO 1675

1675 TO 1773

1773 TO 1815

FROM AFT

1815 ON

LOWER BUNTLINES

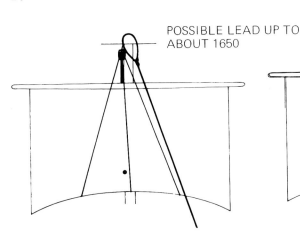

POSSIBLE LEAD UP TO
ABOUT 1650

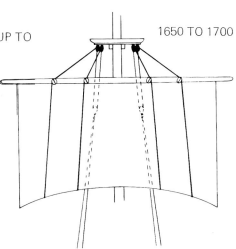

1650 TO 1700

1700 TO 1805

ADDITIONAL LEAD
BLOCKS UNDER THE TOP

fitted as the First Rates of 1675, except that instead of having two blocks stropped together a special long block was used.

From 1773 until about 1815 leechlines rove as follows: one end was made fast to the sail, the other end rove through a block on the yard, through a double block under the fore part of the top, through a double block under the after part of the top, rove through a block, back up through the double blocks and down to the sail. The block through which the leechline rove was stropped to another—head to head—to take the leech whip. In small ships this method of fitting the leechlines was introduced much earlier and in fact some models of 1720 show this method but only, however, on small ships. On some small ships only one leechline was fitted each side, running from the sail through a block seized to the yard, through the outer sheave of blocks under the fore and after ends of the top (the inner sheaves took the buntlines) and led down to deck; sometimes a single block was spliced in the end and a whip rove down to deck.

After 1815 two leechlines were carried on all ships. The leechlines rove from the sail through single blocks seized to the jackstay, through a double block under the fore part of the top and were taken straight down to deck, both leechlines each side being worked individually. When only one leechline a side was carried, this was made fast to the upper bowline bridle cringle; when

two a side were carried one was made fast to the lower reef cringle and the other to the upper bowline bridle cringle.

Leechline falls were in use from about 1675 to 1773, reeving as follows: the standing part was made fast round the head of the topmast; the running part rove through the block stropped together with the leechline leg block, up through a block stropped and hanging just below the topmast crosstrees (this block was usually stropped with a long strop to the topmast head) then down to deck, usually being made fast to the fore bitts. Leechlines were, of course, fitted both port and starboard of the sail. From 1773 a whip was rove through a block stropped to the block on the leechline, the standing part being made fast to the forecastle rails and the running part belayed close to it after being taken through a lead block.

Slab lines when first introduced were designed to lift up the foot of the sail for clear visibility when sailing under a pilot. Two small blocks were seized to the slings of the yard, the lines reeving aft of the sail and hitching to the middle buntline cringles. The hauling parts were made fast to the cross piece of the topsail sheet bitts. During the latter half of the nineteenth century additional slab lines (making two a side) were rove; they were taken through a double block strapped to the yard at the quarter on the fore side of the yard abaft the sail, through blocks seized to the jackstay between

the sail and the yard and were bent to the leech of the sail, the hauling part leading to the topsail sheet bitts. The latter method of rigging slab lines was to assist in furling the sails.

Buntline legs During the early seventeenth century the buntlines, or brails as they were then called, were simply three ropes, one in the centre, the others on either side, which were fastened to the bolt rope on the foot of the sail, led up through probably a treble block seized to the fore stay collar and led aft down to the forecastle rails where they were made fast. By 1650, however, they had become more complicated and four or six lines were rigged, depending on the size of the ship. They were rigged as follows: one end was made fast to the foot of the sail, the other end rove up through a block seized to the yard on the fore side, rove through a block under the fore side of the top, down aft through one sheave of a shoe block, up through another block under the top, down through another block seized to the yard and finally made fast to the foot of the sail. Generally, one pair of buntlines either side was sufficient but First and Second Rates sometimes had another pair in the centre of the yard or at least slightly each side of the centre, rigged with a shoe block as before but with one leg coming on one side of the mast and the other leg on the opposite side. Thus on large ships, six lines came down across the fore side of the sail and four lines on smaller ships. Sometimes the centre pair of

II RIGGING
Rigging to the fore yard and course

LOWER BUNTLINES

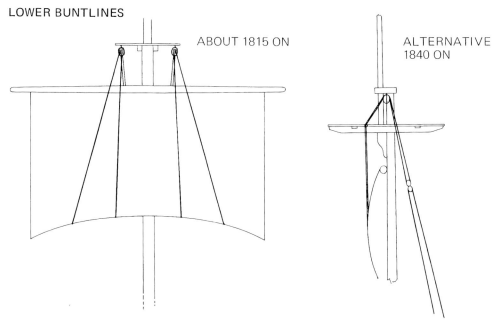

ABOUT 1815 ON

ALTERNATIVE
1840 ON

legs was rove as two single lines and the shoe block dispensed with. Only four buntlines were considered necessary after 1700.

Also after 1700 additional lead blocks (on some ships single blocks, on others double) were fastened under the after side of the top; the buntlines rove through these blocks before leading to deck. Personally I would fit single blocks until about 1745 and double blocks after that. The after blocks under the top were dispensed with after 1805 and the buntlines rove through the forward blocks and down, whip blocks being fitted as before. After 1773 two single blocks were stropped together instead of shoe blocks. Up to 1706 the lead blocks on the yard were secured by a timber-hitch; after this date they were seized to eyebolts set in the top of the yard, until jackstays were introduced, when they were seized to the eyebolts of the jackstay.

Another alternative way to rig the blocks under the tops (on ships carrying only one leechline) was to have the inner buntlines through single blocks and the outer buntlines and leechlines sharing double blocks. Blocks on the yard were dispensed with in about 1815 — I think (but this is only conjecture) at the innovation of jackstays—the buntlines reeving from the bunt of the sail to the blocks

under the top. Also, in about 1840, the buntlines were taken through a hole or sheave in the top, through a double block stropped to the lower cap, down through the whip block, back through another sheave in the double block and down through the top and then made fast to the sail as before. Some ships, however, still led the buntlines under the top as before 1840—it was probably a matter of the master's choice.

Buntline falls were used when buntline legs were fitted with shoe blocks: the buntline falls were actually common whips, one end being made fast to the rails on the after end of the forecastle, the other reeving through the lower sheaves on the shoe block and back down to the forecastle rails where it was belayed.

Bowlines and bowline bridles are discussed together because one cannot be fitted without the other. The bridle was secured to the leech of the sail by means of the bowline cringles; usually it was simply one short length of rope hitched to the bowline cringles and before hitching both ends, the rope was rove through a thimble to which the bowline was seized. On large ships the bridle comprised two pieces of rope; the illustrations will show how this was rigged more clearly than a description. At all times the bowlines led through single blocks lashed to the

bowsprit a little aft of the fore stay deadeyes or hearts; sometimes these blocks were lashed to the head rails, one block on either side of the bowsprit; they then rove either directly to the forecastle rails or bulwarks or through the multiple lead block lashed to the gammon lashing then up to the forecastle. When models are not fitted with sails the bridles are hitched to the fore yard with timber-hitches, a little inboard from the yard arm cleats. It should be noted that about 1819 toggles were introduced to replace cringles on the sails. The bowlines toggled to the bridles, the buntlines and slab lines toggled to the sails and the leechlines toggled to the bowline cringles (see the chapter on sails). The bowline bridle, however, was spliced to the bridle cringles and toggles were not used instead of these cringles.

Reef points were braided and secured to the sail by a knot on each side of the sail. The points, about twice the circumference of the yard in length and usually two to each cloth of the sail, were rove through the holes in the reef band and an overhand knot worked close up to the holes; about two thirds of the reef point hung on the after side and one third on the fore side of the sail.

Reef tackles and pendants were not carried on the lower yards until the early nineteenth century, the courses being reefed by hauling the sail manually up to the yard, assisted possibly in some degree by hauling on the leechlines. The cringles on the leech of the courses by the reef bands were used for earings and not, as on topsails, for reef pendants or tackles. From about 1830 onwards a block was seized to the reef cringle; a line, one end spliced round the yard arm, rove through this block, up through a sheave bolted to the fore side of the yard by the arm cleats, up through a block on the cap and down to the fore bitts.

Reef lines were used for a method of reefing courses from 1719 to 1805 on large ships, whereby a row of holes was sewn in the courses instead of reef points. A reefing line was rove from each yard arm through these holes and round the yard, spirally towards the centre, being hitched, when reefed, to the jeer block strapping. When not in use, the lines were coiled and made up on the yard arm.

Jack line reefing, or French reefing, was an alternate method of reefing sails used on some ships about 1850; instead of having reef points, holes were sewn in the sail. Behind each row of holes a line called the jackstay was placed; spliced at each end into the eyelet holes of the reef cringles, another line called the reef line or naval line was middled and each end passed from aft to forward through the centre hole, one end above, the other end below the jackstay. Then, working each way from the centre to each leech, the ends were taken through the next holes, forward to aft, taken round the jackstay and crossed over its own part, back through the same hole from aft to forward, and repeated through the other holes; the ends were then spliced

into the eyelet holes of the reef cringles—this sounds more complicated than in fact it is, as the illustrations will show. To reef the sail, reef beckets with a toggle in one end and an eye in the other were seized to the jackstay on the yard, just below the toggle. When reefing, the end of the becket was taken under the reef line and toggled up. By an Admiralty order dated 30 December 1857, all topsails and courses were to be fitted with beckets and the toggles had to be secured to the yards and not to the jackstays.

Clue garnets had their standing part made fast to the yard about one third from the centre of the yard, up to the early nineteenth century, after that, a little nearer to the centre, either with a timber-hitch or, after 1815, seized to the jackstay; it was then rove through the clue block secured to the clue of

the sail, led up through another block seized under the yard close to and a little inboard from the standing part and led down to the fore bitts. After 1670 an additional lead block was made fast to the yard, close to and just outboard of the quarter blocks; the clue garnet then rove as before but also led through the inner block prior to leading to the bitts. From 1680 the outer clue blocks on the yard were made with shoulders but those on the clue of the sail were ordinary ones, as were the inner lead blocks. It was about 1719 before blocks on the clue were changed to shoulder blocks but the inner lead blocks were always common ones. The method of fitting the clue block to the clue of the sail is illustrated; it is sufficient to say that the clue block, sheet block and tack were all secured together. In about 1773 the additional lead blocks were

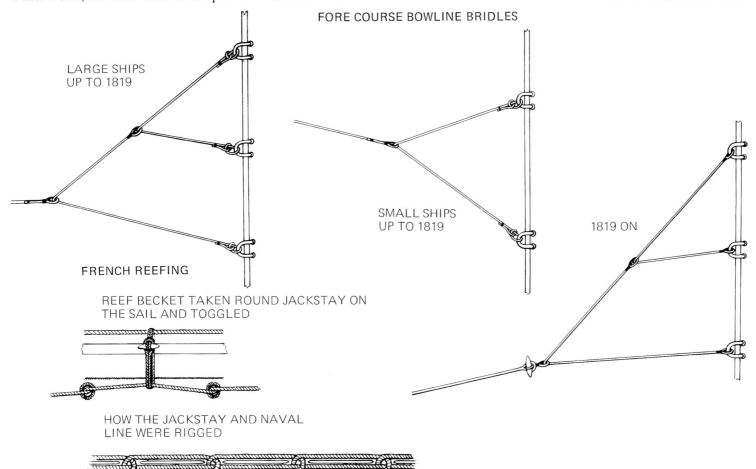

FORE COURSE BOWLINE BRIDLES

LARGE SHIPS
UP TO 1819

SMALL SHIPS
UP TO 1819

1819 ON

FRENCH REEFING

REEF BECKET TAKEN ROUND JACKSTAY ON
THE SAIL AND TOGGLED

HOW THE JACKSTAY AND NAVAL
LINE WERE RIGGED

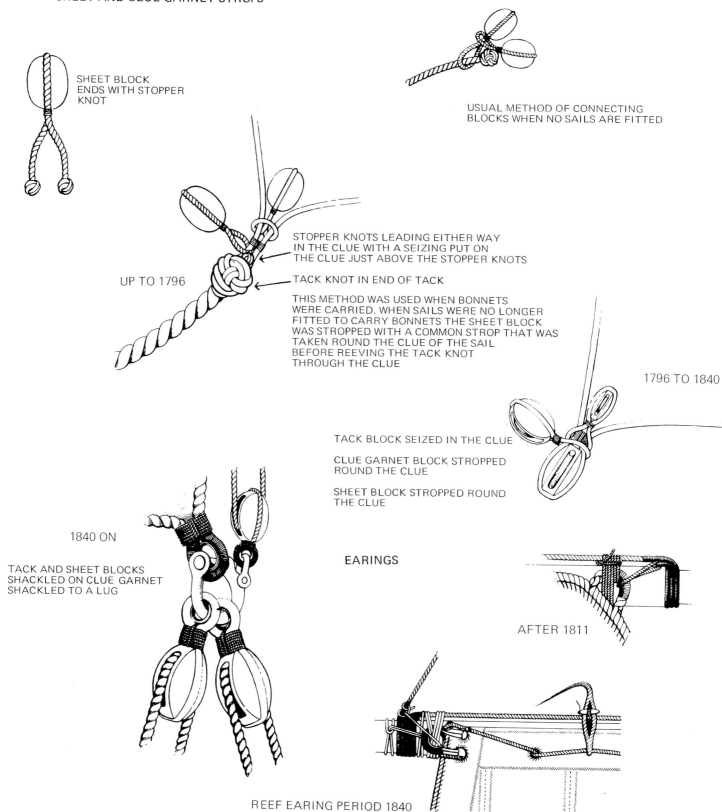

SECURING OF THE TACK
SHEET AND CLUE GARNET STROPS

SHEET BLOCK
ENDS WITH STOPPER
KNOT

USUAL METHOD OF CONNECTING
BLOCKS WHEN NO SAILS ARE FITTED

STOPPER KNOTS LEADING EITHER WAY
IN THE CLUE WITH A SEIZING PUT ON
THE CLUE JUST ABOVE THE STOPPER KNOTS

UP TO 1796

TACK KNOT IN END OF TACK

THIS METHOD WAS USED WHEN BONNETS
WERE CARRIED. WHEN SAILS WERE NO LONGER
FITTED TO CARRY BONNETS THE SHEET BLOCK
WAS STROPPED WITH A COMMON STROP THAT WAS
TAKEN ROUND THE CLUE OF THE SAIL
BEFORE REEVING THE TACK KNOT
THROUGH THE CLUE

1796 TO 1840

TACK BLOCK SEIZED IN THE CLUE

CLUE GARNET BLOCK STROPPED
ROUND THE CLUE

SHEET BLOCK STROPPED ROUND
THE CLUE

1840 ON

TACK AND SHEET BLOCKS
SHACKLED ON CLUE GARNET
SHACKLED TO A LUG

EARINGS

AFTER 1811

REEF EARING PERIOD 1840

dispensed with and the shoulder blocks changed to common blocks; this innovation remained to the end of the sail era.

Sheets altered very little during the sail era and in fact the only alteration was in the position of the sheave in the bulwarks to lead the sheet inboard; until about 1670 the standing part and the sheave were about half way between the fore and main masts; after that they were nearer the main mast—in fact, almost abreast of it. The standing part was seized or hitched to an eyebolt in the ship's side. The running part was rove through the sheet block fastened to the clue of the sail, led aft through the sheave in the bulwarks and secured to the cleats or kevels on the inside of the bulwarks.

The tack, up to 1670, was single and led forward from the clue of the sail, through holes in the stem, and inboard to the forecastle, the tack on the starboard side of the sail being made fast to port, the port tack to starboard. After 1670 and up to about 1706 the tacks, still single ropes, led through ornamented dead blocks between the timbers of the head and up to the forecastle, again port tack to starboard and starboard to port.

Bumkins were introduced in about

1710, first of all on the Sixth Rates, and then gradually on the other Rates, so that by 1745 all Rates were so fitted. I would suggest 1710 for the Sixth, 1719 for the Fifth, 1733 for the Fourth, and 1745 for the First, Second and Third. The tacks rove through a block on the bumkin then through the dead block and up to the forecastle head; they did not cross, port tack being taken to port and starboard tack to starboard. A few years after the introduction of bumkins the dead blocks were dispensed with and the tacks led straight from bumkin to forecastle head. From 1796 tacks were doubled, the standing part being spliced round the bumkin and, the hauling part being rove through a block at the clue of the sail and forward through the bumkin block to the forecastle. After 1815 the standing part was secured to the bumkin by means of a slip. When the tack was single a knot was made in the end to secure it to the clue of the sail. At all times the tack was tapered in its making, the taper starting 10 yards from the knot or splice end and so graduating as to be half the circumference of the outer end at the inboard end.

Earings spread the upper corners of

the sail out to the yard arm. One end was spliced into the head cringle, the other end taken round the yard arm outside of the rigging and back through the cringle about three times; turns were then taken round the yard within the rigging and through the cringle until the earing was expended, two half-hitches finishing it off. Each earing was between 5 and 6 fathoms long. It must be noted that when jackstays were fitted on the yard, earings were fitted in exactly the same manner as before but the sail was made to lie on top of the yard and not underneath. Earings were also spliced into the reef earing cringles and used as before when the sail was reefed.

Robands or rope bands fastened the head of the sail to the yard or jackstay, whichever was applicable, and mostly consisted of braided rope about three times the circumference of the yard in length when jackstays were not fitted and about 3 feet long when jackstays were used. The method of lacing the rope bands is better illustrated than described. There were as many rope bands per sail as there were reef points in one reef band. The centre rope band was taken round the tye or jeer block strop.

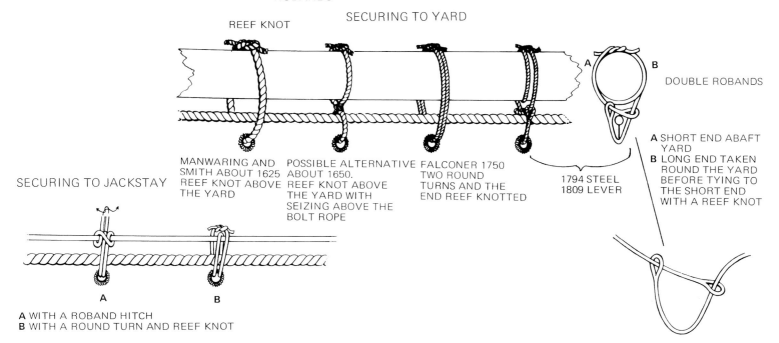

ROBANDS

SECURING TO YARD

REEF KNOT

DOUBLE ROBANDS

MANWARING AND SMITH ABOUT 1625 REEF KNOT ABOVE THE YARD

POSSIBLE ALTERNATIVE ABOUT 1650. REEF KNOT ABOVE THE YARD WITH SEIZING ABOVE THE BOLT ROPE

FALCONER 1750 TWO ROUND TURNS AND THE END REEF KNOTTED

1794 STEEL 1809 LEVER

A SHORT END ABAFT YARD
B LONG END TAKEN ROUND THE YARD BEFORE TYING TO THE SHORT END WITH A REEF KNOT

SECURING TO JACKSTAY

A WITH A ROBAND HITCH
B WITH A ROUND TURN AND REEF KNOT

II RIGGING
Rigging to the main yard and course

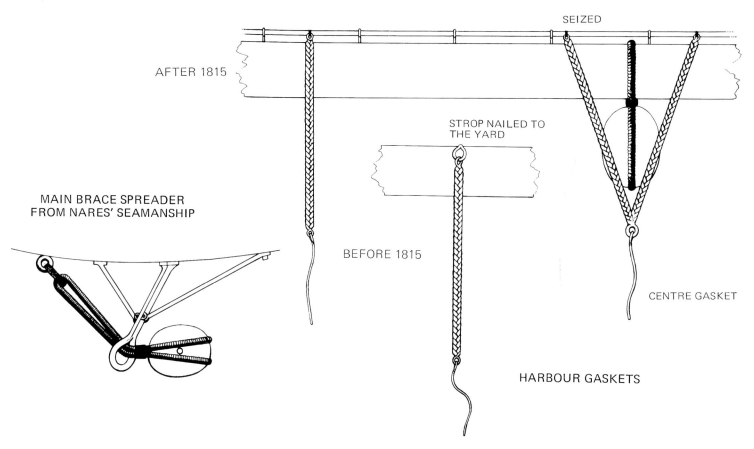

SEIZED

AFTER 1815

STROP NAILED TO
THE YARD

MAIN BRACE SPREADER
FROM NARES' SEAMANSHIP

BEFORE 1815

CENTRE GASKET

HARBOUR GASKETS

Harbour gaskets were used to keep the sail furled; between eight and twelve harbour gaskets were required for the sail, the number depending on the size of the sail. After 1815 when jackstays were fitted, these gaskets were seized at one end to the jackstay and rove through it and round the sail when in use. Before this, gaskets were spliced at one end into a short strop nailed into the top of the yard and when in use rove round the sail and yard, up through the short strop and were hitched to their own part. The centre gaskets had two legs which were secured to the yard on each side of the quarter blocks; they were then taken round the yard and sail as before, making in effect two V shaped gaskets on either side of the centre of the sail, one gasket per seam of the sail being the usual number carried. These harbour gaskets seem to have been an early nineteenth century innovation. On some ships the centre gaskets were ordinary ones, but crossed each other when put on.

Sea gaskets or furling lines were intro-duced in about 1650 and were used at sea for furling the sail. From the late seventeenth century large ships carried eight, medium sized ships six, and small ships four, equally spaced along the yard. They were spliced round the yard or to the jackstay and wound spirally round the sail, yard, booms and so on. When furling sails for har-bour in the nineteenth century, harbour gaskets were used and the sea gaskets coiled and made up on the yard. Dur-ing the seventeenth century two long gaskets were fitted to each yard at the ties; they were wound round the sail and yard, working towards each yard arm, the sail on the extreme ends of the yard being furled with rope yarns. It was not until the late seventeenth century that these long gaskets gave way to a number of short ones.

RIGGING TO THE MAIN YARD AND COURSE

The truss
The ties
The halliard
The jeers
The slings
The parrel rope
The breast rope
The nave line
Truss pendants and falls
Lifts
Span for the cap
Jigger tackle
Stirrups
Brace pendants

All these elements of rigging were fitted as on the fore yard.

Footropes or horses were fitted as on the fore yard but they were introduc-ed earlier—about 1640.

The braces, up to about 1815, had their standing part hitched to an eyebolt in the quarter piece or to the ship's side close to the quarter gallery or even, in some cases, to the top of the quarter galleries. The running part rove through the pendant block or block on the yard, back through either a block on the transom level with the bulwarks or through a sheave in the poop bulwarks (whether a sheave or not depends upon the ship's design, the sheave being an integral part when fitted). The brace was belayed to a cleat on the inside of the bulwarks. From about 1805 on, a spreader was bolted to the ship's side above the quarter gallery; a block was seized to this spreader. The standing part of the brace was hitched to an eyebolt just below the spreader and the running part rove through the brace block on the yard, from out to in, back through the block on the spreader, through a sheave in the poop bulwarks to a cleat inside the bulwarks. After 1815, on some ships, a tackle comprising two single blocks was secured to the standing part, the running part of the tackle reeving through a sheave in the bulwarks close to the sheave for the brace.

A brace span, after about 1790, was fitted to the main brace to trice up the brace. Up to 1850 the span comprised a rope with two legs, into each of which a thimble was spliced and the hauling and standing part of the brace rove through these thimbles. The rope itself, up to 1810, was hitched to the mizen shrouds close to the futtock staves. From 1810 to 1850 the span was made as before but a block was seized to the third mizen shroud close to the futtock stave and the span rope rove through this block down to the pin rail by the mizen shrouds. After 1850 the span comprised a length of rope rove through a

single block; the ends of the rope rove from inboard out through a double block seized to the mizen shrouds; in each end a thimble was spliced to take the brace. The single block on the span had another rope spliced round it, this rope being made fast to the pin rail by the mizen shrouds.

Preventer braces were only used in wartime and were temporary fittings up to about 1815. However, after that date preventers became a permanent fixture. Up to 1815 the standing part of the brace was hitched to the after shroud of the fore mast, close up to the futtock stave. The running part rove through blocks seized to the fore side of the yard arms, forward through blocks seized under the trestletrees of the fore mast and led down to the fore bitts. After 1815 yard blocks were stropped on and a double block seized to the cheeks of the fore mast; the brace rove up through one sheave of the double block, through the yard block, forward through the other sheave of the double block, both ends being taken through sheaves in the fore bitts.

Yard tackle pendants
Yard tackle falls
Yard tackle tricing lines
Martnet legs
Martnet falls
Leechline legs
Slab lines

All the above were fitted as on the fore yard.

Leechline falls were fitted as on the fore yard, but note that after about 1740 leech blocks were shoe blocks and not like those on the foresail.

Buntline legs, up to about 1680, were rigged in the same way as the fore buntlines. From 1680 main buntlines were taken forward, being rove as follows: one end of the buntline was made fast to the cringle on the sail, the other end rove through a block on the yard, through a block under the fore end of the main top, through one sheave of a shoe block, back up through another block under the fore end of the main top, through another block on the yard and down to another buntline cringle. Through the other sheave of the shoe block a rope was rove, both ends being made fast to the forecastle rails.

From 1773 two single blocks stropped together head to head were used instead of shoe blocks. As on the foresail, after about 1815 the blocks on the yard were removed and buntlines rove straight from the sail to the blocks under the top. From 1805 to 1820 the fall was taken to the bitts abaft the fore mast instead of leading to the forecastle rails. From 1820 to 1850, the falls were made fast to an eyebolt and cleat close to the stem on the inside of the fore bulwarks. After 1850

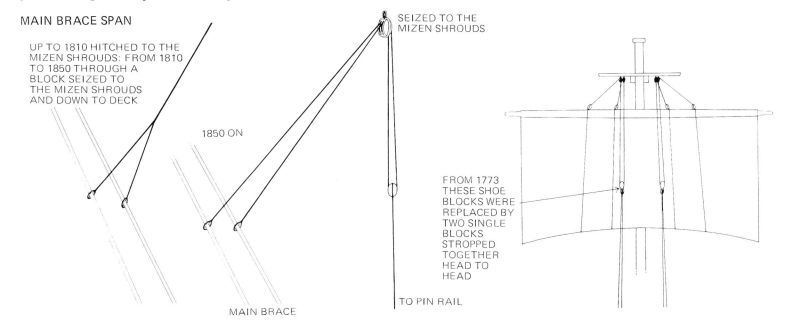

MAIN BRACE SPAN

UP TO 1810 HITCHED TO THE MIZEN SHROUDS: FROM 1810 TO 1850 THROUGH A BLOCK SEIZED TO THE MIZEN SHROUDS AND DOWN TO DECK

1850 ON

SEIZED TO THE MIZEN SHROUDS

FROM 1773 THESE SHOE BLOCKS WERE REPLACED BY TWO SINGLE BLOCKS STROPPED TOGETHER HEAD TO HEAD

TO PIN RAIL

MAIN BRACE

II RIGGING
Rigging to the main yard and course

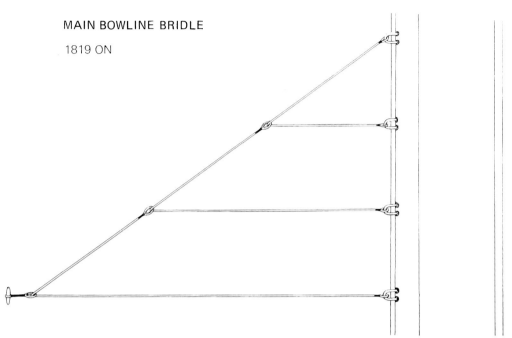

MAIN BOWLINE BRIDLE

1819 ON

the main buntlines were rigged the same as those on the foresail.

Bowlines and bridles Up to about 1670 bowlines rove through blocks seized about half way along the bowsprit, coming in on the forecastle. During the last quarter of the century, First to Fifth Rates had a tackle on them comprising two long-tackle blocks, the upper block being spliced into the bowline, the lower one being seized to the bowsprit; the running part of the fall rove from the lower block to the forecastle. Sixth Rates had a similar arrangement comprising a double and single block. After 1690, bowlines rove through a double block strapped to the fore mast about 5 feet from the forecastle deck, the starboard bowline being taken through one sheave and made fast on the port side of the forecastle. The port bowline rove through the other sheave and was made fast to the starboard side. No tackles were rigged, the bowline going straight to the timber heads; from 1733 bowlines led straight to the fore jeer bitts. After 1805 a pendant was formed on the bridle by splicing a long strop round a thimble on the bridle, this thimble being seized in the bight; another thimble was seized in the other bight and through this a rope was rove with the ends belayed and hitched to the cross pieces of the bitts

abaft the fore mast. This pendant was about 4 feet long. The bridle was fitted the same as that on the fore course. An extra part, however, was rigged: when the bridle on the fore course was made of one piece of rope, the main course bridle was made of two pieces; when the fore bridle was made of two pieces, the main was made of three pieces.

Reef points
Reef tackles and pendants
Reefing lines
Jack line reefing
Clue garnets
The same practice was followed for the above, as for the foresail.

Sheets had the block at the clue of the sail secured in the same way as that on the fore course. Up to 1733, the standing part of the sheet was seized to an eyebolt close to the quarter gallery and on a level with the main deck. The hauling part rove through the block on the sail, back through a lead block seized to another eyebolt just forward of the standing part, forward through a gunport just forward of the break of the quarterdeck and was belayed to a cleat in the inside of the bulwarks in the waist. From 1733 to 1815 the eyebolt for the standing part was level with the mizen mast and the main deck. The hauling part rove through the block on the sail, back

through a lead block just forward of the standing part, was taken through a hole in the ship's side just forward of the break of the quarterdeck and belayed to a cleat, as before. By 1745 the hole in the side was replaced by a sheave, the sheet leading as before. After 1815 a spreader was fitted to the ship's side to enable the lead block to stand out about 4 feet from the side; the spreader was in roughly the same position as the eyebolt in previous years. The standing part was made fast to the spreader. The hauling part, after reeving through the block on the spreader, rove through a sheave in the side—in the same position as in previous years. The spreader was the same shape as that for the main brace.

The tack was single and fastened to the sail in the same way as on the fore sail up to 1790. Up to 1655, on two decked ships or below, the tack was taken through a hole in the side of the ship on the upper deck and was belayed to a cleat on the inside of the bulwarks; this hole was just abaft the fore shrouds, but on three decked ships was in the side of the middle deck and was ornamented. By 1706, instead of a hole in the side, a piece of wood called a chesstree was bolted to the outside of the ship just abaft of the fore shrouds. This chesstree had a hole or sheave in it and the tack rove through this, leading through a port just forward of the chesstree to a cleat inside of the bulwarks on the main deck. By 1706 this chesstree had become the fender just abaft of the fore channels, a sheave being fitted in it as before and the tack reeving the same way. Sometimes, instead of leading finally through a port forward of the chesstree a sheave was let in the side and the tack rove through this.

On large ships after 1790 and on all ships by 1800, all tacks were double. When rigged double, the standing part was hitched to an eyebolt in the chesstree. The hauling part rove through a block on the sail, through the chesstrees and through a sheave forward of the chesstrees to a cleat inside the bulwarks. After 1815 the standing part of the tack was seized to an eyebolt on the upper deck, just inside of the bulwarks on a level with the aftermost fore shroud. The hauling part rove through the block on the sail, from forward to aft through a lead block seized to an eyebolt just aft of the hauling part and was taken to a cleat on the bulwarks.

Earings were rigged the same way as on the fore course.

Robands or rope bands were rigged the same way as on the fore course.

Gaskets (long and harbour) were rigged the same way as on the fore course.

Quarter pendants and tackles were rigged on large ships, hanging from the quarters of the yard, between about 1733 and 1810. The pendant was spliced round the yard, and the tackle and pendant were similar to the yard arm pendant and tackle of up to 1733; but instead of a block being spliced into the pendant, a thimble was used, the upper block of the tackle being hooked into this thimble. When not in use, the tackle was taken down and the pendant was seized to the foremost shroud.

RIGGING TO THE CROSSJACK

Slings were used during all periods for taking the weight of the yard since no jeers were carried on the crossjack. Up to 1773 a single block was strapped to the centre of the yard, the sheave running athwartships. The sling comprised a length of rope, one end of which had a small eye spliced into it; the other end rove through the block from starboard to port, up round the back of the mast above the trestletrees and was rove through the small eye, taken back and seized to its own part. From 1773 the slings of the crossjack were rigged the same as those of the fore yard. After 1793 chain slings could be used when requested.

A truss which was simple like that on the spritsail yard, was used up to 1773 since no parrel was fitted. After that date it was rigged as follows: a thimble was stropped abaft the yard, port side of the slings; the truss pendant was seized round the yard, starboard side

of the slings, taken round the mast through the thimble and led down to deck. On all but the smallest ships, a double block was seized on the end, connecting with a fall to a single block hooked in the mizen channel. Small ships used single blocks throughout. The double blocks were long-tackle blocks until 1810, after which date they were ordinary double ones. After 1850 chain replaced the rope truss, one strop each side of the slings being lashed on, the starboard one having a small shackle for the pendant, the port one a larger bow shackle. The pendant rove round the mast, through the bow shackle and down to deck, made fast as before with a fall in the channels, the block at the pendant end being shackled on.

Lifts similar to those of the fore and main yards were fitted up to about 1670. After 1670 standing lifts were introduced; these were spliced round the yard a quarter in from the yard arms, and were set up with deadeyes

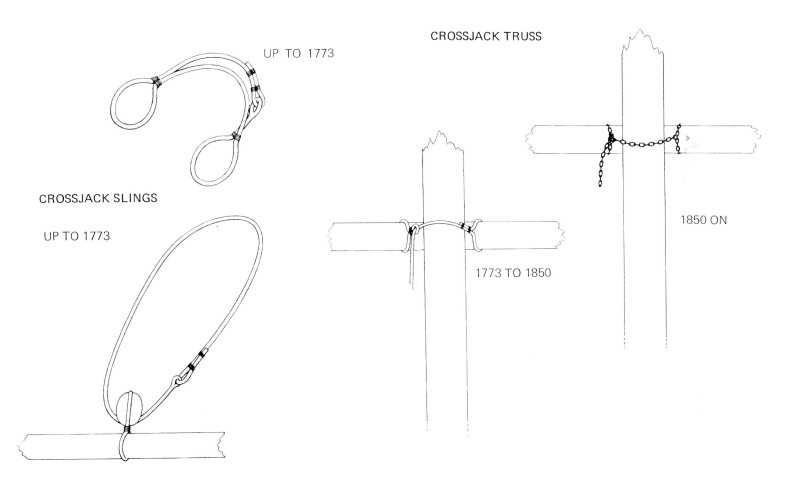

CROSSJACK TRUSS

UP TO 1773

CROSSJACK SLINGS

UP TO 1773

1773 TO 1850

1850 ON

and lanyards to deadeyes secured to the mizen cap with a span. After 1719 a lift was once more a running one; single blocks were secured to the mizen cap with a span, the blocks coming about 2 feet out from the cap; another block was stropped to the topsail sheet block as on the fore and main yard. The standing part of the lift was spliced into the span on the upper blocks; the lifts then rove through the blocks on the yard, up through the span blocks and were taken to deck. No tackles were used in the lower end, the lift being belayed to either cleats at the foot of the mast or to the bitts. From 1805 the lifts were single, spliced round the yard arms, rove through blocks seized to eyebolts in the mizen cap and set up with thimbles and lanyards to eyebolts in the deck at the foot of the mast; the thimbles were spliced into the end of the lifts.

Footropes were fitted in the same way as on the fore yard. Only about two stirrups each side were fitted, even on large ships, and as no jackstays were fitted to the yard, the stirrups and footrope were always carried directly from the yard. On some ships footropes were not used on the crossjack.

Brace pendants were fitted the same way as on other yards but the pendant was taken along the fore side and a seizing put on close to the pendant block to hold the pendant to the yard; this gave a better lead for the braces when led forward (pendants were only taken along the fore side of the yard and seized after 1670).

Braces, up to about 1670, were single and taken aft, being spliced round the yard arms and led in onto the poop via lead blocks seized to eyebolts in the transom. When ships were sailing close by the wind the braces were taken forward, rove through blocks seized to the aftermost shrouds of the main mast (about the length of the head of the mast below the trestletrees) and made fast to the rails. The braces, when taken forward, crossed each other, port brace reeving through the block on the starboard shroud, starboard brace reeving through the port block.

After 1670 braces were double and were always led forward. Blocks were seized to the main shrouds as before; the standing parts of the braces were hitched and seized to the shrouds just above the blocks, the running parts reeving through the pendant blocks, forward through blocks on the shroud and down to deck; the braces crossed as before. From 1805 there were no pendants, the block being stropped directly to the yard arms; the braces, however, rove as before.

From about 1815 the standing parts of the braces were made fast round eyebolts in the main mast, the length of the head below the trestletrees, by means of running eyes; blocks were seized or hooked to these eyebolts. The braces rove through the blocks on the yard, through the blocks on the eyebolts and down to deck. From 1805 the lead blocks of the braces were very often double ones; one sheave, the outer one, was used for the braces and the inner sheave used for the mizen topsail bowline. After about 1815 braces no longer crossed and the port brace led to port, the starboard to starboard.

9 The topsail yards and sails

RIGGING TO THE FORE TOPSAIL YARD AND SAIL

The tie, up to about 1650 was a single rope seized to the centre of the yard and rove through a sheave in the fore topmast hounds; whether this sheave was to port or starboard I do not know, though I am inclined to think that it was to port; after reeving through the sheave a single block was seized in the end. From 1650 until about 1685 the tie was seized round the fore topmast head and led down the starboard side of the mast through a single block strapped in the centre of the yard (the sheave running athwartships), up through a single block hanging by a long strop or pendant from the topmast head—the block itself hanging below the topmast crosstrees on the port side of the mast—and was taken down towards the deck; a long-tackle block was seized in the end. From 1685 to 1706 the ties were double; that is, a double block strapped to the yard and a tie from each side of the mast rove through. A single block was hung as before below the crosstrees but now there was one on each side. Thus one tie came to port and one to starboard, long-tackle blocks being seized into the end of each tie. From 1706 to 1805 ties rove as before but instead of long-tackle blocks being seized in the ends, flat, thin single blocks were used. From 1805, on large ships, there were sometimes double thin blocks seized in the ties. From about 1810 two single blocks were strapped on the yard, the sheaves running fore and aft; the ties were rigged as before except that they led forward of the foremast crosstrees, through the blocks on the yard, up through blocks seized to eyebolts under the topmast trestletrees and were taken down towards deck; double or single thin blocks (depending on the size of the ship) were seized in the ends. During all periods the block in the end of the tie was connected by a strop to a loose bullseye on the topmast backstay (usually the second backstay from forward) though during the latter part of the sail era, from 1840 onwards, a special line was rigged from the aftermost topmast

shroud at the upper end and seized to the upper deadeye of the second topmast backstay; the bullseye was then fitted to this line and the tie block secured to it. This strop between the bullseye and the block was about a foot long and the same circumference as the tie, as was also the line from the topmast shroud to the after backstay deadeye.

From 1840 the tie blocks on the yard were often shackled to eyebolts on the sling hoops of the yard instead of being stropped to the yard.

The runner of the tie was used when ties were single; one end was made fast to an eyebolt in the deck, starboard side, while the other end rove through the block in the tie and had a block seized into the end. On small ships during the early part of the seventeenth century the runner was used by itself and no block was seized in the end, in

which case the end of the runner led straight down to deck where it was belayed. The runner ceased to be used after about 1685.

The halliard of the tie, up to 1650, was formed by a single block seized or hooked to an eyebolt in the deck close to the bulwarks, port side, and rove between this block and a single one in the end of the runner; the standing part made fast to the upper block. From 1650 to 1685 the halliard rove between a long-tackle block in the end of the runner of the tie and a single block seized or hooked to an eyebolt near the top of the bulwarks on the outside of the ship; this eyebolt was just abaft the stay that carried the bullseye for the tie strop. After 1685 and up to 1706, two halliards were used, one for each tie and rigged as before. From 1706 halliards rove as before, but thin, flat single blocks were

FORE AND MAIN TOPSAIL TIES

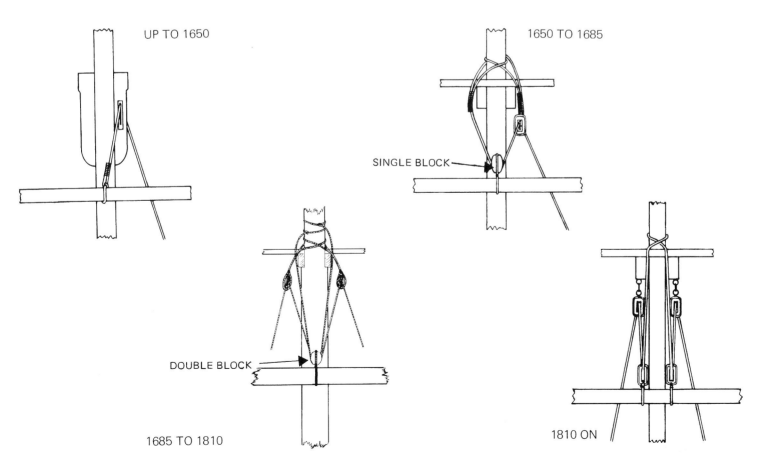

UP TO 1650

1650 TO 1685

SINGLE BLOCK

DOUBLE BLOCK

1685 TO 1810

1810 ON

II RIGGING
Rigging to the fore topsail yard and sail

TOPSAIL YARD PARRAL
UP TO ABOUT 1806

TOPSAIL YARD TRUSS
FROM ABOUT 1806

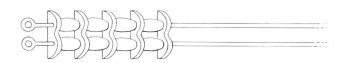

LT GREEN'S PATENT TRUSS PROPOSED 1823
USED ON SOME SHIPS ABOUT 1830

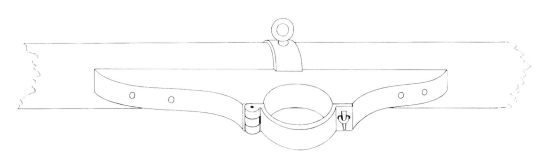

used instead of long-tackle blocks, thin blocks for both upper and lower blocks. The lower blocks were always seized or hooked close abaft and in-board of the second topmast backstay, or the stay carrying the bullseye. When the stay came to a stool, the halliard block came to an eyebolt in the ship's side, and when the stay came to the fore channels the halliard block was secured to an eyebolt in the channels. After 1805 double blocks were some-times used as upper halliard blocks, though on some ships the starboard halliard blocks were two single blocks and the port one of a single and a double block; however as long as the running part leads from the upper block one should experience no diffi-culty in rigging halliards.

Parrel ropes Up to about 1806, parrels with ribs and trucks were used. There were only two rows of trucks and only two holes in each rib. The two parrel ropes each had an eye spliced in one end, these eyes being seized to-gether on the fore side of the yard. The parrel ropes, after reeving through the ribs and trucks, were taken round abaft the topmast and from there, one was taken over the top of the yard, the other below; they were then both

taken round the yard and led over the ribs in the grooves provided, round the yard by the ends with eyes spliced in, and so on until the ropes were used up; the ends were seized to an adjacent part and the ropes frapped together. Allowance was made in the parrels to allow the yard to be braced sharply and so they were not made to fit too tightly round the mast.

Truss parrel After about 1806 and up to the end of the sail era a truss was used, consisting of a length of rope served over all, one end having an eye spliced into it; this end was taken round the starboard side of the yard at the slings and seized to its own part so that the eye was just clear of the seizing. The other end was taken abaft the mast round the port side of the yard where it was again seized to its own part; the end then rove through the eye, was taken back and seized to itself. Some ships in about 1830 were fitted with a metal clamp which was fitted round the mast and onto the yard but usually the normal truss parrel was used.

Topsail lifts acted also as topgallant sheets up to 1790. A block was hung on pendants on either side of the top-mast head, the pendants coming inside

of the stay and long enough for the blocks to hang just below the trestle-trees. The lifts ran from the clues of the topgallant sail, through blocks stropped to the topsail yard arms, up through the pendant blocks and down to deck, via holes in the lower top; usually they were belayed or hitched to the middle lower shroud. If for some reason topgallant sails were not carried, the ends of the lifts usually fastened to the clues were taken up to the topmast cap instead; for this pur-pose a short length of rope with a small eye in each end was clove-hitched round the cap; sometimes a toggle was spliced into the end of the lift to obviate hitching. When sails are not set on a model the best thing to do is to secure the lift to the strop of the topgallant clueline block, thus enabling the topgallant yard to be held down in position. There was a period of about twenty years between roughly 1715 and 1733 when the lifts were separate from the topgallant sheets. Why this odd period broke the continuity I do not know, but contem-porary rigged models of this period show the different method used. The lifts came from the topmast cap, through the yard arm block, through the pendant block to deck, rigged like this both when carrying a topgallant sail and when not. After 1733 they reverted to the normal method of combining lifts and sheets until 1790, when once again the lifts were rigged on their own and remained so until the end of sail. The lifts were hooked to a becket round the topmast cap, rove through a block on the topsail yard, up through the lower sheave of a sister block seized between the first and second topmast shrouds as far up as possible and led down to the pin rail by the lower shrouds. During the latter part of the sail era—1830 onwards—the standing part of the lift was made fast round the topmast head instead of to the topmast cap. On frigates and smaller ships after 1805 the lifts were often rove single, the standing part spliced round the yard arm and led through the sister block down to deck, the block on the yard being dispensed with.

Footropes were introduced about 1680 and fitted on the outer end with a small splice to fit around the yard. The inner end had a smaller eye spliced into it; when parrels were fitted the footrope was seized to the parrel rope through this eye. When trusses were used, the footropes crossed each other in the middle of the yard and were lashed to the yard at the sling cleats in a similar manner to the lower yard footropes. From 1811 footropes still crossed each other as before but were seized to the jackstay.

Stirrups, when the footrope was first used, were not needed and it was not until about 1719 that they were rigged and then only on large ships. Usually capital ships had two stirrups on each side of the yard and medium sized ships, one. By 1745 it seems to have been the practice to fit stirrups to all ships—one a side on small, to three a side on very large, ships. This practice carried on to the end of the sail era. Stirrups were fitted in exactly the same manner as those on the lower yard.

Flemish horses were required on topsail yards when yard arms were made longer; this was an extra footrope. They were spliced round the eyebolt or outer stunsail boom iron on the

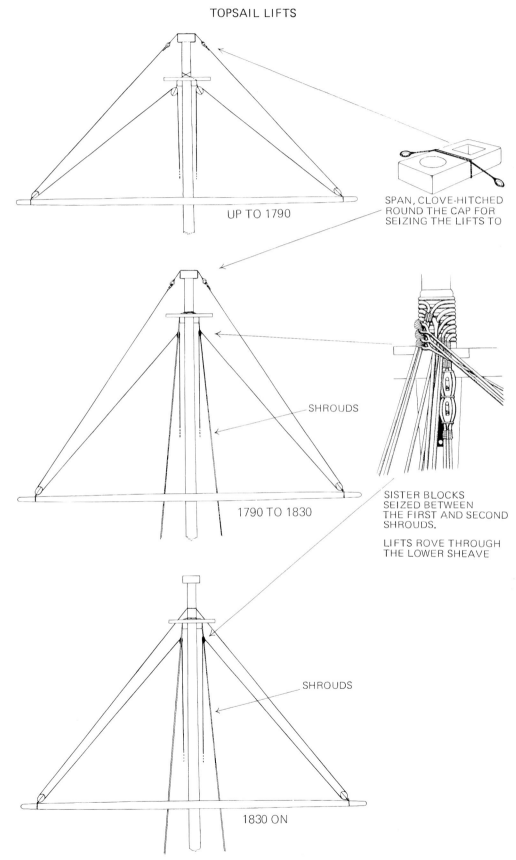

TOPSAIL LIFTS

UP TO 1790

SPAN, CLOVE-HITCHED ROUND THE CAP FOR SEIZING THE LIFTS TO

SHROUDS

1790 TO 1830

SISTER BLOCKS SEIZED BETWEEN THE FIRST AND SECOND SHROUDS.

LIFTS ROVE THROUGH THE LOWER SHEAVE

SHROUDS

1830 ON

FORE TOPSAIL YARD BRACES

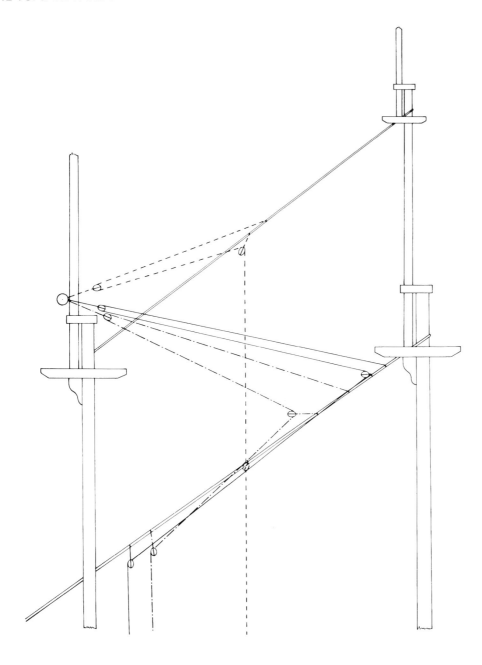

UP TO 1733

1733 TO 1745

1745 TO 1805

end of the yard; the inner end was either seized to the yard or jackstay, as for the footropes. The flemish horse should be about twice as long as the yard arm; no stirrups were required. They were used from 1760 though large ships sometimes carried them a few years prior to that date. I have seen them rigged on a model of a 60 gun ship of about 1742.

Brace pendants were rigged in exactly the same way as those on the lower yard and were in use up to 1805.

Braces, up to 1733 had the standing part made fast about half way down the main topmast stay. The other end rove through the pendant blocks, back through blocks fastened by a short span to the main topmast stay, just below the standing part, and led down to deck, through lead blocks seized to the main stay directly under the blocks on the topmast stay. After 1733 the standing part was made fast about one fifth down the main stay; the brace led through the pendant blocks, back to blocks on a span a little below the standing part on the main stay, led through another lead block seized to the main stay above the belfry and down to the forecastle rails. There were variations at this period; on some ships in about 1745 the standing part was made fast to the collar of the main stay, leading blocks being just below the standing part and on the main stay above the belfry. With the next positioning of the braces—which was about 1805—the standing part was made fast to the main topmast stay collar, led through a block secured to the yard in a similar fashion to those on the lower yard, back through a block just above the mouse on the main stay collar, through a block under the forward part of the main top and led down to deck. After 1830 the standing part was made fast to the main stay collar, was led through the yard arm blocks, taken through blocks on the main stay collar just above the standing part, through blocks under the main top and down to deck. Another variation at this time was that the standing part was made fast to the main topmast head with a clove-hitch above the rigging; the two parts were seized to the main topmast stay by the collar, led through yard

FORE TOPSAIL YARD BRACES

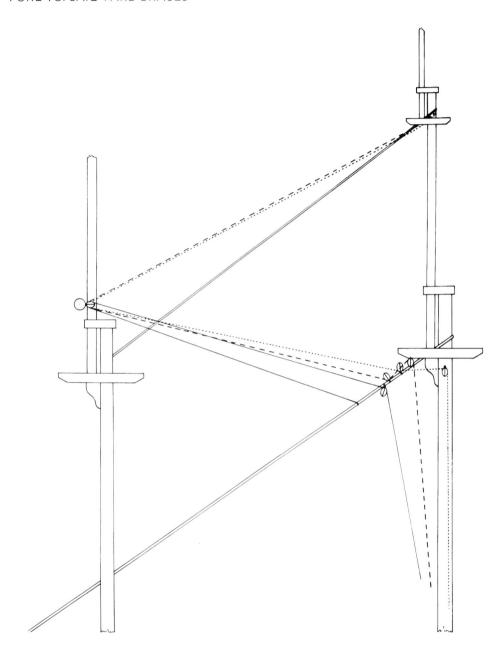

- - - - - - - - - - -
1805 TO 1830

————————
1830 ON

....
ALTERNATIVE 1830 ON

blocks, through lead blocks on the main stay close to the collar, back through blocks seized or shackled to eyebolts on the cheeks of the main mast and down through sheaves in the main bitts.

Leechlines were in use up to about 1790, one end being secured to the upper bowline bridle cringle on the leech of the sail. Up to 1680 the running part rove through a block strapped to the topsail yard close to the ties, and from there up through a block seized to the fore topmast stay collar, and down to deck abaft the yard. From 1680 to 1745 the running part rove through a block seized to the strop of the tie block and was taken down to deck. A block on the yard was not carried during this period. From 1745 to 1805 the running part rove through a block about half way along each side of the topsail yard, was then taken through the block on the tie, up through the inner sheave of a double block seized under the topmast trestletrees and from there to deck. The other sheaves of the double blocks were used for the buntlines.

A buntline on each side of the yard was carried up to 1790. Working in conjunction with the leechline, the standing part was seized or hitched to the buntline cringle in the foot of the topsail. Until about 1745 the running part rove from the buntline cringle up through a block strapped to the topsail yard and from there through a block hanging by a pendant from the topmast head just below the trestletrees, and was taken to deck. After 1745 the buntline rove as before but, instead of a pendant block, the outer sheave of the double block under the trestletrees was used. From 1790, on some ships, two buntlines each side were carried, reeving from the foot of the sail, through blocks on the yard, through double blocks seized to the tie block strop, up through double blocks seized under the trestletrees of the topmast, and down to deck through the square hole of the top, belaying to the topsail sheet bitts. From about 1805 they rove from the sail through a thimble of a lizard hitched round the ties, through either a block under the trestletrees, or a

FORE TOPSAIL BOWLINE BRIDLES

REEF LINE 1655 TO 1668

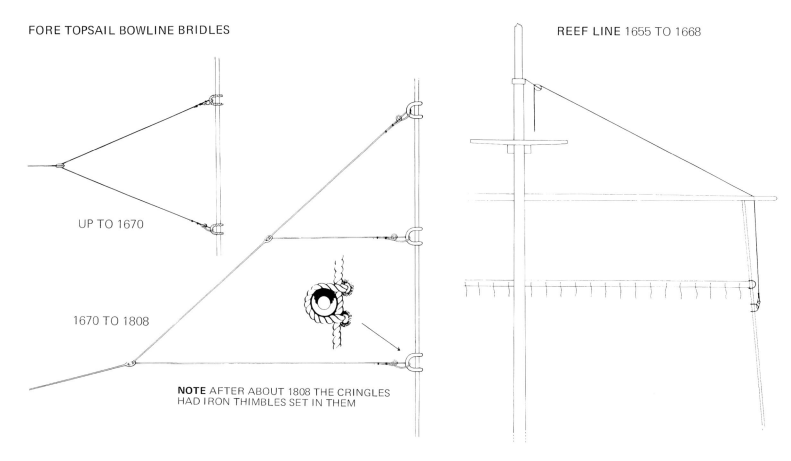

UP TO 1670

1670 TO 1808

NOTE AFTER ABOUT 1808 THE CRINGLES
HAD IRON THIMBLES SET IN THEM

sheave in the trestletrees, and led down to deck. Sometimes at this period a toggle was spliced into the end of the buntline for securing it to the foot of the sail. The buntline blocks were always equally spaced along the yard from the yard arm cleats.

The bridles and bowlines were fitted in the same way as those on the foresail. Up to about 1670 the bridle was one length of rope, but after that it consisted of two. Up to 1680 the bowline ran from the bridle, through one pair of blocks secured to the fore topmast stay on a level with the fore top (these blocks being spliced into a short span hitched to the topstay); it was led down through single blocks strapped to the bowsprit just forward of the fore stay deadeye, through the top sheave of the gammon lashing multiple lead block and up to the forecastle. After 1680, instead of single blocks on the bowsprit, the outer sheaves of a treble block were used, the block being strapped in the same position and the centre sheave of this treble block being used as a lead for the fore top-

mast stay tackle. After about 1733 this treble block was superseded by a single block, seized to eyebolts on either side of the bowsprit cap, but apart from this the bowline rove as usual. After 1773 the bowline led straight to the block on the bowsprit cap and from there straight to the forecastle. About 1850 the bowlines rove from the bridle, through sheaves on the bees of the bowsprit, and in upon the forecastle.

Reef points were made and fitted in the same manner as those on the foresail. Like those points, the method of making reef points altered about 1840.

Reef tackle pendants When reefs were first fitted a line was bent to the reef cringle, taken through a hole in the yard arm, through a block on a span round the topmast cap and taken down to deck. From 1668 to 1790 instead of this line, a pendant was bent to the sail and was taken up through a hole or sheave in the yard arm; it had a single block spliced into the end. From 1790 to 1805 the pendant ran from the sail through the hole or

sheave in the yard arm, up through the upper sheave of the sister block seized between the first and second shrouds of the topmast, and had a double block spliced into the end. After 1805 the pendant was not required as the fall was connected directly to the sail.

Reef tackle falls, up to 1745, rove between the block in the reef pendant and a single block on a pendant from the topmast head, this upper block hanging just below the trestletrees and the standing part made fast to the upper block, the running part leading down to deck. After 1745 the fall rove exactly as before but the standing part was made fast to the topmast cap. From 1790 to 1805, the fall comprised the double block in the reef pendant and another double block seized to the after part of the lower trestletrees; the standing part made fast to the upper block, the running part led down to deck. From 1805 on large ships a block was seized to the reef cringle; the fall was made fast to the outer boom iron neck, led through the block on the sail, through a hole or

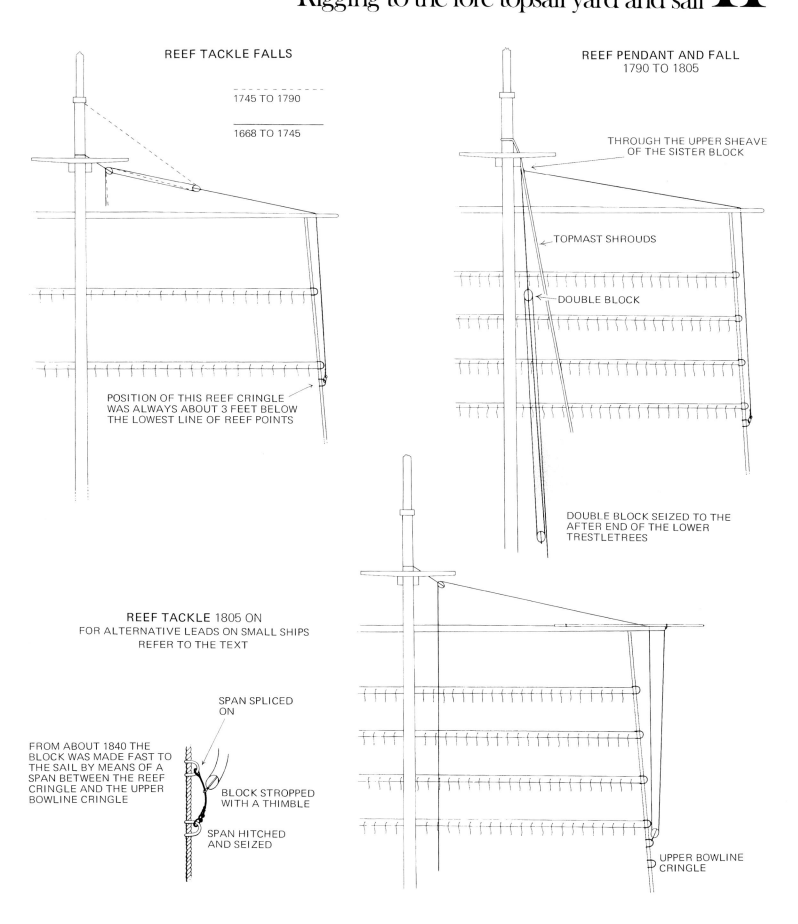

REEF TACKLE FALLS

1745 TO 1790

1668 TO 1745

REEF PENDANT AND FALL
1790 TO 1805

THROUGH THE UPPER SHEAVE
OF THE SISTER BLOCK

TOPMAST SHROUDS

DOUBLE BLOCK

POSITION OF THIS REEF CRINGLE
WAS ALWAYS ABOUT 3 FEET BELOW
THE LOWEST LINE OF REEF POINTS

DOUBLE BLOCK SEIZED TO THE
AFTER END OF THE LOWER
TRESTLETREES

REEF TACKLE 1805 ON
FOR ALTERNATIVE LEADS ON SMALL SHIPS
REFER TO THE TEXT

SPAN SPLICED
ON

FROM ABOUT 1840 THE
BLOCK WAS MADE FAST TO
THE SAIL BY MEANS OF A
SPAN BETWEEN THE REEF
CRINGLE AND THE UPPER
BOWLINE CRINGLE

BLOCK STROPPED
WITH A THIMBLE

SPAN HITCHED
AND SEIZED

UPPER BOWLINE
CRINGLE

sheave in the yard arm, up through a block on a pendant from the topmast head and was taken down to deck. On small ships the fall was made fast to the reef cringle, led up through a block on the yard arm, up through a block strapped to the topmast cap and was taken to deck. Between 1790 and 1830 the upper sheave of the sister block in the topmast shrouds was sometimes used for the lead of the falls instead of pendant blocks from the topmast head.

Jack line reefing came into use in about 1850 and was fitted the same way as on the fore course; the beckets, however, were seized on in pairs, one for the first and third reefs and the other for the second and fourth reefs. When first used only the first and second reefs were fitted this way; the rest of the reefs retained points. In December 1857 all reefs were fitted with jack line reefing.

Reef bands Up to about 1680 one reef band was fitted; from 1680 to 1710 two, from 1710 until about 1788 three, and from 1788 onwards, four reef bands were fitted.

Spilling lines were small pieces of rope, usually eight in number and equally spaced along the fore side of the sail. They were spliced into the lower reef line; an overhand knot was taken round each reef line and the ends spliced into the head of the sail. Spilling lines were used for picking up the reef lines when reefing and were used only in jack line reefing.

Slab reef lines were fitted to the after side of the sail and prevented the sail from flapping about and chafing when reefing. There were as many of these lines for each reef band as there were spilling lines, and again were only used in jack line reefing. Slab reef lines were spliced round each jackstay on the sail and taken through the eyelet hole in the next reef band above, from aft to forward, an overhand knot being worked in the end. The upper lines were spliced round the upper jackstay and taken through the head cringles where an overhand knot was put in the end.

The cluelines, up to 1706 ran from the topsail yard about three quarters of the way in from the yard arms, down

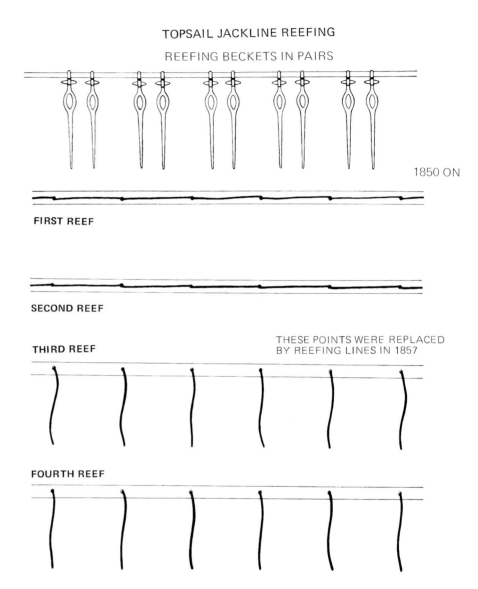

TOPSAIL JACKLINE REEFING

REEFING BECKETS IN PAIRS

1850 ON

FIRST REEF

SECOND REEF

THIRD REEF

THESE POINTS WERE REPLACED BY REEFING LINES IN 1857

FOURTH REEF

through the block secured to the clue of the sail, up through a block strapped under the topsail yard just inboard from the standing part, and led down to deck via a hole in the top. From 1706 to 1719 the clueline rove as before except that a lead block was seized to the fore mast head, about half way down from the cap; the running part rove through these lead blocks before being taken to deck. From 1719 to 1733 an additional block was fitted on either side of the yard. The standing part was made fast nearer to the yard arm, about two thirds in, each side from the yard arms; it ran through the clue block, up through a block just inboard from the standing part, along and through the additional

block strapped under the topsail yard close to the slings, and led down to deck, the block on the mast head being dispensed with. After 1733 this additional block on the centre of the yard was removed and the clues rove from the yard through the clue block, up through the block on the quarters of the yard and led down to deck via the square hole in the top. From 1815, instead of a single block being strapped to the topsail yard, a double block was used. The clueline rove as before but came through the foreward sheave in the double block, the after sheave of the double blocks being used for topgallant sheets.

Sheets of the topsails were very little changed throughout the period. Up to

FORE TOPSAIL 1857 ON

SPILLING LINES

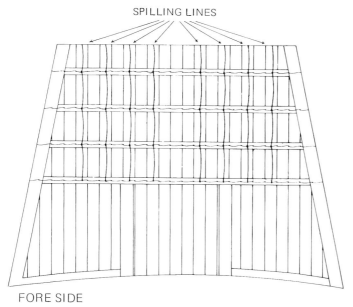

FORE SIDE

SLAB REEF LINES
AFTER SIDE OF THE SAIL

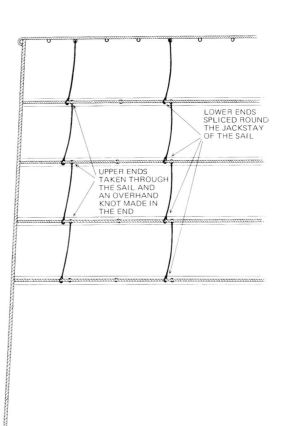

LOWER ENDS SPLICED ROUND THE JACKSTAY OF THE SAIL

UPPER ENDS TAKEN THROUGH THE SAIL AND AN OVERHAND KNOT MADE IN THE END

SECURING TOPSAIL SHEET AND CLUE

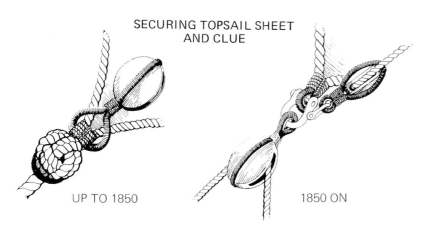

UP TO 1850

1850 ON

1815 two blocks were strapped under the lower yard inside of the sling cleats or just outside the cleats. Another block was strapped to each yard arm of the lower yard; these blocks came on top of the yard. The sheets had a knot worked in them and ran from the sail through the blocks on the yard arms, came along the lower yard on the after side, rove through the centre blocks under the yard and led down to the fore bitts, usually being taken through a sheave in the bitts. From 1815, instead of having blocks strapped to the lower yard arms, a sheave was faired onto the after side of the arms, and the sheet rove through these. Blocks were still used under the centre of the yard

and the sheets rove as usual. About 1850 a block was secured to the topsail clues; the standing part was made fast to the yard arm, rove through the blocks on the clue, down through the sheave on the yard arm and through the centre blocks to deck. Small ships, however, still had the sheets rove as between 1815 and 1850. The method of fastening the sheets to the sail is better illustrated than described.

Earings were fitted the same as those on the course. Additional earings were required for reefing, one being spliced into each reef cringle.

Robands or rope bands were fitted the same way as those on the course.

Gaskets were fitted the same as those on the course. Long gaskets were call-

ed furling lines in the seventeenth century and only one a side was rigged to each yard. At the end of the seventeenth century more gaskets were used though not made so long. Usually two less were required on the topsails than on the courses.

MAIN TOPSAIL BRACES
UP TO 1773

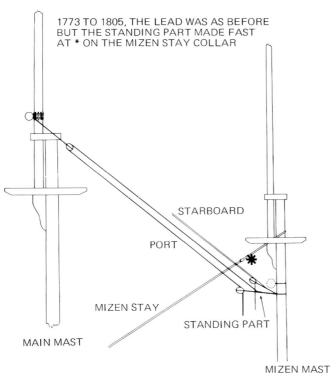

1773 TO 1805, THE LEAD WAS AS BEFORE
BUT THE STANDING PART MADE FAST
AT * ON THE MIZEN STAY COLLAR

STARBOARD

PORT

MIZEN STAY

STANDING PART

MAIN MAST

MIZEN MAST

1805 TO 1810

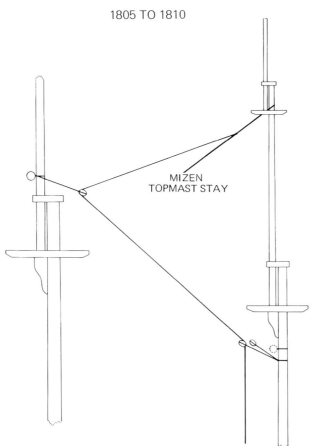

MIZEN
TOPMAST STAY

RIGGING TO THE MAIN TOPSAIL YARD AND SAIL

Ties were rigged the same as on the fore topsail yard. The sheave in the hounds would be on the starboard side.

The runner of the tie was rigged the same as on the fore topsail yard. The standing part of the runner would be on the port side.

The halliard of the tie was rigged the same as on the fore topsail yard. When single ties were used the halliard would be on the starboard side.

Parrel ropes
Truss parrel
Lifts
Footropes
Stirrups
Flemish horses
Brace pendants
These were rigged as on the fore topsail yard.

Braces Up to about 1810 two single blocks were secured by means of a span to the mizen mast, just below the crossjack yard; the blocks were spliced into each end of the span and the span clove-hitched round the mast. The blocks came about 6 feet from the mast. Up to about 1773 the standing part of the brace was seized to the span just behind the blocks; the running part rove through the block in the brace pendant, back through the block on the span and led down to deck, usually being made fast to a timber head or to the rails abreast of the mizen mast, although some large ships had the braces fast to cleats on the mizen mast a few feet up from the deck. From 1773 to 1805 the standing part was made fast to the mizen stay collar. From 1805 on, the standing part was made fast to the mizen topmast stay collar. After 1810 the blocks rigged on the span were shifted to a position about 16 feet down the mizen mast from under the mizen top and were seized to eyes in an iron band round the mizen mast, the run of the braces being exactly the same as before that date.

Leechlines were fitted the same as those on the fore topsail.

Buntlines were fitted the same as those on the fore topsail.

Bowline bridles were fitted to the sail

in the same way as on the fore topsail. Usually the main topsail bridles consisted of one more part than those on the fore topsail.

The bowlines, up to about 1680, rove through blocks seized to the aftermost fore shrouds by the futtock staves and were made fast to the rails on either side of the belfry. From 1680 to about 1705, two single blocks were seized to the rim of the fore top on the after edge; bowlines rove through these and led as before to the rails. From 1705 to 1741 the lead blocks were strapped to the after side of the fore mast head. From 1741 to 1773 the lead blocks were seized to eyebolts in the after end of the fore trestletrees, the bowlines still leading to the rails. From 1773 until about 1830 the lead blocks were once more carried on the aftermost fore shroud but lower than before—about 6 feet below the futtock stave. After 1830 lead blocks were seized to the fore stay collar abaft the mast. From 1773 the bowlines, instead of leading to the rails by the belfry, led to the pin rail by the fore shrouds.

Reef points
Reef tackle pendants
Reef tackle falls
Cluelines
Sheets
Earings
Robands or rope bands
Gaskets
These were all fitted as on the fore topsail.

RIGGING TO THE MIZEN TOPSAIL YARD AND SAIL

The tie, up to between 1670 on large ships and 1690 on small ships, was bent directly to the yard, rove through a sheave hole in the topmast just below the rigging stops and had a long-tackle block spliced in the end; after these dates a single block was strapped to the yard. The standing part of the ties was spliced or seized round the topmast head; the hauling part rove through the block on the yard, through the sheave hole in the mast and had a long-tackle block seized as before. From about 1705 the ties rove as before but had a single block in the end; this remained the general practice for most ships (though some large

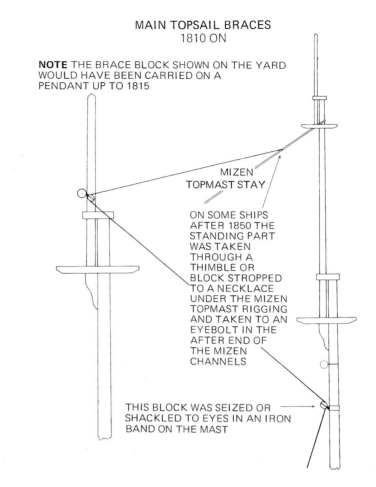

MAIN TOPSAIL BRACES
1810 ON

NOTE THE BRACE BLOCK SHOWN ON THE YARD WOULD HAVE BEEN CARRIED ON A PENDANT UP TO 1815

MIZEN TOPMAST STAY

ON SOME SHIPS AFTER 1850 THE STANDING PART WAS TAKEN THROUGH A THIMBLE OR BLOCK STROPPED TO A NECKLACE UNDER THE MIZEN TOPMAST RIGGING AND TAKEN TO AN EYEBOLT IN THE AFTER END OF THE MIZEN CHANNELS

THIS BLOCK WAS SEIZED OR SHACKLED TO EYES IN AN IRON BAND ON THE MAST

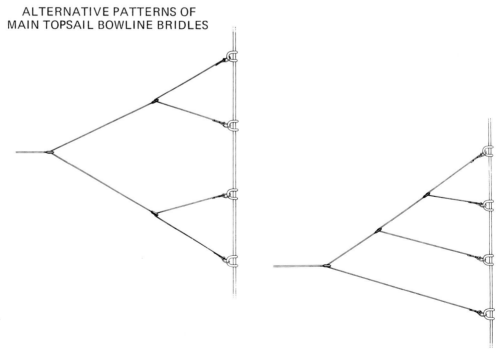

ALTERNATIVE PATTERNS OF
MAIN TOPSAIL BOWLINE BRIDLES

Rigging to the mizen topsail yard and sail

ships had a double block in the end of the tie) until about 1805 when, instead of making a sheave hole in the mast, a block was strapped to the mast head hanging just under the trestletrees, the ties reeving as before. From about 1815 two single blocks were seized, one either side, under the trestletrees; the ties rove through one of these blocks, through the block on the yard and through the other block under the trestletrees, both ends having either a double block spliced in them as on large ships, or single blocks as on small and medium ships.

Halliard of the tie When one halliard was rigged (that was up to about 1815) the halliards always led to starboard with the lower block hooked to an eyebolt in the channels as described for the fore topsail halliards. After 1815 halliards rove either side, again as described for the fore topsail halliards; they were stropped to the backstay in the same manner.

Parrel ropes were rigged the same way as on the fore topsail yard.

The truss parrel was rigged the same way as on the fore topsail yard.

Lifts, until 1670, were spliced round the yard arm and then rove through blocks stropped to the topmast head; single blocks were spliced into the ends which connected up by falls to other single blocks seized to the mizen top; the fall was made fast in the top. From 1670 to 1745 the standing part was spliced to the mizen topmast head. The running part rove through blocks on the yard then up through blocks on a span from the topmast head just below the standing part, thence down to deck. After 1745 the lifts rove the same as other topsail yard lifts.

Footropes
Stirrups
Flemish horses
Brace pendants
These were rigged as on the fore topsail yard.

Braces, up to 1805, led aft with the standing part made fast to the peak of the mizen yard or gaff. The running part rove through the brace pendant blocks, back through single blocks on a span round the mizen yard or gaff just below the standing part and the

brace led down to the rails by the transom. Until about 1670, blocks on the mizen yard were about 8 feet down the yard from the standing part; aften then the standing part and the blocks were very close, about a foot separating them. Blocks on the span were usually about 2 feet from the yard. From 1805 to 1815 the standing part of the brace was seized to the main mast head, rove through blocks on the fore side of the topsail yard and was then taken forward through blocks seized to the aftermost shroud of the main mast, just above the crossjack lead block. The braces crossed like those on the crossjack yard— starboard to port, port to starboard; the braces then led down to deck. From 1815 the standing part and the lead blocks were seized, either to eyebolts under the after side of the main cap or to eyebolts half way down the main mast head on the after side; sometimes the lead blocks were stropped to the main mast head with the standing parts secured to the strops. The braces, as before, led down to deck after passing through the lead blocks, but from 1815 instead of crossing each other, the port brace led down on the port side and the starboard brace led down on the starboard side.

Leechlines were rigged the same way as on the fore topsail.

Buntlines were rigged the same way as on the fore topsail.

Bowline and bridles Up to 1805 blocks were seized to the aftermost main shroud by the futtock stave; bowlines led from the bridles through the blocks on the opposite side shroud; the port bowline rove through the block on the starboard main shroud, starboard bowline through the port block. From 1805 bowlines shared the double block through which the crossjack brace rove, the bowlines reeving through the inboard sheave of the lead blocks and down to deck. Bowlines ceased to be crossed after about 1815. The bridles were similar to the fore topsail bridles.

Reef points were rigged the same as those on the fore topsail with one less row of points. The first row of reef points was introduced in about 1700,

the second in 1710 and the third in about 1788.

Reef tackle pendants
Reef tackle falls
Cluelines
Sheets
Earings
Robands or rope bands
Gaskets
These were rigged as on the fore topsail.

It should be noted that when the mizen topmast was the upper mast on the mizen and no topgallant yard was carried, the mizen topsail yard on Fourth Rates and below was rigged in a similar fashion to the fore and main topgallant yards, no leech or reef lines being used and, in most cases, no buntlines.

10 Topgallant and royal yards and sails

RIGGING TO THE FORE TOPGALLANT YARD AND SAIL

Ties and halliards Up to about 1670, First, Second and Third Rates had the tie hitched round the yard, taken through a sheave in the top of the topgallant mast and taken down towards the lower top; a single block was seized into the end which connected up with a fall to a block seized to the lower top, just on the port side of the main topmast stay. Other rates during this period had a block seized to the yard; the tie was seized round the topgallant mast head, rove through the block on the yard, up through the sheave in the top of the mast and was taken down to the lower top where it was hitched to one of the deadeyes in the top on the port side. The falls or halliards of the First, Second and Third Rates were also made fast in the top. After 1670 all rates had a block on the yard; the tie rove as before but a fall or halliard was also fitted to the lower end and made fast in the lower top. Some of the small ships, however, did not have a halliard; the tie was taken through the top and was belayed to the bitts abaft the fore mast. From about 1765 to 1805 the tie was hitched round the yard, rove through the sheave in the top of the mast, and was set up with a halliard to the starboard

trestletree of the lower mast. The halliard consisted of a double block seized into the end of the tie and a single block seized to the lower trestletree. The hauling part of the halliard was belayed to the bitts abaft the foremast. After 1805 the tie was seized round the yard and rove through the sheave in the mast head; it was then taken straight down through the lower top to the bitts abaft the fore mast, no halliards at all being fitted for any rate.

Parrel ropes were fitted the same way as those on the topsail yard; they were in use until about 1805.

The truss parrel was either fitted the same way as the topsail yard truss parrel or, alternatively, two strops were put on the yard. One of the strops was long enough to go round the yard, leaving enough room for a thimble to be seized in it; the other strop was

longer and was seized close to the yard with a thimble seized in the other end. The two thimbles were united with a lashing.

Lifts Up to about 1815, two blocks were hung on short pendants from the topgallant mast head. A block was stropped on each yard arm. The standing part of the lift was spliced round the topgallant mast head, the running part rove through the block on the yard arm, up through the block on the pendant from the mast head, and was taken to the lower top where it was made fast to a deadeye or cleat. After 1815 lifts were single, no blocks being carried on the yard arm; the lift was spliced round the yard arm, rove through pendant blocks on the topgallant mast head or, as after 1840, through blocks siezed between the shrouds, and was taken down to the fore bitts through the top. After 1773,

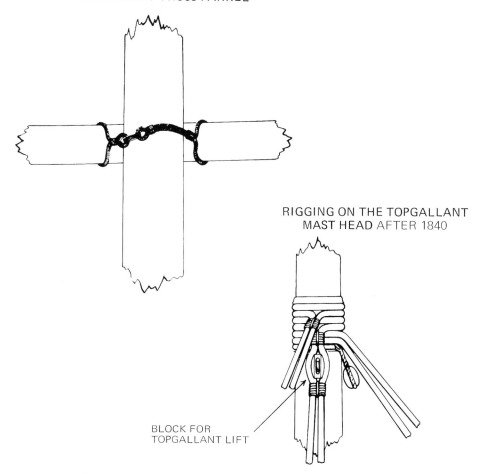

TOPGALLANT TRUSS PARREL

RIGGING ON THE TOPGALLANT MAST HEAD AFTER 1840

BLOCK FOR TOPGALLANT LIFT

II RIGGING
Rigging to the fore topgallant yard and sail

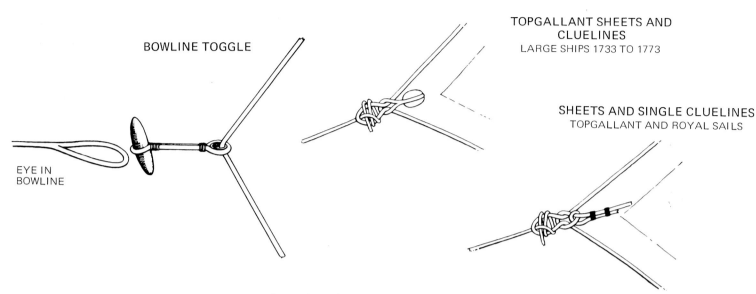

BOWLINE TOGGLE

EYE IN
BOWLINE

TOPGALLANT SHEETS AND
CLUELINES
LARGE SHIPS 1733 TO 1773

SHEETS AND SINGLE CLUELINES
TOPGALLANT AND ROYAL SAILS

on Third Rates and below, lifts were rigged singly and sometimes thimbles were used instead of pendant blocks. (This date of 1773 is only conjectural; single lifts may have been introduced on small ships as early as 1745.)

Footropes were introduced at the same time as those on the topsail yard and fitted in the same way.

Stirrups occurred on very few ships on the topgallant yard — it was during the nineteenth century that they were used and then only on the largest ships, fitting one a side. Stirrups were fitted in the same way as on the topsail yard.

Brace pendants were fitted in the same way as on the topsail yard and were in use for the same length of time.

Braces Up to about 1733 the standing part of the brace was hitched and seized to the main topgallant stay about a quarter of the stay up from the fore mast, rove through the pendant block on the yard, up through one of a pair of blocks hitched by a short span to the main topgallant stay just below the standing part, and was taken down to the rails on either side of the belfry via blocks on short spans on the main topmast stay, and the main stay, directly under the span blocks on the main topgallant stay. From 1733 until about 1805 the standing part was hitched and seized to the main topmast stay collar, was rove through the pendant blocks on the yard, up through blocks seized to the main topmast stay collar just below the standing part; it was then taken

through a block seized to the after end of the lower top of the fore mast and taken down to a cleat on either side of the belfry. Sometimes, instead of seizing blocks to the after end of the top, the blocks were strapped round the fore mast head close to the top, and the brace taken through the top to the cleats. From 1805, the standing part was seized to the first main topmast shroud by the futtock stave, was rove through the block stropped to the yard arm, back through blocks seized to the main topmast shroud just below the standing part, and was taken down to a pin in the pin rail by the main shrouds. On small ships the braces were often single; the standing part was made fast to the yard arm with the running part leading as before. It was sometimes the practice, especially in the latter half of the eighteenth century, to put sheaves in the fore end of the main topmast trestletrees and dispense with the lead blocks and stay collar. This method was used only when the braces were single.

Leechlines were never carred on the topgallant sail.

Buntlines were not used until the late eighteenth century and then only on First Rates. Two blocks were seized to the topgallant mast head, and two thimbles seized to the ties close to the yard. The buntlines were fitted with legs to fasten to the foot of the sail. The leading parts rove through the thimbles, up through the blocks on the mast head and were made fast in

the lower top. After about 1815 thimbles were dispensed with and the buntlines were taken directly through the mast head blocks, being made fast both to the foot of the sail and in the lower top as before.

Bowlines and bridles Bridles comprised single ropes fitted the same way as on the foresail. When sprit topmasts were fitted the foremost end of the bowline rove through blocks hitched to the fore topgallant stay with a short span (up to 1706 these blocks were half way down the stay, after 1706 they were a quarter of the way down the stay); it rove through blocks either stropped round the sprit topmast head as up to 1680, or seized to the top of the aftermost sprit topmast shroud after 1680. They were then taken through the sprit top, through blocks seized to the futtock shrouds of the sprit topmast and led from there through the gammon lashing block to the forecastle. When sprit topmasts were not carried, the bowlines rove through span blocks a quarter of the way down the topgallant stay (on small ships, thimbles were used instead of blocks), then through the two outer sheaves of a treble block on the outer end of the jibboom and were taken to the forecastle via the gammon lashing block; sometimes two single blocks or one double block was used instead of the treble block on the jibboom (the centre sheave of the treble block was for the topgallant stay). After about 1760 no span blocks or thimbles were used — the bowlines rove directly through thimbles stropped round the end of the jibboom, then as before on to the forecastle. The usual method of securing bowlines to bridles was with a toggle on the bridle and an eye in the bowline. This was especially so from 1760 on, though it was not used so much before this date. From 1719 to the end of the sprit topmast era some ships carried the bowlines past the sprit topmast to blocks on the jibboom end and thence in to the forecastle.

Cluelines rove from the clue of the sail up through blocks about 3 feet from the slings and down to the lower top where they were made fast. Between about 1733 and 1773 there was a short period when, on large ships cluelines were fitted the same way as on the topsails, that is, blocks on the clues with the standing parts made fast to the yard rove through blocks on the sail, up through blocks on the yard and down to the lower top; the blocks on the yard were strapped with two lashing eyes. After 1773 the rigging of the cluelines reverted to the method used before 1733.

Sheets Up to 1790 the topsail lifts acted as the topgallant sheets (see entry under this heading) except for the period 1715 to 1733; during this period and after 1790, sheets rove in the same manner as the topsail sheets. They did not alter after 1850 as did the topsail sheets, however, but were rigged in the same way from 1815 onwards. They were bent to the clue with a double sheet bend. After 1815 cheek blocks were fitted to the after side of the topsail yard arms as a lead for the topgallant sheets.

Earings were fitted in the same way as those on the topsail.

Robands or rope bands were fitted in the same way as those on the topsail.

Gaskets were fitted in the same way as those on the topsail. Long gaskets were called furling lines in the seventeenth century and only one a side was rigged to each yard; they were in use before those on the course.

RIGGING TO THE MAIN TOPGALLANT YARD AND SAIL
Ties and halliards
Parrel ropes
Lifts
Footropes
Stirrups
Brace pendants
These were all rigged as on the fore topgallant yard.

Braces, up to 1745 had the standing part made fast to the mizen topmast head. After reeving through the pendant blocks the braces rove through blocks secured to the mizen topmast head by means of a short span — the blocks being about 2 feet from the mast head — and were taken down to deck. After 1745, the standing part was still made fast to the mizen topmast head but the running part, after reeving through the pendant blocks, rove through blocks on the foremost mizen topmast shroud by the futtock stave, and was taken down to deck. From 1805 the standing part was made fast to the mizen topmast stay collar by the mouse; the running part rove through blocks on the yard arm, through blocks seized to the stay just above the standing part, through blocks strapped under the mizen topmast trestletrees, after end, and were taken to deck. When rigged singly as described for the fore topgallant braces, the lead blocks were stropped to the mizen topmast head and the braces led from these blocks straight to deck.

Buntlines were rigged in the same way as on the fore topgallant sail.

Bowlines and bowline bridles The bridles were rigged the same as on the fore topgallant sail. Up to 1745 the bowlines rove through blocks or thimbles on a short span about half way down the main topgallant stay, were taken through blocks seized to the aftermost fore topmast shroud close to the futtock stave, and were made fast in the fore top. After 1745 and up to 1773, the bowlines rove straight to blocks strapped to the after end of the fore topmast trestletrees, and were taken down and made fast in the fore top. After 1773, instead of blocks being strapped to the trestletrees, sheaves were made in the trestletrees, the bowlines reeving through them and belaying in the fore top. The *Victory* of 1737 had the bowlines rigged as after 1745, but this was an exception rather than the rule.
Cluelines
Sheets
Earings
Gaskets
Robands or rope bands
These were rigged in the same way as on the fore topgallant sail.

RIGGING TO THE MIZEN TOPGALLANT YARD AND SAIL
Ties and halliards
Parrel ropes
Lifts
Footropes
Stirrups
These were rigged the same as those on the fore topgallant yard and sail.

The Braces, up to about 1805, led aft and were single; one end spliced round the yard arm and the other end rove through small blocks or thimbles stropped to the peak of the mizen yard or gaff. After 1805 braces led forward, usually singly, though sometimes when they were first taken forward they were rove double; when double, which was between 1805 and 1815, the standing parts were seized to the aftermost main shrouds by the futtock stave; the running parts rove through the brace blocks on the yard arms, through sheaves in the after end of the main trestletrees and thence to deck. After 1815 and up to about 1839 the braces were single and rove through single blocks seized to eyebolts under the main cap after end and thence to deck. After 1839, still single, the braces rove through blocks seized to the main topmast after shroud by the futtock stave and thence to deck. When taken forward the braces did not cross as did those on the topsail yard.

Buntlines were rigged the same as those on the fore topgallant sail.

Bowlines and bridles Bridles were rigged the same as on the other topgallant sails. Up to about 1830, the bowlines rove through blocks, seized to the main topmast crosstree on the outer sides of the trestletrees. After 1830 bowlines rove through a double block seized to an eyebolt in the after edge of the main cap, or on some ships through blocks seized to the aftermost main topmast shroud by the futtock

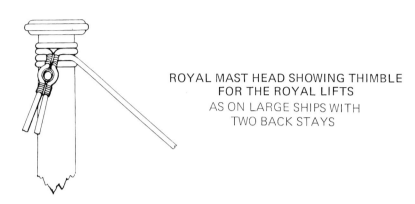

ROYAL MAST HEAD SHOWING THIMBLE
FOR THE ROYAL LIFTS
AS ON LARGE SHIPS WITH
TWO BACK STAYS

stave. In both cases the bowlines were made fast on deck.
Cluelines
Sheets
Earings
Robands or rope bands
Gaskets
These were rigged in the same way as those on the fore topgallant sail.

RIGGING TO THE FORE ROYAL YARD AND SAIL

Ties and truss When first introduced in 1799 (discounting those carried on the *Sovereign of the Seas*) royals were set flying, the tie hitched round the royal yard, rove through a sheave in the royal mast head and made fast in the lower top. Often the yard and sail were stowed by being lashed to the topmast shrouds. After about 1820 the tie was still rigged in the same way but a simple truss was fitted similar to that on the topsail yard.
Braces were spliced round the royal yard arms and rove through blocks on either side of the main topgallant shrouds — seized to the foremost shroud close up to the topgallant mast head — and taken down to the pinrail by the main shrouds. When royals were set flying braces were often omitted.
Buntlines were not rigged.
Footropes were not often rigged but, sometimes, after 1820 a simple one without stirrups was rigged.
Bowlines Simple rope bridles were fitted. The bowlines led forward through blocks seized to the flying jibboom end and were taken in on the

forecastle; they were toggled to the bridles. When royals were set flying bowlines were not rigged.
Lifts spliced round the yard arms, rove through thimbles seized to the royal backstay and were made fast in the lower top. When royals were set flying no lifts were rigged.
Cluelines were always rigged the same way, hitched to the clues, rove through blocks near the slings, and taken down to deck, the blocks on the yard being secured in the same way as those on the topgallant yard.
Sheets were fastened to the clues and rove through sheaves in the topgallant yard just inboard from the yard arms; from the sheaves they rove through blocks under the topgallant yard close to the slings and were taken down to deck. Sometimes the topgallant clue-lines and the royal sheets shared double blocks under the topgallant yard, the sheet in the after sheave; this was especially so after 1820.
Earings
Robands or rope bands
Gaskets
These were fitted in the same way as those on the topgallant sail.

RIGGING TO THE MAIN ROYAL YARD AND SAIL

Ties and truss were rigged in the same way as those on the fore royal yard.
Braces rove singly, one end spliced round the yard arm, the other taken through blocks, seized to the top of the mizen topgallant foremost shroud, and belayed to a pin by the mizen shrouds.

Footropes were rigged in the same way as those on the fore royal yard.
Bowlines and bridles The bridles were single ropes bent at each end to the cringles in the sail. The bowlines rove through blocks strapped to the fore topgallant mast and were made fast in the fore top.
Lifts
Cluelines
Sheets
Earings
Robands or rope bands
Gaskets
These were rigged in the same way as those on the fore royal yard and sail.

RIGGING TO THE MIZEN ROYAL YARD AND SAIL

Ties and truss were rigged the same as those on the fore royal yard.
Braces were spliced round the yard arms, rove through sheaves in the after ends of the main topmast trestletrees, and made fast to the pin rail by the main shrouds; they did not cross as those of the crossjack did. This method of rigging the braces was used from 1815; before then the royal sail was set flying and no braces were used.
Bowlines and bridles The bridles were the same as on the other royal sails. The bowlines rove from the bridles through blocks seized well up to the main topmast after shrouds and were made fast in the main top.
Footropes
Lifts
Cluelines
Sheets
Earings
Robands or rope bands
Gaskets
These were rigged in the same way as those on the fore royal yard and sail.

11 Sprit and sprit topsail yards and sails

spliced into the strap of the block on the yard, rove through one sheave of a long-tackle block strapped to the bowsprit end, through the block on the yard, through the other sheave of the long-tackle block and through the gammon lashing to the forecastle. Usually the halliards were rove through the starboard gammon block, though not always. About 1805, instead of halliards, the yard was held by a lanyard rove between a thimble stropped to the yard and an eyebolt set in the after side of the bottom of the bowsprit cap; this eyebolt was used from about 1773, the fiddle block from then to 1805 being stropped to it. From about 1815 chain was used instead of the halliard or lanyard, shackled to a thimble stropped to the yard, and shackled to the eyebolt in the bowsprit cap. Another method in use before chain was to make a long strop, served

RIGGING TO THE SPRITSAIL YARD AND SAIL

Parrel Up to about 1640 the spritsail yard was fitted with a parrel exactly the same as those fitted to the fore, main and mizen topsail yards.

Slings superseded the parrel in 1640. the sling was made of a length of rope with a small eye spliced into each end and was served all over; one end was taken round the yard and a seizing put on both parts; the other end was taken over the bowsprit and round the other side of the yard; another seizing was put on and a lashing taken through the two eyes: the illustration makes this abundantly clear. Another way was to have an eye put in one end only; this end was taken round the yard and seized to its own part; the other end was taken over the bowsprit, round the yard. Another seizing was put on and the end then rove through the eye, was backed and seized to its own part.

The halliard, up to 1640, rove from the end of the bowsprit, where it was fitted on with an eye splice, through a single block strapped to the centre of the yard, through another single block strapped to the end of the bowsprit, through the multiple gammon lashing block and up to the forecastle head. After 1640 the standing part was

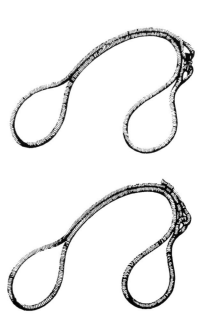

TWO TYPES OF SPRITSAIL YARD SLINGS

II RIGGING
Rigging to the spritsail yard and sail

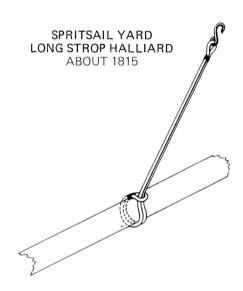

all over, with a thimble and hook set on it, the strop seized together by the thimble; the other end was taken round the yard and the hook and eye rove through it; the strop was pulled taut, and a round seizing put on close to the yard; the hook was taken to the eyebolt in the cap.

Preventer slings, between about 1760 and 1805, were used instead of a halliard when in port; the outer end of the sling had a hook spliced into it which was hooked to the eyebolt under the cap; the other end was hitched round the spritsail yard at the slings.

Garnets were in use up to 1675 and assisted in bracing the spritsail yard. A block was stropped either side of the spritsail yard about half way between the centre of the yard and the yard arms; the garnet was middled and clove-hitched round the fore stay, about half way up the stay; the ends rove through the blocks on the yard, through blocks on a short span round the fore stay just below the standing part, down through blocks seized to the headrail and up to the forecastle.

Standing lifts Pendants were eye-spliced round the spritsail yard, about a quarter way in from each yard arm, and had deadeyes spliced into the ends; these set up with lanyards to deadeyes stropped to the bowsprit a few feet forward of the slings. Sometimes knots were worked in them as on horses; sometimes, instead of splicing the end round the yard, a small eye was made

in the end and it was seized to the yard.

Brace pendants were fitted the same way as on the other yards. They ceased to be used in about 1805.

Braces were made from a length of rope middled and clove-hitched round the fore stay. The position of the standing part altered during various periods as follows: up to 1700 it was half way up the fore stay; from 1700 to 1719 the standing part was seized to the spritsail yard, just inside the lifts, with a seizing through a small eye in the braces; from 1719 the standing part was once more secured to the fore stay, but this time it was up by the mouse of the stay; from about 1733, it again started half way down the stay;

about 1760 it was taken from the fore stay by the mouse, and remained in this position until 1815; from then the standing part was led from an eyebolt under the fore mast forward trestle-tree in large ships, and from the yard arm in smaller ships. By this time some ships had changed the spritsail yard for spreaders. Up to 1700 the running part of the braces rove through the blocks on the brace pendants, up through blocks on a short span, clove-hitched, just below the standing part, down through blocks seized to the head and into the forecastle. From 1700 the standing parts ran from the yard up through blocks on a short span, hitched round the fore stay about half way or a little above half way up the

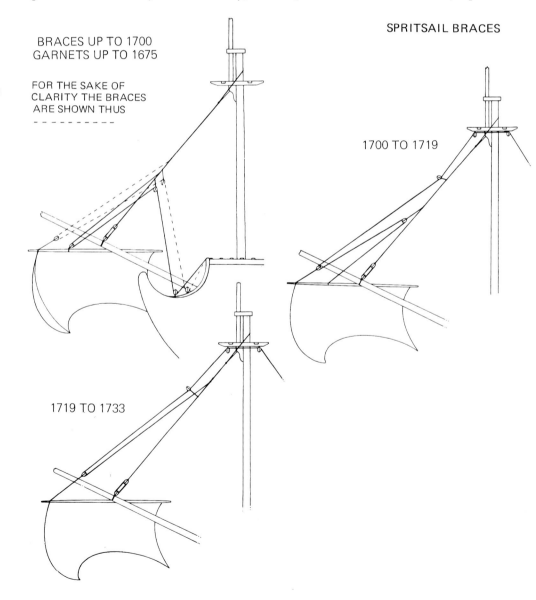

BRACES UP TO 1700
GARNETS UP TO 1675

FOR THE SAKE OF
CLARITY THE BRACES
ARE SHOWN THUS

SPRITSAIL BRACES

1700 TO 1719

1719 TO 1733

stay, down through the brace pendant blocks, up through another pair of blocks on a short span two thirds up the fore stay, through blocks seized under the fore part of the fore top, through other blocks under the after end of the fore top, through blocks on a short span on the main stay, level with those on the fore stay, and were taken down to deck and made fast to a cleat on the bulwarks abaft the fore-castle bulkhead. From 1719 the brace ran from the stay through the brace pendant blocks, through blocks on a span two thirds up the fore stay, and then through blocks under the fore top and on the main stay as those of 1700. From 1733 the braces rove as before but came straight down to deck

from the after block under the fore top. From 1773 the blocks were under the trestletrees and were double ones, the spritsail braces reeving through the outer sheave. As the standing part was taken further up the stay, the lead blocks on the short span were no longer required and from about 1760 the braces rove from the pendant blocks to those under the fore top. From 1815 only the foremost block was used, but instead of it being a double one, a single block was seized to an eyebolt in each trestletree, the brace leading from the yard arm through the block under the trestle-tree and taken straight down to the fore bitts. After about 1830 when only a few ships still retained the spritsail yard

a double block to take both braces was seized to an eyebolt in the centre of the foremost crosstree of the fore mast. The braces were single, leading from the yard through the double block down to the bitts.

Spritsail running lifts were also used as sheets for the topsail yard when a sprit topsail yard was carried; when used as topsail sheets, the ends had a knot worked in them and were secured to the topsail cluelines. There were blocks strapped on the spritsail yard arms through which the sheets rove; they were then taken through blocks on a span round the bowsprit, and led to the forecastle via the gammon lash-ing blocks. Up to 1670, the span round the bowsprit was by the knee of the

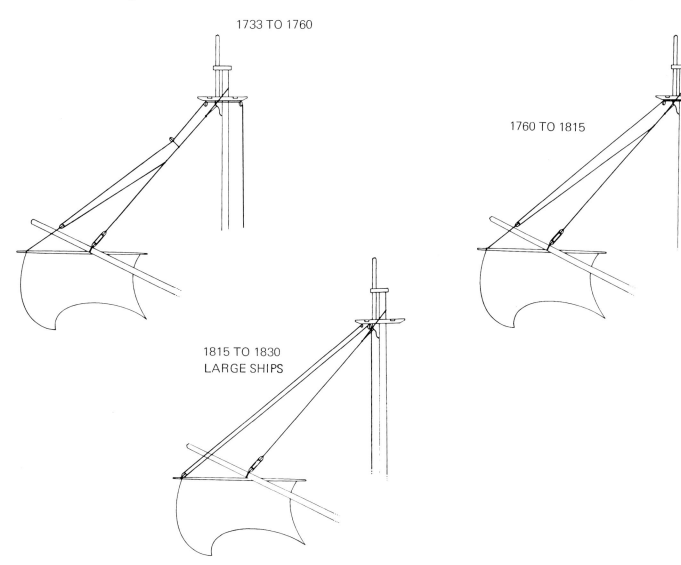

1733 TO 1760

1760 TO 1815

1815 TO 1830
LARGE SHIPS

II RIGGING
Rigging to the spritsail yard and sail

sprit topmast, reeving through a hole in the knee and taken round the bowsprit. After 1670, eyebolts were set into the bowsprit by the knee and the lead blocks seized to them, the lifts running as before. From about 1733 to 1760 the lead blocks were seized to the fore preventer stay collar; after then the lead blocks were seized to eyebolts in the side of the bowsprit cap. When the sprit topsail was not carried, the standing parts of the lifts were spliced to eyebolts set in the sides of the bowsprit cap, the lifts running from the eyebolts through the blocks on the yard, through blocks seized to eyebolts in the bowsprit cap just under the standing part eyebolts, and were led to the forecastle rails via

the gammon lashing blocks. When no sail was carried on the spritsail yard, the lifts were often rove by splicing the standing part round the spritsail yard arms, reeving the other ends through blocks on the bowsprit cap and making them fast on the forecastle head.

Sheet pendants were used up to 1655, and from 1680 to 1690; a knot was formed in one end which was taken through the clue of the spritsail; a single block was spliced in the other end. From 1690 to 1790 a strop was used instead of a pendant, and between 1690 and 1750 a special block called a spritsail sheet block was introduced; this block is described in the chapter devoted to blocks. The strop rove

through the holes in the block and a spritsail sheet knot formed in the end. The strop was secured to the clue of the sail in the same way as the sheet pendant. The strop was also twisted in the making so that it formed a double cable. After 1790 pendants or strops were no longer used. When the special block went out of fashion in 1750, a block similar to a clueline block was used.

Sheets, up to about 1670, had their standing parts hitched to the outer timber heads on the forecastle head-rails. The running part rove through the blocks in the pendants or, as between 1655 and 1680, through the blocks on the clues of the spritsail and were taken through sheaves in the bulwarks, about two thirds of the distance between the fore and main mast, from the fore mast, where they were made fast to the cleats on the inside of the bulwarks, just forward of the sheaves. From 1670 to about 1705, the standing parts were hitched to timber heads in the rails abreast of the fore mast, the running parts reeving as before through sheaves in the bulwarks, under the sheaves through which the fore sheets rove. From 1705 to 1745 the standing parts were seized to eyebolts, either just above the lead of the main tack in the bulwarks, as on large ships, or to eyebolts set in the forward end of the fore channels, or set in the side just above the fore channels, as on smaller ships. The running parts rove as before, through sheaves just below the foresail sheet sheaves. From 1745 until about 1773, the standing part was hitched round the first deadeye on the fore channels, or to a timber head by the first shroud; the running part rove as before. After 1773 the standing part was either seized to the eyebolt to which the standing part of the foresail sheet was secured or, as was the method about 1790, to eyebolts in the bows by the catheads. Up to about 1790, the running parts rove through sheaves below the foresail sheet sheaves; to keep the running parts of the sheets clear of the sea, a wooden thimble was put on them and a length of rope was spliced round this thimble and hitched to the lower part of the fore shrouds — usually to the third shroud; this rope I

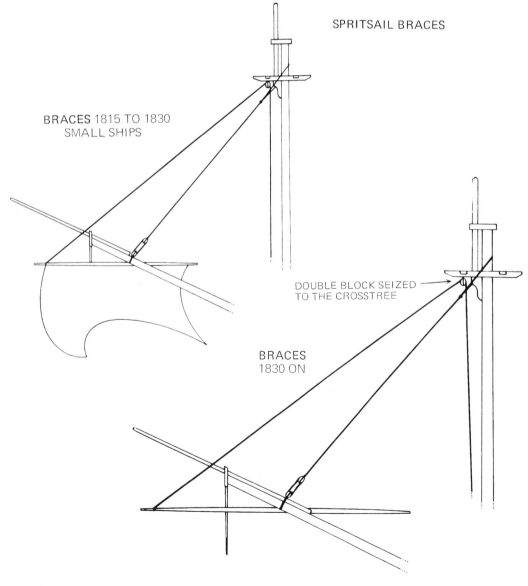

SPRITSAIL BRACES

BRACES 1815 TO 1830
SMALL SHIPS

DOUBLE BLOCK SEIZED
TO THE CROSSTREE

BRACES
1830 ON

have called the sheet tricing line in the Appendix. After 1790 the running parts were taken to the forecastle. By Admiralty Order of December 1815 the sprit topsail was no longer issued to HM ships.

Cluelines had their standing parts timber-hitched round the spritsail yard, two thirds in from each yard arm. The running parts rove through the blocks at the clues of the sail, were led through blocks stropped to the yard a little in from the standing parts and, up to about 1773, rove through blocks seized to the headrails and thence up to the forecastle. After 1773 the running parts rove straight to the forecastle rails from the blocks on the yard. In some ships the clues led through the gammon lashing block instead of through blocks on the headrails; the usual lead, however, was through the blocks on the headrails.

Footropes Usually only one footrope was carried, spliced round each yard arm, and seized in the centre to the halliard block strop.

Stirrups were seldom fitted, though there was a period from about 1719 to 1775 when, on large ships, two stirrups each side of the yard were fitted. Before and after that period no ships had stirrups.

Reef points were fitted in the same way as on the fore topsails and reef bands on spritsails ran diagonally across the sail. No tackles were rigged, the sail being reefed by hand.

Earings

Robands or rope bands

Gaskets

These were fitted in the same way as on the foresail.

Buntlines During the seventeenth century, small and medium sized ships had a single buntline bent to the foot of the sail in the centre and rove through a single block strapped to the bowsprit, just above the slings of the yard; there seems to be no particular side for this block to lay, and the buntline rove through a sheave of a gammon lashing block to the forecastle. Up to about 1680 very large ships had buntlines rigged through long, double blocks; there were four leads to the foot of the sail though actually only two ropes, the ends of the ropes being bent to the sail after reeving through one sheave of the long double blocks; a whip was rove through the other sheave, coming in straight to the forecastle. The standing parts bent to the forecastle timber heads and the hauling parts hitched to the rails. Thimbles or small blocks were seized to the upper side of the yard as a lead for the buntlines, the long double blocks laying aft of the yard when the sail was set. After about 1680 two buntlines were rigged on all ships, reeving from the foot of the sail through thimbles strapped about 3 feet out from the centre of the yard, through the gammon lashing blocks and in on to the forecastle. From about 1773 large and medium sized ships had the same buntlines as just mentioned, but instead of leading through thimbles on the yard, they led through thimbles strapped to one side of the bowsprit, just above the slings and were taken straight in to the forecastle. On small ships one buntline only was rigged, but legs were formed in the end; these legs bent to the foot of the sail. The hauling part rove through a thimble seized to the sling of the yard and was taken in on to the forecastle.

RIGGING OF THE SPREADERS

Jaw ropes The spreaders were secured to the bowsprit by means of a rope knotted at one end; the other end rove through a hole in the jaw of the spreader, was taken round the bowsprit, through the hole in the other side of the jaw and a knot worked close up to the hole. Each spreader had individual jaw ropes.

Fore guys were cut and spliced to fit snugly round the jibboom end; the other ends were spliced round the outer ends of the spreader. Usually four stranded rope was used, wormed, parcelled and served.

After guys had one end spliced round the spreaders; the other ends had thimbles spliced in them, which set up to eyebolts in the bows just forward of the catheads. The after guys were usually four stranded rope wormed and so forth, as the fore guys.

Lower guys were fitted in the same way as the after guys; they were set up with lanyards to a span shackle each side of the cutwater and wormed, parcelled and served as before. The order of rigging the spreaders was first the lifts, then lower guys, after guys and the forward guys. After about 1850 the lower guys led through a block at the cutwater and were set up with a tackle on the forecastle head. These lower guys were sometimes referred to as jumpers.

Braces were required to enable a spritsail to be set on the spreaders. There were two methods of rigging these — double and single. When rigged double, a block was stropped to the end of each spreader; other blocks were seized to eyebolts in the hounds of the fore mast, just below the trestletrees; the standing parts were clenched to eyebolts or spliced into the strop of the blocks at the hounds; the running parts rove through the blocks on the spreader, through the blocks at the hounds, through blocks seized to eyebolts in the deck at the foot of the mast, and were made fast to the bitts. When rove singly, the standing part was spliced round the end of the spreader; the running part rove as before, through a block at the hounds and led down; a single block was spliced into the end which connected up with a fall to a double block, seized to an eyebolt in the deck at the foot of the mast; the standing part of the fall was made fast to the upper block, one sheave of the lower block being used as a lead up to the bitts. When a spritsail was used on the spreaders, clues, bunts and so forth were fitted temporarily, but this mode of spreading a spritsail was up to the individual commanders of the ships; one would not expect models to be fitted with sails on the spreaders.

Lifts were spliced round the end of the spreader and secured with a lanyard and thimble to eyebolts in the side of the bowsprit cap.

RIGGING TO THE SPRIT TOPSAIL YARD AND SAIL

The parrel was fitted in a similar way to the topgallant yard parrel and remained the same during all periods, not being superseded by slings.

Ties were used when the yard was carried on the topmast. Up to 1719 a

II RIGGING
Rigging to the sprit topsail yard and sail

single rope was used as a tie, one end being bent to the centre of the yard, the other taken through a sheave set into the sprit topmast or, in some cases, through a block on a short strop from the sprit topmast head. In the end of the tie a block was spliced; up to 1680 a single one, after 1680 a long-tackle block was used. After 1719 ties and halliards were incorporated in one rope.

Halliards, up to 1680 had the standing part spliced into the strop of the block of the tie, rove through a single block seized to an eyebolt in the sprit top, through the upper block and finally made fast in the top. After 1680 and up to 1719 the standing part was made fast to the lower single block (seized as before to an eyebolt in the top); the running part made up the fall with the long-tackle block in the tie, and made fast again in the fore top, either to cleats in the top or hitched round a deadeye plate. After 1719, the halliard was spliced round the sprit topmast

head and rove through a block strapped to the centre of the yard, was taken through a sheave or block at the topmast head, and rove through a sheave of the gammon lashing block to the forecastle head. When the yard was carried on the jibboom, the standing part of the halliard was made fast to the strop of a block secured to the outer end of the jibboom; the hauling part rove through a block on the yard, through the block on the jibboom, and belayed to a pin in a rack over the bowsprit inboard, or to a timber head on the forecastle.

Lifts When the yard was carried on the sprit topmast the standing parts of the lifts were made fast to the sprit topmast head, either with eye-splices round the mast, or bent to short pendants from the sprit topmast cap; the hauling parts rove through blocks stropped to each yard arm, through blocks stropped to the sprit topmast head and were made fast in the top. When the yard was carried on the

jibboom, the standing parts were eye-spliced round the yard arm; the hauling parts rove through thimbles, seized each side of a strap round the jibboom end and led inboard, either through the gammon lashing blocks or through the fairlead collar on the bowsprit.

Brace pendants were fitted in the same manner as on other yards and ceased to be used by about 1773.

Braces When the yard was carried on the sprit topmast, the standing part of the brace was made fast to the fore stay, level with the sprit top; the hauling parts rove through the pendant blocks, through blocks on a short span on the stay just below the standing parts, through a double block strapped to the bowsprit, directly under the blocks on the stay, and were made fast on the forecastle. When the yard was carried on the jibboom, the standing parts were spliced round the yard arms; the hauling parts rove through blocks under the forward end of the fore top, through blocks under the

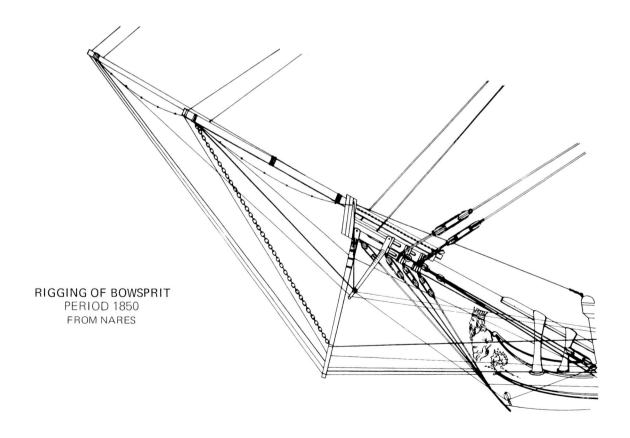

RIGGING OF BOWSPRIT
PERIOD 1850
FROM NARES

104

after end of the top and led down to the after rail of the forecastle. From 1773, braces shared the same double blocks under the fore top as the spritsail yard braces. Until 1773 both the sprit-sail braces and sprit topsail braces rove through single blocks stropped under the fore top.

Sheets were incorporated with spritsail lifts when the sprit topmast was carried. These are described under that heading. When the yard was carried on the jibboom, the sheets rove from the clue of the sail, through blocks stropped to the spritsail yard arm, through blocks lashed either side of the bowsprit just forward of the spritsail yard slings, and were made fast on the forecastle.

Cluelines, when the yard was carried on the sprit topmast, were made fast to the clues on the sail, rove through blocks, stropped to the yard about 2 feet without the slings, through blocks on a span which rove through and was hitched to a hole in the knee of the sprit topmast, (these blocks being just clear of the after edge of the sprit top) and finally led to the fore-castle via the gammon lashing blocks or fairlead collar. When the yard was carried on the jibboom, the clues rove from the sail, through blocks or thimbles stropped to the yard, 2 feet without the slings, and were led to the forecastle via the lead collar on the bowsprit. From 1719 whenever a jib-boom was carried in conjunction with a sprit topmast, lead blocks were carried on a span clove-hitched round the upper part of the knee, just below the bowsprit cap, the clues leading as before, being taken through the outer holes in the fairlead collar and then to the forecastle.

Earings

Robands or rope bands

Gaskets

These were fitted in the same way as on the fore topgallant sail.

The footropes comprised a single length of rope spliced to each yard arm and seized to the yard on each side of the slings. No stirrups were fitted.

12 Mizen yards and sails

RIGGING TO THE MIZEN YARD AND SAIL

The parrel was made of ribs and two rows of trucks. Up to 1670 the parrel rope had a two hole deadeye seized in the bight and after that date, a wood-en thimble; the two ends rove through the ribs and trucks; then, after the parrel was taken round the mast, the two ends were taken through the dead-eye or thimble and were spliced together. The distance between the thimble or deadeye and the spliced ends was about 3 feet; this enabled plenty of slack to be obtained on the parrels when eased off. The parrel was secured to the yard by seizing the throat of the deadeye or thimble to the strap of the jeer block on the yard, the deadeye or thimble hanging just clear of the yard. The yard was gener-ally carried on the starboard side of the mast.

A truss parrel superseded the parrel of ribs and trucks in about 1773 and com-prised a piece of rope served all over; this rope was taken round the yard and a seizing put on so that the yard was seized tightly in the bight; the two ends were taken round the mast and rove through an iron thimble, seized to the jeer block strop close to the yard; the two ends were spliced together and a thimble seized in the bight.

Truss was the name given to the tackle or, as during the first part of the sixteenth century, the rope by which the parrel or truss parrel was tightened to the mast. Up to 1640 a rope was bent to the spliced ends of the parrel, probably with a sheet bend, and was made fast to a cleat at the foot of the mizen mast; after 1640 a tackle com-prising a long-tackle hook block and a single hook block was used. The long-tackle block hooked to the parrel rope and the single hook block hooked to an eyebolt in the deck, at the foot of the mast, with the fall belayed to a cleat bolted to the mast about 4 feet up from the deck. After 1773, the upper block was hooked to the iron thimble in the bight of the parrel; the lower block was secured in the same position as before. From 1733 to 1773, instead of hooking the lower block to an eyebolt on deck, the block was

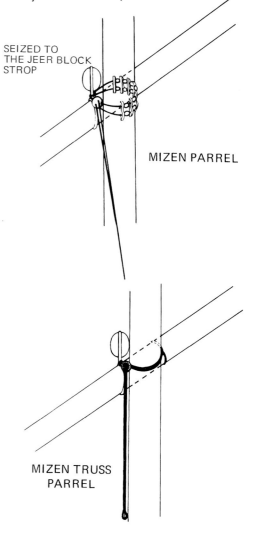

SEIZED TO THE JEER BLOCK STROP

MIZEN PARREL

MIZEN TRUSS PARREL

II RIGGING
Rigging to the mizen yard and sail

MIZEN LIFTS

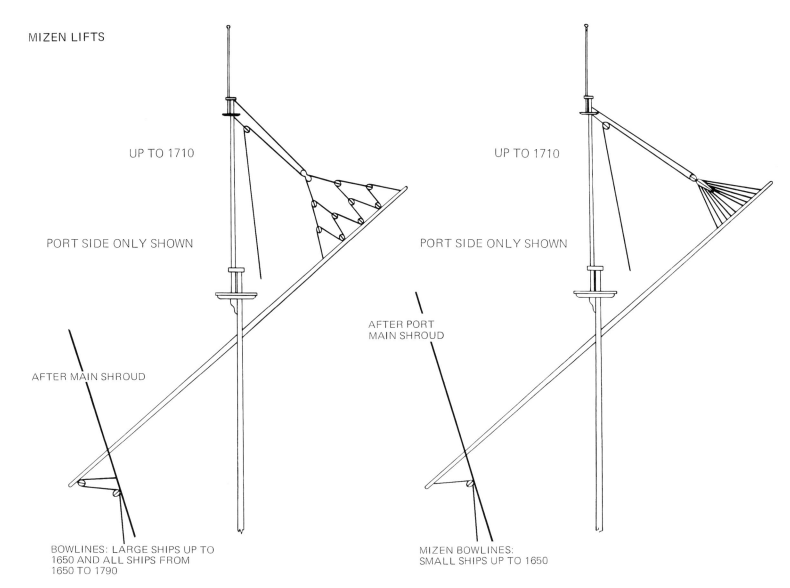

UP TO 1710

PORT SIDE ONLY SHOWN

AFTER MAIN SHROUD

BOWLINES: LARGE SHIPS UP TO
1650 AND ALL SHIPS FROM
1650 TO 1790

UP TO 1710

PORT SIDE ONLY SHOWN

AFTER PORT
MAIN SHROUD

MIZEN BOWLINES:
SMALL SHIPS UP TO 1650

stropped to the lower end of the mizen yard, forward of the yard arm cleats, and the running part made fast to the strop of the lower blocks. The fall made up in a coil on the yard.

Sling During the last few years before the mizen yard was replaced by a gaff – that was from about 1790 – the yard was held close to the mast by a sling similar to that of the spritsail yard. The yard was not required to be lowered and hoisted and a truss was not fitted as in previous years.

The tie was hitched round the centre of the yard, the other end being taken from aft, forward through a sheave in the mizen mast just below the top; it then led forward of the mast and a single block was spliced into the end;

this block connected by a fall to a sheave in the knighthead before the mast; there were two sheaves in the knighthead and the standing part of the fall was made fast to the upper block and the fall was belayed to the knighthead.

Jeers were used from about 1640 in conjunction with the tie and comprised a single block stropped to the centre of the yard and another single block, hanging by a long strop from the mizen mast head on the opposite side of the yard. The standing part of the jeer was spliced round the mizen mast head, rove through the block on the yard, up through the block from the mizen head, and was taken down to deck, generally being made fast to a timber head on the bulwarks abreast

of the mizen mast, or to the opposite mizen channel to the one to which the truss was made fast. By 1670 jeers superseded the tie entirely: a double block was strapped to the mizen yard and a treble block hung by a long strop from the mizen mast head; the strop was double and was seized to the mast head above the rigging; the block hung below the trestletrees with the strop between them. The standing part of the jeer was spliced round the yard just forward of the jeer block. The hauling part led down and was made fast to one of the deadeyes on the starboard mizen channels. This method of reeving the jeers remained until the mizen yard was replaced by the gaff. On Second Rates and below,

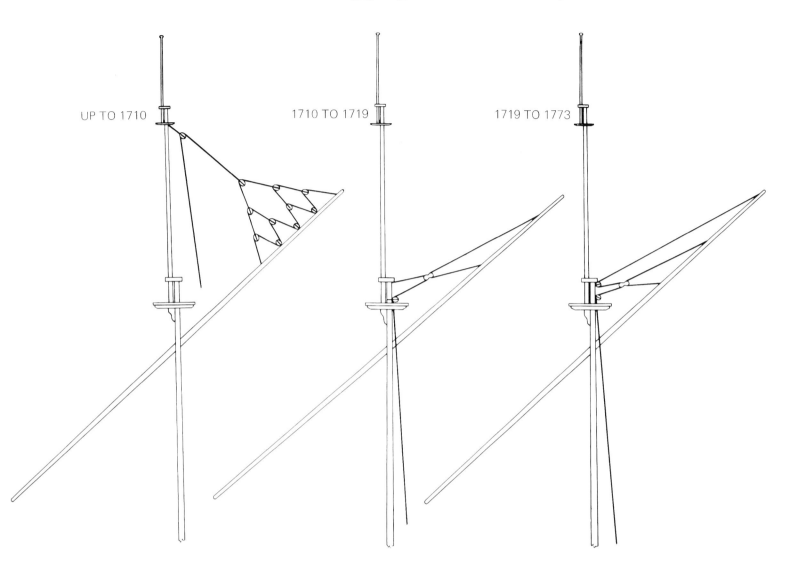

UP TO 1710

1710 TO 1719

1719 TO 1773

two double blocks were used instead of one treble and one double block. **Lifts,** during the seventeenth century, and up to 1710, were the rather complicated pattern of crowsfeet shown in the illustrations; a block was strapped to the mizen mast head and the hauling part was rove through it, leading down to and being made fast in the port mizen chains. After 1710 the lifts were much simpler: from 1710 to 1719, a span was clinched or spliced to the after part of the mizen yard, one end at the peak or a few feet down from the peak, the other end half way down the after part of the yard; before securing, the span rove through a long double block similar to the blocks used for the leechline legs but the lift

block was a single unit and not two single blocks spliced together. The fall of the lift was seized to the mizen mast head under the cap, rove through the block on the span, was taken through a block strapped to the mizen mast head just above the rigging and taken down to the port mizen chains. From 1719 to 1773, the span was secured further down the yard, the after end one third of the way down the after half of the yard, the forward end two thirds down; the same type of block was used on the span. The standing part of the fall was spliced round the peak of the yard; the fall was then taken through a block strapped round the mizen cap, through the block on the span, through a block strapped to

the mizen mast head just above the rigging, and taken down and made fast to the port mizen chains; after 1773 a double block was strapped round the mizen cap and a single block strapped half way down the after half of the yard. The standing part of the lift was spliced round the peak; the lift rove through the starboard sheave of the double block, through the single block on the yard, through the other sheave of the double block and was led down and made fast in the port mizen chains. **Bowlines** were rove singly on small ships up to about 1650; the bowlines were cut-spliced round the forward end of the mizen yard; one end rove to port, the other to starboard, and they were taken through blocks seized to

II RIGGING
Rigging to the mizen yard and sail

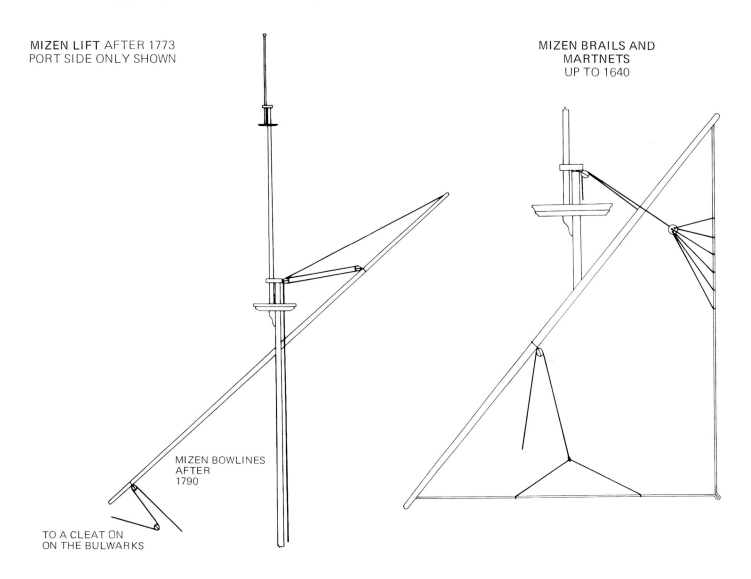

MIZEN LIFT AFTER 1773
PORT SIDE ONLY SHOWN

MIZEN BRAILS AND
MARTNETS
UP TO 1640

MIZEN BOWLINES
AFTER
1790

TO A CLEAT ON
ON THE BULWARKS

the aftermost main shrouds on a level with the forward end of the mizen yard, and made fast to a timber head or the rail by the aftermost main shrouds. Large ships at this period, and all ships after 1650 and up to about 1790, had a pair of blocks stropped to an eyebolt in the end of the yard; bowlines were seized to the aftermost main shrouds, taken through blocks on the yard, through blocks seized to the shrouds a few feet below the standing part, and were made fast as before to the rails. After 1790 the standing part and the lead block were moved to eyebolts in the deck at the side near the aftermost main shroud and the bowlines were belayed to a cleat in the bulwarks, blocks being stropped to the

yard as before.

Mizen sheets, up to about 1650, were rigged in the same way on all ships: the standing part was seized to an eyebolt in the centre knee of the transom; the sheet rove through a block hooked to the clue of the sail, through a lead block seized to an eyebolt just below the standing part, and was belayed to a cleat in the side, well aft. After 1650, small ships only were rigged in this fashion. The rest had a single block hooked to the sail, with the standing part spliced into the strop of this block; the sheet rove through one sheave of a double block seized to an eyebolt in the centre knee of the transom, through the block hooked to the sail, through the other sheave of

the double block and belayed as before. From about 1706 all ships had the sheets rigged the same as on large ships in previous years, except for the First Rates which had a long-tackle block hooked to the sail; the standing part of the sheet was spliced into the strop of a single block hooked to the eyebolt in the knee; the fall rove between these two blocks and was belayed as before to the side. When the mizen sail was laced to the mast — that is from about 1730 — sheets were rigged in all ships without exception in the manner of the large ships of the period 1650 to 1706.

Martnets were in use before 1640 and were the predecessors of the mizen brails, though brails were used on the foot of the sail in conjunction with the martnets. Martnets consisted of three ropes, passed through a three hole deadeye, thus forming six legs which were bent to the leech of the sail; these spread along the upper part of the leech taking up a quarter of the sail (the second quarter from the peak). The deadeye was spliced into a rope which, in turn, rove through a double block strapped to the mizen mast head and was taken down to deck. I have described one martnet but there were, however, two, one on each side of the sail and the double block was shared by both falls.

Brails, when used at the same time as martnets, required a span fitted to either side of the foot of the sail; one end of the span was bent one third along from the nock and was rove through a thimble that was spliced into another rope; the other end of the span was then bent a quarter way in from the clue; the rope rove through blocks stropped to the forward half of the yard. The blocks shared one strop which was large enough to fit round the yard and round the two blocks; seizings were then put on between the blocks and the yard to hold the strop and blocks tightly round the yard. The brails, after reeving through the blocks, were taken to the rails on either side of the ship. The blocks on the yard at

this period were just below the centre of the yard, or a quarter of the way down the forward half of the yard from the centre. For periods after 1640 I am taking the brails separately since describing them collectively would lead to confusion. At all times brails were rigged each side of the sail.

Peak brails, during the periods before the mizen sail was laced to the mast, were bent a quarter way down the leech, rove through blocks stropped one third down the after half of the yard, through a block spliced into a rope which led to the rails either side, up through blocks stropped two thirds down the after half of the yard, and bent once gain to the sail half way down the leech. Thus peak brails had two parts fastened to the sail leading to one hauling part.

Throat brails, during the same period as mentioned above, were bent to the leech three quarters of the way down, rove through blocks stropped just above the centre of the yard and were then taken to the rails just abaft the mizen mast.

Foot brails, during this same period, were bent to the foot of the sails with an equal distance along the foot between each brail, the tack and cringles. They led through blocks to the forward half of the yard; the aftermost brail blocks stropped just forward

of the centre of the yard, the others equal distances apart between the aftermost blocks and the forward end of the yard. The average number of brails was three a side; on large ships, four, on small ships, two. The brails, after leading through the blocks on the yard were rove through blocks seized to the aftermost main shrouds, these blocks being level with the blocks on the yard. Thus the aftermost brail was taken through the upper block and the foremost brail through the lowest block. The brails were made fast to the rails by the main shroud.

Peak brails, when the mizen sail was laced to the yard and mast, rove from just under one quarter way down the leech through blocks stropped one third down the after half of the yard, and led to the rails or to a pin on each quarter.

The middle brails, when the mizen sail was laced to the yard and mast, rove from half way down the leech, through blocks stropped two thirds down the after half of the yard, and led through thimbles seized half way up the after mizen shroud, to be belayed to a cleat seized to the foot of the shroud, or to a pin in the rail by the shroud.

Throat brails, during the above period, rove from three quarters of the way down the leech, through blocks stropped by the centre of the yard and led

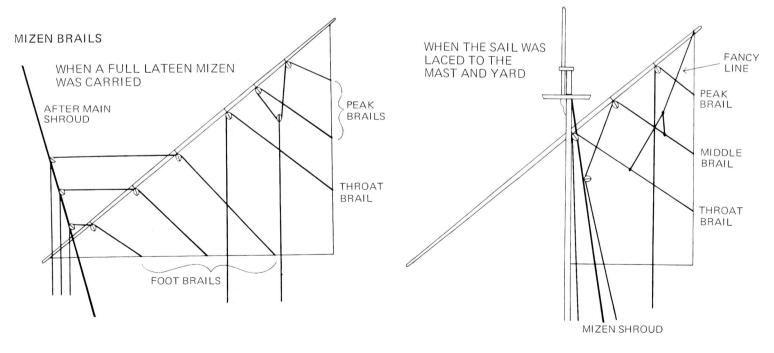

MIZEN BRAILS

WHEN A FULL LATEEN MIZEN WAS CARRIED

AFTER MAIN SHROUD

PEAK BRAILS

THROAT BRAIL

FOOT BRAILS

WHEN THE SAIL WAS LACED TO THE MAST AND YARD

FANCY LINE

PEAK BRAIL

MIDDLE BRAIL

THROAT BRAIL

MIZEN SHROUD

down the mast to cleats in the deck at the foot of the mizen mast, or to cleats bolted to the mast.

Fancy lines, during the period mentioned above, were rigged each side of the sail. Their purpose was to keep the brails clear of the lee side of the sail when the sail was set. Each line had a span with a thimble spliced in each end; one of the thimbles had the throat brail rove through it and the other end had the middle brail rove through it. The span itself was rove through a thimble which was spliced into the end of a rope; this rope rove through blocks seized to the peak of the yard and led down to the taffrail.

Vang pendants and falls were rigged when the sail was laced to the yard and mast. Vang pendants were one length of rope, clove-hitched in the centre to the peak of the mizen yard; a double block, usually a long-tackle block, was spliced into each end which connected to a single block hooked to an eyebolt in the quarter piece each side, the fall belaying to a cleat in the side by the taffrail.

Smiting lines were used to enable the sail to be set quickly. Spliced round the lower end of the yard when the sail was furled along the yard, the line was taken in with the lashings, the end thus coming out at the peak of the sail and was taken down to deck. When the sail was required to be set, a sharp pull on the smiting line broke the lashings and the sail was unfurled. The lashings were usually rope yards. This smiting

line was used only when a full mizen sail was carried.

Lacings to the yard or mast, and earings The sail was laced to the yard in a spiral fashion from the peak, and laced down to the forward end or nock. When the forward part of the sail was cut off, the lacings were two pieces of rope, one reeving from peak to throat round the yard, the other from the throat to the tack round the mast. Lacings were spliced round the peak for the yard lacing and round the earing cringle for the mast lacing. Earings were also fitted in the usual manner, one at the peak and one at the nock or throat, dependent on the cut of the sail. The method of lacing down the mast is illustrated, with the driver and mizen sail carried together.

A tack was not required on the mizen sail until bonnets were no longer fitted to the sail; then, instead of the sail being a true lateen it was cut with an additional piece on the foot, as if the bonnet were permanently fixed to the sail. The tack, a single piece of rope, was spliced into the cringle in the lower forward corner of the sail and was hitched to an eyebolt in the deck on whichever side of the ship the fore part of the sail was required to be fastened. A tack was also required when the fore part of the sail was removed and the sail laced to the mast; this tack was a piece of rope, spliced into the tack cringle at the foot of the sail, and was rove through an eyebolt

in the deck abaft the mast and through the tack cringle alternately until the tack was used up.

Reef points After 1680 a diagonal reef band was put on the sail from nock to one third down the leech. Reef points, one to every seam, were put in as illustrated in the Seamanship Part. No reef tackle was used. When the fore end of the sail was cut off the reef band ran parallel to the foot, one third up the luff.

RIGGING TO THE MIZEN BOOM GAFF DRIVER AND SPANKER

Gaff parrel When the gaff replaced the mizen yard it was fitted to the mast by means of a simple parrel. The jaws of the gaff had a hole in each side; a rope with a wall and crown in one end was rove through one hole, threaded through an appropriate number of trucks, taken round the mast and rove through the hole in the other side of the jaws; an overhand knot was then worked down the rope so that the parrel was held moderately tight to the lower mast—not too tightly, however, as the gaff was hoisted up and down the mast. When trysails were fitted the gaff and boom were fitted by parrels in the same way as when fitted directly to the mizen mast.

Gaff topping lift or peak halliards When first introduced the topping lift was rigged in the same way as the lift on the mizen yard. During the last few years of its use—from about 1805—a double block was seized or hooked to

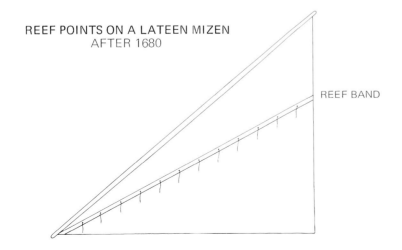

REEF POINTS ON A LATEEN MIZEN
AFTER 1680

REEF BAND

GAFF TOPPING LIFT

an eyebolt in the after side of the mizen cap; a single block was stropped half way down the gaff and the standing part of the lift was spliced round the peak, rove through the starboard sheave of the double block, through the block on the gaff, through the port sheave of the double block, and was made fast to the bitts on the port side abaft the mast. This method of rigging the lift seems to have remained the same to the end of the sail era. On some ships there were slight variations: one of them was the fitting of an eyebolt in a band round the peak for the standing part to be spliced into; also, instead of stropping the block to the gaff, an iron hoop with an eyebolt on it was driven down the gaff and the block hooked and moused to the eyebolt—this was from about 1818; also another variation on large ships, from about 1840, was to make the standing part fast to an eyebolt abaft the mizen topmast cap, (hooked and moused usually), and the lift then rove through a single block a quarter of the way down the gaff, (hooked to an eyebolt in a hoop), up through the starboard sheave of a double block (hooked to an eyebolt in the after side of the mizen mast cap), through another block (hooked to an eyebolt in another hoop half way down the gaff) through the port sheave of the double block, and was made fast to the port bitts abaft the mizen mast. No definite way of rigging the lifts during the last few years seems to have been made, and

the reader will not go far wrong if he follows either of the last two ways.
Gaff vangs, pendants and falls were rigged in the same way as those mentioned for the mizen yard up to 1818. After 1818, vang pendants were seized, (through a thimble spliced into the end), to eyebolts in a band round the peak—the same band that the topping lift rove from; in the lower end of the pendants a single block was spliced; a whip was rove through this block with the standing part bent to an eyebolt on the inside of the bulwarks by the taffrail, and the hauling part to a cleat by the standing part. Another lead for this whip was to bend the standing part to an eyebolt in the quarter piece either side; the hauling part rove through a block seized to the eyebolt in the side that the main brace standing part was made fast to; the hauling part then rove through a hole or sheave in the side, just forward of the lead block and was made fast to a cleat inside the bulwarks.
Gaff throat halliards used an eyebolt set into the jaws of the gaff on the upper side; a double block on large ships and a single block on small ships was hooked to this eyebolt, and a fall rove between this block and one hanging from the mizen mast head on a long strap, the block coming between the trestletrees aft; the fall led down the starboard side of the mast to the bitts on the starboard side. From 1818, instead of a block from the mast head, sheaves were let into the after cross-

tree between the trestletrees, the sheaves running fore and aft. There were two sheaves and only a single block on the gaff. The standing part was spliced round the strop of the single block and the hauling part taken as before to the bitts.
The boom truss parrel comprised a piece of rope, rove through holes in the boom jaws and had a stopper knot worked in each end, the truss fitting round the mast or trysail mast.
The boom topping lift, up to about 1805 was middled and clove-hitched, or cut and cut-spliced, round the after end of the boom; the two ends then rove through single blocks strapped to the mizen mast head on either side and led down outside of the top; a double block was spliced into each end connecting up by the falls to single blocks hooked to eyebolts in the mizen channels aft; the hooks were moused and the hauling parts were belayed to cleats on the mizen mast a few feet from the deck. From 1805 to 1815 the topping lift led through blocks seized to eyebolts under each trestletree, aft of the mizen mast, instead of through blocks from the mast head. The lead and fall was the same though the hauling parts were belayed to pins in the rail by the mizen shroud instead of to the mast. A span with a thimble in each end was sometimes hitched round the boom about 12 feet in from the after end; each half of the span was about 4 feet long. The lifts were rove through these

BOOM TOPPING LIFT

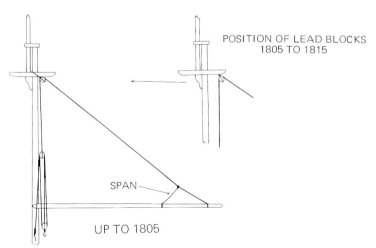

POSITION OF LEAD BLOCKS
1805 TO 1815

SPAN

UP TO 1805

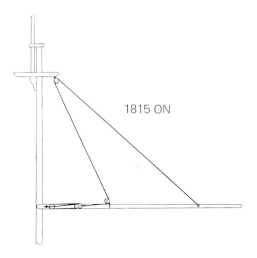

1815 ON

thimbles before being rove through the blocks on the trestletrees. I should imagine that the purpose of these spans was to provide a spring to the lifts, so that if a sudden strain came on the boom the span would give way rather than the lifts. After 1815 the lifts were separate and were spliced round thimbles set round eyebolts each side of the boom, just outside the taffrail, or were spliced round the boom and held there with thumb cleats. The other end of the lifts rove either through blocks strapped to eyebolts under the trestletrees or through sheaves let into cheeks bolted on the outer side of the mizen trestletrees (especially so after 1840); they then rove through single blocks, either side of the boom on eyebolts set two thirds in from the after end, or, snatched into snatch cheeks, bolted to the boom in the same position as the blocks. Thimbles were spliced into the ends and long-tackle blocks were hooked to these thimbles connecting with a fall to single blocks, hooked to eyebolts by the jaws, or to thimbles in a strap round the jaws. A cleat was bolted each side of the boom by the jaws for the falls to belay to.

Boom sheets sometimes had a horse fitted for the lower sheet block to run on, but generally the block was strapped to an eyebolt and this is the method I will describe. When a horse was to be fitted, the sheets were rigged exactly the same, except that the lower block stropped to an iron thimble running along the horse. A double block was seized into a strap round the boom inside the taffrail; another double block was strapped to an eyebolt in the transom. The standing part of the sheet was made fast to the strap of the lower block, and the hauling part belayed to a cleat in the deck. Often on large ships a single block as well as the double blocks, was strapped to either a thimble on the horse or to a thimble on an eyebolt in the transom; a thimble, just large enough to take the sheet, was seized on the strap of the double block on the boom; the end of the sheet was timber-hitched round the boom just abaft of the double block, and the sheet then rove through the lower and upper

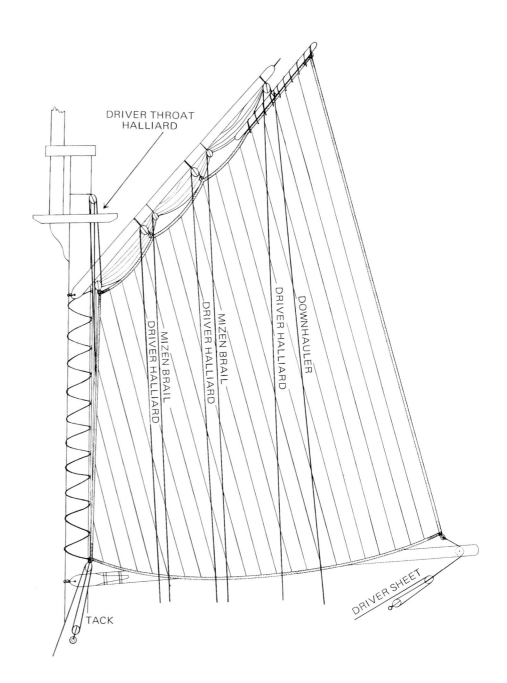

DRIVER SET WITH MIZEN SAIL BRAILED

DRIVER THROAT HALLIARD

MIZEN BRAIL
DRIVER HALLIARD

MIZEN BRAIL
DRIVER HALLIARD

DRIVER HALLIARD

DOWNHAULER

DRIVER SHEET

TACK

double blocks with the hauling part leading through the single block. There was another method of rigging the boom sheets and that was in conjunction with the boom guys.

Boom sheets and guys A thimble was set into an eyebolt in each quarter piece and a double block strapped to each thimble. Two single blocks, one each side, were seized into a grommet round the boom, just outside the taffrail, or to eyebolts on the boom after 1840. The rope for the sheets and guys was cut in the middle and cut-spliced round the boom end, or was spliced into eyebolts set in the boom on either side. The ropes rove each side through one sheave of the double block (the outer one) on the quarter, through the single block on the boom, through the other sheave in the double block and through a hole or sheave in the side and were finally made fast to cleats in the deck or on the inside of the bulwarks. This method of fitting the guys and sheets together was in use from about 1818, but was not used in all ships.

Boom guys pendants and tackles Up to 1818 the outer ends of the pendants were hooked to thimbles, seized in a strop round the boom end. After 1818 the ends were hooked to eyebolts in a band round the boom end. At all times single blocks were spliced into the other ends of the pendants; these connected up with a fall to other single blocks strapped to eyebolts in the quarter pieces. The standing part of the fall was made fast to the block on the pendant and the hauling part brought inboard either via sheaves in cheek blocks bolted on the top of the taffrail either side or through other lead blocks seized to the iron outrigger (to which the main brace was fastened) and through holes in the side to cleats on the inside of the bulwarks or, finally, in some instances, straight in over the taffrail to the cleats. On some ships the standing part was made fast to the quarter blocks and the hauling part rove from the quarter blocks, through leading holes or sheaves in the side to the cleats, this last method being in use from about 1840.

Horses or footropes were required, owing to the overhang of the boom

RIGGING OF A SPANKER
SHOWING THE SAIL IN THE PROCESS
OF BEING BRAILED UP PERIOD 1850
FROM NARES

over the stern; the outer ends were either spliced round thimbles on an eyebolt at the very end of the boom or they were put on as one piece of rope middled over the boom and seized underneath. There were overhand or diamond knots worked in the horses. The inner ends had an eye spliced in them and were seized to the boom by the sheet blocks strop. There were two horses to each boom and the knots were about 18 inches apart.

The driver sail was used only in light winds and was really a fine-weather secondary sail to the shortened mizen sail in use up to 1810. The mizen sail was not carried on a boom but was loose footed. The driver was, however,

fitted to a boom and the gaff or mizen yard; also, part of the head was laced to a yard, slung from a block at the outer end of the gaff. A short yard was laced to the after head of the sail; this yard had a halliard bent to the centre which rove through a tail block secured round the end of the gaff and was made fast to a pin or cleat at the side. The head of the sail was bent to the gaff or mizen yard by two halliards rove through tail blocks spaced down the gaff or yard, and leading to the side like the yard halliard. The throat halliard consisted of a luff tackle—one single block strapped round the mizen mast head, the other hooked to the throat cringle. The tackle came on the

TRYSAIL SHEETS

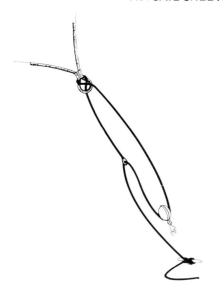

same side as the tack, the fall leading to the after bitts, the standing part on the lower deck.

A downhauler was needed on this sail; it was bent to the driver yard by the halliard and made fast to the taffrail. **The tack** comprised a fall with two small single blocks, one hooked into the tack cringle, the other to an eyebolt by the foot of the mast, starboard side of the boom. Sometimes a double and single block was used, the double on the sail, the lower block sometimes hooked to an eyebolt in the upper side of the boom jaws.

Sheets were made fast with a sheet-bend to the clue and rove through a sheave in the boom. A single block was spliced into the end which connected by a fall to another single block hooked to an eyebolt in the centre of the taffrail, the fall leading in upon the quarterdeck. Sometimes a traveller was put round the boom and the sheet seized to it close by the clue; this kept the sheet close to the boom; an out-hauler bent to the traveller was rove through the sheave in the boom and made fast to a cleat under the boom. **The spanker** is referred to by many authorities as another name for the driver; however to assist in clarifying the various alterations to this sail I prefer to refer to the spanker as the sail that was evolved from the driver,

thus giving us three sails in the evolution of the mizen—namely the mizen sail, the driver and finally the spanker. This sail was laced to the gaff, and the luff was either laced to the mast or was seized to hoops round the trysail mast when fitted. On some small ships, hoops were used round the mizen mast but only when wooldings or bands were not fitted. The peak and throat were also secured with earings.

Brails were four in number. The peak brail led from the sail through blocks seized or strapped one third down the gaff; up to about 1818, it was taken from there straight to the poop rails and, after 1818, was taken through the inner sheave of a double block, seized to eyebolts either side of the gaff jaws, thence to deck. The middle brails rove from the sail, through blocks seized or strapped two thirds down the gaff, through the outer sheaves of the double blocks at the gaff jaws and down to deck. The throat brails rove from the sail, through either the inner sheaves of the double block, as up to 1818, or through single blocks seized to an eyebolt under the gaff jaws after 1818, thence to deck. The foot brails rove from the sail, through blocks seized half way down the luff of the sail and then to deck. After 1818, sheaves were bolted to the gaff instead of the lead blocks on the gaff. Brails were middled and seized to the cringles ; on the leech of the sail; these cringles were put in to coincide with the lead blocks on the gaff so that when brailed up, the sail was carried snugly down the gaff.

A spiral gasket was used to furl the sail as on the mizen sail, harbour gaskets being put on one to a cloth when required in port.

Reef points, in up to three rows, were carried across the foot of the sail.

Tacks were fitted the same way as on the driver.

Sheets A single block was hooked into the sheet cringle. The standing part of the sheet was spliced round the end of the boom. The other end rove through the block in the sail, through a sheave let into the boom, a few feet in from the end, and was belayed round a cleat bolted under the boom by the jaws. An eyebolt was put in the boom upper

side of the jaws for hooking the sheet block to when the sail was not rigged or was harbour-furled.

RIGGING TO THE FORE AND MAIN TRYSAILS

Trysails were introduced in 1815; the main trysail was first, followed a few years later by the fore trysail; they took the place of the mizen and main staysails. The head was laced to the gaff and the luff seized to hoops on the trysail mast.

Parrels were rigged the same way as on the spanker gaff.

Throat halliards only required a single rope, spliced into an eyebolt in the upper side of the jaws. The other end was taken between the trestletrees, taken round the mast head and seized to its own part. The halliard had only to be of such a length to rig as mentioned.

A peak span was spliced round the gaff one end a few feet in from the outer end, the other end one third of the gaff, from the jaws. A thimble was put on the span before being spliced; a long pendant was spliced round the thimble. This pendant, when the gaff was hoisted into position with temporary tackles, was either taken round the mast head and seized to its own part or taken through a thimble strapped round the eyes of the lower rigging, and made fast to its own part.

Vangs were fitted the same as the spanker vangs.

Peak, middle, throat, and foot brails were rigged in the same way as on the spanker, and made fast to the bitts.

The tack comprised one piece of rope spliced into the tack cringle, and rove between there and an eyebolt in the deck at the foot of the mast until expended; the parts were then frapped together.

Sheets comprised a length of rope with a thimble spliced into one end, bent to the clue with a sheet-bend so that the end with the thimble was one third of the length of the other end. A single block with a hook and thimble was hooked to a ringbolt on deck either side of the mast abaft the mast the trysail was on; the long end of the sheet was rove through the block then through the thimble in the short leg and belayed well aft.

The outhauler was sometimes rove single and sometimes double. When single, one end was spliced into the head clue, rove through a sheave in the end of the gaff, through a block hooked to an eyebolt in the lower mast head, and had a block spliced in the end for a whip to reeve through. When double, the whip was dispensed with and a block shackled to the head clue; the standing part was spliced to the gaff end, rove through the block on the sail, through the sheave in the gaff, through the block at the mast head and down to deck.

The inhauler was spliced into the peak cringle, taken through a block shackled or hooked to the throat of the gaff and had a block spliced in the end for a whip to reeve through.

13 Stunsail yards, booms and sails

RIGGING TO THE FORE LOWER STUNSAIL

Stunsail The actual date for the introduction of stunsails seems to be open to doubt, the earliest mention being 1655 for the main and 1690 for the fore. Also information prior to 1790 is unfortunately not to be found: I can therefore only give details of stunsail rigging from 1790 onwards, and suggestions before that date I have enclosed in brackets. I must emphasize that the part in brackets is my own idea and is not based on contemporary authority.

The outer halliard was seized round the stunsail yard, one third along from the inboard end up to about 1840 (after then in the centre) and rove through a block seized to the outer boom iron on the fore yard, through a block secured to the fore mast cap by means of a span and led down to deck. This method of rigging the outer halliard was altered in about 1745 when, seized as before to the yard, it was led through a block seized to the outer end of the stunsail boom on the lower yard, was taken through the block on the cap span and led down to deck; it will be noted that this change enabled much wider stunsails to be carried. (I would rig the halliards as shown in the first instance up to 1745 —bearing in mind that the stunsail was

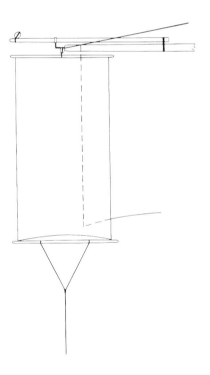

LOWER STUNSAIL
PRIOR TO 1745

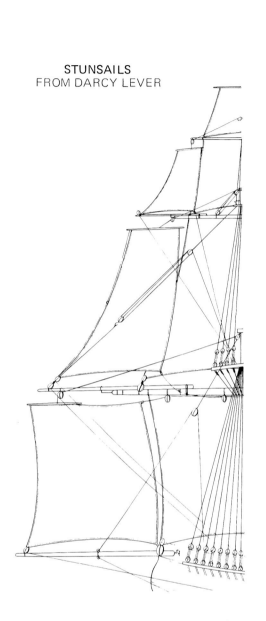

STUNSAILS
FROM DARCY LEVER

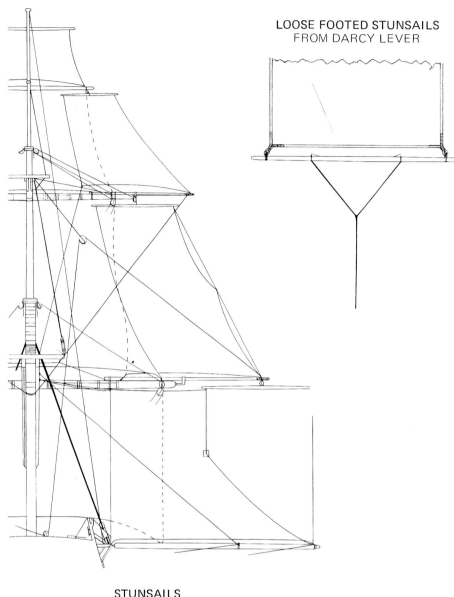

STUNSAILS
FROM NARES

LOOSE FOOTED STUNSAILS
FROM DARCY LEVER

probably quite narrow when first introduced— and rig a shorter yard up to 1745 and a longer one from 1745. I should imagine that the period 1745 to 1829 saw very little change in the shape of the stunsail.)

The inner halliard was bent to the upper inner cringle of the stunsail, rove through a tail block on the outer quarter of the lower yard, through another one on the inner quarter and was taken down to deck. No change was made in this rigging during the nineteenth century. (Before 1745, I should be inclined to fit the outer stunsail halliard in the centre of the

yard and to dispense with the inner halliard altogether, the head of the sail being laced right along the yard. After 1745 I should fit the inner halliard as shown in the first instance.)

Sheets were middled, and the bight bent to the clue, one sheet leading forward and the other aft. (These probably remained unaltered from the innovation of the stunsail to the end of the sail era.)

The tripping line was used from about 1840 and rove from the tack where it was bent, through a thimble secured to the centre of the stunsail, through a tail block bent to the inner end of the

stunsail yard, through another tail block bent to the fore mast close under the top and led down to deck. On large ships it was often rigged double and, in this case, the thimble on the sail was not required. The standing part of the tripping line was bent to the stunsail boom iron of the fore yard, rove through a tail block bent to the stunsail tack, through another tail block bent to the boom iron close to the standing part, through a tail block on the fore mast, then taken to deck. Sometimes the tail block on the fore mast was dispensed with and the fall led straight to deck from the block on the boom iron. The tripping line could be rigged either on the fore side or on the after side, the latter being most recommended. The use of the tripping line was to assist in taking the wind out of the sail when striking it.

The tack rove through a block on the end of the lower or swinging boom and, up to about 1810, was rove through a block lashed to the main chains, led up through a gunport and made fast inboard. After about 1810, a double sheave was fitted in the bulwarks at the after part of the waist netting; the tack led through the upper sheave direct and did not have a leading block in the main chains. (I should imagine that the foot of the sail during the early periods was loose footed on small ships and would not therefore be rigged with tacks as described here. I believe that the lower boom and tacks as described were first introduced in 1690 for larger ships and were not generally used until about 1733.) Up to about 1805/1810 large and medium ships would be expected to carry a swinging boom and small ships would be loose footed. After 1805/1810 all ships had swinging booms.

The swinging booms either hooked to a plate on the fore channels, to an eyebolt in the ship's side just forward of the channels or, on three-deckers, to an eyebolt abreast of the fore end of the fore channels but just above the lower gunports; the inner end was held down by a tackle between the inner end and an eyebolt in the wale directly under the inner end. Up to about 1810, a thimble was strapped midway along the boom, it being on top of the boom; to this thimble a topping lift was clinched which rove up through a block on a long span round the lower mast head and down to deck. After 1810 eyebolts on a spider band were used instead of a thimble strapping; the lift then rove from the eyebolt, through a clump block seized to the fore yard with a tail, up through another clump block seized between the second and third shroud of the fore rigging, and thence to deck; the clump block on the fore yard was taken out on the yard prior to the using of the boom, and when the

boom was not in use this block would be secured to the fore shrouds, ready for when it was required. Another way of rigging the topping lift — in use about 1850 — was to seize a block half way up, or sometimes higher, to the second shroud; the topping lift was rove through the block seized to the shroud, and taken down to deck. On some ships a luff tackle was hooked to the topping lift to assist in hoisting up the boom.

Guys, up to 1810, were clinched round the boom in the centre; after that date they were spliced round thimbles in eyebolts on the boom. The forward guy led from the boom, through a block lashed round the end of the spritsail yard — or spreader, whichever was applicable — through a sheave in the bees, then through a fairlead in the forecastle bulwarks, or straight from the spritsail yard block to the forecastle, the latter method being used up to about 1810. The after guy led from the boom, through a block lashed to a timber head by the gangway, and led inboard or, as was the case after 1810, through the lower sheave in the bulwarks at the after end of the waist netting. On some ships, even to the end of the sail era, the guys and the lift were spliced round the boom, no eyebolts being fitted, in which case cleats were nailed on the boom to keep the rigging in place.

Loose footed stunsails had a yard secured to the foot of the sail by the two lower cringles, thus dispensing with the stunsail tack though still retaining the sheets; a span was fitted to each end of the yard and a guy made fast to the middle of the span by means of an eye seized in the centre of the span; this guy was taken aft, led through a block lashed in the main chains and led inboard via a gunport, where it belayed to a cleat in the waist. (This is the method I recommend for all ships up to 1745 and for small ships up to 1805/1810.)

Rope bands secured the stunsails to the upper yards in the usual manner. In some cases a spiral lashing was used.

RIGGING OF THE MAIN STUNSAILS

Stunsail As with the fore stunsail notes, much of the following is conjectural; the main stunsail was introduced before the fore stunsail, its earliest mention being 1655; the fore stunsail did not come into general use until 1690. By Admiralty Order in 1801, the main stunsail was no longer issued, but sizes for it were given as late as 1845. It is possible that this order was rescinded in 1829 when an Establishment of sail sizes was ordered and undoubtedly the main stunsail was still used in the years between 1801 and 1829; it was probably made onboard ship.

Outer stunsail halliard
Inner stunsail halliard
Stunsail sheets
These were rigged exactly as on the fore stunsail.

Stunsail tacks were rigged the same as on the fore stunsail and led through a block seized to an eyebolt by the transom or to a timber head well aft on the quarterdeck.

The swinging boom topping lift was rigged the same as on the fore stunsail.

The swinging boom guys were rigged the same as on the fore stunsail; lead blocks were seized to the fore channels and mizen channels, or fore channels and an eyebolt in the quarterdeck.

Loose footed stunsails were rigged the same as on the fore stunsail; lead blocks seized to an eyebolt by the transom or to a timber head aft on the quarterdeck. This method of carrying stunsails was seldom used for the main stunsail except possibly prior to 1745.

Tripping lines
Rope bands
These were fitted as on the fore stunsail.

RIGGING OF THE FORE TOP STUNSAILS

Stunsails Like the stunsails on the lower yard, very little information is obtainable prior to about 1790; as the method of rigging them altered very little after that date I have no reason to think that the method of carrying them was any different before 1790. They were fastened to the stunsail yard in the same way as the lower stunsails.

II RIGGING
Rigging to the main top stunsails

Halliards A block was seized to an eyebolt on the extreme end of the topsail yard arm, or to the boom iron on the end of the yard; this block had a thimble stropped to it through which the seizing was taken. The halliard was bent to the stunsail yard, was rove through the block on the end of the topsail yard, taken through a block, fastened with a span to the topmast cap, and led down to deck. There were, of course, two blocks on the span — one for the port stunsail halliard, the other for the starboard halliard. The halliard was bent to the stunsail yard with a stunsail-bend (see the description of knots, bends and hitches). Up to about 1840 it was bent one third out along the yard; after 1840, the halliard was secured to the centre of the yard.

The sheets were doubled, one leading forward to deck, the other aft to deck; they were secured to the inner corner of the stunsail in the same way as jib and staysail sheet pendants. Stunsail sheets did not have pendants, being fastened directly to the sail; the fore sheets led in to the forecastle, the after sheets to the upper deck abaft the fore shrouds.

The tack bent to the outer clue of the sail, rove through a block stropped to the outer end of the stunsail boom on the lower yard, was then taken aft down to deck outside of the backstays, through a lead block by the gangway, and made fast inboard close to the lead block.

The downhauler made fast to the outer end of the stunsail yard and rove through a thimble seized half way down the outer leech of the sail, through a block lashed to the outer clue of the sail, and was taken down to deck at the waist close to the tack.

The stunsail boom tackle was used to run the stunsail boom out and comprised two double blocks, one made fast to the outer boom iron, the other stropped to the hole in the inner end of the boom; the fall led in along the yard and was made fast to the centre of the yard. As an additional support to the boom when run out, the top burton tackle hooked into a thimble stropped to the centre of the boom. The inner end of the boom was also lashed to the yard after being run out.

Stunsail boom strop When the stunsail boom was hauled in, as an addition to the inner lashing a strop was sometimes put round the fore yard and the end taken through the bight thus forming a loop; a toggle was seized to the boom end and was toggled through the loop; the strop was long enough to go round the yard with about 2 feet to spare.

RIGGING TO THE MAIN TOP STUNSAILS

Stunsails were rigged in the same way as those on the fore topsail yard, with the tacks leading to lead blocks on the rails close to the stern shrouds, and the downhauler running adjacent to it.

RIGGING OF THE FORE TOPGALLANT STUNSAILS

Stunsails were introduced on the topgallant yard in about 1773; heads of the sails were secured to the stunsail yards in the usual way.

The halliard was bent one third along the yard up to about 1840 (and after then bent to the centre of the stunsail yard) and rove through a jewel block seized to an eyebolt in the end of the topgallant yard, up through a block stropped to the head of the topgallant mast, and was taken down and made fast in the lower top.

Sheets were double like those on the top stunsails, the forward one leading to the quarter of the topsail yard, the after one taken to the fore top and made fast to the topmast shrouds.

Tacks rove from the outer clue, through a block or thimble on the end of the stunsail boom on the topsail yard, and were either taken to the main chains as up to about 1815, or through a block seized to the after deadeye in the fore top, and down to the pin rail by the fore shrouds as after 1815.

The downhauler was made fast to the outer stunsail yard arm, and was taken to the fore top leading abaft the stunsail.

The stunsail boom strop was fitted the same as on the fore yard.

RIGGING OF THE MAIN TOPGALLANT STUNSAILS

Stunsails were rigged the same way as those on the fore topgallant yard, the tacks reeving to the mizen chains up to 1815, and after then to the main top, as the fore ones to the fore top.

14 The staysails and jib

RIGGING OF THE FORE STAYSAIL

Halliards Staysails were seldom fitted on the fore stay, and one would expect only large ships from the late eighteenth century on to be so rigged. The standing part of the halliard was hitched or seized to an eyebolt under the port trestletree of the fore mast. The running part rove through a block, seized to the head of the sail, up through a block, seized to an eyebolt under the starboard trestletree, and was taken down to deck.

Sheets were double, the bight being put through the clues and the ends reeving through the bight. Single blocks were spliced in the ends and a whip was rove through each of these blocks; the standing part of the whip was made fast to an eyebolt in the bulwarks, or deck close to the bulwarks, abreast of the fore mast; the running part was brought to the pin rail, either directly, or through a snatch block on the deck. After about 1840 the sheets were often shackled or lashed to the clue as illustrated on the jibsail.

The tack was a piece of rope spliced into the cringle in the tack of the sail and made fast to the fore preventer stay heart. or round the bowsprit close to the preventer stay.

The downhauler was fastened to the head of the sail, and rove through a few hanks, was taken through a single block seized to the preventer stay, lanyard, or collar, and was then taken to the forecastle where it was belayed. **A long gasket,** made fast to the head cringle, and wound spirally round the sail, was used at sea. In harbour the sail was secured by individual pieces of rope yarn or sennet gaskets as the harbour gaskets on other sails.

RIGGING OF THE MAIN STAYSAIL

The staysail stay, up to about 1810, was an additional stay required for taking the staysail; after 1810 the sail was hoisted up the main stay. This sail, however, was not often rigged and if I were rigging a model I would not worry about rigging a staysail on the main mast. However, for the record, up to 1745, the upper end of the stay was seized round the main stay, just below the mouse; the lower end was secured with hearts or deadeyes and a lanyard to the fore mast, the staysail stay running in a line with the main stay. After 1745 and up to 1810, the upper end of the stay was clinched round the main mast head above the rigging; the lower end of the stay was taken through the collar of the main stay, and was set up with thimbles and a lanyard to the fore mast, running as before in a line with the main stay. The dates given here are conjectural but should be approximately correct.

The main staysail halliards, up to 1745, were rigged in the same way as the fore topmast staysail halliards. After 1745, the standing part of the halliards was seized to the main mast head; the hauling part was rove through the block on the sail, up through a block, seized to

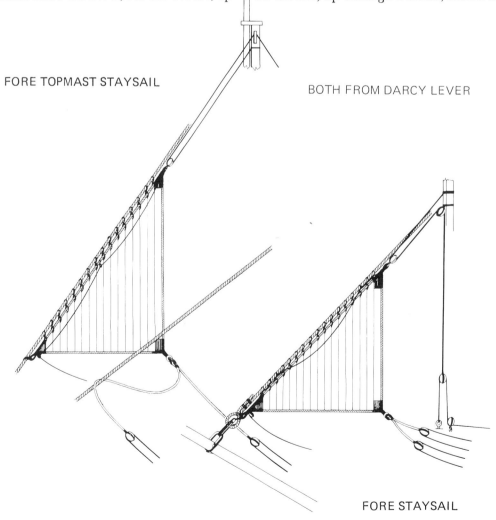

FORE TOPMAST STAYSAIL

BOTH FROM DARCY LEVER

FORE STAYSAIL

the rigging under the main top on the starboard side, and a double block was seized in the end; this block connected by a fall to a single block, hooked to an eyebolt in the deck, close to the side just abaft the main mast; the fall was belayed in the rail by the main shrouds. After 1815, the standing part was seized to an eyebolt under the port trestletree; the running part rove through the block on the sail, through a block seized to an eyebolt under the starboard trestletree, and was then taken directly to the pin rail by the main shrouds.

Sheets were rigged as those of the fore topmast staysail; the standing and running part of the whip was taken to timber heads at the fore part of the quarterdeck, or to the bulwarks just abaft of the main mast.

The tack fastened round the foot of the fore mast or to an eyebolt in the deck by the mast, since this staysail was only three sided.

The downhauler was rigged the same as that on the fore topmast staysail; no lead block was required, however, the downhauler being belayed to the bitts abaft the fore mast.

Gaskets were rigged as on the fore staysail.

RIGGING OF THE MIZEN STAYSAIL

A staysail must have been impossible to set together with a lateen mizen sail, but as engravings and paintings of ships do show a staysail furled on the stay, I conclude that sometimes the staysail was used when the lateen was brailed up. Of course, when the mizen sail was laced to the mast no trouble arose in setting the staysail, the brails and so on being no longer in the way. To set the staysail, a special staysail stay was required; this staysail stay was used until about 1810, when the staysail was carried on the mizen stay or, if one was rigged, on the preventer stay. On small ships, the staysail was carried on the mizen stay earlier than 1810—perhaps as early as 1745, though this date is conjectural.

The staysail stay had its upper end clinched round the mizen mast head, and the lower end rove through a thimble strapped round the main mast, after side, and half the distance between the main deck and the underneath of the trestletrees. The stay had a thimble spliced in the end, and was set up with a lanyard to an eyebolt abaft the mast.

The halliard was usually double, with a block on the head of the sail. The standing part of the halliard was seized to the head of the mast; the running part rove through the block on the sail, up through a block strapped to the port mizen trestletree, on the fore side of the mast, or to a block strapped to the port side of the mizen mast head and was taken down to the rails by the mizen shrouds, or alternatively hitched to the mizen stay collar. The lead block at the mast head was mainly used when the sail was carried from the staysail stay.

The sheets consisted of one length of rope, bent to the sail to form a long and short leg; a block or thimble was spliced into the end of the short leg; the long leg rove through a block seized to an eyebolt in the deck at the side or in the bulwarks, was then rove through the block or thimble in the short leg, and made fast to a cleat by the block on the deck. There was a block each side of the deck so that when the sheets were required to be rigged on the other side of the ship it was not necessary to move the block.

Tacks Between 1760 and 1840, the staysail had four sides, and consequently required two tacks: the upper one secured the forward upper corner of the sail to the thimble strapping of the staysail stay, or the equivalent on the mizen stay or preventer stay, whichever the staysail was on; the lower tack was made fast to an eyebolt in the deck at the foot of the main mast. When the sail was triangular—up to 1760 and after 1840—the tack made fast to the eyebolt in the deck, or round the main mast by the deck, as after 1840. Before 1760 the tack was made fast as described for the upper tack between 1760 and 1840.

The downhauler was made fast to the head of the sail, rove through a few hanks half way down the sail, through a block seized to the stay by the tack, and was made fast to the bitts abaft the main mast.

MAIN STAYSAIL FROM DARCY LEVER

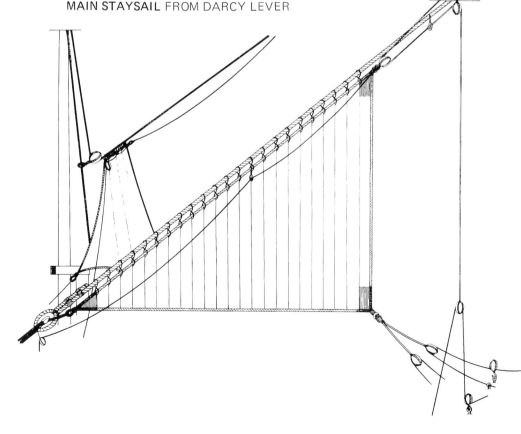

MIZEN STAYSAIL FROM DARCY LEVER

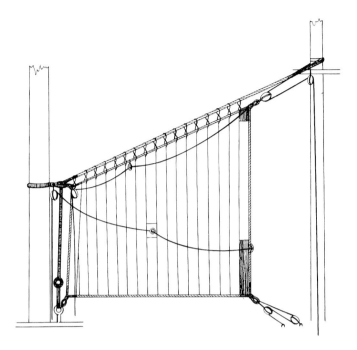

Brails were used only when the sail was four sided, the brails coming on both sides of the sail; the centre of the brail was seized to the leech. In the centre of the sail, a thimble was set into a patch on both sides of the sail, or a small piece of rope with a thimble in each end was put through the sail, thus forming a lizard on either side of the sail in the centre. The brail rove through these thimbles, through two single blocks, lashed on either side of the sail by the upper tack, or through one double block strapped to the collar on the main mast, and were made fast to the bitts.

Gaskets were rigged as on the fore staysail.

RIGGING TO THE FORE TOPMAST STAYSAIL

Staysail stay (1660 to 1815) The topmast staysail was introduced in about 1660 and an additional stay was required for carrying it because of the rigging and lead blocks seized to the fore topmast stay. This additional stay became known as the fore topmast staysail stay; it was seized to the fore topmast stay, two thirds up the stay,

and was made fast with either dead-eyes or hearts to the bowsprit, just a little way down from the topmast stay. When a fore topmast preventer stay was introduced, the staysail stay was no longer required, the sail being carried on the preventer stay. There was a period, however, when the stay-sail stay was again used—from about 1745 to 1815. The staysail stay was then secured round the bowsprit with a running eye, between the bees and spritsail yard truss; the upper end rove through the upper sheave of a cheek block, bolted to the port side of the topmast head, and led down; a double block was spliced into the end; this double block connected up with a single block, seized to the after part of the port lower trestletree, the end running down to deck and fastening to the bitts. After 1815 the staysail was once more carried on the fore topmast preventer stay.

Halliard When the staysail stay was carried, a single block was seized to the topmast stay, just above the upper part of the staysail stay. Another small block was seized to the head of the sail. The halliard rove between these

two blocks, the standing part being made fast to the upper block; the running part led straight down to deck. After the introduction of the topmast preventer stay, the upper block was seized to the preventer stay in the same position as when on the topmast stay. Before 1719, however, the upper block was secured by a pendant from the topmast head, the pendant coming on the fore side of the foremost cross-tree with the block hanging just below the crosstree on the port side of the mast. Though large ships still carried a block on the head of the staysail, the medium and small ships had the halliard made fast directly to the sail, and rove through the pendant block down to deck. When the sail was fitted with a block, the standing part of the halliard was seized to the fore topmast stay collar, on the starboard side; the running part rove through the block at the head of the sail, up through a pendant block, and was taken to deck. After 1745, instead of a block from a pendant, the halliard rove through the lower sheave of a cheek block, bolted to the port side of the topmast head, and so to deck. After 1815, instead of the cheek block, a block was seized to an eyebolt in the port trestletree, or under the top on the port side, the halliard reeving as before. After 1805, all ships had the halliard fastened directly to the peak of the sail and none carried a block on the sail.

Sheets At all times pendants were doubled, and consisted of a single block spliced into each end of a piece of rope; the bight of the rope rove through the clue, and the ends were taken through the bight, thus forming a bend in the clue. A whip rove through a block in each end, one to port, one to starboard; the standing part of the whip was made fast to an eyebolt by the cathead, or to a timber head close to the cathead; the standing part was taken in on the forecastle, either directly to the pin rail, or through a lead block by the forecastle deck, thence to the rail. Before pin rails came into general use, whips were hitched to a timber head near the fore shrouds.

The tack was spliced into the tack cringle, and consisted solely of a length

II RIGGING
Rigging of the main topmast staysail

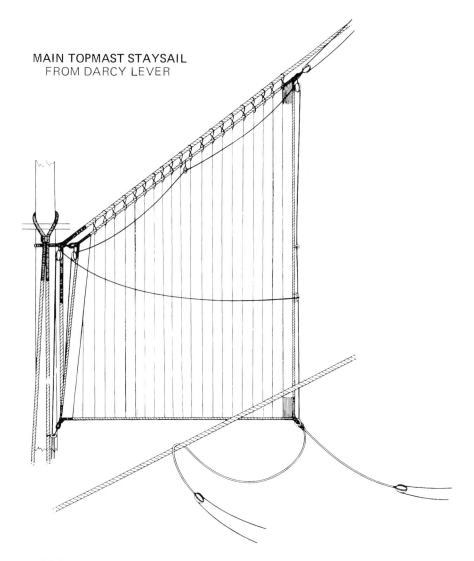

MAIN TOPMAST STAYSAIL
FROM DARCY LEVER

block on the stay, and down to deck. When the staysail was carried on the main topmast preventer stay, the halliard was single, one end clinched to the head of the sail; the running part rove through the upper sheave of a cheek block at the main topmast head, on the starboard side, and was taken down and belayed to a pin on the fife rail abaft the main mast. From 1773 to 1815, the halliards were double, the standing part being seized round the main topmast head, the running part reeving through a block on the sail, up through the cheek block and so to deck. After 1815, a block was seized to an eyebolt in the starboard trestletree, as for the fore topmast staysail; this block took the place of the cheek block, the halliard reeving as before.

Sheets and pendants were double as on the fore topmast staysail. The whips rove through the blocks in the end, and one end of the whip was made fast to an eyebolt in the boat skid on the deck at the side, just forward of the main mast; the running part was made fast either to the boat skid or to a cleat close to the standing part.

Tacks Up to about 1760, the sail was three sided and only one tack was required. After that date the sail was four sided and two tacks were needed, one on the upper and one on the lower cringle of the fore side. The tack on the three sided sail, and the upper tack of the four sided sail, was a single rope, spliced into the cringle and made fast to the foot of the stay. The lower tacks on the four sided sail were double, fastened to the lower cringle by reeving the bight through the cringle, and reeving the ends through the bight; one of the ends was taken to port, the other to starboard, and they rove through blocks seized under the shrouds a few feet above the deadeye—usually to the second shroud—and were made fast to the pin rail by the shrouds, or to a cleat secured to the shrouds.

The downhauler was secured to the head of the sail when the sail was three sided, taken through a few hanks half way down the sail, through a block seized to the stay deadeyes or preventer stay lead block strop and was taken down to deck.

of rope which rove from the cringle to the lower deadeye of the fore topmast preventer stay, or staysail stay or, when the stays rove through the bees, was taken round the bowsprit.

The downhauler was hitched to the head of the sail, was taken through a few hanks, rove through a block seized to the foot of the stay and led in to the forecastle.

A netting was required to keep the topmast staysail clear of the bowsprit when furled. Two stretchers, with a hole in each end, were secured to the bowsprit horses by reeving the horses through the holes, a net was then formed between the stretchers and the horses; the length of the net was sufficient to take the sail when tightly furled.

Gaskets were rigged as on the fore staysail.

RIGGING OF THE MAIN TOPMAST STAYSAIL
The staysail stay was an additional stay required to hoist the staysail on, before the introduction of the preventer stay: the staysail stay was seized about a quarter of the way down the main topmast stay and was set up with deadeyes and a lanyard to the after part of the collar of the fore stay.

Halliard When a staysail stay was carried, a block was seized to the main topmast stay just above the end of the staysail stay. The standing part of the halliard was spliced into the strop of this block, rove through a block on the peak of the sail, up through the

MIDDLE STAYSAIL   MIZEN TOPMAST STAYSAIL

BOTH FROM DARCY LEVER

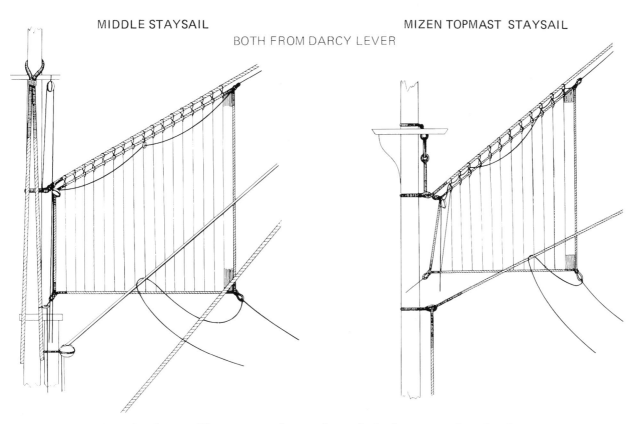

The brails also served as a downhauler. The brails came either side of the sail, and were only used on the four sided sail; the centre of the brail was seized to the cringle about half way down the leech, the brail reeving through the cringle; the ends came forward, through blocks seized to the topmast preventer stay at the lower end, and up to 1805 rove through blocks siezed to the strop of the main bowline block, and made fast to the bitts. After 1805, brails rove straight from the blocks on the topmast preventer stay to the pin rail by the shrouds.

Gaskets were rigged as on the fore staysail.

RIGGING OF THE MIDDLE STAYSAIL

The middle staysail was introduced in about 1773 and was carried on a special stay (the middle staysail stay) between the main topmast staysail and the main topgallant staysail. The lower end was seized to a thimble in a grommet or strop round the fore topmast under the fore topsail parrel; this grommet or strop was loose enough to slide up and down the fore topmast.

The upper end rove through the lower sheave of a cheek block on the port side of the main topmast head, and a double block was seized in the end, a fall was rove between this block and a single block lashed to the main trestletree. The hauling part was made fast on deck. By an Admiralty Order of December 1815, middle staysails were no longer issued to HM ships.

The halliard was always single and rove through the upper sheave of the port cheek block at the main topmast head, the end leading straight to deck.

Sheets were rigged double and had no whips; they led straight to a block on the gunwale by the gangway, thence either to a cleat on the boat skid or to a pin in the pin rail.

Tacks Being a four sided sail two tacks were required; the upper one was secured to the thimble by which the lower part of the stay was made fast; the lower tack was double as on the main topmast staysail, and rove through thimbles on the fore topmast shrouds, just above the upper deadeyes and was made fast in the top.

The downhauler A single block was seized to the stay by the tack; the

downhauler was made fast to the head of the sail, was taken through a few hanks half way down the sail, rove through the block at the tack and led down to deck.

The tricing line was clinched to the grommet or thimble around the mast and rove through a block, strapped under the port fore topmast crosstree close to the trestletree, and was taken down and made fast in the top.

No brails were required on the middle staysail.

Gaskets were rigged as on the fore staysail.

RIGGING OF THE MIZEN TOPMAST STAYSAIL

The staysail halliard was always single; the end bent to the sail and rove through a block strapped to the starboard side of the mizen topmast head (or through a hole in the mast just above the rigging when no topgallant masts were carried), thence down to deck. The staysail was secured by hanks to the mizen topmast stay. By Admiralty Order of December 1815, this sail was no longer issued to HM ships.

II RIGGING
Rigging to the main topgallant staysail

MAIN TOPGALLANT STAYSAIL

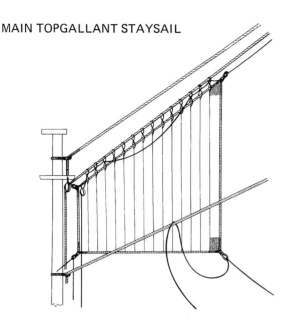

MIZEN TOPGALLANT STAYSAIL

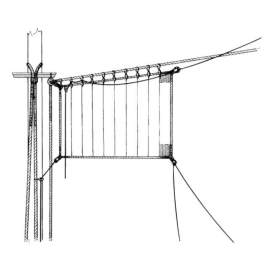

BOTH FROM DARCY LEVER

Sheets were rove double, like the sheets of the middle staysail, and the ends rove through thimbles seized to the forward mizen shrouds below the crossjack yard and were taken down to the rails by the mizen shrouds.
Tacks From 1760, when the sail was four sided, the upper tack was secured to the collar round the main mast where the mizen topmast stay was made fast; the lower tack was rove double like those on the middle staysail, and the ends taken through thimbles, seized inboard on the second shroud of the main shrouds about half way up the shrouds; they were then taken to the pin rail by the main shrouds. Before 1760, the sail was three sided and the tack was rove like the upper tack.
The downhauler was made fast to the head of the sail and rove through a few hanks half way down the sail, through a block seized by the tack, thence down to deck.
Gaskets were rigged as on the fore staysail.

RIGGING TO THE MAIN TOPGALLANT STAYSAIL
The staysail stay, up to 1810, had the upper end spliced into the main topgallant stay close to the collar; the

lower end rove through a thimble or block strapped either to the after port crosstree of the fore topmast close to the trestletree, or to the fore topmast head close above the crosstree, and was made fast in the top. After 1810, the upper end of the stay was spliced round the main topgallant mast head; the lower end rove as before. When the sail was furled the stay was slackened off and the sail made up in the fore top. Consequently the stay must be long enough to allow the bight of the stay to reach the top.
The halliard was always single and rove from the sail through a sheave hole in the main topgallant mast head just above the hounds and was made fast to the bitts abaft the main mast.
Sheets and tacks were rove in a similar fashion to those on the middle staysail, with the tack thimbles just abaft those of the middle staysail. This sail was three sided up to about 1760; after then, until about 1810, it was four sided; from 1810 onwards, it reverted to being a three sided sail. The sheets led directly to the pin rails.
The downhauler rove from the head of the sail, through a block seized to the strapping of the thimble through which the stay rove, and was made

fast abaft the fore mast.
Gaskets were rigged as on the fore staysail.

RIGGING OF THE MIZEN TOPGALLANT STAYSAIL
The halliards were single, bent to the peak of the sail and rove through a hole above the rigging on the mizen topgallant mast head, or through a block seized in the same position. The halliard was taken down to deck and belayed to the pin rail aft on the port side. The staysail was carried on the topgallant stay.
Sheets were rove double, the ends reeving through thimbles, seized to the foremost mizen shrouds by the futtock stave, and belaying to the pin rail by the shrouds; alternatively they were taken directly to the pin rails.
Tacks were made fast in a similar fashion to the mizen topmast staysail; the lower tacks rove through thimbles, seized well up to the second main topmast shrouds, inboard side; the tacks were made fast in the main top. This sail was only in use between about 1802 and 1815.
The downhauler rove as that on the mizen topmast staysail, and was made fast in the main top.

Gaskets were rigged as on the fore staysail.

A main royal staysail was carried on the royal stay, when this latter was fitted to the main mast. The staysail was rigged in a similar manner to the topgallant staysail, the halliard reeving through a hole above the royal rigging, and being taken down to deck. The downhauler made fast in the fore top, and the sheets were taken through lead blocks just abaft the topgallant staysail sheet lead blocks. This sail was not used on all ships: usually only the largest ships carried them. When first introduced, the sail was four sided, and the lower tacks made fast in the fore top, via lead blocks on the topgallant shrouds. After about 1805 the sail became three sided.

RIGGING TO THE JIB
The jib was introduced in about 1705 and was carried in two ways; set flying—that is, without a stay, the head of the sail being supported only by the halliard (this method was used when the sail was first carried, and in a few ships during the last quarter of the eighteenth century); the other way was to fit a stay called the jibstay, the sail being hoisted by the halliards up this stay and secured to it by hanks. About 1719 saw this stay introduced, the lower end being seized to a thimble on the traveller (for a description of this traveller see the chapter devoted to furnishings of masts and yards). Up to about 1745, the upper end of the stay rove through a block stropped to the topmast cap on the starboard side; it was then led down to the stool abaft the fore channels, where on small ships it was hitched round a deadeye or, as on larger ships, secured by means of a fall taken to the stools; the falls consisted of two single blocks, the lower one stropped to a deadeye on the stool; the deadeyes mentioned are those holding the backstay down. After 1745, the stay was rove the same way but, instead of a block at the cap, a cheek block was **bolted** to the topmast head, the stay reeving through the upper sheave in the cheek block. In about 1815, the stay was secured at the topmast head with a long eye-splice; the lower end, instead of going

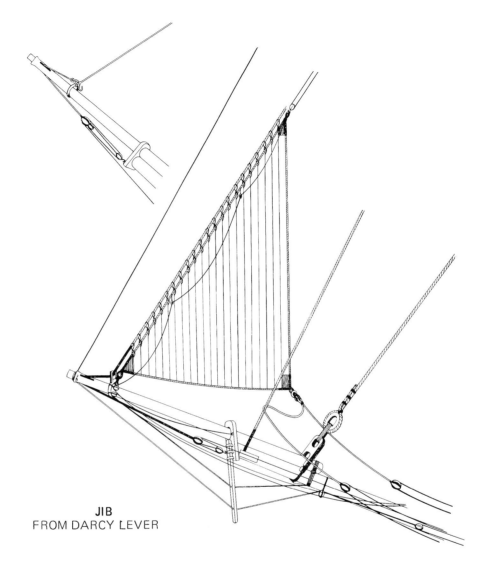

JIB
FROM DARCY LEVER

to a traveller, was rove through a sheave in the jibboom end, rove through a hole in the upper part of the martingale, and was made fast to an eyebolt in the bows close to the bowsprit, by means of two single blocks which formed a tackle on the starboard side; the hauling part of the tackle made fast on the forecastle. After 1850, the lower end was spliced round the jibboom end; the upper end rove through a block, bolted to an eyebolt under the starboard trestletree of the topmast and was set up by a tackle to the fore starboard channels.

Halliards When the jib was set flying, a block was seized to its head; another block was strapped to the topmast head on the starboard side.

The standing part was seized round the topmast head on the port side, rove through the block on the sail, up to the block on the mast head and down to deck. After 1719, a block was stropped to the topmast cap on the starboard side and the halliard was seized round the topmast head on the port side, rove through a block at the head of the sail, up through the block of the cap and taken to deck; on small ships the block on the sail was dispensed with and the end of the halliard was seized to the sail, taken up through the block on the cap and down to deck. After 1765 the halliard was single on all ships, and instead of a block on the cap, the halliard rove through the lower sheave of the cheek block on

125

Rigging of the flying jibsail

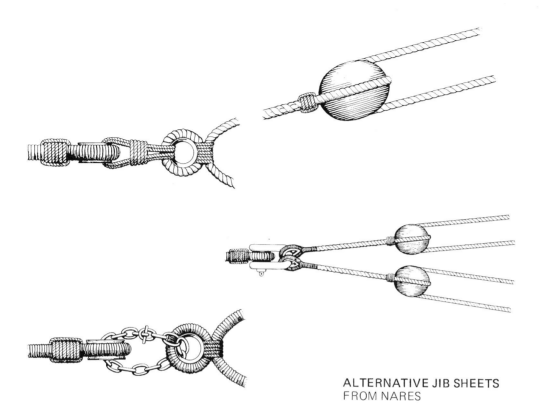

ALTERNATIVE JIB SHEETS
FROM NARES

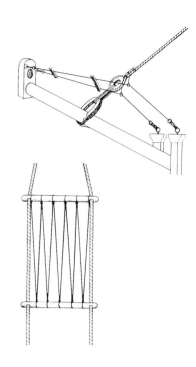

BOWSPRIT NETTING
FOR THE FORE TOPMAST
STAYSAIL

the starboard side of the topmast head, and was taken down to deck. After 1815, a block was seized to an eyebolt under the upper starboard trestletree; the halliard rove through this block down to deck. Sometimes when the jib was set flying–from 1705 to 1719, on some small ships up to 1733, and though not the general rule, on some ships between 1760 and 1790–halliards were rove double, both ends coming down to deck. A block was stropped either side of the topmast head, the halliards reeving from the deck on one side, up through one block, through the block on the sail, up through the other block, and down to deck on the other side. Between 1745 and 1815, cheek blocks instead of ordinary blocks were bolted to the topmast head, in which case the topmast staysail stay rove through the lower sheave of the port cheek block; the halliard of this sail rove through the lower sheave of the starboard cheek block, and the jib halliards rove through the upper sheave of the cheek blocks.

A **downhauler** was required when the sail was carried on a jibstay, and was rove in a similar fashion to that on the topmast staysail, the lead block being seized to the traveller; the downhauler, after reeving through this block, was taken to the forecastle head via the gammon lashing lead block when carried, or straight to the forecastle when a gammon block was not carried. When a traveller was not fitted, the lead block was seized to the foot of the jibstay. The downhauler also acted as an inhauler when a traveller was used.

The outhauler was seized to the shackle of the traveller, was rove through a sheave in the end of the jibboom and from there was taken towards the bows. A single block was seized into the end, which set up with a fall to another block, seized or hooked to an eyebolt in the bows, close alongside the bowsprit on the port side. On small ships a tackle was dispensed with and the outhauler taken straight to the forecastle, but when a tackle was used the hauling part was taken in on the forecastle.

Sheets were fitted in exactly the same way as the staysail sheets and were taken to the forecastle adjacent to and just inboard of the staysail sheets.

The tack cringle, when a traveller was fitted, was put over the hook on the traveller. When no traveller was carried, the tack was rigged as that on the staysail and was made fast round the jibboom, close to the foot of the jibstay.

Gaskets were rigged as on the fore staysail.

RIGGING OF THE FLYING JIB

Flying jibs were used when flying jibbooms were introduced. They were secured to the flying jibstay with hanks; usually the flying jibstay rove through a sheave in the flying jibboom end, and was made fast on the forecastle via a sheave in the dolphin striker. On a few ships the stay was rove through a roller or block on a traveller on the flying jibboom, prior to reeving through the flying jibboom sheave. Another method was to take the stay through a block on the traveller and then lead it to the forecastle; the traveller would have an outhauler reeving through the sheave in the flying jibboom.

Halliards were single, being made fast to the head of the sail; they were

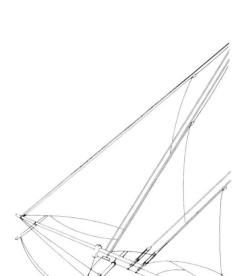

BOWSPRIT
FROM DARCY LEVER

taken through a block stropped to the topgallant mast head on the port side and taken down to deck. On some ships a sheave was let into the topgallant mast pole, just above the rigging stop, instead of the block at the topgallant head.

The downhauler rove from the head of the sail, through a few hanks, through a block seized either to the topgallant stay by the flying jibboom, or seized to the traveller, and was taken straight to the forecastle. This downhauler also acted as an inhauler for the traveller.

Sheets were double, the bight being rove through the clue and the ends taken through the bight; they were then taken straight to the forecastle without having whips on them.

Tacks were rigged in the same way as the jib, but to the flying jibboom instead of to the jibboom.

Gaskets were rigged as on the fore staysail.

15 Miscellaneous ropes

Rope jackstays A piece of rope, the length of the yard, was eye-spliced at each end to fit the yard arms. The rope was then cut in the middle and rove through eyebolts along the yard. Thimbles were spliced into the centre ends, and the jackstays set up with a lanyard through the thimbles.

Bunt gaskets There was an optional ornamental harbour fitting, consisting of a triangular piece of rope with a diamond netting worked inside it. One side of the triangle was long enough to stretch between the two quarter blocks. The two other sides met to form the apex of the triangle, which was large enough to support the sail. In each corner a thimble was seized. The gasket was seized to the jackstay under the sail. The apex thimble had a piece of long sennet middled and seized to it. The gasket was then put round the bunt of the sail, and the two ends of the sennet taken round the mast, thus bowsing the sail well in to the mast.

Bonnet and drabler lacings The method of lacing the bonnets to the courses was exactly the same as the method of lacing the drablers to the bonnets, therefore the following applies to both sails: at the head of the sail and sewn to the sail and bolt rope was a rope called a latchet, which was sewn so that it formed loops. These loops rove through holes in the foot of the sail above, so that each loop was put through a hole and then through the bight of the previous loop, thus forming a chain. I should imagine that the latchets were put on from the centre, working outwards towards the clues. The last loops were hitched to the ends of the latchet rope. The earing cringles of the bonnet or drabler were also lashed to the clues of the sail above. The sheets and tacks from the courses would be moved to the bonnet or drabler clues.

Cat falls were used for catting the anchor. The fall of the tackle was rove, running from a treble hooked block, called a cat block, and through the sheaves in the end of the cathead. The standing part of the fall was clenched to an eyebolt under the cathead, and

BUNT GASKET
LACED TO THE
JACKSTAY

JACKSTAY

II RIGGING
The back rope

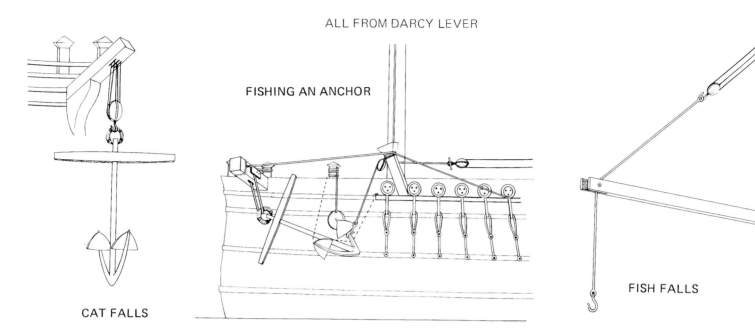

ALL FROM DARCY LEVER

FISHING AN ANCHOR

CAT FALLS

FISH FALLS

the hauling part led in on to the fore-castle from the cathead, generally to a cleat bolted to the inboard end of it, or sometimes to a timber head close by. On some small ships the cat block had only two sheaves, as did the cat-head. The fall, however, led as above. Prior to 1719, most ships had double blocks; after 1719, only Sixth Rates had double blocks.

The back rope or cat-back was a piece of rope, one end of which had another piece spliced in, making a fork. These forked ends were spliced round thimbles stapled to each cheek of the cat block; the other end was taken to the forecastle and was used to assist in hooking the cat block into the ring of the anchor when catting it. Another rope was secured to the back of the hook and was led inboard. It also assisted when catting. All cat ropes were sometimes led through lead blocks on the bows or the head.

The cathead stopper was spliced to an eyebolt in the cathead. The other end was taken through the ring of the anchor and made fast inboard when the anchor was at the cathead. It was wormed and parcelled all over with a smaller rope bent to the end to assist in bringing the stopper inboard. In the latter years of sail it was made of chain and was shackled on.

The shank painter comprised a length

of chain with a rope tail spliced in one end. The chain was lashed through the end link to an eyebolt in the side, or in the fore end of the fore channel. The end with the tail was taken round the inside arm and shank of the anchor and brought up and hitched to a tim-ber head on the forecastle. It was used for securing the shank, as the stopper does the stock.

Fish pendant tackle and guys Up to about 1773, the fish davit was carried across the forecastle, the inner end held down by a square shackle called the span shackle. To the outer end of the davit a large single block was secured, stropped on with a double strop. Through this block rove the fish pendant. One end of this pendant was spliced round a long-tackle block. The other end had a large hook, the fish hook, spliced on. The tackle rove between the block on the pendant and a single hook block, which was hooked to an eyebolt in the main chains when required. Some ships had no tackle, the pendant being taken to the cap-stan via a lead block in the main chains. After 1773, the fish davit was much shorter and was secured in position on the fore channels by a shoe; ; an eyebolt was fitted to the upper side on the outer end and another one on each side on the outer end. The upper one was for a topping lift, the

others for a fore and aft guy respec-tively. Sometimes the upper eye was dispensed with and the topping lift spliced round the davit head. In the inboard end of the topping lift a thimble was spliced and, when the davit was topped, (generally this was done with a deck tackle) the topping lift was seized round the fore mast head. Sometimes no thimble was put in the end, and the topping lift was hitched round the fore mast head. The outer end of the topping lift was either spliced round a thimble, set on the upper eyebolt in the davit, or spliced round the davit. The fore and after guys were spliced to thimbles in the eyebolts on the davit. The fore guy was hitched to the cathead, the after guy to the after end of the fore chan-nels. Up to about 1840 the fish pen-dant and tackle were the same as prior to 1773. After 1840, a double and single block were stropped to the davit head, and a double hook block was used in the end of the fish tackle. No pendant was used. The standing part of the fall was secured to the lower block, and after reeving through both double blocks, the hauling part was taken through the single block from forward to aft through a lead block by the gangway, thence inboard. The fore and after guys were spliced round the neck of the davit.

The fish back was a rope secured to the back of the fish hook and was led up on the forecastle. It assisted in fishing the anchor.

Anchor cables were clinched to the ring of the anchor up to about 1850 when the method of splicing the cable to a shackle and shackling onto the ring was introduced. The cable, when at sea, was often unrove from the anchor and secured along the deck with ring stoppers. The inboard end of the cable was clinched to beams in the cable locker and the cable flaked down. To clinch to the ring, the end was taken through the ring, brought over the part leading through round the cable and seized to itself, thus forming a noose round its own part. Three seizings were put on. An inside clinch was usually used, though an outside clinch was sometimes fitted.

The cable messenger was of such a length as to go round the capstan and through the viol block, forward and back to the capstan. The two ends had an eye spliced into them and were set up together with a lanyard. This formed a continuous rope, used for bringing up the cable (see notes on viol block).

The swifter was a length of rope with an eye spliced into one end. The other end was hitched in turn to the end of each capstan bar. Finally, the end rove through the eye and was hitched and seized to its own part. The capstan bars, by using a swifter, were held tightly to the capstan. Some ships had holes in the end of the capstan bars to reeve the swifter through, the ends being secured together as before.

Nippers were small pieces of rope used to hold the cable and messenger together when bringing up the anchor. They were held on by hand and removed just before they reached the capstan.

Hook ropes were ropes with a hook spliced into one end and were used for flaking down the cable in the cable locker.

Deck stoppers were spliced or hooked to ringbolts along the deck and had a knot and a tail formed on the end. They were used to secure the anchor cable along the deck. Ring stoppers were spliced into the ringbolts along the deck to check the cables. Bitt

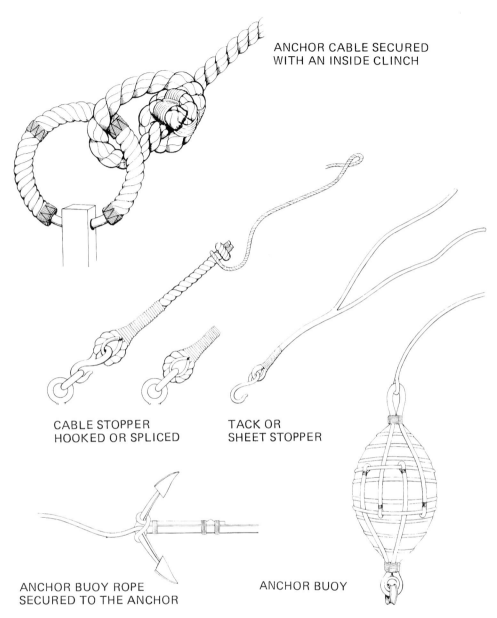

ANCHOR CABLE SECURED
WITH AN INSIDE CLINCH

CABLE STOPPER
HOOKED OR SPLICED

TACK OR
SHEET STOPPER

ANCHOR BUOY ROPE
SECURED TO THE ANCHOR

ANCHOR BUOY

stoppers were spliced round the fore bitts to hold the cable when taking it round the bitts. Tack and sheet stoppers were used to stopper the tacks or sheets before belaying them, and were fitted with hooks to be used wherever necessary. Various other stoppers were used as temporary measures, such as mooring up, and so forth. The stoppers for use on the cable had a wall knot in the end with a small lanyard spliced round just below the knot. The other stoppers were ropes with the ends plaited, or sometimes halved, to form a fork. They were about 2 fathoms long.

Anchor buoy rope's length depended on the depth of the water expected to

anchor in. One end of the rope had a buoy knot worked in it; this end was clove-hitched round the crown of the anchor, one half-hitch being on each side of the crown. A seizing was put on close to the crown, one close to the knot and one on the end, the end being laid up the shank. The other end was spliced into a thimble on the buoy.

Anchor buoy slings were made of a piece of rope nine times the length of the buoy. From this piece, two pieces were cut off to form two hoops to go tightly round the buoy, just on either side of its widest part. The remaining rope was cut into four pieces: each piece had an eye spliced into each end;

they were then wormed, parcelled and served. Two of these pieces made the slings for the upper part of the buoy and the other two for the lower slings. Through the eyes of the upper slings the rope to make one hoop was rove; the ends, after reeving through, were spliced together to form the hoop – this hoop was the one to fit round the lower part of the buoy. Through the eyes in the lower slings rove the upper hoop rope. The upper slings were taken under the upper hoop before reeving through the lower hoop and the lower hoop was taken over the lower slings before being spliced together. The bights of the slings were seized together with a round seizing. In the lower bight, a thimble was seized to take the buoy rope. The upper bight was left without a thimble and a lanyard spliced into it for securing the buoy when the anchor was up. The buoys, when inboard, were lashed to the foremost fore shroud with this lanyard.

Rudder pendants Chains were shackled to eyes in the rudder, coming up each side of the rudder to under the transom. To the end of the chains large rings were fitted and into these rings were hooked the rudder pendants. These pendants had a thimble in each end with the hooks set round the thimbles. The hooks were moused. The pendants were seized to eyes or hooks set under the transom – one by the side of the rudder post, one half way along, and one under the quarter gallery. The end of the pendants were seized to the after end of the mizen channels. When required, a long tackle was hooked in the ends. The fall hooked to an eyebolt in the mizen chains and led in through a port.

Tiller ropes had between five and seven turns taken round the wheel barrel. The centre of the tiller rope was nailed to the barrel. Each end rove through holes in the deck under the barrel, through sheaves under the holes, through sheaves in the side of the ship, back through eyes in a hoop on each side of the tiller end and were made fast by having a thimble spliced into the ends, which were set up by lanyards to eyebolts a little down the tiller. Other methods were used accord-

ing to the size of the ship, but so long as the ropes lead down, then to the side, and back to the tiller, there should be no difficulty in rigging them. Cowhide ropes were used after 1815.

Quarter davit gear Boats were carried on the quarters from davits fitted by the mizen shrouds from about 1810. The guys and span up to about 1830 were made of rope. The span had a thimble spliced into each end and was set up by lanyards to eyebolts in the head of the davits. The guys had similar thimbles spliced into each end, set up with lanyards to eyebolts in the side of each davit: the forward guy was set up by lanyard and thimble to an eyebolt in the side forward of the mizen channels, the after guy set up in a similar manner to an eyebolt aft of the channels. The topping lift, up to 1830, also of rope, was set up to eyebolts on top of the davits. A rope was lashed to an eyebolt in a hoop, half way between the deck and top of the mizen mast; the outer end of the rope had another rope spliced into it, thus forming a fork. The ends of the fork were secured to the davits. After 1830, chain took the place of rope for the guys, span and topping lift. The guys and span were fitted as before, being either set up with lanyards or shackles. The topping lift was made of two chains, one from each davit, and these were set up to a pair of eyebolts on the hoop round the mizen mast. The falls rove through a single hook block and two sheaves in each davit, the standing part of the fall made fast to the lower block, the hauling parts made fast to cleats inside the bulwarks by each davit. Two man-ropes, each long enough to reach the water, were seized to the span by each davit, and in each rope overhand knots were worked, spaced about 2 feet apart.

Stern davit gear The falls were similar to those on the quarter davits. Spans and man-ropes were sometimes fitted in a similar way to those of the quarter davits.

Breech ropes were clinched to the large ringbolts on either side of the gunport, and taken round the cascabel of the gun or, from about 1790 when the guns were made with an eye by the cascabel, through this eye. (When

first introduced, this eye was cast with the gun, and the breech rope had to be rove through it before being clinched. After about 1838 the ring could be opened to give access to the breech rope. When the cascabel had no eye it was sometimes the practice to form a cut-splice in the centre of the breech rope and slip the cascabel through this. This was especially so during the the last half of the eighteenth century.

Gunport tackles were small tackles required to open the port lids. A rope was hitched to the ring in the outside of the port lid and rove through a small hole in the ship's side. The end of the rope had a thimble spliced into it which enabled one end of a tackle consisting of two hook blocks to be hooked to it; the other end hooked to an eyebolt in the deck head.

Gun tackles usually three in number and consisting of double and single hook blocks, were required for each gun. One tackle, used for hauling the gun inboard and keeping it steady while being loaded, was hooked to an eyebolt in the centre of the after axle on the gun carriage and to a ringbolt in the deck behind the gun. The other two tackles were hooked to eyebolts in the side of the carriage and to eyebolts on either side of the gunport; they were used for hauling the gun out ready for firing.

Futtock staves were made of rope, wormed, parcelled and served. They were seized to the under side of the shrouds on all masts that carried futtock shrouds and were long enough to stretch from the first shroud to the last shroud. They were placed the same distance below the upper side of the trestletrees as the under side of the cap was above the trestletrees. The size of the rope was the same size as the futtock shrouds.

Rigging of the bumkin Up to 1773, only one shroud was used on each bumkin and this was eye-spliced round the end of the boom and hooked or seized to eyebolts in the stem. After 1773, an additional shroud was fitted, leading from the bumkin to an eyebolt above the cheeks of the head. After about 1805, yet another shroud was fitted, leading to an eyebolt in the bows underneath the bumkin. Some ships after about 1840 had chain shrouds instead of rope. When first used, the bumkin was also lashed down in the head to the main rail; this lashing was probably not used after the introduction of the second shroud. Thimbles, or deadeyes and lanyards were sometimes used for securing the shrouds to the end of the bumkin, especially during the latter part of the eighteenth century. For the first few years after the introduction of the bumkin no rigging was fitted except for the lashing to the headrail, the bumkins then being made with a downward curve.

The triatic stay was seized to the fore and main masts a few feet from deck; thimbles were seized in the stay and the lower blocks of the stay tackles were hooked into these thimbles when the tackles were not in use, thus keeping the tackles clear of the deck.

The timenoguy was a rope used to keep the sheet or tack of a course from fouling up when working the ship; it was secured to any convenient point and one would not expect to see a timenoguy rigged on a model.

The payaree was a rope rove through the clues of the fore course to guy the fore course out to the swinging boom when running before the wind; this again would not be usually seen on a model.

26 *Endeavour* model showing the fore topmast staysail netting.

27 Bowsprit and fore mast rigging of the *Medway,* 1742.

II RIGGING
Rigging on models

28 Gammon lashing block, main stay collar, and so on, of the *Breda*, 1692. Note the lead of the fore tack through the deadblock. (This block should fit between the headrails).

29 *Breda*, 1692. Sprit top-mast. Note the backstay crowsfeet.

II RIGGING
Rigging on models

II RIGGING

30 Details of the
Endeavour, 1768. Model
made in the National
Maritime Museum and
rigged by the author.

31 Details of the
Endeavour model.

II RIGGING
Rigging on models

32 Topsail halliard block of a 20 gun ship of about 1710. Note how the thimble runs on the backstay.

33 Close up of the main top and yard of the *Medway*, 1742.

34 *Endeavour* model. Mizen mast at the top.

35 *Breda*, 1692. Mizen topmast and mizen yard.

36 *Endeavour* model. Rigging at the main mast head.

37 *Endeavour* model. Main yard and top.

38 Contemporary model of about 1717. Detail of the mouse on the fore stay.

39 Main top of a 20 gun ship of about 1710.

40 Lower end of the fore topmast stay of a 20 gun ship of about 1710.

41 The main stay of the *Medway*, 1742, showing the stay tackles.

42 Main stay of a 20 gun ship of about 1710. Note the cable laid rope.

II RIGGING
Rigging on models

43 *Breda.* Main top from aft.

44 *Breda*, 1692. Main top from aft showing crowsfeet of mizen topmast stay.

45 *Breda*, 1692. Note the futtock shrouds.

46 *Breda*, 1692. Fore mast.

II RIGGING
Rigging on models

47 Plate from
Anthony Deane's
*Doctrine of Naval
Architecture,* 1670,
of a fifth rate ship.

48 Plate from
Sutherland's
*Shipbuilding
Unveiled.*

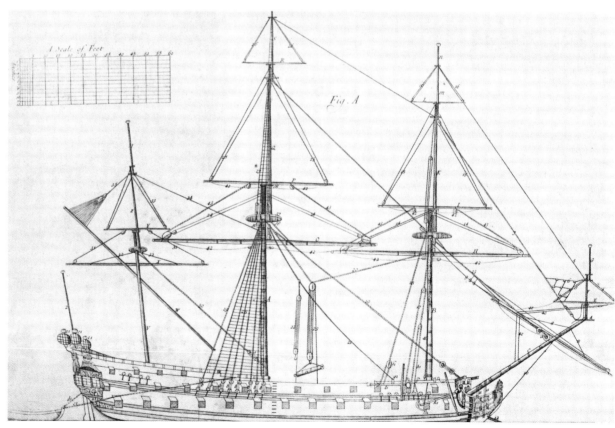

49 Rigging plan of the 1719 establishment. Note the lead of the main brace on this plan. The normal lead was aft, not to the foremast as shown here. This was either a draughtsman's error or possibly an idea put forward but not adopted.

II RIGGING
Rigging on models

50 HMS *Albion*, 1842. Lithograph by Dutton. Note the brails on the main trysail.

Sailmaking   III

III SAILMAKING
Width of the head

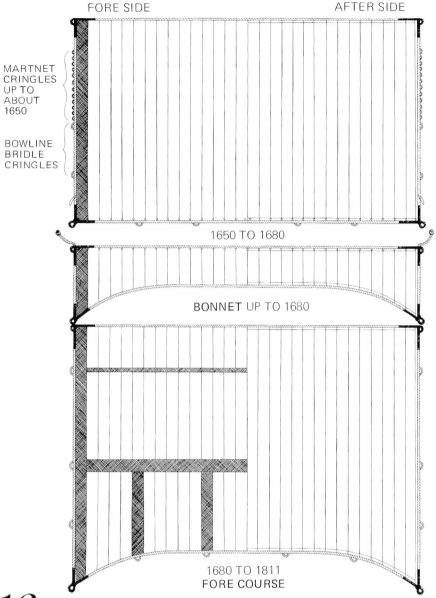

FORE SIDE   AFTER SIDE

MARTNET CRINGLES UP TO ABOUT 1650

BOWLINE BRIDLE CRINGLES

1650 TO 1680

BONNET UP TO 1680

1680 TO 1811
FORE COURSE

16 Square sails

NOTE: ALL SQUARE SAIL DRAWINGS SHOW THE FORE SIDE ON THE LEFT AND THE AFTER SIDE ON THE RIGHT OF THE CENTRE LINE

Although books are available describing the methods of sailmaking in the late eighteenth and nineteenth centuries, very little information is available for earlier periods. The only source of information is from paintings and drawings, but unfortunately the artists show only such obvious things as reef bands and entirely omit other cloths that must have been sewn on the sails.

The following notes are based upon sails from about 1794, Steel's book on sailmaking being the earliest work on the subject. However it is possible to give the position of reef bands, buntlines and so on and I recommend that one should look at sailmaking for the earlier periods from a seaman's point of view, and ask oneself whether the sails would have required strengthening at various places as was the case in later years. Of course for small models it is usually sufficient to show only the seams and reef bands, but larger models would obviously require more

detail. If making sails for earlier periods I would certainly put on top linings and mast cloths, as these are the places on the sails that take most wear.

At the time of writing the earliest contemporary model with original sails at the National Maritime Museum is the *Tartar,* a 20 gun ship of 1734. There are only a few models fitted with sails in any case, which to my mind seems a great pity.

Now as regards the mainly conjectural dates I have given for the changes in the sails during the nineteenth century, one must remember that in a lot of cases the sailmaker had his own methods of making sails, probably passed down to him from his predecessors, and that even the Admiralty Orders regarding sails mention that such things as goring the seams are up to the discretion of the individual sailmaker. Apart from all this I think the reader will not err too greatly if he follows the dates I have given.

The following are the main points to note before attempting to make any sails:

Width of the head During all periods the head of the lower sails came to within 18 inches from the yard arm cleats, the main and fore topsails to within 18 inches, the mizen topsail to within 12 inches, all topgallants to within 6 inches and all royals to within 4 inches.

Width of the foot The topsails, topgallants and royals spread the width of the cleats of the yard below. The fore course was usually the same width at the foot as at the head, though it was sometimes the practice to have the foot narrower than the head by the width of two cloths. Up to the nineteenth century, the main course was wider at the foot by the width of two cloths, and in the nineteenth century, by the width of four cloths.

Depth of the sail at the leech With regard to topsails and above, the depth or hoist depended upon the length of the appropriate mast, the depth being the height of the mast from the heel to the hounds (or, in the case of the topgallant or royal masts, the rigging stop). The fore course was low enough to just clear the main stay. The main course was cut to just clear the boats in the waist. In referring to the depth of the courses I include the bonnets and drablers, carried as additions to the courses in the seventeenth century, for these sails were seamed and cut as if they were one sail, extra allowance on the measurement being made for the tabling of the bonnet and drabler. These were then cut off, so that by tabling the course, bonnet and drabler, the sailmaker finished up with three sails that were sure to fit each other. The proportions of the depth of the sails when bonnet and drabler were fitted were: the course nine thirteenths, the bonnet three thirteenths and the drabler one thirteenth.

A naval sailmaking order of 1845 gives the following positions for the hoist of the various yards: main and fore yards to be the equivalent of one tenth the length of the topmast below the hounds; topsail yards to be one half the length of the mast head below the hounds; topgallant yards to be one tenth the length of the topgallant mast below the hounds. The depth of the sails were to be: main course to come 7 feet from the deck; fore course on flush decked ships to come 3 feet from the forecastle, and on ships not flush decked to come 6 feet 6 inches from the deck; topsails to be the length of the topmasts minus the head; topgallants to be from the fid hole to the hounds plus one thirty-sixth of this length; royals to be the length of the royal mast. This method of arriving at the lengths seems to tie up very closely to lengths in previous periods and should be a good guide to follow.

Shape of the foot Many people think that all sails had a hollow foot, mainly due to impressions given in paintings and prints by artists; this, however, is erroneous. The courses certainly had a hollow foot, or roach, which was the technical term, the mizen topsail always had a roach, the rest of the topsails were straight footed up to 1802 as were the topgallants and royals up to that date. The depths of the roaches were: Fore course, the centre 3 feet higher than the clues. This curve started from the outer buntline cloths, the centre section being straight. The main course was only cut

like this after 1811; prior to that date the curve extended along the entire foot. From 1802 the roach of the fore and main topsails was about 1 foot 9 inches, curved along the whole foot. Up to 1802 the depth of the roach of the mizen topsail was 2 feet 3 inches; after then the roach was 3 feet. The topgallants on the main and fore roached between 3 and 4 feet, while

the mizen topgallant was roached about 5 feet 6 inches. The fore and main royals were roached 1 feet 6 inches, the mizen royal 2 feet. These depths of the roaches depended mainly upon the sail being able to clear the stays when the topsails were close reefed, consequently the above measurements are only a guide and not a hard and fast rule. Allowance also had

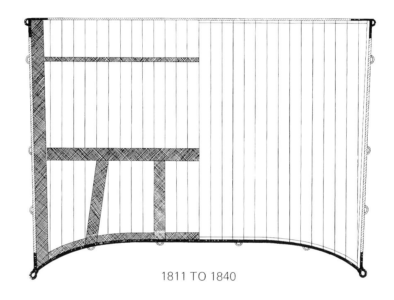

1811 TO 1840

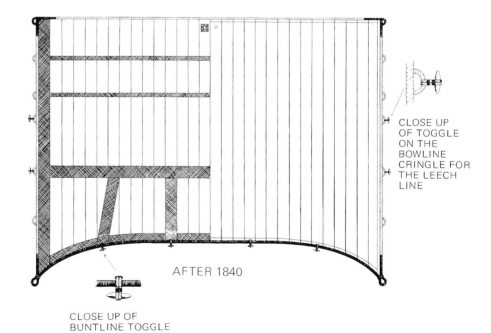

CLOSE UP
OF TOGGLE
ON THE
BOWLINE
CRINGLE FOR
THE LEECH
LINE

AFTER 1840

CLOSE UP OF
BUNTLINE TOGGLE

FORE COURSE

III SAILMAKING
Linings, bands and cloths

to be made on the mizen topgallant sail for clearing the main topgallant braces, thus the depth of 5 feet 6 inches is not as excessive as it seems.

Linings, bands and cloths To strengthen sails and to prevent chafing, extra cloths were sewn on wherever they were needed. On the after side of the topsails, in the way of the tops, additional cloths were sewn on; these were called the top lining. During the nineteenth century, linings were also put on the topgallant sails in the way of the crosstrees. The leech and foot of all square sails were lined on the fore side of the sails. Where reef points were carried, a band called the reef band was sewn across the fore side of the sail, and also on the fore side of the sails, cloths were required in the way of the bunt- and leechlines. Extra cloths called the mast linings were sewn on the after side of the sails to prevent chafe against the masts. Finally, across the fore side of courses and topsails, a cloth called the middle band was sewn. Before describing the individual bands or linings I must point out that the usual width of a cloth, (and a cloth, by the way, is the sailmaker's term for the canvas he uses) was 24 inches though, in the seventeenth century a 25, 26 and 30 inch width was used. Also, an 18 inch cloth was often used for staysails and jibs in the nineteenth century.

The reef bands of courses were one third of a cloth broad and those on the topsails were half a breadth. The edges in all cases were sewn under the leech lining to give a double thickness. The positions of the reef bands on the courses were as follows: when one band was fitted, it came about one sixth of the sail down from the head, when two bands were fitted the first came one sixth down and the second one third. The topsails, when only one band was carried, had it one eighth down; with two bands, the first at one eighth and the second at one quarter; with three bands one eighth, one quarter, and three eighths; finally with four bands one eighth, one quarter, three eighths and one half. Reef bands on the spritsail ran diagonally across the sail, from about 4 feet in from each earing cringle, to about 2

feet 3 inches up the opposite leech from the clue cringle.

Leech linings The leeches of the courses and the topsails were always lined from earing to clue on the fore side of the sail; this lining was sewn over the reef bands and middle bands. On the courses, the lining was one width of cloth all the way down, on the topsails up to 1811 the lining tapered from a full cloth's width at the foot to half a cloth at the head. After 1811,

the cloth ceased to be tapered and a full cloth was taken right down the leech. Before 1811, the leech of the main topgallant sail only had the outer cloth lined from the clue; in effect, this was just a doubling of the outer cloths. On the fore and mizen topgallant sails, pieces were sewn on the outer cloths only, coming up a distance of 9 inches from the clues; on the fore, main and mizen topgallant sails, pieces were also sewn on by the

1650 TO 1680

MARTNET CRINGLES UP TO 1650

BOWLINE BRIDLE CRINGLES

BONNET UP TO 1680

1680 TO 1811

MAIN COURSE

earings, a cloth's width but only 9 inches long. After 1811, on all the top-gallants, the leeches were lined right down with half a width of cloth. Before 1811, no linings or pieces were sewn on the royal sails; after 1811, earing pieces were sewn on a cloth's width and 9 inches long. No extra cloths were put on the clues.

Foot linings were only used after 1811. On the courses they stretched from clue to clue and were sewn under the

leech linings; they were half a cloth wide. On the topsails they stretched from clue to buntline cloth, and were half a cloth wide. On the topgallants the lining covered one third of the foot from each clue, again half a cloth in width. The royals had the whole of the foot covered with a third of a cloth's width.

Middle bands were sewn on the fore side of courses and topsails and, in all cases, were a full breadth of cloth;

they stretched from leech to leech, and were sewn under the leech linings. On some small ships and frigates during the nineteenth century, the mizen topsail was not fitted with a middle band; instead of this, reef tackle pieces were sewn on the after side of the sail (see the notes on this subject). I have not come across any evidence showing a middle band on any sails prior to the introduction of reef bands; I conclude, therefore, that it was only required when sails were made to be reefed and carried in rougher weather. The middle band was usually positioned half way between the lower reef band and the centre of the foot.

Buntline cloths The courses generally had four buntline cloths, each one breadth of cloth, running from the foot of the sail to the middle band; the middle band was sewn over the ends of the bunt cloths. The cloths were spaced equally along the foot. Up to about 1811, the cloths ran vertically up the sail, and after 1811, only the inner cloths were vertical—the outer cloths sloped inwards by one cloth of the sail at the middle band. The topsail had two buntline cloths, each a cloth wide, sewn on one third of the foot from each leech like those on the courses sewn under the middle band; the topsail bunt cloths were vertical at all periods. All bunt cloths were sewn over the foot linings. I have seen no evidence of buntline cloths in use prior to the introduction of the middle band; probably they were not found necessary when the sails were relatively small. Topgallant and royal sails were not fitted with buntline cloths.

Reef tackle pieces When the mizen topsail was not fitted with a middle band, two bands were sewn on the after side of the sail, running from the reef tackle cringles of the lower reef to the corners of the top lining. On the larger ships where the mizen topsail carried a middle band, the reef tackle pieces were still sewn on the after side of the sail. Fore and main topsails, however, had the reef tackle pieces sewn on the fore side of the sails, running from the lower reef cringles to the top of the bunt cloths, sewn under the leech lining and the middle band.

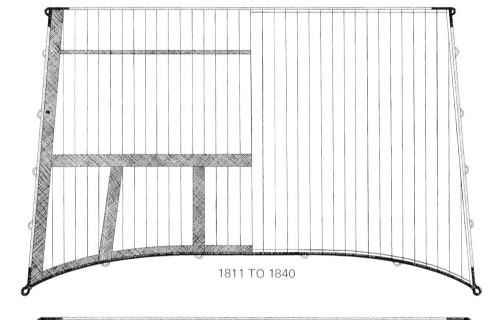

1811 TO 1840

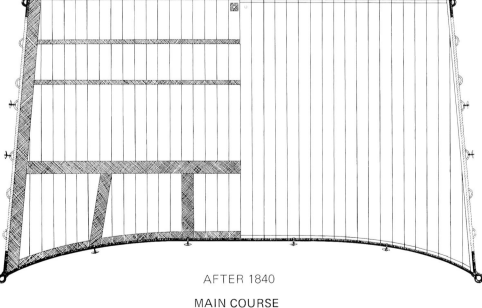

AFTER 1840

MAIN COURSE

III SAILMAKING
Mast cloths

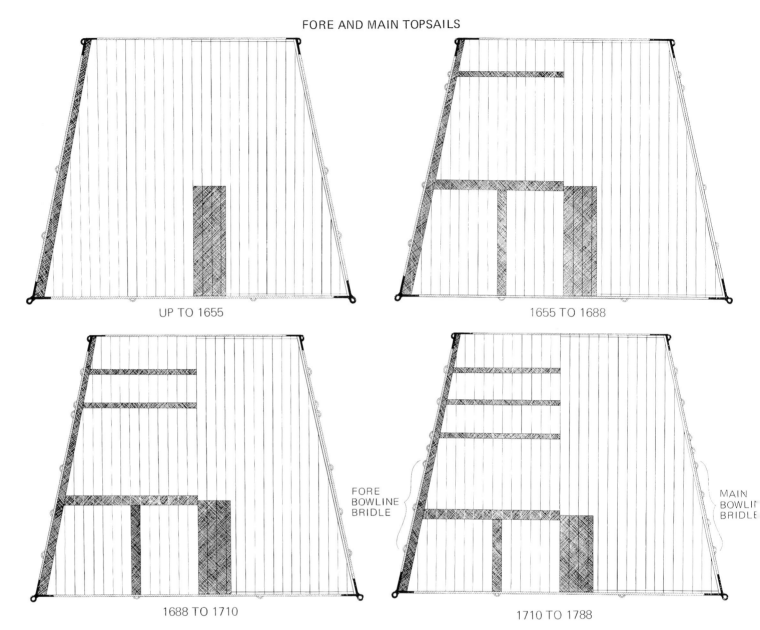

FORE AND MAIN TOPSAILS

UP TO 1655

1655 TO 1688

1688 TO 1710

FORE
BOWLINE
BRIDLE

1710 TO 1788

MAIN
BOWLIN[
BRIDLE

On all topsails, the reef tackle pieces tapered from two thirds of a cloth at the leech to one third at the inboard end. The reef tackle pieces were not in general use until about 1811..

Mast cloths To prevent chafing against the mast, extra cloths were sewn on the after side of the topsails. They were two cloths wide and extended from the top lining to the lower reef band up to 1811, from then to about 1845 they extended to the second reef band (first reef band on mizen topsails) and finally they were taken right up to the head. From about 1845 the topgallant sails were also fitted with a

mast cloth, one cloth wide extending from the top lining to the head. It is possible that on large ships the topgallants had mast cloths as early as 1829, but I can find out nothing definite about this. All mast cloths ran down the centre and either side of the centre of the sails. They were probably introduced about 1788.

The top linings prevented chafing of the sails against the tops or crosstrees. They were only required on the topsails and topgallant sails. Though the topsails probably had top linings during all periods, they were introduced on the topgallants at the same time as

mast cloths. The top linings were sewn on the after side of the sails, extending from the foot to the level of the centre of the middle band or, in the case of the topgallants and the mizen topsails not fitted with a middle band, they extended one third up the sail. They were carried in the centre of the foot, covering one fifth of the breadth of the sail up to 1811 and, by 1845, they had been increased to cover one third of the sail's breadth.

Bunt strops From about 1840, on the courses and topsails, strops were fitted to the sails to assist in their bending or unbending. Two holes, equidistant

FORE AND MAIN TOPSAILS

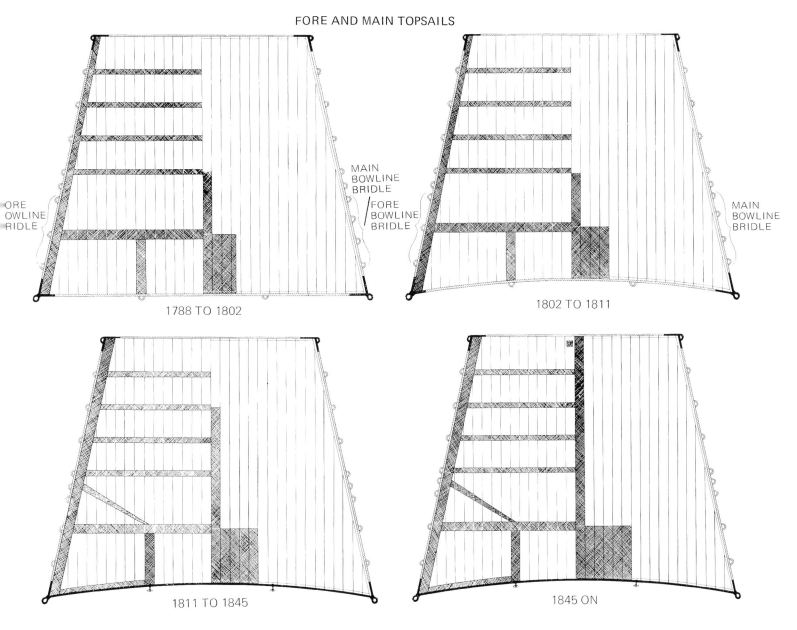

MAIN
BOWLINE
BRIDLE

FORE
BOWLINE
BRIDLE

ORE
OWLINE
RIDLE

MAIN
BOWLINE
BRIDLE

1788 TO 1802

1802 TO 1811

1811 TO 1845

1845 ON

from the centre, were made in the sail about 1 foot apart and 1 foot from the head; sometimes a square of canvas was sewn on in the way of these holes for extra strength. Through these holes a rope was placed and was formed into a strop just large enough to ride easily between the holes; the strop was then covered in canvas. When bending or unbending the sails, a tackle could be hooked in the strop thus hoisting the sail from the bunt.

Bolt ropes were ropes sewn round the edges of the sails. They took their name from the positions they were sewn—the leech rope on the leech, the

foot rope on the foot and the head rope on the head; they were known collectively as the bolt ropes. The sizes of the bolt ropes varied to such an extent that it would take a volume to give all the different sizes for all the various ships over the periods that this book covers. I think that for the modelmaker it is sufficient to give an average size based upon the size of the stays and so on. The use of the bolt rope was to strengthen the sail so that any strain should fall upon the rope and not the canvas. Of the three ropes the head rope was the smallest, the leech and foot ropes were the same

size. The following proportions are for the leech and foot ropes: main course one third the size of the main stay; fore course one third the size of the fore stay, all topsails two thirds of their respective stays, all topgallants one half the size of their respective topsail leech and foot bolt ropes, sprit-sail three fifths the size of the fore course leech and foot bolt ropes, sprit topsail the same as the fore topgallant sail, lower and top stunsails two fifths the size of the fore course leech and foot bolt ropes, topgallant and main and fore royals two thirds of the mizen topsail leech rope, mizen royal

III SAILMAKING
Bolt ropes

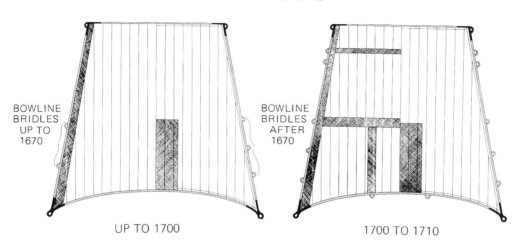

BOWLINE
BRIDLES
UP TO
1670

BOWLINE
BRIDLES
AFTER
1670

UP TO 1700

1700 TO 1710

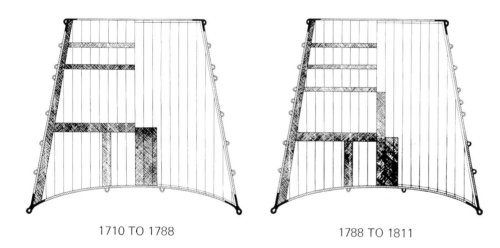

1710 TO 1788

1788 TO 1811

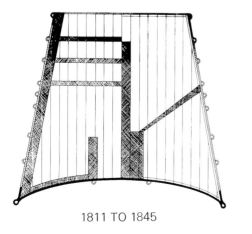

1811 TO 1845

1845 ON

one third of the fore course leech and foot bolt ropes.

The proportions for the head ropes were: courses, all topsails, main and fore topgallants, spritsail and sprit topsail two fifths the size of their respective leech and foot bolt ropes; mizen topgallant, all royals, topgallant stunsails, five ninths the size of their respective leech and foot bolt ropes; lower and top stunsails five eighths of their leech and foot bolt ropes. The bolt rope was sewn on the after side of the sail, a stitch to every strand of rope. The part of the bolt rope either side of the clues was served and, instead of being sewn to the sail, was marled on; this comprised passing marling through small holes pricked in the canvas and taking it round the bolt rope. Up to about 1811, these marled sections stretched from the outer buntline cringle to the lower bowline cringle on the main course; on the fore course, from the outer buntline cringle to one eighth up the leech; the main and fore topsails, 3 feet either way from the clues; spritsail and mizen topsail, 2 feet either side of the clues; the topgallant, royals, and sprit topsails were not marled. After 1811, the main and fore courses were served and marled all along the foot and between 2 and 3 feet up the leeches; the main and fore topsails were served and marled along the foot and 3 feet up the leeches; the mizen topsail along the foot and between 18 inches and 2 feet up the leeches; the topgallants, main and fore royals along the foot and 18 inches up the leeches; the mizen royal was served and marled only 18 inches either side of the clues. The stunsails were not marled on until 1811, and then only at the tack, the topmast stunsails were served and marled 18 inches either side of the tack cringle, the topgallant stunsails 12 inches either side of the tack, the lower stunsail was sometimes served and marled at the middle of the foot for a distance of a quarter the length of the foot to prevent chafing against the lower boom.

Cringles were made of a single strand of rope which was half of an inch smaller than the leech bolt rope. This strand was put through a hole made in

MAIN TOPGALLANT

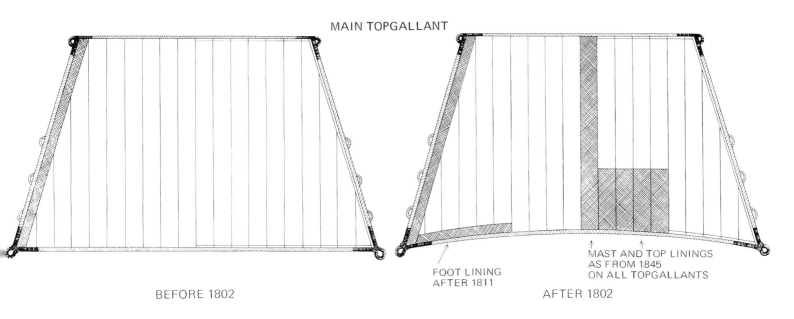

FOOT LINING
AFTER 1811

BEFORE 1802

↑ MAST AND TOP LININGS
AS FROM 1845
ON ALL TOPGALLANTS

AFTER 1802

FORE AND MIZEN TOPGALLANTS

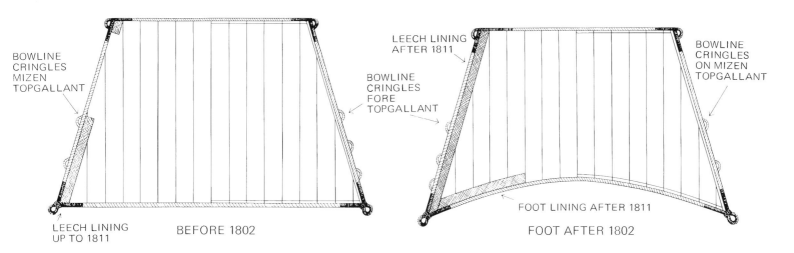

BOWLINE
CRINGLES
MIZEN
TOPGALLANT

LEECH LINING
UP TO 1811

BEFORE 1802

LEECH LINING
AFTER 1811

BOWLINE
CRINGLES
FORE
TOPGALLANT

BOWLINE
CRINGLES
ON MIZEN
TOPGALLANT

FOOT LINING AFTER 1811

FOOT AFTER 1802

FORE, MAIN AND MIZEN ROYALS

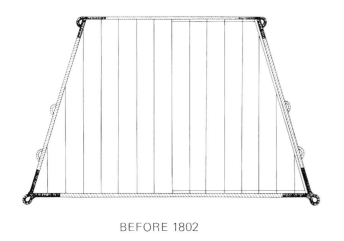
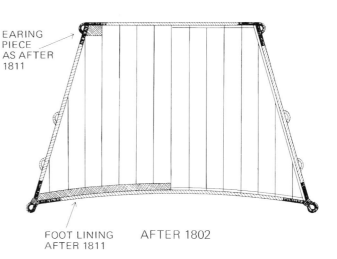

BEFORE 1802

EARING
PIECE
AS AFTER
1811

FOOT LINING
AFTER 1811

AFTER 1802

the sail just in from the bolt rope so that one third of the strand was one side and two thirds the other; the two ends were laid up together to the size of the required cringle; both ends were then taken through another hole made in the sail, one from one side the other from the other side. The short end was then laid under two strands of the bolt rope, the long end was backed and laid up with the original two ends, thus forming a three-stranded rope; finally the end was tucked under the strands of the bolt rope. On cringles worked in the leech ropes it was the usual practice to tuck the lowest end of the cringle a couple more times than the upper end, for the lowest end always took most strain and was liable to draw out if additional tucks were not taken. Each cringle was about four

turns of bolt rope in length, the bow-line, leechline, slab line and buntline cringles were superseded in 1819 by toggles.

The positions where the cringles were placed also applied to these toggles and the following should show the approximate positions: either end of each reef band; the centre of each bunt cloth; when martnets were used twelve cringles on each leech were required, equally spaced with the upper one, one sixth down the sail and the lowest one half way down; reef pendant cringles were placed 3 feet below the lowest reef cringle; reef tackle cringles were either 3 feet below the lowest reef cringle, or between the upper bowline cringle and the lower reef cringle; the bowline cringles on the royals and mizen topgallant sail came

half way down the leech and three quarters down; those on the fore and main topgallants were three on each leech, the upper one half way down, the others equally spaced from there to the clue; the topsails had three bow-line cringles on each leech in the same position as the fore and main top-gallants; the main course also had three bowline cringles each side, equally spaced between the lower reef and the clue, or between the reef pendant cringle and the clue; the fore course had two cringles each side, the upper one half way down the leech the lower one three quarters down. The date when the various cringles were needed can be ascertained from the rigging section of this book.

I have only given the positions of some of the cringles for with the various alterations of such items as bunt-lines, especially during the earlier periods, it would only confuse the situation if I gave all the possible positions; as long as the reader bears in mind that these cringles were placed so they all had a fair share of strain, and consequently were equally spaced, he should have no trouble in placing the cringles in the right positions. I find it the best policy to put the cringles on after I have set the sail; by this means I can obtain the best lead for the buntlines or slab lines and so on.

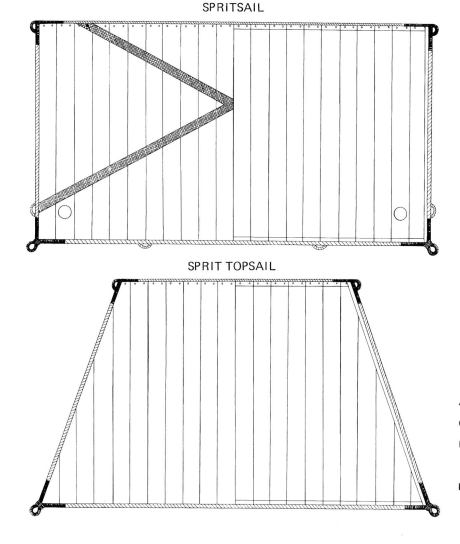

SPRITSAIL

SPRIT TOPSAIL

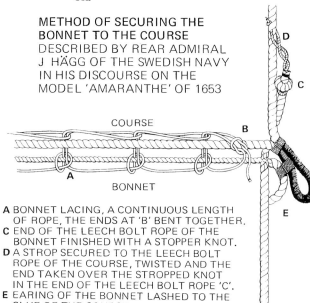

METHOD OF SECURING THE BONNET TO THE COURSE
DESCRIBED BY REAR ADMIRAL J HÄGG OF THE SWEDISH NAVY IN HIS DISCOURSE ON THE MODEL 'AMARANTHE' OF 1653

A BONNET LACING, A CONTINUOUS LENGTH OF ROPE, THE ENDS AT 'B' BENT TOGETHER.
C END OF THE LEECH BOLT ROPE OF THE BONNET FINISHED WITH A STOPPER KNOT.
D A STROP SECURED TO THE LEECH BOLT ROPE OF THE COURSE, TWISTED AND THE END TAKEN OVER THE STROPPED KNOT IN THE END OF THE LEECH BOLT ROPE 'C'.
E EARING OF THE BONNET LASHED TO THE CLUE OF THE COURSE

Toggles were used instead of cringles after 1819 for securing slab, leech-, and buntlines to the sails. The toggle was fastened to the sail by means of two small strops formed through a hole in the foot of the sail and the two strops were then seized together close to the bolt rope; the toggle was then seized into the bight of the strops; by using toggles instead of cringles the time taken to bend or take down a sail was more than halved.

Roband and reef point holes Holes to take the robands and reef points were made in the sail with a fid or spike, and small grommets made out of rope yarns were sewn round the edge of the holes. Up to about 1811, two holes were made in each cloth for robands and all reefs; after 1811, the holes for the robands were staggered. Two holes were made in the cloths either side of the centre cloth, one hole in the centre of the next cloth, two in the next and so on; the centre cloth had no hole made in it but instead, a small cringle was put on the head rope which not only helped in keeping the centre of the sail to the yard but was also of assistance in making sure that the centre of the sail lined up with the centre of the yard when bending the sail. After 1845, the sequence of two and one holes was also applied to the two upper reefs of the topsails; the other reefs were still fitted with two holes per cloth.

Tablings The hemming round the edge of the sail was called tabling. On the square sails the tabling was always put on the after side of the sail. The width of the tabling depended upon the size of the sail and the following will give a good idea of the average widths (in inches):

	Head	Leech and foot
Main and fore courses	4–6	3–5
Spritsail and all topsails	3–4½	3
Topgallant and sprit topsail	3	2½
Royals	2½	2

The head of the stunsails varied from 3 to 4 inches, the leech from 1½ to 2 inches, and the foot from 2 to 3 inches.

FORE LOWER STUNSAIL UP TO 1745

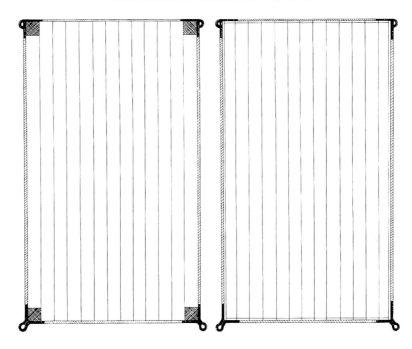

NOTE STUNSAILS SHOW FORESIDE ON LEFT AND AFTER SIDE ON RIGHT

MAIN LOWER STUNSAIL UP TO 1745

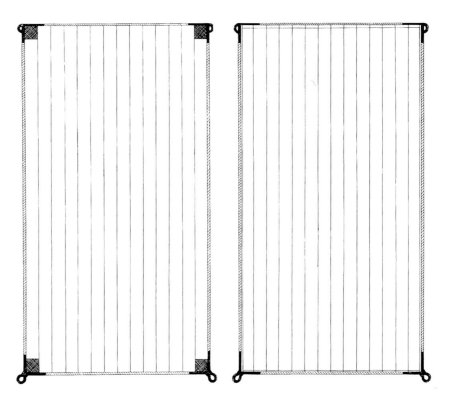

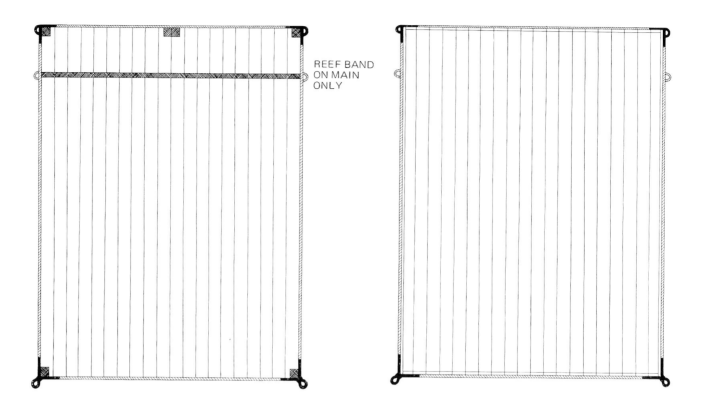

REEF BAND
ON MAIN
ONLY

FORE AND MAIN LOWER STUNSAILS 1745 TO 1829

Water holes To allow water to escape from the spritsail, two holes were cut in the sail, one in the centre of the second cloth each side, level with the reef cringle. Each hole was between 4 and 6 inches in diameter.

Clues were made by splicing a slightly larger rope into the foot and leech bolt ropes and forming a loop by seizing both parts together at the corner of the sail. This rope was called the clue rope; it was wormed and served. The amount of slack left on the clue rope to form the loop was the length of fourteen turns of rope. When bonnets were carried, a small strop was spliced into the clue rope, just a little way up the leech; this was to take the knot formed on the bonnet leech rope by the earings. After about 1840, iron thimbles were seized in the clues and the tacks, sheets and cluelines were shackled on. Only one shackle was used on each clue, on the topsails and above; the sheet block was strapped with an iron thimble seized in the strap and the shackle was put through

this thimble and the pin of the shackle through the clue. On the side of this shackle was a small lug which took the pin of a smaller shackle for securing the clueline. The same principle applied on the courses, except that the large shackle took both sheet and tack; the clue garnets shackled to the lug on the large shackle.

Earings were formed by leaving an additional length on the leech rope, usually equivalent to fourteen turns of the rope. This extra length was turned back and spliced into the leech rope and the splice was always stitched to keep the ends from drawing. The head rope was spliced into the earing. The earings on the bonnet and drablers were made in a slightly different manner: a short length was left on the leech rope and a stopper knot formed in the end; the earing itself was either formed with the head rope, in which case the extra length on the leech rope had to be unlaid and intertwined with the head rope before being laid up again to form the stopper knot or —

and this I think the more feasible — an extra length of rope was spliced into the leech rope from which the earing was made. As there is no definite information as to which method was the correct one, it is up to the individual rigger to select the method he prefers. The end of the leech rope with the stopper knot worked in it was taken through a small strop in the leech of the course (the strop being twisted to hold the knot firmly). By means of this stopper knot, the strop in the course, and a seizing between the clue cringle of the course and the earing of the bonnet, the sails were united firmly. The drabbler was fitted the same way to the bonnet. I have illustrated the method of lacing the bonnet and drabbler on, and the reader should have no problems in this respect.

Seams It was by varying the widths of the seams that the sailmaker actually shaped his sails, however, for model-making, seams the same width all the way down are quite satisfactory. The width of the seams was between 1 inch

FORE SIDE (AFTER SIDE THE SAME AS IN PREVIOUS YEARS)

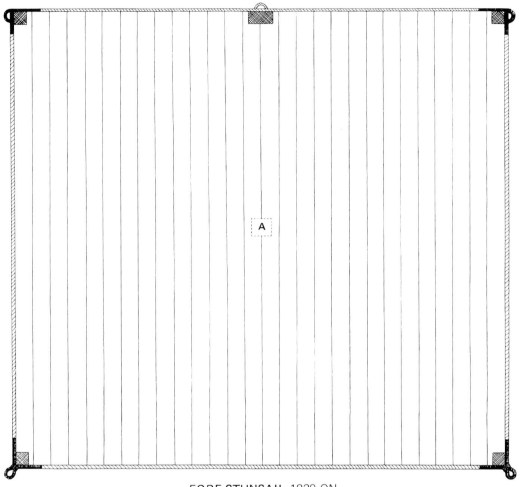

FORE STUNSAIL 1829 ON
MAIN STUNSAIL WHEN CARRIED WAS SIMILAR TO THE FORE

A THE POSITION
OF THE PIECE
TO TAKE THE
THIMBLE FOR THE
TRIPPING LINE
AFTER 1840

CLOSE-UP OF 'A'

and 1 1/2 inches, depending upon the size of the sails; large ships' courses and topsails usually 1 1/2 inches, topgallants and royals 1 1/4 inches, smaller ships' courses and topsails 1 1/4 inches and the rest of the sails 1 inch.
Stunsails were made of a lighter canvas than the other square sails; they were not lined, but instead they had a small square of cloth sewn on each corner, on the fore side of the sail. Up to 1829, these squares were 2 feet square, after 1829, they were 1 foot square. After 1829, the lower stunsail had an extra piece sewn on the fore side at the centre of the head, 2 feet wide and 18 inches deep. The earings were formed in the same way as those of the other square sails; the tack and clue cringles were made by leaving

slack on the foot and leech bolt rope and seizing them into a bight. They had iron thimbles seized in them after 1840; before then they were served as were the earings during all periods. The bolt rope was sewn on all round the sail, the clues were not marled. The lower stunsails had a cringle in the centre of the head rope which was also served. The main lower and main topmast stunsails had a reef band made of a 6 inch width of cloth, sewn on the fore side of the sail one eighth the depth of the sail from the head. I should imagine that these reef bands were not fitted before about the middle of the eighteenth century. After about 1811, a reef band was also put on the fore topmast stunsail, the same position down the sail as the others.

Reef earing cringles were required on either end of the bands. Up to 1829, a cringle was put on the outer leech of the fore and main top stunsails, half way down the leech; this was for the downhaul lead. After 1829, instead of the cringles, the downhaul was led through a hole in the leech, one third from the head, and another one, two thirds from the head, both holes near the edge of the sail. Also after 1829, the tack was served on the top stunsails a distance of 18 inches either side of the cringle. I had better point out here that the tack of a stunsail was the lower outer corner, and the clue was the lower inner corner.
The seams of the stunsails always ran parallel to the inner leech. The depth of the inner leech of the lower stun-

III SAILMAKING
Stunsails

FORE TOPMAST STUNSAIL UP TO 1811

MAIN TOPMAST STUNSAIL UP TO 1811

sails varied a great deal according to the build of the ship; however, the following should be a good guide:
Main — 2 or 3 yards deeper than the main course leech. Fore — up to 1829 1 or 2 yards deeper than the fore course leech, after 1829 — 2 feet deeper than the fore course leech.
Topmast stunsails — up to 1829 1 yard deeper than their respective topsails, after 1829 3/4 of a yard deeper than their respective topsails.
Topgallant stunsails — half a yard deeper than their respective sails.
The width of the head of the stunsails can be given from about 1790; however, I think that the only stunsails where difficulty may possibly arise in this respect are the lower ones. It is a very simple operation to arrive at the width of the upper stunsails by means of paper patterns set between the yards and the booms; with the lower stunsails where the method of carrying them altered in 1745, one can only arrive at a conjectural width and I hope that the widths that I give will answer the purpose.
Width of the head:
Fore and main lower up to 1745 — one tenth the length of their respective course yards; main 1745 to 1829 — between two cloths more and one cloth less than the number of yards in the inner leech of the stunsail, (large ships two more and small ships one less); fore 1745 to 1829 — one cloth less than the main stunsail; 1829 on — both main and fore were about one half the width of their own course, though on three-deckers they were slightly narrower, being five twelfths the width of the course. Although by Admiralty Order the main lower stunsail was no longer issued after 1801, I have included the width here because on some training ships the sail was used until quite late and the size of the main stunsail was given in the Navy Dockyard Sailmakers Guide of 1845.
Main topmast stunsail — at all periods had six cloths less on the head than yards deep of the inner leech of the top stunsail.
Fore topmast stunsail — at all periods one cloth less than the main topmast stunsail.
Main and fore topgallant stunsails — up to 1829 large ships had three cloths

more and small ships one cloth more,
than yards deep of the inner leech of
the topgallant stunsails; from 1829 on
there was one cloth more on three-
deckers, and the same number on
two-deckers and below, of yards deep
of the inner leech.
Width of the foot:
Lower stunsails — the same as the
head.
Topmast stunsails — at all periods four
cloths more than the head.
Topgallant stunsails — up to 1829 two
cloths more than the head; after 1829
four cloths more than the head.
These extra cloths on the foot were
gored on the outer leech. The lower
stunsails were the only ones where the
leeches were at right angles to the
head, all the others sloped slightly
outwards from the inner earing. The
amount that the leeches sloped depended entirely upon the angle of the
topsail or topgallant sail leech. The
following is only intended to be a
rough guide:
Topmast stunsails — 4 inches per cloth.
Topgallant stunsails — 3 to 5 inches
a cloth.
After 1811 the foot of the top stunsails
was cut at a sharper angle to the head,
sloping downwards 1 inch per cloth
more than the head. Also after 1811 on
the topgallant stunsails both head and
foot sloped downwards 6 inches per
cloth. I know from experience that
the fitting of stunsails is a very difficult operation; I do find that stunsails
are best made after the other square
sails are put in position, for no matter
how accurately the sail plans are
copied, small discrepancies creep in
and the stunsails are found to be slightly out of shape to the leech of the
square sails. However, if the stunsails
are left until last, paper patterns can be
cut in their place and the stunsails cut
to the finished patterns.

FORE AND MAIN TOPMAST STUNSAILS 1811 ON

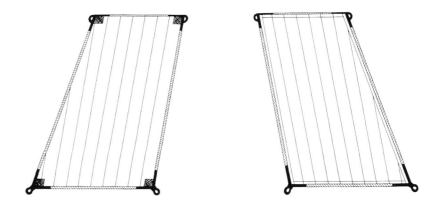

FORE AND MAIN TOPGALLANT STUNSAILS

17 Fore and aft sails

STAYSAILS AND JIBS

All fore and aft sails were tabled and roped on the port side. The upper corner was called the 'peak', the corner to which the sheet was fastened was the 'clue', the third corner on a three sided sail was termed the 'tack' or, in the case of a four sided sail, the upper one was the 'nock tack' and the lower the 'tack'. The side of the sail between the peak and the clue was the 'leech', that from the clue to the tack was the 'foot', the side between the peak and the tack or nock was the 'stay' and the side of a four sided sail between the nock tack and the tack was the luff. Staysails and jibsails were strengthened on the corners with additional pieces of canvas: at the peak, running from the first seam, and cut so that it was at right angles to the leech, one piece of cloth was sewn on the port side and over the tabling. Another piece of cloth a full cloth's width was sewn on the clue running two yards up the cloth next to the leech, and cut at right angles to the leech, sewn on the port side over the tablings. At the tack on a three sided sail, the first cloth from the tack was doubled, while on the bunt of a four sided sail, a half breadth of cloth was sewn the entire length of the bunt again on the port side and over the tablings. The foot of staysails was cut at right angles to the leech, the luffs of the mizen, mizen

top and main topmast staysails were cut at an oblique angle; other four sided staysails were cut square at the bunt. The foot of the mizen had two more cloths than at the stay, the foot of the mizen topmast staysail one more cloth and the main topmast staysail two more cloths. The stay of the sails was cut with a slight curve, though on a model they are best cut straight.

On pictures and drawings, the foot of the jib and flying jib are usually depicted as having an upward curve; this, however, is the complete opposite. The foot was cut with a downward curve or roach so that when the sail was filled out the foot only appeared to have the upward curve. The tack of the jib was usually higher than the clue, a matter of 3 inches per cloth on the foot and the flying jibsail was usually cut with the tack level with the clue. The cloths of all staysails and jibs were seamed parallel to the leech. The width of the tabling depended upon the size of the sail, an average being between 2 and 3 inches on the leech, 3 to 3½ on the stay, and between 2 and 2½ inches on the foot and luff. It is very difficult to give exact measurements for fore and aft sails; one either has to draw up a sail plan, as practised by sailmakers, or make patterns first as I advise modelmakers. To assist the reader in gauging the correct proportions for the jibs and staysails, I will give a few proportions as laid down in various sailmaking books. Before getting on to the actual sizes I think I had better describe the shape of the sails. Sails with four sides were not introduced until 1760; consequently before this date the sails were relatively small. The jib was introduced when jibbooms were carried, flying jibs were used from 1794 and when the flying jibboom was introduced, both these sails were always three sided. The fore staysail was introduced in 1773, the main staysail in 1660 and remained in use until 1815 when it was ousted by the trysail; both these lower staysails were always three sided. The mizen staysail was introduced in 1660 and was a three sided sail up to 1760; from 1760 to 1815 it was four sided; it was replaced by the main trysail in 1815. The fore

topmast staysail was the only other sail that was always three sided and was introduced in 1660. The main topmast staysail was three sided from its introduction in 1660 until 1760; from 1760 the sail was four sided and remained so until the end of the sail era. The mizen topmast staysail was introduced in 1709 and was three sided until 1760, when it became four sided; this sail ceased to be used after 1815. The main topgallant staysail was another sail introduced in 1709; it was a three sided sail from 1709 to 1760, and from 1810 on; between 1760 and 1810 the sail was four sided. The mizen topgallant staysail had a relatively short life, only being used between 1760 and 1815; it was always four sided. Finally, the main royal staysail was introduced in 1719, was three sided from 1719 to 1760, and from 1805 onwards; between 1760 and 1805 it was four sided. The middle staysail was always four sided but was only used for a short time, from 1773 to 1815.

Prior to the introduction of four sided staysails in 1760, information is very sparse, in fact almost non-existent; consequently the following notes must only be regarded as conjectural and not historical fact. The only method I have been able to use has been to proportion the sails according to furled sail depicted in contemporary pictures and prints.

The length of the stay of the sails was proportionate to the length of the appropriate stay and should be about four sevenths for the fore topmast staysail, two thirds for the main topgallant staysail, four fifths for the main topmast staysail, seven eights for the mizen topmast staysail and eight ninths for the mizen staysail. The leech of the main and fore staysails was the same depth as the centres of their respective courses, the foot was just over half the width of the head of their respective courses, and as the clue was cut at right angles, the length of the stay of the sails was worked out correspondingly. The length of the leeches on the top staysails was the same as the depth of their appropriate square sails, that is the main top staysail was the same as the main topsail and so forth. The leech of the main topgallant staysail was half the length of the main top-gallant stay. The foot of all the stay-sails was about two thirds the depth of the leech.

As regards the jib, the stay of the sail was about three quarters the length of the jibstay, or when set fly-ing, three quarters the distance between the outer end of the jibboom and the fore topmast hounds. The leech was about three fifths the length of the jibstay, the foot, cut with a downward curve or roach was about the length of the jibboom. I must emphasize that these proportions should only be used as an approximate guide.

After 1760, we enter the periods where much more information is available, and the following descriptions of the proportions of four sided staysails, three sided staysails and jib and flying jibs are based on authentic data. The modelmaker must bear in mind that all proportions given by various contemporary authorities were intend-ed to assist the sailmaker and were not strictly adhered to, the latter adjusting the proportions according to his own ideas as to the best interpretation. That is why I always advocate making pat-terns first before cutting out the actual sail.

Fore topmast staysail The leech was the same depth as the fore topsail, the foot was two thirds the depth of the leech, the clue was cut at right angles. These proportions remained the same to the end of the sail era.

Fore staysail The leech was the same depth as the centre of the fore course, the foot had two more cloths than half the number of cloths in the head of the fore course, the clue was cut at a right angle and the proportions re-mained the same to the end of the sail era.

Main staysail The leech was the same depth as the centre of the main course, the foot was five eighths the width of the head of the main course, the clue was cut at right angles and these pro-portions remained the same until the staysail was superseded in 1815 by the fore trysail.

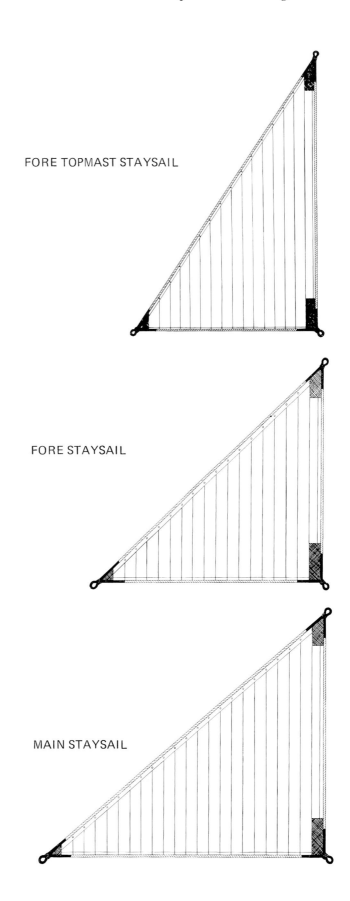

FORE TOPMAST STAYSAIL

FORE STAYSAIL

MAIN STAYSAIL

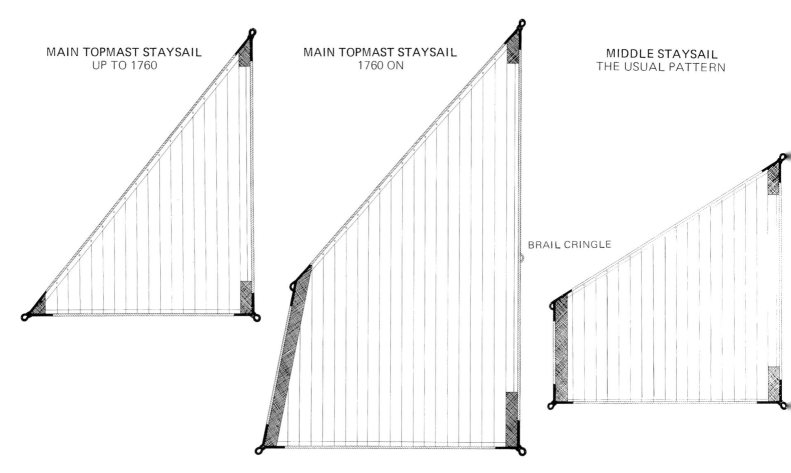

MAIN TOPMAST STAYSAIL
UP TO 1760

MAIN TOPMAST STAYSAIL
1760 ON

MIDDLE STAYSAIL
THE USUAL PATTERN

BRAIL CRINGLE

Main topmast staysail The leech was 5 yards deeper than the leech of the main topsail, the foot was two thirds the depth of the leech, and the luff was two fifths the leech; there were two cloths gored at the luff and the clue was cut at right angles. Reference to the drawings of the sails will show what is meant by having cloths gored at the luff These proportions remained the same to the end of the sail era.

Middle staysail The leech was about 6 yards deeper than the main topgallant sail, the foot was half the width of the foot of the main course, the luff was five twelfths the leech, both lower tack and clue were cut at right angles. (It is impossible to give an exact proportion for the leech as the cut of this sail depended upon the angle that the middle staysail stay was required to be rigged.) The illustrations of the middle staysail show the usual cut of the sail and a cut of the sail at the end of its life on some vessels.

Main topgallant staysail Up to 1810, the leech was one and a half times the depth of the main topgallant sail, the

foot was the same as the head of the topgallant sail and the luff was two fifths the leech; both lower tack and clue were cut at right angles. From 1810 onwards, the leech was one and three quarter times the depth of the main topgallant sail, the foot was the same as the leech and the stay of the sail was one and a third times the length of the leech.

Main royal staysail The leech was one and a quarter times the depth of the main royal sail, the foot was the same as the head of the main topgallant sail, and the stay of the sail was one and a half times the length of the foot.

Mizen staysail The depth of this sail depended upon the height of the quarterdeck; the foot of the sail had to clear the deck by between 6 and 7 feet. The foot was half the width of the head of the main course and the luff was between three fifths and two thirds the depth of the leech; the clue was cut at a right angle, and two cloths were gored on the luff. The best method of making these sails where the bunt had gored cloths is to cut

them at right angles, then cut off the sail from lower tack to the first or second seam from the nock tack, dependent upon whether one or two cloths require to be gored.

Mizen topmast staysail The leech was between 1 and 2 yards deeper than the mizen topsail, the foot was half the width of the head of the fore course and the luff was two fifths the leech, the clue was cut at right angles and one cloth was gored on the luff

Mizen topgallant staysail There seems to have been no set rules for the proportions of this sail for it was only used for a few years and not on all ships. The shape of the sail depended upon the angle of the stay to the main topmast. The leech was about the same depth as the mizen topgallant sail, the luff about two fifths of the leech, and the foot about the same width as the mizen topgallant sail head; when cutting out this sail it is essential to draw out a plan to work out the angles of the four corners.

Jib Up to 1811, the leech was twice the depth of the leech of the fore stay-

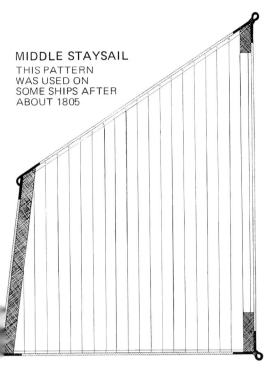

MIDDLE STAYSAIL
THIS PATTERN
WAS USED ON
SOME SHIPS AFTER
ABOUT 1805

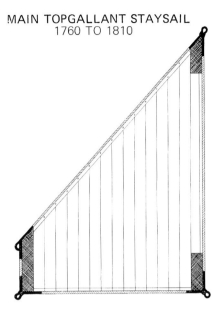

MAIN TOPGALLANT STAYSAIL
1760 TO 1810

MAIN TOPGALLANT STAYSAIL
1810 ON

MAIN ROYAL STAYSAIL
UP TO 1805

MAIN ROYAL STAYSAIL
1805 ON

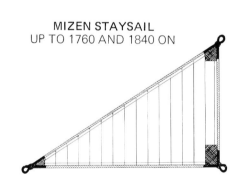

MIZEN STAYSAIL
UP TO 1760 AND 1840 ON

MIZEN STAYSAIL
1760 TO 1840

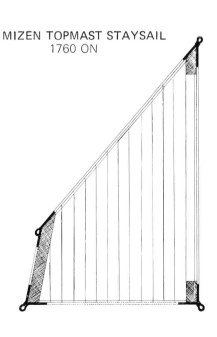

MIZEN TOPMAST STAYSAIL
1760 ON

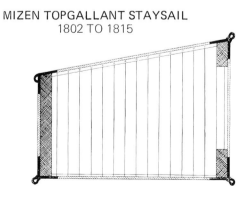

MIZEN TOPGALLANT STAYSAIL
1802 TO 1815

FLYING JIB

JIB

FORE TOPMAST
STAYSAIL

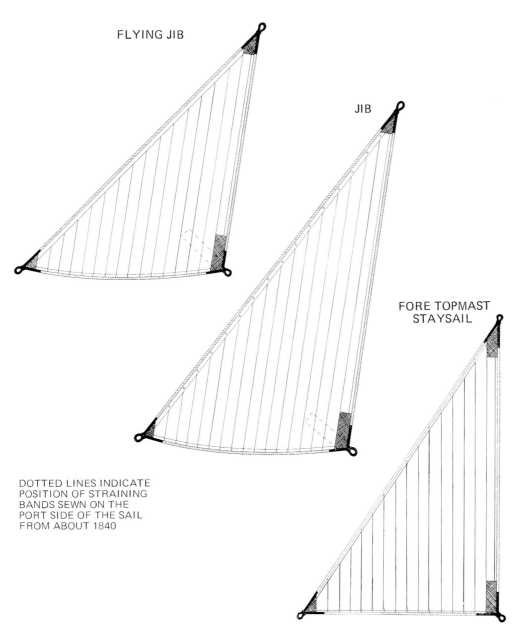

DOTTED LINES INDICATE
POSITION OF STRAINING
BANDS SEWN ON THE
PORT SIDE OF THE SAIL
FROM ABOUT 1840

stay of the sail and finally made fast to the tack cringle. This latter method was used prior to 1745 on the staysails, and nearly always used for the jib and flying jib.

Bolt ropes On three sided sails, this was the same size all round; on four sided sails, the head rope was almost twice the size of the leech, luff and foot, and in some cases exactly double. The following are the approximate proportions of the main topmast stay; when the head rope needs to be larger, the sizes can be worked out from these given proportions. For example, if the given proportion is 1/3, the proportion of the head rope would be 3/5.

Fore, main and mizen	2/5
Fore, main and mizen topmast staysails	1/4
All topgallant staysails	1/4
All royal staysails	1/5
Jib	1/5
Jib (head or luff)	2/5
Middle staysail	1/5
Middle staysail (head)	2/5

I must emphasize that the above are only approximate proportions, but they will answer as far as the modeller is concerned.

MIZEN SAIL

Up to about 1680, the mizen sail was triangular, the three corners called the peak, the clue and the nock. However, to give more sail area a bonnet was sometimes carried which was fitted to the foot of the sail and was about one fifth of the depth of the leech of the mizen sail; it was oblong in shape. This bonnet was secured to the mizen sail in the same manner as the bonnets on the courses. After 1680, the sail was cut combining both mizen sail and bonnet, giving a four sided sail. The four corners were known as the peak, the clue, the nock and the tack. The head of the sail ran from the peak to the nock, the leech from the peak to the clue, the foot from the clue to the tack, (or nock on a three sided sail) and the luff from tack to nock. The cloths were parallel to the leech and the clue was always cut at right angles. The angle at which the yard was carried does not seem to have been laid down, as indeed the angle of

sail, the foot was two thirds the leech plus 2 feet; the length of the stay of the sail has to be worked out for the foot was gored a matter of 3 inches per cloth decreasing from the tack to the clue; this goring of 3 inches continued until 1845. From 1811 to 1845 the foot was five sixths the length of the jib-boom, the leech was one and a half times the length of the foot. After 1845 the foot was the length of the jibboom, the leech was one and a quarter times the length of the foot minus 1 yard and the foot was gored 4 inches per cloth.

Flying jib The foot was two thirds

the length of the foot of the jib, the leech was one and a quarter times the length of the foot plus 1 yard and the foot was gored 6 inches per cloth decreasing from the tack to the clue.

Note There were two methods used for securing staysails to the stays: the most usual method was by hanks. For a description of these hanks, reference should be made to the section of this book devoted to the furnishings of the masts and spars. The other method was to lace the sails to the stays by means of a line, spliced into the peak cringle and taken spirally down the stay, reeving through the holes in the

the gaff in later years depended upon the individual sailmaker; however, it seems to have been the general rule to have the yard at the same angle as the mizen stay.

The size of the bolt rope was: head, one quarter the size of the mizen stay; leech, foot and luff, half the size of the mizen stay. The clue rope was 1/2 inch larger than the leech rope and was about 18 feet long.

The tabling at the head was between 3 and 4 inches wide, that on the leech 3 inches, the luff 3½ to 4 inches, and the foot between 2 and 3 inches. Pieces were sewn on all the corners similar to the staysails; the peak piece was one yard long, the nock piece formed a triangle and the leech was lined 5 yards up from the clue. When the sail was four sided, the nock piece was dispensed with and the luff was lined from the nock to the tack. All these pieces and linings were one cloth wide.

With regard to the various cringles, I think it would be best if the reader referred to the rigging section of this book to find out their exact positions. The cringles were formed in the same way as those described on the square sails. The peak earing cringle was formed with the leech bolt rope, the clue cringle with the clue rope (which was spliced into the foot and leech bolt ropes); the nock and tack cringles were formed from the head bolt rope and the luff bolt rope respectively. After 1680, when sail and bonnet were combined, a reef band was sewn across the sail, running from the nock to about one third down the leech, the sail being reefed up to the yard. This reef cloth was a quarter cloth's width and was put on the port side of the sail. The depth of the leech was of such a length as to allow the foot of the sail to clear the poop by about 6 feet. The mizen yard was generally hoisted up so that the parrel came just under the upper catharpins. Holes for the reef points were made in every seam of the sail, and holes for the head lacing were made two to a cloth.

After 1730, and up to 1745 on small ships and 1780 on large ships, the fore part of the sail was cut off and the luff laced to the mizen mast. The holes for the luff lacing were 27 inches apart, with the lowest hole just above the reef tack cringle. The reef band, a quarter cloth's width, ran parallel to the foot of the sail, one fifth the length of the leech up from the foot; the reef was then taken in at the foot and the reef cringles were put in either end of the reef band. The holes for the head lacing and the reef points were two to a cloth. The luff was not lined but instead a piece was sewn on at the nock 1 yard long and a full cloth wide. The foot was cut with a downward curve of 1 inch goring per cloth running towards the centre of the foot; the early type of mizen sail had a straight foot. The peak and clue had similar pieces sewn on as in previous years though it was not found neces-

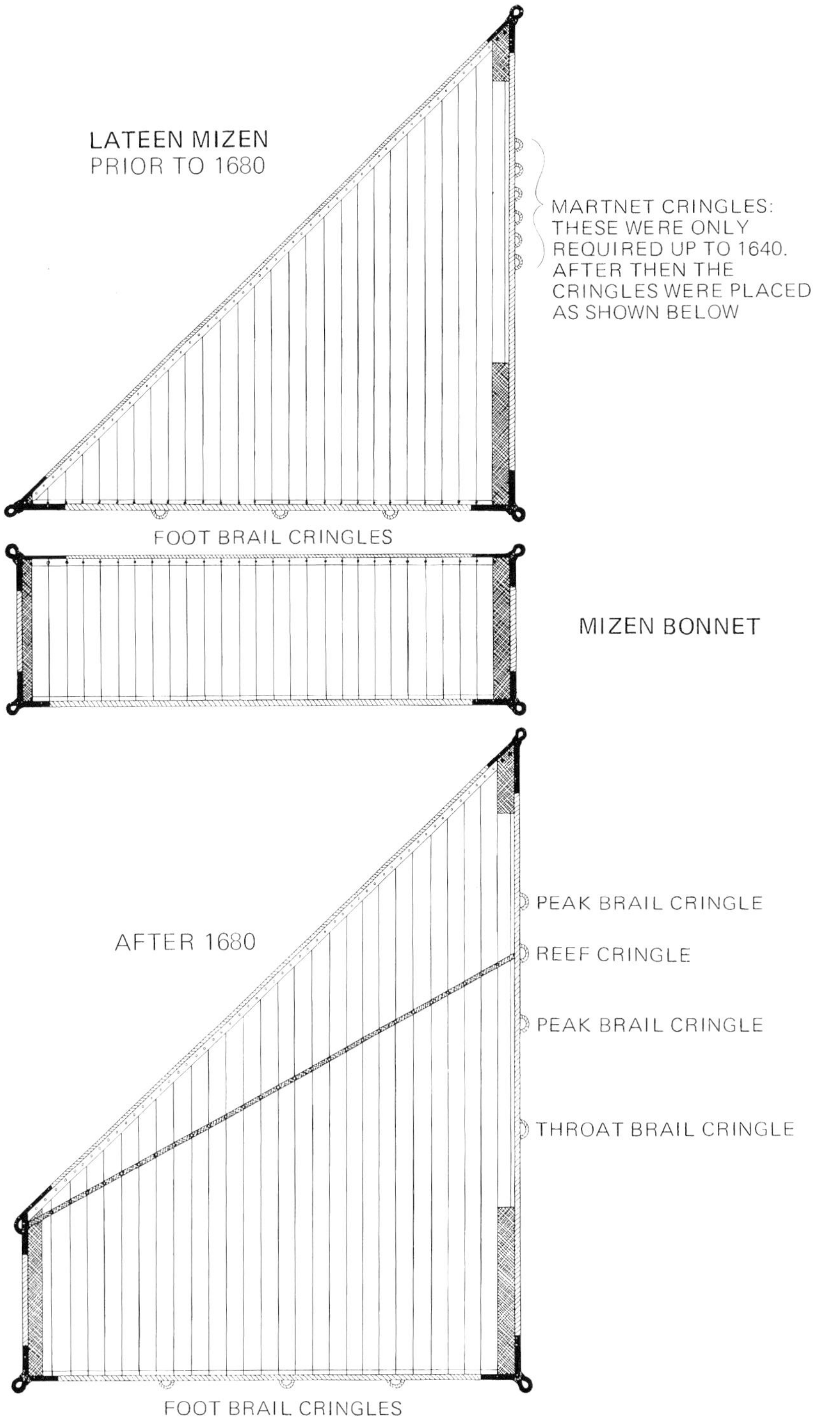

LATEEN MIZEN
PRIOR TO 1680

MARTNET CRINGLES: THESE WERE ONLY REQUIRED UP TO 1640. AFTER THEN THE CRINGLES WERE PLACED AS SHOWN BELOW

FOOT BRAIL CRINGLES

MIZEN BONNET

AFTER 1680

PEAK BRAIL CRINGLE

REEF CRINGLE

PEAK BRAIL CRINGLE

THROAT BRAIL CRINGLE

FOOT BRAIL CRINGLES

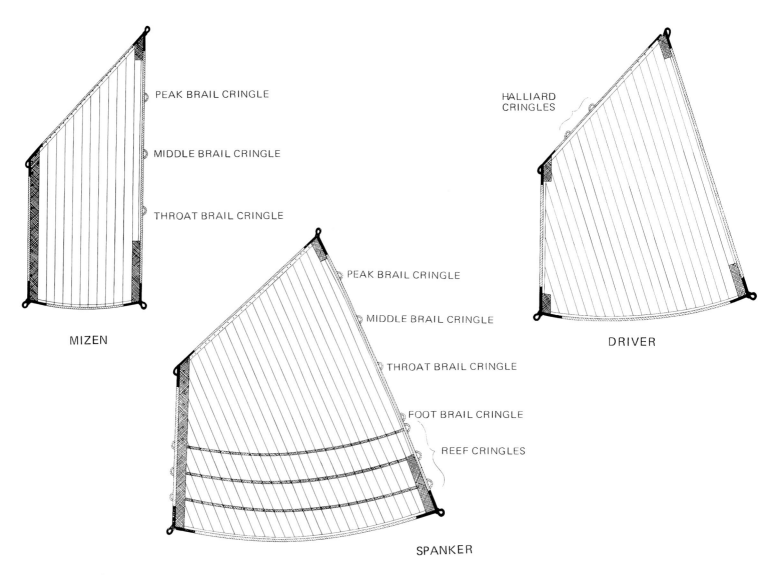

PEAK BRAIL CRINGLE

MIDDLE BRAIL CRINGLE

THROAT BRAIL CRINGLE

MIZEN

HALLIARD
CRINGLES

DRIVER

PEAK BRAIL CRINGLE

MIDDLE BRAIL CRINGLE

THROAT BRAIL CRINGLE

FOOT BRAIL CRINGLE

REEF CRINGLES

SPANKER

sary to put a piece on the tack. When gaffs were fitted, which was from 1745 on small ships and 1780 on large ships, the mizen sail was cut exactly as just described; the angle of the gaff, though still left to the discretion of the sailmaker, was usually lifted at a slightly higher angle than the mizen stay.

The mizen sail was always loose footed, that is, no boom was ever fitted; it was only when the permanent driver replaced the mizen in 1810 that the boom became a permanent feature.

SPANKER

As I mention in the rigging section I prefer to call the permanent driver by its other name, the 'spanker'; this helps in differentiating between the two

sails. The linings and tablings were exactly similar to those of the mizen sail except that the leech tabling was narrower in the middle of the leech than at the peak and clue; this gave an outward curve at the leech which straightend out when the sail was filled with wind.

It was sometimes the practice to form the cringles at the corners so that instead of protruding, they came inside of the bolt rope. The method of making these cringles was to sew the bolt rope round the sail, then seize iron thimbles between the bolt rope and the sail; the thimbles were then marled onto the corners of the sail. The clue cringle, however, was always formed on the earlier system and was about 9 inches long. Iron thimbles

were also sometimes used for the reef cringles, seized inside the usual rope cringles.

The head bolt rope was about one quarter the size of the mizen stay, the leech, foot and luff bolt ropes were one and two thirds the size of the head bolt rope, the clue rope was 1/2 inch larger than the leech rope and was 12 feet long. The head of the spanker was laced to the gaff and the luff either laced to the mast or trysail mast or seized to hoops on the mast or trysail mast. Reef bands ran parallel to the foot, and were a quarter of a cloth wide; small ships only had one reef band, put on one sixth the length of the luff from the foot, medium size ships had two bands, the lower one sewn on one sixth of the luff from the foot, and the upper band one third from the foot and the large ships were fitted with three reef bands the upper one half way up the luff, and the others equally spaced between the upper band and the foot. When two or three bands were fitted, the lower one ran parallel to the foot, while the others were 6 inches wider apart at the leech than at the luff.

The holes for the head lacing were one in one cloth, two in the next, one in the next, and so on; the holes for the luff lacing started just above the upper reef cringle, and were spaced 30 inches apart up to the nock and the holes for the reef points were made in each seam.

The foot was cut with a downward curve as described on the mizen sail. It was, however, much wider than the foot of the mizen and consequently there were more cloths in the foot than in the head. The cloths ran parallel to the leech and the extra cloths were gored on the luff. (Goring was the technical term for the slanting cut of a cloth.)

With regard to the position of the brail cringles, the text on rigging will show their positions.

DRIVER

Up to 1810 the driver was a temporary sail, rigged as described in the rigging section. The tablings and linings were the same as on the spanker and, in fact, the only difference between the driver and the spanker was at the head, where holes were required for lacing on the driver yard; these holes were one per cloth for the length of the yard. Also along the head bolt rope two cringles were required, spaced equally between the nock cringle and the fore end of the driver yard. The peak, tack and nock pieces were 1 yard long, and the leech was lined 2 to 3 yards up from the clue, all these pieces being a full cloth in width. It was often the practice to line the spanker in the same manner as just described for the driver.

No reef bands were required on the driver, and usually the cringles on the corners of the sail were made in the early fashion as described for the mizen sail.

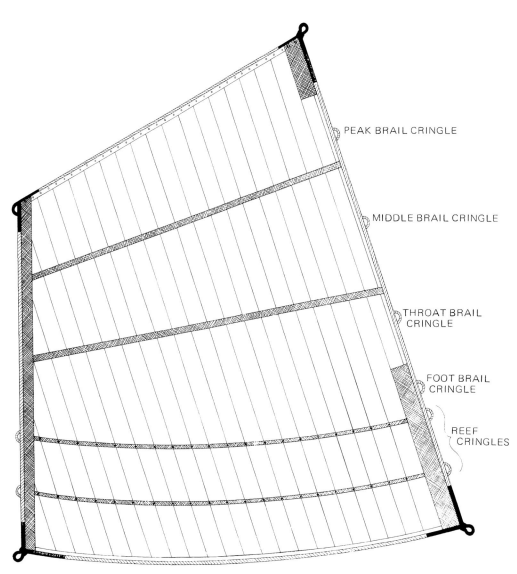

PEAK BRAIL CRINGLE

MIDDLE BRAIL CRINGLE

THROAT BRAIL CRINGLE

FOOT BRAIL CRINGLE

REEF CRINGLES

MAIN AND FORE TRYSAIL

TRYSAILS

Trysails were tabled the same as the spanker. Two reef bands were fitted, the lower band one sixth up the luff, the upper band one third; both bands were parallel to the foot, and each were a quarter cloth's width. The luff was lined with half a breadth of cloth from tack to nock, the leech was lined with a full cloth as far as 4 feet above the upper reef band, and again from the peak a distance of 4 feet 6 inches. To give an additional strength to the sails two bands, each one third of a cloth wide, were sewn across the sail equally dividing the upper reef and the head at both luff and leech. The bolt rope, cringles and so forth were the same as on the spanker. The trysails came to within 1 foot of the end of the gaff, and the gaff was usually peaked at the same angle as the spanker gaff. All the linings were sewn on the port side of the sails. The foot of the trysail had a downward roach as described for the mizen sail.

51 *St Michael*, 1669.

III SAILMAKING
Representative models 1669–1846

52 A 90 gun ship of 1675. Contemporary model with modern rigging.

53 *Breda*, 1692. Contemporary hull and rigging. Trinity House Model.

III SAILMAKING
Representative models 1669–1846

54 A ship of about 1695 (bow view).

55 A ship of about 1695 (quarter view).

56 A 50 gun ship of about 1710.

57 *Royal William*, 1719. Contemporary model with modern rigging.

III | SAILMAKING
Representative models 1669-1846

58 *Centurion*, 1732. Contemporary model with modern rigging.

59 *Tartar* of 1734 (bow view). Contemporary model with mainly original rigging.

If undelivered

60 *Tartar* of 1734 (broadside view). One of the few models with contemporary sails.

...AILMAKING
...epresentative models 1669–1846

...ntemporary model of the *Victory* of 1737 (broadside). Modern rigging.

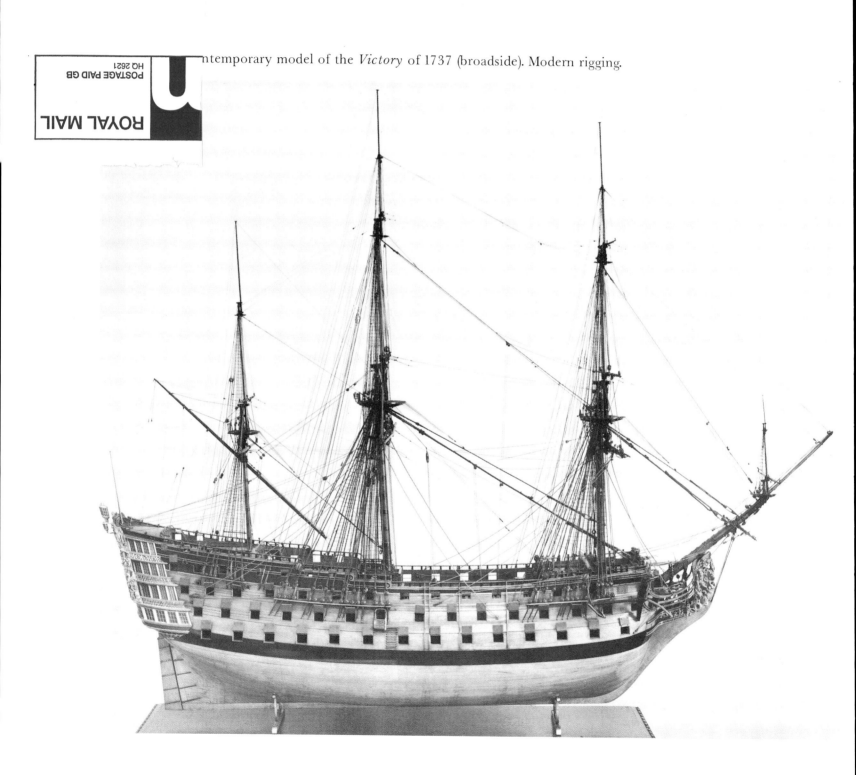

62 Large scale model of the *Victory* of 1737 (bow view).

III SAILMAKING
Representative models 1669-1846

63 A contemporary model of a 60 gun ship of about 1735 — a fine example of eighteenth century craftsmanship.

64 *Endeavour* (1768) model, made in the
National Maritime Museum and rigged by
the author. (Bow view).

65 *Endeavour*, 1768 (broadside).

III SAILMAKING
Representative models 1669–1846

66 Contemporary model of a frigate of about 1805 with original sails and rigging (quarter view).

67 Frigate of about 1805 (broadside).

68 *Hastings*, 1818. Contemporary model with mainly original rigging.

III SAILMAKING
Representative models 1669–1846

69 *Constance*, 1846. Contemporary model with original rigging.

Seamanship IV

18 Order of dressing the masts and yards

ORDER OF DRESSING THE MASTS AND YARDS

Lower masts Pendants of tackles, shrouds, stay, preventer stay (on small ships it was sometimes the practice to carry the preventer stay under the stay). After 1810 the preventer was under the stay on all ships.

Topmasts Burton pendants, shrouds, backstays, preventer stay, stay.

Main and mizen topgallant masts Stay, shrouds, backstay.

Fore topgallant mast Stay, flying jib-stay, shrouds, backstay.

Royal masts Stay, backstay.

Fore yard Head earing strop, jackstay, yard tackle, brace, lift, footrope.

Main yard Head earing strop, jackstay, yard tackle, preventer brace, brace, lift, footrope.

Crossjack Jackstay, brace, lift, footrope.

Topsail yards Head earing strop, jackstay, brace, lift, footrope.

Topgallant and royal yards Footrope, head earing strop, jackstay, brace, lift. The above order is for the end of the sail era; however it is only necessary to deduct ropes not carried during other periods to arrive at the order for any year required.

Note Under the rigging on all masts and before the rigging on all yards, grommet strops were placed to obviate any chafing on the rigging.

ORDER OF DRESSING THE BOWSPRIT

The following orders are based on those shown on models and in contemporary books; it will be seen that although there were a few variations the general trend was the same. All the following are from the inboard end of the bowsprit.

Period 1850 Inner bobstay, starboard shroud, port shroud, fore preventer stay collar, middle bobstay, starboard shroud, port shroud, fore stay collar, outer bobstay, cap bobstay.

Period 1818 Inner bobstay, starboard shroud, port shroud, fore preventer stay collar, middle bobstay, starboard shroud, port shroud, forestay collar, outer bobstay.

Period 1810 and 1805 Inner bobstay, starboard shroud, port shroud, forestay collar, outer bobstay, fore preventer stay collar.

Period 1773 Fore stay collar, Inner bob-stay, starboard shroud, port shroud, fore preventer stay collar, outer bobstay.

Period 1733 Fore stay collar, inner bobstay, starboard shroud, port shroud, outer bobstay, fore preventer stay collar.

Period 1719 Inner bobstay, starboard shroud, port shroud, fore stay collar, outer bobstay, fore preventer stay collar.

Period 1710 Fore stay collar, starboard shroud, port shroud, bobstay.

It should be noted that during all periods, the first collar put on the bowsprit came approximately one third the length of the visible part of the bowsprit down the bowsprit, from the outer end. There was also a space of about 2 feet between the bobstays, consequently when three bobstays were carried the various collars were spaced in three batches; when two bobstays were carried the collars were in two batches, and where the stay collars were fitted before the bobstays, the space of 2 feet applied to the stay collars. The cap bobstay was a separate bobstay carried just abaft the bowsprit cap.

ORDER OF DRESSING THE JIBBOOM

Footropes, guy pendants, martingale stay.

ORDER OF DRESSING THE FLYING JIBBOOM

Footropes, flying jib guys, flying martingale stay.

DATES OF CHANGES IN MASTS AND RIGGING

1611/18 Introduction of SPRIT TOPMAST.

1618 By this date SQUARE MIZEN TOPSAILS were in general use.

1623 By this date only two ships in the Royal Navy still retained the BONAVENTURE MIZEN; they were *Royal Prince* and *St Andrew*. By 1640 no ships had more than three masts.

1630 Introduction of JEERS.

1637 ROYALS and MIZEN TOPGALLANT sails carried on the *Royal Sovereign*, the only ship so rigged.

1640 Introduction of bowsprit WOOLDINGS.

1642 First mention of FOOTROPES on the main yard.

1650/70 RAMSHEAD no longer used for lower TIES.

1650 By this date MARTNETS were replaced by LEECHLINES. Large ships carried STAYSAILS. GASKETS were fitted on the lower yards.

1655 Introduction of first row of REEF POINTS on main and fore topsails. First known mention of main STUNSAILS in naval inventories.

1660 Introduction of main, mizen, main top and fore top STAYSAILS.

1668 Introduction of second row of REEF POINTS on the main and fore topsails.

1670 Introduction of mizen topmast. STANDING BACKSTAYS.

1675 Introduction of double TOP ROPES on main and fore topmasts. First mention of FOOTROPES on the fore yard.

1680 FOOTROPES introduced on the topsail yards. Introduction of REEF POINTS on the courses. BONNETS no longer used on the courses, or mizen sail. First mention of BUMKIN. LIFTS taken to the mast head instead of under the tops.

1680/1700 MIZEN STAY secured with deadeyes.
1685 Introduction of YARD TACKLES.
1690 MAIN and FORE STAYS set up with hearts.
STUNSAILS carried on main and fore lower and topsail yards.
1691 BOBSTAYS fitted on large ships.
1700/1712 The after end of the MIZEN TOP was squared off and by 1712 all TOPS were altered in this fashion.

1700 Introduction of the BEES.
Introduction of the fore and main PREVENTER STAYS.
BOBSTAYS on all rates.
Introduction of the first row of REEF POINTS on the mizen topsail.
1705 Introduction of the JIBBOOM and SAIL on small ships.
1706 Introduction of BOWSPRIT SHROUDS.
1709 Introduction of mizen topmast STAYSAIL.
Introduction of main topgallant STAYSAILS.
1710 Introduction of JIBBOOM GUYS.
CROWSFEET no longer used on the mizen yard LIFT.
Introduction of the third row of REEF POINTS on the main and fore topsails and the second row on the mizen topsail.
1710 BUMKINS used on Sixth Rates.
1712 By this date, on 60 gun ships and below, the SPRIT TOPMAST had been replaced by the JIBBOOM.
1719 By this date, on 70 gun ships and below, the SPRIT TOPMAST had been replaced by the JIBBOOM.
Introduction of double BOBSTAYS.
Introduction of JIB STAY.
Introduction of main royal STAY and STAYSAIL on large ships.
1730 Forward edge of the mizen sail was laced down the mast; by 1750 this innovation had spread to all ships.
Shortly after this alteration the DRIVER was introduced to serve as an occasional sail used in fair weather.
1733 Lower CATHARPINS no longer rigged.
1733/45 Introduction of OPEN HEARTS on the fore stay and fore preventer stay collars.
1740 Introduction of SLAB LINES.

1745 BUMKINS carried on all rates.
Introduction of GAFFS on the mizen sail of small ships.
Introduction of BEE BLOCKS.
BELAYING PINS were used on racks on the shrouds of small ships but not seen on large ships until the end of the eighteenth century. By this date on all ships the SPRIT TOPMAST had been replaced by a JIBBOOM.
1750 Introduction of ROPE WOOLD-INGS on the mizen mast of large ships.
1760 MIZEN TOPGALLANT MAST and SAIL were in general use.
Introduction of TRUSS PENDANTS on the fore and main yards.
Introduction of FLEMISH HORSES (large ships may have used them a little earlier).
Introduction of FOUR SIDED STAY-SAILS.
1770 Introduction of the mizen top-mast SHIFTING BACKSTAY.
1773 Introduction of the FORE STAY-SAIL.
Introduction of the MIDDLE STAY-SAIL.
Introduction of the mizen TRUSS PARREL.
Introduction of the topgallant STUNSAILS.
Introduction of the SLINGS on the lower yards.
SPRITSAIL LIFTS were no longer used as sprit topsail sheets.
FISH DAVITS were shorter and set on the channels.
1779 Introduction of the main and fore ROYAL SAILS.
1788 Introduction of the fourth row of REEF POINTS on the fore and main topsails, and the third row on the mizen topsail.
1790 TOPSAIL LIFTS no longer used as topgallant sheets.
General introduction of ROYALS on all masts.
1793 Mizen PREVENTER STAY authorised.
Main PREVENTER STAY taken to the BOWSPRIT.
Mizen sail fitted with a BOOM.
1794 Introduction of the DOLPHIN STRIKER.
Introduction of the FLYING JIB-BOOM.
1796 Introduction of double TACKS.

1800 IRON HOOPS replaced rope wooldings.
1801 Lower STUNSAILS on the main mast no longer issued.
Fore lower STUNSAIL yard carried from the end of the upper stunsail booms.
1805 All SHROUDS were cable laid.
1806 Mizen topsail BRACES led forward.
TRUSS PARRELS superseded PARRELS on the topsail yards.
DRIVER fitted as a permanent sail, replacing mizen sail.
1810 MAIN STAY and PREVENTER STAY made fast on the forecastle.
1811 Introduction of CHAIN CABLE.
Introduction of JACKSTAYS on the yards.
CHAIN SLINGS permanently fitted.
1811/1830 During this period the SPRITSAIL YARD was relegated to a spreader and remained in use as a spreader until it was replaced by prop-er SPREADERS in 1850.
1815 BRACE PENDANTS no longer fitted.
MAIN PREVENTER BRACE a perma-nent fitting.
TRYSAILS replaced main and mizen staysails.
MIDDLE STAYSAIL and MIZEN TOP STAYSAILS were no longer issued to HM ships.
SPRIT TOPSAILS were no longer issued to HM ships.
DOLPHIN STRIKER was fitted with a jaw.
CROSSJACK BRACES no longer crossed each other.
TOPS were made 18 inches wider at the after end than at the first deadeye on the main and fore masts, and 12 inches on the mizen mast. Also the lubber's hole was fitted with a hinged flap.
STAYS were fitted by means of legs instead of a running eye.
The JIBBOOM heel was made square to serve as a mizen topmast if required.
1816 A semi-circle was cut out of the after side of the topsail caps and a clamp fitted, to enable the TOP-GALLANT MAST to be carried abaft the topmast when chasing.
1819 Introduction of TOGGLES on the sails instead of cringles.
1820 Introduction of CHAIN NECK-

LACE to take the futtock shrouds.
1823 Patent TRUSS proposed by
Lieutenant Green and adopted shortly
afterwards.
1835 Introduction of FRAME CROSS-
TREES on topmasts.
1840 SHROUD LANYARDS spliced
to eyes in the channels.
Lower SHROUDS turned in cutter-
stay fashion.
JACK LINE or FRENCH REEFING
introduced and also second reef on
courses.
CHAIN GAMMONING a general
practice.
1850 Chain replaced by rope on JIB-
BOOM CRUPPER, lower TRUSSES
and BOBSTAYS.
Introduction of the CAP BOBSTAY.
1853 Trials took place of the first
screw frigate built for the Royal Navy
with auxiliary engines, namely the
Arrogant, a wooden ship launched in
1848.
The majority of the dates given here
are only approximate but they should
give a good idea of the various changes
that occurred at that period.

**LASHING OF THE JEER BLOCK
STROPS TO THE MASTHEAD**

NOTE THE SHAPE OF THE CLEAT

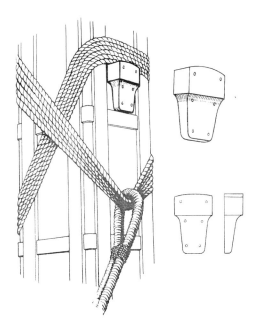

19 Ropework, blocks and other tackle

ROPEWORK

There are so many excellent books
written on the subject that my contri-
bution seems hardly necessary; however, I do not intend to teach the
reader how to make knots, splices,
bends or hitches, but to show where
the various knots and so forth were
used. I cannot recommend too highly
The Ashley Book of Knots for anyone
not conversant with the method of
forming knots. This book, written by
Clifford W Ashley, describes in the
fullest detail all the knots, splices,
whippings, seizings, fancy ropework,
and so on that one could ever come
across on board a ship in this, or any
other century.
The art of seamanship altered very
little through the years, which shows
as nothing else can the quality of our
early seamen. When decorative ropework was called for, it depended
entirely upon the skill of the seaman,
as of course it still does. I have seen
old seamen sitting for hours, patiently
forming elaborate sennet, bell ropes
and various other items, and I have
never ceased to marvel how this skill
has been passed down, and seemingly
will never die out. (I wonder when the
first knot was made and by whom.)
When it comes to working on the rigging of a model, it is of course the best
plan to try and use the same type of
knot that would have been used on

the actual ship, but as this is not always
possible, especially when repairing
rigging, then it is up to the rigger to
use an alternative knot; with experience one soon learns the alternative,
and one should have no difficulty in
making a trim job.
Whipping, pointing and back splicing
are means of finishing off the ends of
ropes. Whipping is the most usual
method and although the common
whipping is the simplest one to make,
I prefer the sailmaker's whipping, both
for neatness and holding power. Pointing is a more elaborate method and
one hardly expects to come across it
in a model; usually only the larger
ropes were pointed to assist in reeving
them through holes or sheaves (and
also to prevent the ends from being
cut off and sold by hard up seamen to
unscrupulous land sharks). Back splicing could only be used if the rope did
not have to be taken through a block.
Seizings Flat seizings were used to
seize two parts of rope together where
there was no strain on the seizing, such
as the upper seizing when turning in
deadeyes and hearts. Throat seizings
were used to seize blocks into their
straps, for the lower seizings of deadeyes and hearts, and also seizing two
parts of rope together where the strain
was equal on both parts, such as the
upper seizing of the shrouds at the
mast head. Racking seizings were used
to seize two parts of rope together
where the strain only came on one
part; on some ships they replaced the
flat seizings on the shrouds and stays.
Cross seizings were used to fasten
hoops to the sails. Rose seizings were
used to secure a rope with an eye-
splice in the end to a spar so that the
eye lay flat along the spar, an example
being the inboard end of footropes.
The lashing most favoured was the
rose lashing, for not only was it firm
but also ornamental. It was used to
lash the ends of the stays together
abaft the masts, and to lash the ends
of block straps together when the
straps were in the form of legs. Cross
lashings were used to lash the inboard
ends of the jackstays together.
Knots, bends and hitches Blackwall
and midshipman's hitches were used to
bend a rope to a hook. A bowline knot

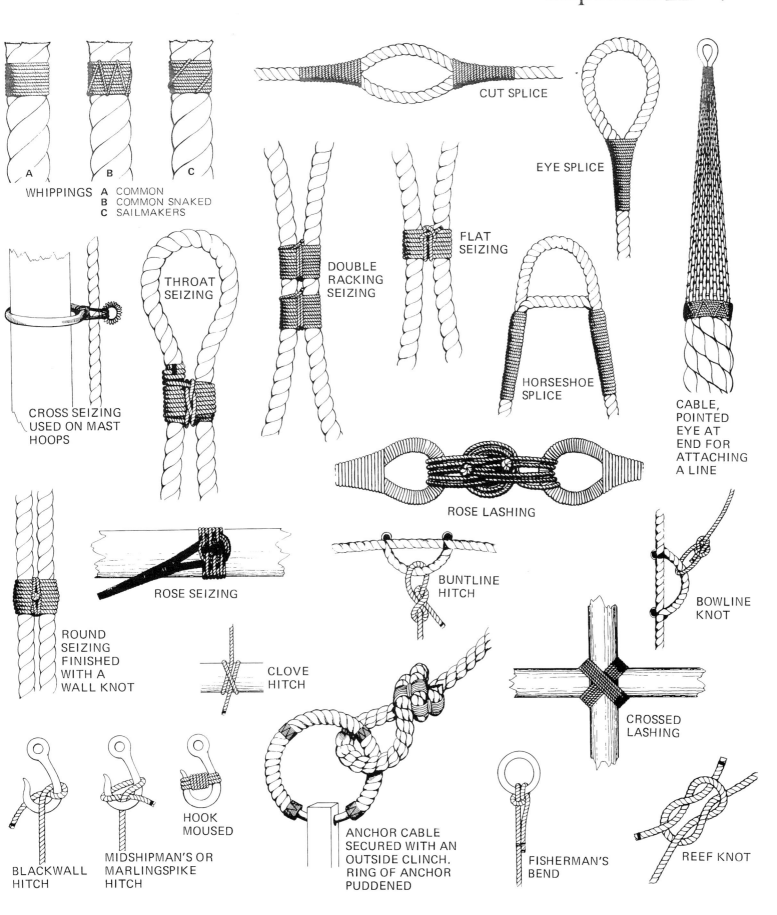

WHIPPINGS A COMMON
B COMMON SNAKED
C SAILMAKERS

CUT SPLICE

EYE SPLICE

FLAT SEIZING

DOUBLE RACKING SEIZING

THROAT SEIZING

CROSS SEIZING USED ON MAST HOOPS

HORSESHOE SPLICE

CABLE, POINTED EYE AT END FOR ATTACHING A LINE

ROSE LASHING

ROUND SEIZING FINISHED WITH A WALL KNOT

ROSE SEIZING

BUNTLINE HITCH

BOWLINE KNOT

CLOVE HITCH

CROSSED LASHING

BLACKWALL HITCH

MIDSHIPMAN'S OR MARLINGSPIKE HITCH

HOOK MOUSED

ANCHOR CABLE SECURED WITH AN OUTSIDE CLINCH. RING OF ANCHOR PUDDENED

FISHERMAN'S BEND

REEF KNOT

IV SEAMANSHIP
Ropework

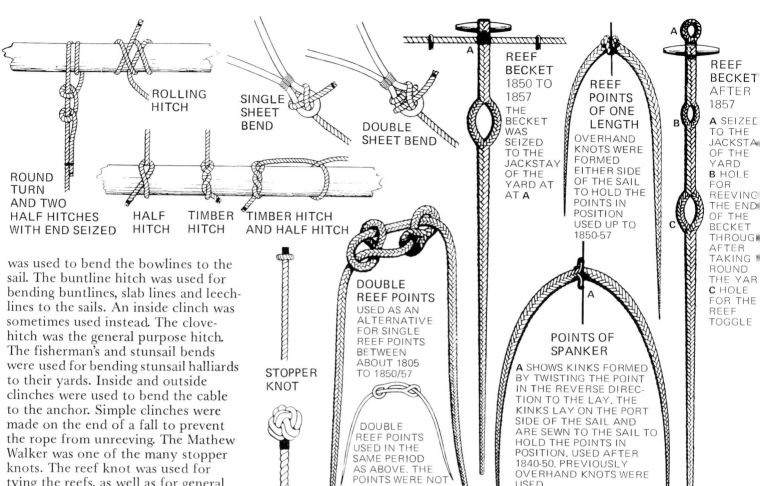

ROLLING HITCH

SINGLE SHEET BEND

DOUBLE SHEET BEND

ROUND TURN AND TWO HALF HITCHES WITH END SEIZED

HALF HITCH

TIMBER HITCH

TIMBER HITCH AND HALF HITCH

STOPPER KNOT

TACK KNOT

DOUBLE REEF POINTS USED AS AN ALTERNATIVE FOR SINGLE REEF POINTS BETWEEN ABOUT 1805 TO 1850/57

DOUBLE REEF POINTS USED IN THE SAME PERIOD AS ABOVE. THE POINTS WERE NOT ROVE THROUGH THEIR OWN EYES BEFORE REEVING THROUGH THE SAIL

REEF BECKET 1850 TO 1857 THE BECKET WAS SEIZED TO THE JACKSTAY OF THE YARD AT AT A

REEF POINTS OF ONE LENGTH OVERHAND KNOTS WERE FORMED EITHER SIDE OF THE SAIL TO HOLD THE POINTS IN POSITION USED UP TO 1850-57

POINTS OF SPANKER A SHOWS KINKS FORMED BY TWISTING THE POINT IN THE REVERSE DIRECTION TO THE LAY. THE KINKS LAY ON THE PORT SIDE OF THE SAIL AND ARE SEWN TO THE SAIL TO HOLD THE POINTS IN POSITION. USED AFTER 1840-50. PREVIOUSLY OVERHAND KNOTS WERE USED.

REEF BECKET AFTER 1857 A SEIZED TO THE JACKSTAY OF THE YARD B HOLE FOR REEVING THE END OF THE BECKET THROUGH AFTER TAKING ROUND THE YARD C HOLE FOR THE REEF TOGGLE

was used to bend the bowlines to the sail. The buntline hitch was used for bending buntlines, slab lines and leech-lines to the sails. An inside clinch was sometimes used instead. The clove-hitch was the general purpose hitch. The fisherman's and stunsail bends were used for bending stunsail halliards to their yards. Inside and outside clinches were used to bend the cable to the anchor. Simple clinches were made on the end of a fall to prevent the rope from unreeving. The Mathew Walker was one of the many stopper knots. The reef knot was used for tying the reefs, as well as for general purposes and the roband hitch was for securing robands to the jackstay. The rolling hitch was for bending smaller ropes to larger ropes, such as when tail blocks were required. A round turn and two half-hitches were used for making a standing part fast, usually with the end stoppered back. The sheet bend (double and single) was used for bending the sheets to the clues. The timber-hitch was used for securing cluelines and clue garnets to the yards; it was also used for bending the truss to the lower yards in the seventeenth century. The tack knot was a stopper knot placed in the outer end of the tack when single tacks were used. Flat sennet was used for reef points, robands and sea gaskets; they were all tapered in the making. Reef beckets were also made out of flat sennet, with eyes formed in the sennet for the toggles. French sennet was used for making harbour gaskets.
Strapping of blocks was done in a number of ways, all of them for a par-

ticular purpose. It is, however, only a matter of commonsense as to which strap goes where. If the reader bears in mind that all blocks, no matter where they are carried, should be able to be unrigged with the minimum amount of trouble, for the purposes of maintenance, no difficulty should arise in selecting the right strap. As regards the question of whether to serve the straps of the blocks or not, there are two trends of thought — some like to serve them to keep the weather out of the strap, while others like to leave the straps unserved so that any signs of wear or rot are visible. Personally I prefer an unserved strap, having seen a strap part and injure a shipmate; however it certainly was the practice to serve such exposed straps as those round the tack block, where the sea could easily get to them. I therefore

suggest serving all large and all exposed straps, all straps where they could be chafed, such as those on the yards, and leave the rest of the straps unserved.
Straps made in the form of strops were used where blocks had to be seized in position, or where the blocks were carried on the yardarms — in fact, anywhere that it was possible to carry a block without lashings. Blocks carried on pendants never had the pendant spliced round them, for if this was done the blocks could never be brought to deck for inspection without renewing the pendant which was a very wasteful procedure. Instead, a long eye was spliced in the pendant and the block seized in this eye with a racking seizing. Blocks lashed on the yards were seized into a strap made from one length of rope with a small

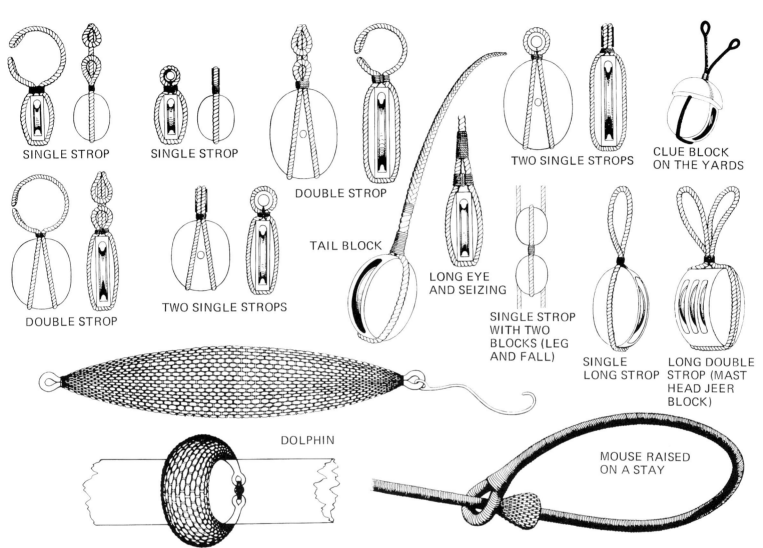

SINGLE STROP

SINGLE STROP

DOUBLE STROP

TAIL BLOCK

TWO SINGLE STROPS

CLUE BLOCK ON THE YARDS

DOUBLE STROP

TWO SINGLE STROPS

LONG EYE AND SEIZING

SINGLE STROP WITH TWO BLOCKS (LEG AND FALL)

SINGLE LONG STROP

LONG DOUBLE STROP (MAST HEAD JEER BLOCK)

DOLPHIN

MOUSE RAISED ON A STAY

eye spliced in each end; the block was not lashed in the centre of the strap, but was so done to have one long leg and one short leg. Thus, the lashing came on the after side of the yard. Spans in which two or more blocks were seized, such as those carried at the mast heads or at the caps for the lifts, were made in the same fashion as the other lashing straps just described except that equal lengths were left on both ends of the span. Thimbles were seized in the straps only when the blocks were shackled on, or when the blocks were fitted with hooks; at all other times the straps were made with soft eyes. Some blocks were carried with double straps of which there were two types, one comprising two single straps, the other made of one long strop doubled, with the block seized in the bight. This was necessary

because on some blocks the eye of the strap had to run in line with the sheave, in which case the first method was used, but if the eye had to run in a contrariwise direction, the second method was called for. Double strapped blocks were only required where great strain came on the blocks such as the jeers, crossjack slings and so on.

Topsail halliard blocks were strapped with a long strop which had a hook and thimble seized in the end, which allowed the block to be carried a few feet from the channel, thus keeping the block as far as possible from the sea. Working tackles such as quarter tackles and yard arm tackles, stay tackle falls and so forth, often had the lower block spliced into a long pendant with a hook and thimble spliced into the other end. Brace blocks, when

they were not carried on pendants, were fitted to the yards by means of a dog and bitch strop which comprised two interlocked thimbles; round one thimble a strop was formed into which the block was seized, round the other thimble a strop was formed to be seized round the yard arm. The straps of clueline and spritsail sheet blocks had to be rove through the holes in the cheeks of the blocks before the ends were either spliced together as on the clueline blocks, or formed into a knot as on the spritsail sheet block. All splices, by the way, should lay on the arse of the block. I hope that the illustrations will help to clear up any questions the reader may want answering.

Servings and other means of protection Any part of the standing rigging where it could suffer from chafing was always served: for instance, the top-mast backstays in the way of the lower tops, or the foremost shroud where the lower yard could rub against when braced round. It was also the practice to lash mats, made from rope yarn, where needed; however, I have never seen such mats on a model. I have seen one contemporary model carrying dolphins, which were rope fenders or puddings lashed a few feet up the lower masts. They were used to allow the lower yard to be lowered so that the centre was supported on the dolphin.

There were various methods for securing the standing part of a fall to the block, the most popular way being to splice the standing part round the block strapping at the arse of the block. Another way was to seize a thimble into the strap and make the end fast through the thimble; this method was used when the end was shackled on. A less usual way was to make a small becket and place it through the block strap, splicing the fall to both parts of the becket, so that the strain and chafe was taken on the becket and not on the block strap. Finally, on double and treble blocks a method sometimes practised was to splice the end of the fall round the block strap at the head of the block, then seize the rope with two seizings to the block strap at the side of the block, thus the standing part led from one side of the block and the hauling part from the other side, keeping the blocks level when hauling on them.

BLOCKS, DEADEYES, HEARTS AND OTHER TACKLE

The shape of blocks altered very little over the years and although machines were produced to make the blocks in the nineteenth century, the principle of construction remained the same. Some blocks were cut out of one piece of wood while others were built up of four or more pieces. The actual method of construction is immaterial to the modelmaker; what is far more important is using the correct type of block and having the blocks to the right proportions.

The common block (single) had a width of sheave that was one tenth more than the diameter of the rope; the diameter of the sheave was four times the width of the sheave. The width of the sheave hole was one sixteenth more than the width of the sheave and the length of the sheave hole was one and one third the diameter of the sheave. The length of the shell was eight times the width of the sheave hole; the width was two fifths the length of the shell; the breadth was six times the width of the sheave; and the position of the pin was eleven twenty-firsts from the top of the block. The edges of the sheave hole were chamfered off and the shell slightly rounded. The pin was made of wood on small blocks and iron or brasss on larger blocks. When metal pins were used, the block was coaked: that is, brass plates were set in the shell of the block for the pin to bear on. The pin was held in place by the strap of the block. This strap was one quarter the length of the block in circumference. The score for the strap was half the depth of the strap at the top and bottom of the block, diminishing to nothing at the pin.

Common blocks (double and treble) were made to the same proportions as the single blocks except in the width of the shell. This was increased by the separating piece or pieces between the sheaves which were five sixths the width of the sheaves. The common block as the name suggests was the most popular type of block and was used for all purposes except where specific types of blocks were called for.

Jewel blocks were small common blocks carried on the end of the upper yards to take the stunsail halliards; they were seized or toggled on.

External iron bound blocks When blocks were used for such purposes as the lead of the top ropes, they were iron bound instead of having a rope strap because of the extreme strain taken by the blocks. The proportions of these blocks were the same as for the common blocks, but instead of scoring the shell, an iron strap was let into the block. This strap was only let into the shell at the top and bottom, similar to the method of fitting the rope strap. The iron strap in the way of the pin was made wider and a hole cut out of the strap to give access to the pin; the pin, strangely enough, does not seem to have had contact with the strap but was borne on coaking set in the cheeks of the blocks. The strap was formed into a hook at the head of the block, an ordinary hook when single blocks were used, but when two iron bound blocks formed a tackle the lower block was fitted with a swivel hook; this enabled turns to be taken out of the fall.

Although the top tackle blocks used in the seventeenth century were iron bound, I do not think that swivel blocks were introduced until the middle of the eighteenth century and I have not come across them on a model earlier than 1737. The size of the iron strapping varied according to the use of the block. On the blocks taking the minimum amount of strain the strap was only 1/4 inch thick, while on the blocks taking the maximum strain, the strap was at least 1 inch thick; the breadth of the strap was about three times the thickness. The faces of external bound blocks were usually flatter than the faces of the common blocks.

Internal iron bound blocks were made to the same proportions as the external bound blocks, but the iron binding was placed inside the shell, and only extended from the head of the block to just below the pin. On this type of block the pin was borne by the strap as there was no need for a score to be cut on the outside of the shell. Some of these blocks were made with the strapping extending to the arse of the block, with a leg to take the standing part of the fall; also, instead of being fitted with hooks, the blocks were shackled on, and consequently the strap at the head of the block was formed into a ring. The blocks previously fitted with swivel hooks were fitted with swivel eyes and were introduced about 1840.

Shoulder blocks were made like single common blocks, except that the head of the block had a shoulder on one edge. The purpose of this shoulder was to prevent the rope reeving through the block from jambing in the sheeve. They were used on the lower yard

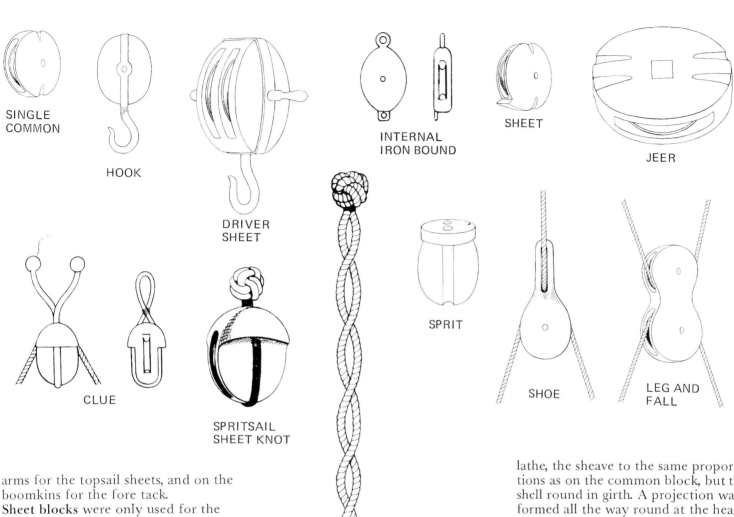

SINGLE
COMMON

HOOK

DRIVER
SHEET

INTERNAL
IRON BOUND

SHEET

JEER

CLUE

SPRITSAIL
SHEET KNOT

SPRIT

SPRITSAIL
SHEET
STROP

SHOE

LEG AND
FALL

arms for the topsail sheets, and on the boomkins for the fore tack.

Sheet blocks were only used for the lower block of the mizen sail or driver sheets, the only difference between these blocks and the common blocks being that the pin extended on either side of the block, to enable the sheets to be belayed to it. This type of block was only required when the ship was fitted with a horse to take the lower block. They were either double stropped, or external iron bound, in both cases with a hook.

Double scored blocks were large common blocks made to be fitted with double straps. Instead of a centre score, two scores were cut in the shell, either side of the centre; these scores either ran down alongside each other the whole length of the shell, or were alongside at the head, then separated to lie just under the sheave holes at the bottom of the block. All jeer blocks were double scored, as were the topsail sheet blocks carried from the quarters of the lower yards.

Clue blocks differed from common blocks in that the clue blocks had a shoulder formed on either side, extending from the head to just above the pin. This shoulder was circular and had a hole in the way of the strapping score to admit the strap.

Spritsail sheet blocks, as the name suggests, were only used for the spritsail sheets. They were turned on a lathe, the sheave to the same proportions as on the common block, but the shell round in girth. A projection was formed all the way round at the head of the block and a hole was bored through this projection either side of the block for the strap to reeve through; the score for the strap was taken right round the shell as far as the projection. This type of block was used from about 1690 to 1750; after then blocks similar to clue blocks were fitted.

Shoe blocks were similar to two single common blocks, placed together head to head, with the sheaves running in a contrariwise direction. Both sheaves were the same size, the shell was cut out of one piece of wood, and no strap was required. The proportions of shoe blocks were the same as two single common blocks.

The leg and fall blocks, like the shoe blocks, were similar to two single common blocks, placed head to head, but both sheaves ran in the same direction. Again no strap was used and consequently no score was required. The proportions were the same as two

165

common blocks. On some ships instead of using a leg and fall block, two single blocks were used strapped together head to head.

Long-tackle or fiddle blocks had a width of sheave that was one tenth more than the diameter of the rope. The diameter of the upper sheave was four and three quarter times, and the diameter of the lower sheave three and a half times, the width of the sheave. The width of the sheave holes was one sixteenth more than the width of the sheave. The length of the upper sheave hole was one and one third times the diameter of the upper sheave and the length of the lower sheave hole was one and a half times the diameter of the lower sheave.

The length of the shell overall was fourteen times the width of the sheaves and the length to the neck was eleven twentieths the overall length of the shell, from the head of the shell. The width of the shell was one fifth the length of the shell. The breadth of the upper shell was half the length of the shell; the breadth of the lower shell was three eighths the length of the shell; and the breadth of the neck of the shell was three twenty-fifths the length of the shell. The position of the upper pin was three tenths the length of the shell from the head and the position of the lower pin was eleven fiftieths the length of the shell from the arse.

The block was scored down to the two pins. The upper edge of the upper sheave hole was two twenty-fifths the length of the shell from the head, the lower edge of the lower sheave hole was two twenty-fifths the length of the shell from the arse; this left the centre of the block solid for a distance of seven fiftieths the length of the shell. The pins were similar to those of the common block. These long-tackle blocks were used to make up falls where the tackle was carried along a yard such as yard arm tackles, or in positions where ordinary double blocks could foul up. The strap of the block was secured at the nect with a round seizing.

Sister blocks were double blocks with the sheaves one above the other in a vertical line. The sheaves were the same proportions as on the common block, but the shell was almost spherical, being only slightly flattened on the sides. A dovetail was formed at both ends of the shell to take seizings and a seizing was also put on at the necking. This necking came proportionately between the two halves of the shell, (the upper sheave was slightly smaller than the lower sheave) and the length of the necking was the same proportions as on the long-tackle blocks. The score was taken right down each side of the block so that the topmast shrouds could lie in them. The dovetails were half the length of the top or bottom halves of the shell respectively; the width of the dovetails and the necking coincided with the distance apart of the topmast shrouds where the block was to be seized. When a necklace was fitted on the topmasts for the hanging blocks, (after 1840), the sister blocks were rigged with a double strop and were shackled to the necklace. When fitted like this the lower dovetail was omitted and the bottom rounded, the score was taken all round the block and the strop was seized at the necking and the upper dovetail. The shell was spherical and the sheaves proportionately the same as those of the earlier sister blocks; the depth of the shell was proportionate to the sheaves.

Topsail halliard blocks were flat thin blocks. The sheave was one tenth wider than the diameter of the rope and its length six times the width. The length of the shell was one and one third times the diameter of the sheave, the breadth of the shell was five sixths the length and the width one third the length. The block had a single score.

Ramshead block The following is conjectural, based upon the description in Smith's *A Sea Grammar,* and upon scrutiny of various seventeenth century paintings. As the name suggests the block was shaped like a ram's head, having three sheaves for the halliard in what could be called the crown of the head, and a hole for the ties in what I call the jaws, this hole running in line with the pin of the sheaves. The sheaves would be one tenth more than the diameter of the halliard in width,

and their diameter would be four times their width. The proportions for the cheeks, width of the sheave holes etc would be the same as for the common treble block. The length of the shell would be about twelve times the width of the sheave holes, with the hole for the ties half way between the top of the sheave holes and the top of the block; this hole was one tenth wider than the diameter of the ties. The shell tapered towards the head of the block and, to prevent chafe, the edges of the tie hole were chamfered off. The outer edges of the block were rounded off. No score was required for the block was not strapped. The pin of the sheaves was positioned about ten twenty-firsts from the bottom of the block. Other information about this block is unfortunately lacking; however one made to the description I have given should answer very well for the purpose.

Snatch blocks were of two types. One was a wooden shell with an opening for snatching ropes in; it had a hole in the head to take a becket in which a thimble and hook were seized. The block was egg shaped and came in various sizes. The sheave was one tenth wider than the rope's diameter and its length was four times the width. The length of the shell was eight times the thickness of the sheave hole. The opening in the block was cut diagonally down to the sheave and was slightly wider than the sheave hole. The width of the shell was one fifth its length, the taper of the block was half the diameter at the head than at the sheave. The hole for the becket was one sixth the length of the shell from the head, and ran the same way as the sheave. The pin was one third from the arse of the block. This type of block was only used for light purposes and when a sturdy block was called for the second type was used.

This block was iron bound with a strap that hinged over the slot of the snatch, secured by a forelock pin or toggle. The proportions were the same for the bound block as they were for the unbound one, but instead of having a hole for a becket the strap terminated in a swivel hook. The model

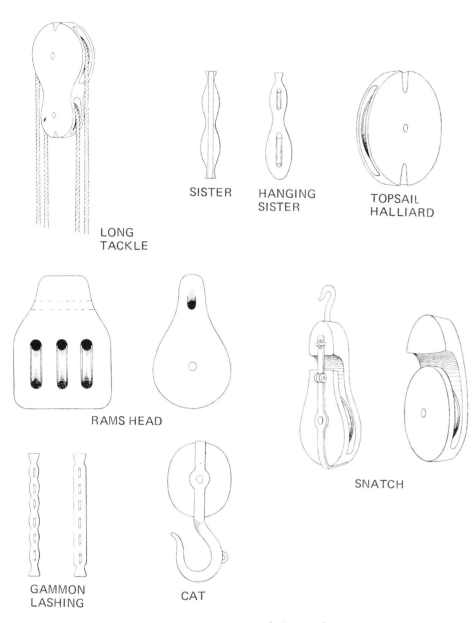

LONG TACKLE

SISTER

HANGING SISTER

TOPSAIL HALLIARD

RAMS HEAD

SNATCH

GAMMON LASHING

CAT

FISH HOOK

SLIP HOOK

of the *Medway,* a 60 gun ship of 1742 has an unbound snatch block hanging from a deck beam, and is now in the National Maritime Museum at Greenwich.

The viol block was the largest block used on board a ship. The width of the sheave was one tenth more than the diameter of the viol. The diameter of the sheave was seven times its thickness, the sheave hole was three eighths wider than the thickness of the sheave. The length of the sheave hole was one and one third times the diameter of the sheave. The length of the shell was ten times the thickness of the sheave hole, the breadth of the shell was eight times the thickness of the sheave, and the thickness of the shell was two sevenths of its length. The block was double scored and had an iron pin the same diameter as the width of the sheave. When hoisting up the anchor, the block was lashed to the main mast. It was only used when the jeer capstan was manned instead of the main capstan, for weighing anchor. The viol, when the main capstan was used, was taken straight to the capstan and the block was not required. The viol block was not used on ships below 36 guns, and was only in use from the latter part of the seventeenth century to when chain cables were used. An interesting print in the National Maritime Museum shows how the viol was used when manning the main capstan in the eighteenth century; the viol, after the turns were taken round the capstan, ran over a series of rollers lashed to the deck beams overhead; between these rollers, men were stationed to haul the bights to the next roller, by the hawse hole a long upright roller was clamped between the deck head and the deck and this led the viol round and into position for nipping onto the cable.

Thick and thin quarter blocks are mentioned by Steel but I do not intend to include them, for they were only an unpopular experiment which lasted but a short time, and were not used in many ships.

Gammon lashing or rack blocks were long blocks either in the form of single blocks placed head to tail, or a straight length of wood with a number of vertical sheaves. I have seen both types on models. The number of sheaves varied though on an average six seemed to have been the most popular. I have seen double sheaves but only on one model. On either end of the block a dovetail was formed to take a lashing; no score was required, the blocks being held in position on the gammoning by the lashings.

The cat block was always iron bound with a large hook at its head. The hook was formed with the iron strap and was as long as the length of the shell. There were either two or three sheaves,

IV SEAMANSHIP
Blocks, deadeyes, hearts and other tackle

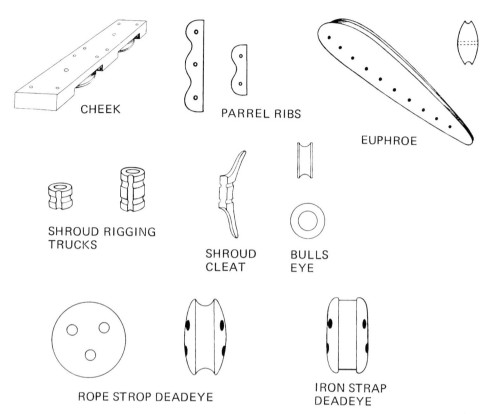

CHEEK

PARREL RIBS

EUPHROE

SHROUD RIGGING
TRUCKS

SHROUD
CLEAT

BULLS
EYE

ROPE STROP DEADEYE

IRON STRAP
DEADEYE

depending upon the size of the ship.
The proportions of the cat block were
the same as the common block.

The fish hook was about one and a
half times the diameter of the cat
block hook and had an eye in the top
running through a thimble, which was
to take the fish pendant.

Hanging blocks From about 1840, a
chain necklace was placed round the
topmast, below the rigging and under
the bolster. Iron bound blocks were
shackled there for the topsail ties, jib
and staysail halliards.

Bee blocks and cheek blocks I have
described in the section of this book
devoted to masts and spars.

The parrels for the yards comprised
ribs and trucks, those on the lower
yards made up of three rows of trucks,
and the other parrels made up of two.
The length of the ribs on the lower
parrels were one and a half times the
diameter of the yard, those on the
mizen yard, the topsail yards (except
the sprit topsail) and the spritsail yard
were one and a half times the diameter
of their yards; finally those on the sprit
topsail, and all the topgallant yards,

were twice the diameter. The depth of
the ribs was equal to the diameter of
the trucks and the width of the ribs
was a quarter the diameter of the trucks.
The trucks' diameter was one fifth the
rib's length on parrels of three rows,
and one third the length on parrels of
two rows. The length of the trucks
was one and a quarter times their
diameter. A hole was bored through
the trucks to take the parrel rope;
holes were also bored through the ribs
for the same purpose. The trucks were
positioned so that 1/2 inch of truck
protruded beyond the back of the rib.
There was a slight cavity in the ribs in
the way of the trucks. Though the
above description may sound complicated, reference to the illustration
should clarify the situation. Parrels for
the gaff and boom did not require ribs;
the trucks were similar to the others
and were about three eighths the diameter of the gaff or boom.

The euphroe was one quarter the
length of the appropriate mast head
long, the width at the upper end was
one seventh the length and it tapered
to half this width at the lower end; the

thickness was one seventh the length
all the way down. The number of
holes varied, but twelve to fourteen on
the main and fore and eight to ten on
the mizen was a good average. These
holes were equally spaced down the
euphroe and a score was cut right
round the euphroe for the strop.

Rigging trucks were small spherical
pieces of wood with a hole bored
down the centre. A groove was cut
down the outside for the shroud to
lay in, and a horizontal groove cut
round the centre to take a seizing.
They were used during all periods,
seized to the inboard side of the lower
shrouds; their purpose was to lead the
running rigging through. Sometimes
they were made longer than the
diameter, in which case two grooves
were cut for the seizings, one on the
top and one on the bottom. The trucks
were usually from 4 to 6 inches in
diameter.

Shroud cleats were seized to the
shrouds, were made of wood and had
a groove on the underside to take the
shrouds. Two more grooves were cut,
one at the top and one at the bottom
for the seizings. Usually they were
seized just above the deadeyes, and
were probably in use in most periods.
Their purpose was to provide additional belaying points to the timber
heads or pin rails.

Bullseyes were wooden rings with a
groove round the outside edge, mostly
used on bowline bridles. The diameter
of the ring was twice the diameter of
the hole, which was one tenth more
than the diameter of the rope required
to reeve through it. The groove on the
outside came almost to the face of the
bullseye. The width was about three
quarters the width of the hole.

Deadeyes in thickness were slightly
more than half their diameter, which
was one and a half times the circumference of the shroud or stay. The
groove round the deadeyes fitted to
the chains was as wide as the link of
the chains, those that fitted the shrouds
or stays were the diameter of the
appropriate shroud or stay. However
when the shrouds were turned in
cutter-stay fashion, the groove was a
little wider to take both parts of the
shroud. The depth of all grooves was

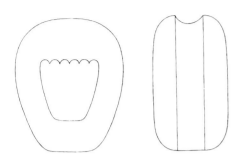

CLOSED HEART

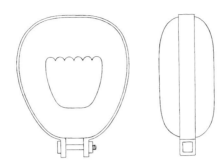

IRON STRAPPED HEART
1810 ON

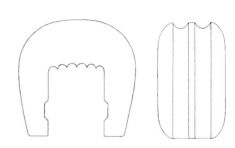

OPEN HEART
DOUBLE SCORED

half the diameter of the rope or link. The three holes were one tenth wider than the lanyard's diameter, and the faces of the deadeyes were grooved slightly from the holes in the way of the lanyard for a distance of a few inches. The holes were rounded on the edges and formed a triangle one quarter the deadeye's diameter in from the edge.

Closed hearts had a length that was about one and a half times the circumference of the stay, the diameter was three quarters the length, and the thickness twice the diameter of the stay. The lower heart was the same size as the upper heart. A groove was cut round the outside, except at the top; this groove was the same diameter of the stay or collar, and half as deep. The hole in the centre was made so that the wood left where the lanyard lay was one third the diameter, decreasing to one quarter the diameter at the sides and top. In order that the lanyard could lay evenly, scores were cut inside the hole, as many as possible to fit the size of the lanyard. The edges of the hearts were rounded off. When the hearts were shackled to the deck, the groove was made to fit the strap. Consequently, as this iron strap was narrower than a collar, the heart was rounded more, still being the same thickness. When the hearts were turned in cutter-stay fashion, two grooves were made round the heart, the thickness being the same as before, but the faces were flatter. Hearts for the bowsprit rigging were made to the same

proportions as those on the stays or collars.

Open hearts had proportions that were the same as given for the closed heart, the only difference being that they were made in the shape of a horseshoe. The opening was at the bottom of the heart. A score was cut at each end to take the seizings to the collar. This type of heart was used on the fore stay and fore preventer stay collars to allow the collar to go round the bowsprit, leaving enough room for the jibboom.

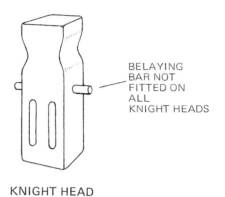

IV SEAMANSHIP
20 gun ship of about 1719

20 Belaying

20 GUN SHIP OF ABOUT 1719
Taken from a contemporary rigged model in the National Maritime Museum.

RIGGING OF THE MAIN MAST
Falls of tackles Ringbolt between the sixth and seventh deadeyes on the main channels.
Stay tackle fall Taken along the stay and hitched round itself.

RIGGING OF THE FORE MAST
Falls of tackles Ringbolt between the fifth and sixth deadeyes on the fore channels.

RIGGING OF THE MIZEN MAST
Burton pendant falls Aftermost timber head.

RIGGING OF THE MAIN TOP MAST
Stay tackle Centre of the fore jeer bitts.
Burton falls Hitched to an eyebolt in the main top by the second shroud.

RIGGING OF THE FORE TOP MAST
Burton falls Hitched to an eyebolt in the fore top by the second shroud.

RIGGING OF THE MAIN YARD
Jeers Main jeer bitts via the inner sheave.

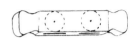

BELAYING BAR NOT FITTED ON ALL KNIGHT HEADS

KNIGHT HEAD

CAVEL CLEAT

BELAYING PIN

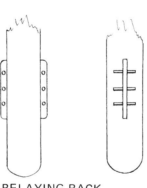

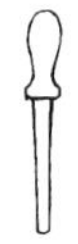

BELAYING RACK ON FOOT OF MIZEN MAST

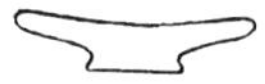

CAVEL BLOCK

CLEAT

TIMBER HEAD

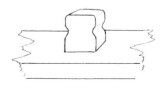

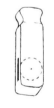

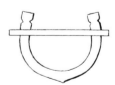

KEVEL

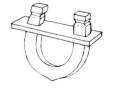

Nave line Hitched to the mizen stay collar.

Lifts Hitched round the first shroud of the main mast.

Braces Kevel between the main and mizen masts via a sheave in the poop rails.

Yard tackle falls Hitched round itself.

Sheet Made up for harbour, seized to the mizen shrouds; would normally be belayed to a cleat on the bulwarks abreast of the main mast.

Tack Timber head by the first shroud of the fore mast.

Clue garnet Main topsail sheet bitts via lead blocks between the bitts.

Leechline Hitched to the third shroud of the main mast.

Buntlines First and second timber heads of the belfry rails.

Bowline Hitched to the fourth shroud of the fore mast.

RIGGING OF THE FORE YARD

Jeers Fore jeer bitts via the inner sheave.

Nave line Collar of the main preventer stay.

Lifts Timber head by the first shroud of the fore mast.

Braces Cleat inside the bulwarks just abaft of the fore topmast backstay.

Yard tackle falls Made fast down the main preventer stay round itself.

Sheet Cleat inside of the bulwarks just abaft of the fore brace cleat.

Tack First timber head of the forecastle head, port tack on the starboard side and the starboard tack on the port side.

Clue garnet Fore topsail sheet bitts via lead blocks between the bitts.

Leechline First and second timber heads of the belfry rails.

Buntlines Second and third timber heads of the belfry rails.

Bowlines Inner timber heads of the forecastle head.

RIGGING OF THE CROSSJACK YARD

Lifts Timber head by the second shroud of the mizen mast.

Braces Hitched to the deadeye of the fifth main shroud.

RIGGING OF THE MIZEN YARD

Truss tackle First deadeye of the

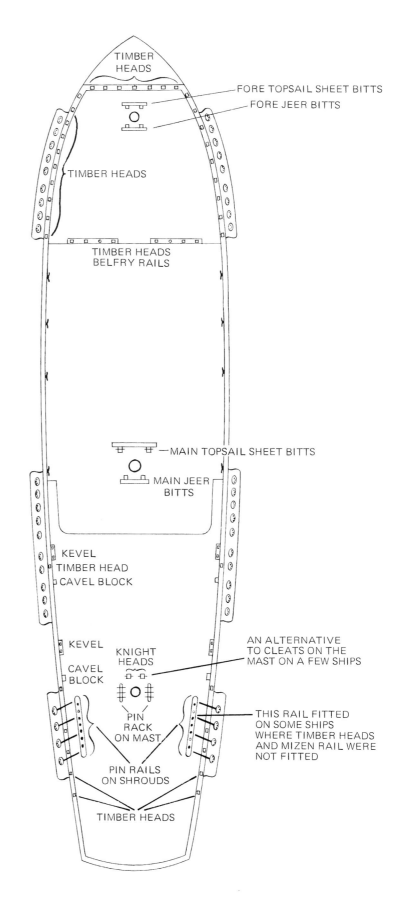

mizen shrouds on the port side.
Jeers Cavel block abreast of the mizen mast on the starboard side.
Bowlines Timber head by the sixth shroud of the main mast.
Peak brails Timber head by the mizen topmast backstay.
Throat brails Timber head abaft the mizen shrouds.
Foot brails Hitched to the after deadeye of the main shrouds.

RIGGING OF THE MAIN TOPSAIL YARD

Halliards Cavel block abaft the aftermost main shroud.
Lifts Hitched to the second deadeye of the main shrouds.
Braces Cavel block on the side just forward of the mizen mast.
Sheets Main topsail sheet bitts via the inner sheave.
Clueline Bitts abaft the main jeer bitts.
Bowline Fore jeer bitts via the outer sheave.
Reef tackle After deadeye in the main top.

RIGGING OF THE MAIN TOPMAST STAYSAIL

Halliard Hitched round the main topmast preventer stay deadeye.

RIGGING OF THE FORE TOPSAIL YARD

Halliard Cavel cleat just inside the bulwarks at the break of the forecastle.
Lifts Timber head by the second shroud of the fore mast.
Braces With the braces of the fore yard.
Sheets Fore topsail sheet bitts via the inner sheave.
Cluelines Belfry rails between the second and third timber heads.
Bowlines Inner timber head on the forecastle head.
Reef tackle After deadeye in the fore top.

RIGGING OF THE FORE TOP STAYSAIL

Staysail halliard Hitched to the fore topmast stay deadeye.

RIGGING OF THE JIB

Halliard Starboard forecastle head rails between the second and third timber heads.

Downhauler Hitched to the fore topmast stay strop.
Outhauler Hitched to the fore topmast stay strop.

RIGGING OF THE MIZEN TOPSAIL YARD

Halliard Starboard rails just forward of the mizen topmast backstay.
Lifts Middle deadeye in the mizen top.
Braces Cleats either side of the staff on the transom.
Sheets Cleats on the foot of the mizen mast.
Cluelines Timber head by the third mizen shroud.
Bowlines Belayed with the crossjack braces crossing each other. Port bowline to starboard and starboard bowline to port.

RIGGING OF THE MIZEN TOP STAYSAIL

Halliard Hitched to the mizen topmast stay deadeye.

RIGGING OF THE MAIN TOPGALLANT YARD

Halliard Inner rail of the break of quarterdeck rails.
Lifts Centre crosstree of the main topmast.
Braces Rail by the first shroud of the mizen mast.
Cluelines Second deadeye in the main top.
Bowlines Hitched to the fore topgallant backstay deadeye.

RIGGING OF THE MAIN TOPGALLANT STAYSAIL

Halliard Fore topmast after crosstree.

RIGGING OF THE FORE TOPGALLANT YARD

Halliard Cleat on the port side of the belfry.
Lifts Centre crosstree of the fore topmast.
Braces With the halliards (cleats either side of the belfry).
Cluelines Third deadeye in the fore top.
Bowlines Centre timber head on the forecastle head.

RIGGING OF THE SPRITSAIL YARD

Halliard Hitched to the gammon lashing.

Lifts Second timber head on the forecastle head.
Braces Belfry rails close to the belfry.
Sheets The standing part seized to the second timber head on the forecastle rails, the running part belayed on the fore sheet cleat.
Cluelines First timberhead on the forecastle head.

FIRST RATE OF THE 1733 ESTABLISHMENT
Taken from the contemporary rigged model of HMS Victory, 1737.

RIGGING OF THE MAIN MAST
Fall of the tackles After fall hitched to the tenth and forward fall hitched to the sixth deadeye plates on the main channels.
Stay tackle fall Eyebolt in the deck on the starboard side of the main hatch.
Fore hatch stay tackle fall Eyebolt in the deck on the starboard side of the capstan.

RIGGING OF THE FORE MAST
Falls of the tackles After fall hitched to the ninth and the forward fall hitched to the sixth deadeye plates on the fore channels.

RIGGING OF THE MIZEN MAST
Burton pendant falls Timber head just abaft the mizen shrouds.

RIGGING OF THE MAIN TOP MAST
Stay tackle Centre of the main top bowline bitts.
Burton falls Hitched to an eyebolt in the main top by the third deadeye.
Running breast backstay runner Seized to the third deadeye plate in the main channels.
Running breast backstay falls Hitched to the fifth deadeye plate in the main channels.
Top rope falls Made fast round itself to a ringbolt by the companionway.

RIGGING OF THE FORE TOP MAST
Stay tackle Hitched to the fore preventer stay strop.
Burton falls Hitched to an eyebolt in the fore top by the third deadeye.
Running breast backstay runner Seized to the third deadeye plate in the fore channels.
Running breast backstay falls Hitched to the fourth deadeye plate in the fore channels.
Top rope falls Made fast round itself to a ringbolt forward of the hatchway under the belfry.

RIGGING OF THE MAIN YARD
Jeers Main jeer bitts via the inner sheave.

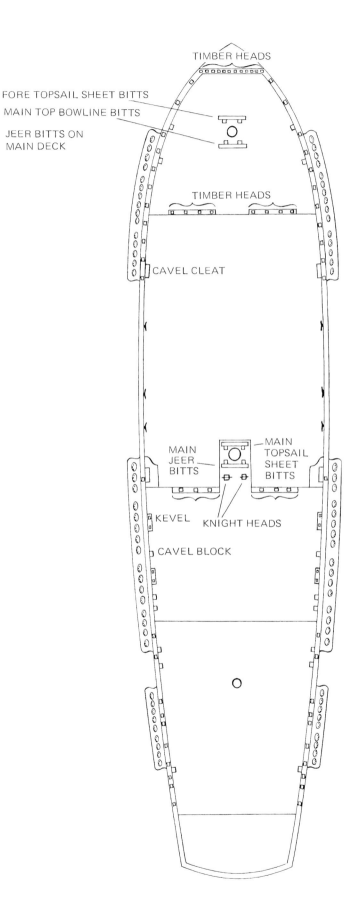

TIMBER HEADS

FORE TOPSAIL SHEET BITTS

MAIN TOP BOWLINE BITTS

JEER BITTS ON MAIN DECK

TIMBER HEADS

CAVEL CLEAT

MAIN JEER BITTS

MAIN TOPSAIL SHEET BITTS

KEVEL   KNIGHT HEADS

CAVEL BLOCK

Nave line Centre of the main jeer bitts.
Lifts Timber head by the second main shroud.
Braces Kevel between the main and mizen masts via a sheave in the poop rails.
Yard tackle falls Hitched round the third deadeye plate in the main channels.
Quarter tackle falls Hitched to an eyebolt in the gunwale abaft the fore stool.
Sheet Cleat forward of the entry port.
Tack Cleat aft of the entry port.
Clue garnet Main topsail sheet bitts via the outer sheave.
Leechline Standing part seized to the second timber head in the break of the quarterdeck rails, running part belayed to the knightheads abaft the main jeer bitts via the outer sheave in the knighthead.
Buntlines Second and third timber heads of the belfry rails.
Bowlines Main top bowline bitts crossing each other, port to starboard and starboard to port.

RIGGING OF THE FORE YARD
Jeers Fore jeer bitts via the inner sheave.
Nave line Main top bowline bitts in the centre.
Lifts Timber head by the first fore shroud.
Braces Cleat inside the bulwarks midway between the fore and mizen masts.
Yard tackle falls Hitched to the third deadeye plate in the fore channels.
Sheet Cleat inside the bulwarks just abaft the fore brace cleat.
Tacks Third timber head of the forecastle head (crossing each other).
Clue garnet Fore topsail sheet bitts via the outer sheave.
Leechline First and second timber heads of the belfry rails.
Buntline Second and third timber heads of the belfry rails.
Bowline Third timber head of the forecastle head.

RIGGING OF THE CROSSJACK YARD
Lifts Timber head by the first mizen shroud.
Braces Outer stanchions of the break

of the quarterdeck rails (crossing each other).

RIGGING OF THE MIZEN YARD
Truss tackle Made fast down the yard.
Jeers Timber head by the fourth mizen shroud port side.
Lifts Timber head by the fourth mizen shroud starboard side.
Bowlines Timber head by the aftermost main shroud.
Sheets Hitched to an eyebolt in the centre knee on the transom.
Peak brails Timber head by the mizen topmast backstay.

RIGGING OF THE MAIN TOPSAIL YARD
Halliard Kevel by the sixth main shroud via a sheave by the ninth shroud.
Lifts Timber head by the fourth main shroud.
Braces Timber head just forward of the first mizen shroud via a sheave by the first shroud.
Sheets Main topsail sheet bitts via the inner sheave.
Cluelines Main jeer bitts via the outer sheave.
Buntlines Knighthead abaft the main jeer bitts via the inner sheave.
Bowlines Main top bowline bitts via the outer sheave.
Reef tackle Timber head by the sixth main shroud.

RIGGING OF THE MAIN TOP STAYSAIL
Halliards Second stanchion of the break of the quarterdeck rails starboard side.

RIGGING OF THE FORE TOPSAIL YARD
Halliards Aftermost timber head on the forecastle.
Lifts Timber head by the fourth fore shroud.
Braces Cleat inside of the bulwarks just abaft halfway between the main and fore masts.
Sheets Fore topsail sheet bitts via the inner sheave.
Cluelines Main top bowline bitts via the inner sheave.

Buntlines Main top bowline bitts.
Bowlines Fifth timber head on the forecastle head.
Reef tackle Timber head by the fifth fore shroud.

RIGGING OF THE FORE TOP STAYSAIL
Halliard Belfry rails starboard side.

RIGGING OF THE JIB
Halliard Timber head by the eighth fore shroud starboard side.
Downhauler Inner timber head of the forecastle head.
Outhauler Fourth timber head of the forecastle head starboard side.

RIGGING OF THE MIZEN TOPSAIL YARD
Halliard Rails by the timber head just forward of the mizen topmast backstay starboard side.
Lifts Timber head by the third mizen shroud.
Braces Mizen rails just aft of the peak brails.
Sheets Cleats on the mizen mast.
Cluelines Timber head by the fourth mizen shroud.
Bowlines Belayed with the crossjack braces (crossing each other).

RIGGING OF THE MIZEN TOP STAYSAIL
Halliard Timber head just forward of the mizen topmast backstay port side.

RIGGING OF THE MAIN TOPGALLANT YARD
Halliard Inner rail of the break of the quarterdeck rails.
Lifts Rail by the after mizen shroud.
Cluelines Timber head between the sixth and seventh main shrouds.
Bowlines Timber head between the seventh and eighth fore shrouds.

RIGGING OF THE MAIN TOPGALLANT STAYSAIL
Halliard Outer rail of the break of the starboard quarterdeck rails.

RIGGING OF THE FORE TOPGALLANT YARD
Halliard Inner starboard belfry rails.
Lifts Centre crosstree of the fore topmast.

Braces Belayed with the halliards either side of the belfry.
Cluelines Timber head by the seventh fore shroud.
Bowlines Fifth timber head on the forecastle head.

RIGGING OF THE SPRITSAIL YARD
Halliard Hitched to the gammon lashing.
Lifts Third timber head on the forecastle head.
Braces Belfry rails close to the belfry.
Sheets Standing part seized to the second timber head on the forecastle running part belayed to a cleat just abaft the break of the forecastle.
Cluelines Fourth timber head on the forecastle head.

RIGGING OF THE SPRIT TOPSAIL YARD
Halliard Fifth timber head on the forecastle head port side.
Lifts Centre deadeye plate on the sprit top.
Braces Belfry rails just outboard of the spritsail braces.
Cluelines Fifth timber head on the forecastle head.

HMS MEDWAY, 1742
Rigging of about 1763

RIGGING OF THE MAIN MAST
Fall of tackle (forward) Eyebolt in the channel between the third and fourth shrouds.
Fall of tackle (after) Eyebolt in the channel between the seventh and eighth shrouds.
Stay tackle fall Made fast round itself.
Fore hatch stay tackle fall Made fast round itself.
Main tackle fall Cleat in the bulwarks starboard side in the middle of the waist.

RIGGING OF THE FORE MAST
Fall of tackle (forward) Timber head by the first fore shroud.
Fall of tackle (after) Round itself by the after fore shroud.

RIGGING OF THE MIZEN MAST
Burton pendant falls Third deadeye plate in the mizen channels.
Stay tackle Round itself.

RIGGING OF THE MAIN TOPMAST
Stay tackle Round itself.
Burton falls Third deadeye in the main top.
Top rope falls Round itself.

RIGGING OF THE FORE TOPMAST
Stay tackle Round itself.
Preventer stay tackle Round itself.
Burton falls Second deadeye in the fore top.
Top rope falls Round itself either side of the fore hatch.

RIGGING OF THE MAIN TOPGALLANT MAST
Stay Round the collar of the fore stay.

RIGGING OF THE FORE TOPGALLANT MAST
Stay Round the fore stay collar starboard side.

RIGGING OF THE JIBBOOM
Guy pendant Outer timber head of the forecastle head rails.

RIGGING OF THE MAIN YARD
Jeers Main jeer bitts, via the inner sheave.

Lifts Cavel block on the bulwarks by the first main shroud.
Braces Cleat on the bulwarks just forward of lead sheave on the poop.
Yard tackle falls Third shroud of the main mast.
Yard tackle outer tricing line Third shroud of the main mast.
Yard tackle inner tricing line Gallows next to the upright.
Quarter tackle falls Eyebolt in the side below the main channels between the second and third deadeyes round itself.
Sheets Not belayed but should turn up to a cleat on the bulwarks a little forward of the main sheet sheave.
Tack Cleat on the bulwark just forward of the chesstree.
Clue garnet Main topsail sheet bitts via the outer sheave.
Buntlines Third timber head of the belfry rails.

RIGGING OF THE FORE YARD
Jeers Fore jeer bitts via the inner sheave.
Truss pendant falls Round itself to an eyebolt in the deck at the foot of the fore mast each side.
Lifts Timber head by the first shroud of the fore mast.
Braces Main jeer bitts via the outer sheave.
Yard tackle falls Second shroud of the fore mast.
Yard tackle inner tricing line Third shroud of the fore mast.
Yard tackle outer tricing line Fore topsail sheet bitts next to the upright.
Sheet Cleat on the inside of the bulwarks just forward of the main mast.
Clue garnet Fore topsail sheet bitts via the outer sheave.
Leechline First timber head of the belfry rails.
Buntline Second timber head of the belfry rails.
Slab line Fore topsail sheet bitts in the centre.
Bowline Third timber head of the forecastle head.

RIGGING OF THE CROSSJACK YARD
Lifts Third pin in the rail by the second mizen shroud.
Braces Cleat on the deck beam at the break of the quarterdeck via the inner sheave of the cavel.

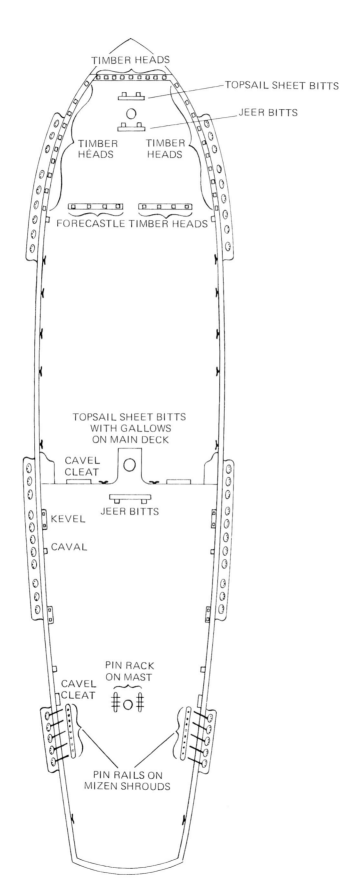

TIMBER HEADS

TOPSAIL SHEET BITTS

JEER BITTS

TIMBER HEADS

TIMBER HEADS

FORECASTLE TIMBER HEADS

TOPSAIL SHEET BITTS
WITH GALLOWS
ON MAIN DECK

CAVEL CLEAT

JEER BITTS

KEVEL

CAVAL

PIN RACK ON MAST

CAVEL CLEAT

PIN RAILS ON MIZEN SHROUDS

RIGGING OF THE MIZEN YARD

Truss tackle Round itself to an eye-bolt abaft the mizen mast.
Jeers Timber head between the fourth and fifth mizen shroud port side.
Lift Timber head by the fourth mizen shroud starboard side.
Bowlines Timber head by the seventh main shroud.
Peak brails Timber head by the mizen topmast backstay.
Throat brails After pin in the rack on the mizen shrouds.

RIGGING OF THE MIZEN STAYSAIL

Halliards Second shroud of the mizen mast.
Downhauler Cross piece of the main jeer bitts port side.

RIGGING OF THE MAIN TOPSAIL YARD

Halliards Cavel block on bulwark by the aftermost main shroud.
Lift Fourth main shroud.
Braces Cavel cleat on bulwarks by first mizen shroud.
Sheets Main topsail sheet bitts via the inner sheave.
Cluelines Third eyebolt at foot of the main mast.
Leechlines Second eyebolt at foot of the main mast.
Bowlines Fore jeer bitts via the outer sheave.
Reef tackle Fourth eyebolt at the foot of the main mast.

RIGGING OF THE MAIN TOP STAYSAIL

Halliard Cavel block between the main topmast backstay and the first mizen shroud, starboard side.
Downhauler Hitched to a lead block seized to the foremast by the main preventer stay heart starboard side.

RIGGING OF THE MIDDLE STAYSAIL

Stay halliard fall Round itself on the after crosstree of the main mast.
Staysail halliard Cavel block opposite to the main top staysail knighthead.
Downhauler Hitched to a block seized to the strop of the main bowline lead block.

RIGGING OF THE FORE TOPSAIL YARD

Halliard Cavel block on the bulwarks by the break of the forecastle.
Lifts Third shroud of the fore mast.
Braces Belfry rails next but one to the belfry.
Sheets Fore topsail sheet bitts via the inner sheave.
Cluelines Round the lead block on the fourth eyebolt in the deck either side of the fore mast.
Buntlines Round the lead block on the second eyebolt in the deck either side of the fore mast.
Bowlines Fourth timber head on the forecastle head.
Reef tackle Round the lead block on the third eyebolt in the deck either side of the fore mast.

RIGGING OF THE FORE TOP STAYSAIL

Stay halliard fall Round itself to the after crosstree of the fore mast, port side.
Staysail halliard Timber head between the sixth and seventh fore shroud, port side.
Downhauler Fourth timber head in the forecastle rails starboard side.
Outhauler Fourth timber head in the forecastle rails starboard side.

RIGGING OF THE JIB

Jib stay halliard fall Round itself starboard side of the fore top.
Jib halliard Timber head between the sixth and seventh fore shroud starboard side.
Downhauler Fourth timber head in the forecastle head rails starboard.
Outhauler Third timber head in the forecastle head rails starboard.

RIGGING OF THE MIZEN TOPSAIL YARD

Halliard Timber head between the mizen topmast backstay and the after mizen shroud.
Lifts Third mizen shroud.
Braces Mizen rails just aft of the vangs.
Sheets Cleats on the mizen mast.
Cluelines Third pin by the second mizen shroud.
Bowlines Belayed with the crossjack braces via the outer sheave of the cavel block.

RIGGING OF THE MIZEN TOP STAYSAIL

Halliard On the timber head with the port peak and middle brails.
Downhauler Cross piece of the main jeer bitts starboard side.

RIGGING OF THE MAIN TOPGALLANT YARD

Halliard Cross piece of the main jeer bitts at the centre.
Lifts Third deadeye in the main top.
Braces Fourth pin between the second and third mizen shrouds.
Cluelines Second main shroud.
Bowlines After timber head on the forecastle.

RIGGING OF THE MAIN TOPGALLANT STAYSAIL

Halliard Cleat on the beam at the break of the quarterdeck port side.
Downhauler Hitched round the lead block on the mast by the main stay on the port side.

RIGGING OF THE FORE TOPGALLANT YARD

Halliard Centre of the fore jeer bitts.
Lifts Third deadeye in the fore top.
Braces Belfry rails next to the belfry.
Cluelines Second fore shroud.
Bowlines Fourth timber head on the forecastle rails.

RIGGING OF THE SPRITSAIL YARD

Lifts Fourth timber head on the forecastle head.
Braces Timber head next to the belfry.
Sheets Cleat inside the bulwarks just aft of the forecastle.
Cluelines Second timber head of the forecastle head.
Buntlines Fourth timber head of the forecastle head.

RIGGING OF THE SPRIT TOPSAIL YARD

Halliard Third timber head of the forecastle head.
Lifts Fifth timber head of the forecastle head.
Braces Timber head by the belfry.
Cluelines Fourth timber head of the forecastle rails.

FRIGATE OF ABOUT 1810
RIGGING OF THE MAIN YARD

Jeers Main jeer bitts when rove.
Truss pendant falls Fifth pin of the main pin rail.
Nave line Centre of main jeer bitts.
Lifts Second pin of the main pin rail.
Braces Cleat in bulwarks near the transom.
Yard tackle outer tricing line First pin in the quarterdeck rails.
Yard tackle inner tricing line Second pin in the quarterdeck rails.
Sheet Cleat on the bulwarks between the main and mizen masts.
Tack Cleat on the bulwarks just aft of the main sheet cleat.
Clue garnet Main topsail sheet bitts via outer sheave.
Leechlines Seventh pin of the main pin rail.
Buntlines Second pin of the fore jeer bitts.
Bowline First pin of the fore jeer bitts.
Slab line Centre of the break of quarterdeck rails.

RIGGING OF THE FORE YARD

Jeers Fore jeer bitts when rove.
Truss pendant falls Fifth pin of the fore pin rail.
Nave line Centre of the fore jeer bitts.
Lifts Fore jeer bitts.
Braces Main jeer bitts via the inner sheave.
Yard tackle outer tricing line First pin of the fore pin rail.
Yard tackle inner tricing line Fore jeer bitts.
Tack First timber head on the forecastle.
Clue garnet Fore topsail sheet bitts via the outer sheave.
Leechlines Fourth pin on the fore pin rail.
Buntlines First timber head on the forecastle.
Bowline First timber head on the forecastle.
Slab line Centre of the fore topsail sheet bitts.
Sheets Cleat on the bulwarks abreast of the main hatch.

RIGGING OF THE MAIN TOP STAYSAIL

Halliard Hitched to the after main shroud on the port side.
Sheets First pin of the main pin rail.

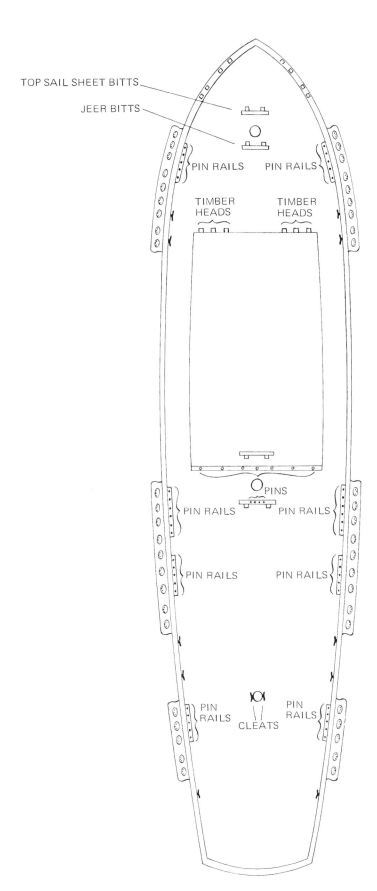

TOP SAIL SHEET BITTS

JEER BITTS

PIN RAILS   PIN RAILS

TIMBER HEADS   TIMBER HEADS

PINS

PIN RAILS   PIN RAILS

PIN RAILS   PIN RAILS

PIN RAILS   PIN RAILS

CLEATS

Tacks First pin of the fore pin rail.
Downhauler Fore jeer bitts on the starboard side.
Brails Fore jeer bitts.

RIGGING OF THE MIDDLE STAYSAIL

Stay halliard fall Hitched to the rail in the fore top.
Staysail halliard Hitched to the after starboard main shroud.
Sheets Outer pin of the break of the quarterdeck rails.
Tacks After deadeye in the fore top.
Downhauler Rails of the fore top.
Brails Rails of the fore top.

RIGGING OF THE FORE TOPSAIL YARD

Halliard Cleat in the bulwarks abreast of the break of the forecastle.
Lifts Third pin of the fore pin rails.
Braces Main jeer bitts.
Sheets Fore topsail sheet bitts via the inner sheave.
Cluelines Fore jeer bitts.
Buntlines Fore topsail sheet bitts.
Bowlines First timber head on the forecastle.
Reef tackle Fourth pin of the fore pin rails.

RIGGING OF THE FORE TOP STAYSAIL

Staysail halliard Cleat in the bulwarks just forward of the fore topsail halliard cleat.
Sheets Third timber head of the forecastle.
Downhauler First timber head on the forecastle port side.

RIGGING OF THE MIZEN TOPSAIL YARD

Halliard Cleat on the bulwarks between the mizen shrouds and the stern.
Lifts (standing) Seized to the mizen stay collar.
Braces Eighth pin of the main pin rails.
Sheets Cleats on the mizen mast via blocks on deck at the foot of mast.
Cluelines Second pin of the mizen pin rail.
Buntlines First pin of the mizen pin rail starboard side.
Bowlines Ninth pin of the main pin rails.
Reef tackle Fourth pin of the mizen pin rail.

RIGGING OF THE JIBBOOM AND JIB

Jib guys Second timber head on the forecastle.
Jib halliard Cleat in the bulwarks just abaft of the starboard fore shrouds.
Sheets Third timber head on the forecastle.
Downhauler First timber head on the forecastle port side.
Outhauler First timber head on the forecastle starboard side.

RIGGING OF THE FLYING JIBBOOM AND FLYING JIB

Flying jib guys Second timber head on the forecastle.
Halliard Fifth pin of the fore pin rail port side.
Sheet Fourth timber head on the forecastle.
Downhauler First timber head on the forecastle starboard side.
Outhauler First timber head on the forecastle starboard side.

RIGGING OF THE CROSSJACK YARD

Truss pendant Fifth pin of the mizen pin rail starboard side.
Braces Tenth pin of the main pin rail.

RIGGING OF THE BOOM, GAFF AND SPANKER

Boom topping lift Hitched to the aftermost mizen shrouds.
Peak halliard Third pin of the mizen pin rail starboard side.
Throat halliard Fifth pin of the mizen pin rail port side.
Vangs Cleats on the transom close to the bulwarks.
Boom guys Cleat on the bulwark near the transom.
Boom sheets Hitched round lower sheet block on the transom.
Spanker sheets Hitched on the boom.
Peak brails Hitched to the hammock rails near the transom.
Middle brails Third pin of the mizen pin rail.
Throat brails Third pin of the mizen pin rail.
Foot brails Hitched to the boom jaw rope.

RIGGING OF THE MAIN TOPSAIL YARD

Halliard Cleat in the bulwarks abaft the main shrouds.
Lifts Fourth pin of the main pin rails.
Braces Cleat in the bulwarks aft of the topsail halliard cleat.
Sheets Main topsail sheet bitts via the inner sheave.
Cluelines Main jeer bitts.
Buntlines First pin of the main jeer bitts.
Bowlines Fore jeer bitts via the outer sheave.
Reef tackle Sixth pin of the main pin rail.

RIGGING OF THE MIZEN TOP STAYSAIL

Halliard Cleat on the bulwarks just aft of the port mizen pin rail.
Tacks First main shroud.
Sheets First mizen shroud.
Downhauler Rail of the main top.

RIGGING OF THE MAIN TOPGALLANT YARD

Halliard Second pin of the main jeer bitts.
Lifts Fourth pin of the main pin rails.
Braces First pin of the mizen pin rail.
Sheets Third pin of the main pin rails.
Cluelines Third pin of the main pin rails.
Bowlines Fifth pin of the fore pin rails.

RIGGING OF THE MAIN TOPGALLANT STAYSAIL

Halliard After deadeye in the main top, port side.
Sheets Second pin of the break of the forecastle rails.
Tacks Third deadeye in the fore top.
Downhauler Rail of the fore top.

RIGGING OF THE FORE TOPGALLANT YARD

Halliard Fore jeer bitts.
Lifts Third pin of the fore pin rail.
Braces Second pin of the main pin rails.
Sheets Second pin of the fore pin rail.
Cluelines Second pin of the fore pin rails.
Bowlines First timber head of the forecastle.

RIGGING OF THE MIZEN TOPGALLANT YARD

Halliard Second pin of the mizen pin rails.
Lifts Second deadeye in the mizen top.
Braces After deadeye in the main top.
Sheets Third pin of the mizen pin rail.
Cluelines Fourth pin of the mizen pin rail.
Bowlines Eleventh pin of the main pin rails.

RIGGING OF THE SPRITSAIL YARD

Braces Second pin of the fore pin rails.

IV SEAMANSHIP
Belaying sequence of about 1850

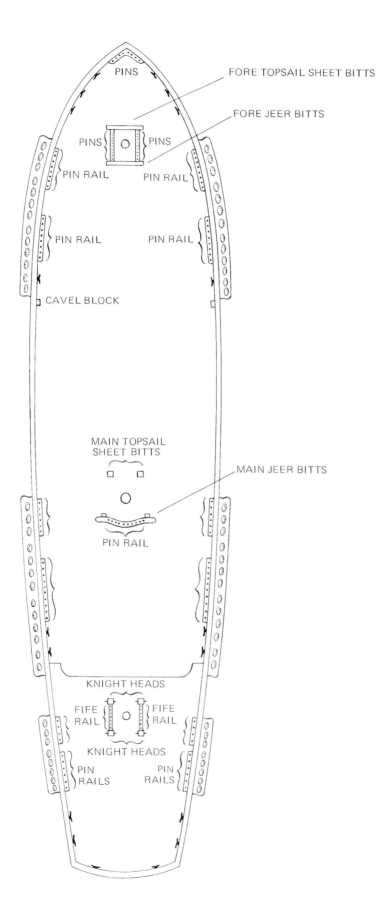

PINS

FORE TOPSAIL SHEET BITTS

FORE JEER BITTS

PINS   PINS

PIN RAIL   PIN RAIL

PIN RAIL   PIN RAIL

CAVEL BLOCK

MAIN TOPSAIL
SHEET BITTS

MAIN JEER BITTS

PIN RAIL

KNIGHT HEADS

FIFE
RAIL   FIFE
RAIL

KNIGHT HEADS

PIN
RAILS   PIN
RAILS

BELAYING SEQUENCE OF ABOUT 1850

BULWARKS

From stem to main mast the order of belaying was:

Fore tack (cleats, port and starboard); flying jib sheets (cleats or belaying pins, port and starboard); jib sheets (cleats or belaying pins, port and starboard); fore topmast staysail sheets (cleats or belaying pins, port and starboard); fore clue garnet (belaying pins, port and starboard); fore topsail cluelines (belaying pins, port and starboard); fore topsail buntlines (belaying pins, port and starboard); fore topsail reef lines (belaying pins, port and starboard); fore topsail lift (belaying pins, port and starboard); fore topgallant cluelines (belaying pins, port and starboard); fore topgallant buntlines (belaying pins, port and starboard); fore topgallant lift lines (belaying pins, port and starboard); fore royal clue- and buntlines (belaying pins, port and starboard); fore royal lift (belaying pins, port and starboard); fore truss tackle (belaying pins, port and starboard); main tack (cleats, port and starboard); fore topsail halliard (cleats, port and starboard); fore top staysail halliard (cleat, port side only); jib halliard (cleat, starboard side only); flying jib halliard (cleat, port side only); fore sheet (cleats, port and starboard); fore trysail vangs (cleats, port and starboard).

Note Pins are required for the running backstay falls. The position is determined by the hole or sheave in the ship's side for leading the fall inboard. The sequence would be interrupted to allow a pin to be used for this fall. When no pin was available, cluelines and buntlines were belayed together thus releasing a pin for this purpose.

Main mast to mizen mast (Unless otherwise stated all rigging belays to pins on the port and starboard sides): Main clue garnet, main topsail clueline, main topsail buntline, main topsail reef line, main topsail lift, main topgallant clueline, main topgallant buntline, main topgallant lift, main royal clue- and buntlines, main truss tackle, main topsail halliard, main

180

staysail halliards and sheets, main try-sail vangs (cleats, port and starboard), main sheet.

Note The number of pins required for staysail halliards and sheets varied between ships of different rates, the position for belaying them was between the topsail halliard pin and the trysail vang pin.

Mizen mast aft (Unless otherwise stated all rigging belays to pins on the port and starboard sides):
Mizen topsail clueline, mizen topsail buntline, mizen topsail reef line, mizen topsail lift, mizen topgallant clueline, mizen topgallant buntline, mizen top-gallant lift, mizen topgallant sheets, mizen royal clue- and buntlines, mizen royal lift, mizen royal sheets, mizen staysail halliards, mizen topsail halliards, mizen vangs (cleats, port and starboard), main brace, boom guys, boom sheets.

BITTS AND FIFE RAILS

Fore topsail sheet bitts Fore topsail and fore topgallant sheets via sheaves in the bitts; fore royal sheets, fore bowlines, fore top bowlines, fore top-gallant bowlines and fore royal bow-lines, to belaying pins on the cross piece of the bitts.

Note When no cross piece is fitted, sometimes a pin rail is carried forward stepped over the bowsprit; alternately the bowlines can be taken to either side of the mast belayed to pins in the fore and after rail of the bitts.

Main topsail sheet bitts Main topsail, topgallant, and royal sheets via sheaves in the bitts.

Mizen topsail sheet bitts Main topsail brace and mizen topsail sheets.

Fore jeer bitts Port to starboard: main topgallant bowline, main topsail bow-line, main bowline, fore topgallant halliard, nave line, fore royal halliard, main bowline, main topsail bowline, main topgallant bowline. When fitted, the main preventer braces are taken to the bitts, usually via sheaves in the bitts.

Main jeer bitts Port to starboard: fore brace, fore topsail brace, fore top-gallant brace, fore royal brace, cross-jack brace, mizen topsail brace, main leechline, main buntline, mizen topgallant bowline, mizen topsail

bowline, main royal halliard, nave line, main topgallant halliard, mizen top-sail bowline, mizen topgallant bowline, main buntline, main leechline, mizen topsail brace, crossjack brace, fore royal brace, fore topgallant brace, fore topsail brace, fore brace.

Mizen fife rail Port to starboard: main topgallant brace, main royal brace, peak halliard, foot, middle, throat, and head brails, mizen topgallant halliard, mizen royal halliard, head, throat, middle, and foot brails, throat halliard, main royal brace, main topgallant brace. When the rail ran fore and aft the the sequence was from fore pin to after pin as follows: port side; main topgallant brace, main royal brace, peak halliard, brails, mizen topgallant halliard. Starboard side; main top-gallant brace, main royal brace, throat halliard, brails, mizen royal halliard.

OTHER BELAYING POINTS

Cleats at the foot of the masts Lower lifts and slab lines. Staysail brails, downhauls and so forth.

Note The belaying of stunsail gear has not been given; it would however be belayed with the gear of the yard that the stunsail was carried on.

70 Close up of the fore channels of a 20 gun ship of about 1710. Note the method of securing the anchor and the spritsail sheet tricing line.

71 Fore channels of the *Medway*, 1742, showing the anchors and anchor buoy.

IV SEAMANSHIP
Details and sources

72 Close up of the fish davit of the *Medway*, 1742.

73 Beak of a 50 gun ship of about 1710. Note the gammon lashing block.

74 *Breda*, 1692. Main channel.

IV SEAMANSHIP
Details and sources

75 Main channel and entry of the *Medway*, 1742.

76 One of the problems of restoration: this plate and the following three photographs show a contemporary rigged model badly ravaged by woodworm. Model of about 1717.

IV SEAMANSHIP
Details and sources

77 The model of about 1717. The stem had been eaten right away and the gammon lashing and bobstay left hanging (left).

78 Close up of the cathead (right). This model was acquired in this condition and has been restored at the National Maritime Museum.

79 The model of the ship of about 1717 (a 70 gun Third Rate) after restoration.

80 Payne's engraving of the *Sovereign of the Seas*, 1637. This and following illustrations are examples of where information can be obtained.

81 Print by Isaac Sailmaker of the *Britannia*, 1682.

82 An engraving of a Third Rate of 1730.

A THIRD RATE MAN of WAR
According to their Prefent Conftruction.

83 The *Victory* at sea, an oil painting by Swaine. Note the mizen sail cut to fit to the mast.

84 An oil painting of Nelson's Flagships, by Pocock.

85 A plate
from Smith's
*A Seaman's
Grammar*, 1692
edition.

86 A plate from Sutherland's *Ship Building Unveiled*.

87-90 An early printed book (1664) with useful information.

[8]

Rigging *for the* Mizoen Maft.

Halliards Four times the length of the maft from the Deck to the Crofs-trees.
Braytles Two times the length of the maft from the Deck to the Crofs-trees.
Sheet One time the length of the Yard.
Tack Three Fathomes length.
Shroudes One time the length of the maft from the Deck to the Crofs-trees,
Pennants Of the Shroud.
Burtenfal One time the length of the main yard.
Stay One time the length of the maft
Bowlines One time the length of the *Crofsjack* yard

Rigging *for the* Mizoen-Top-Maft.

Pennants Of the Shroud.
Shroudes The length of the maft from the Crofs-trees to the Heel.
Stay 1 & ½ the length of the maft.
Lifts Three times the length of the maft.
Braces 1 &⅓ the length of the Mizoen yard.
Bowlines 1 & ½ the length of the *Crofsjack* yard.
Crofsjack braces 2 & ⅓ the length of the *Crofsjack* yard.
Sheets 2 & ½ the length of the *Crofsjack* yard.
Clulines 2 & ⅓ the length of the *Crofsjack* yard.
Halliards 1 & ⅓ the length of the Mizoen yard.
Tye One time the length of the top-maft from the Crofs-trees to the Heel.

FINIS.

A PLAIN and EASIE RULE
TO
RIGGE
ANY
SHIP
BY

The LENGTH of his *MASTS*, and *YARDS*.

Without any further Trouble.

LONDON,

Printed for *William Fifher* at the *Poftern-Gate* neer *Tower-Hill*. 1664.

6.

---

[3]

A Plain and Eafie RULE *to* RIGGE
any SHIP *by the Length of his* MASTS
and YARDS, *without any further Trouble.*

For the Spritfail-Yard.

Halliards **T**Hree times the length of the Yard.
Lifts Three times the length of the Yard.
Clulines Two times the length of the Yard.
Braces Two times the length of the Fore-yard.
Buntlines Two times the length of the Yard.
Sheets Three times the length of the Yard.
Pennants One third of the Yard.

For the Spritfail-Top-maft.

Shroudes Moft be the length of the Maft from the Heel to the Croftrees.
Halliards Three times the length of the Maft.
Lifts Three times the length of the Maft.

A 2   *Clulines*

[4]

Clulines Two times the length of the Spritsail Yard.
Braces Two times the length of the Spritsail Yard.
Cranlines Two times the length of the Topsail yard.

For the Fore-Mast.

Pennants ¾ Of the length of the Shroudes.
Shroudes ⅘ Of the Mast.
Stay One time the length of the Mast wanting ⅛.
Lifts Three times the length of the Shroudes.
Clugarnets Three times the length of the Shroudes.
Buntlines Two times the length of the Mast from the Deck to the Crostrees.
Leechliues Two times the length of the Main Yard.
Braces Two times the length of the Main Yard.
Foresheets 2 & ½ times the length of the Main Yard.
Jeeres Four times the length of the Mast from the Deck to the Crostrees.
Buntlines Two times the length of the Main Yard.
Topsail-sheets Two times the length of the Main Yard.

For the Fore-Topmast-Rigging.

Pennants Of the Shroudes. Shroudes.

[5]

Shroudes One time the length of the Mast from the Crostrees to the feed hole.
Burtons One time the length of the Foreyard.
Lifts 2 & ½ times the length of the Foreyard.
Clulines Three times the length of the Foreyard.
Braces 2 & ½ times the length of the Foreyard.
Bowlines 2 & ½ times the length of the Foreyard.
Leechline Two times the length of the Foretopsail Yard.
Tye One time the length of the Topmast.
Runner 1 & ½ time the length of the Foreyard.
Halliards Three times the length of the Foreyard.
Stay 1 & ½ the length of the Mast.
Backstays 1 & ½ the length of the Foreyard.
Buntlines Two times the length of the Foreyard.

The Fore-Top-gallant-Rigging.

Shroudes One time the length of the Mast from the Crostrees to the feed hole.
Stay 1 & ½ times the length of the Foreyard.
Lifts Three times the length of the Mast.
Braces 2 & ½ times the length of the Foreyard.
Bowlines 2 & ½ times the length of the Foreyard.
Halliards 2 & ½ times the length of the Foreyard.

For the Main-Mast-Rigging.

Pennants ½ Of the Shroudes.

Shroudes

[6]

Shroudes ½ Of the Mast.
Stay The length of the Mast.
Jeers Four times the length of the Mast from the Deck to the Crostrees.
Lifts Three times the length of the Main yard.
Braces 2 & ½ times the length of the Main yard.
Bowlines One time the length of the Main yard.
Clugarnet 2 & ½ times the length of the Main yard.
Buntlines Four times the length of the Mast for Falls and Leges.
Leechlines Two times the length of the Main yard.
Tacks One time the length of the Main yard.
Runners One time the length of the Main yard.
Tacklefals Three times the length of the Runners.
Sheets 2 & ½ the length of the Main yard.
Eknave-line Two times the length from the Crostrees to the Deck.
Topsail-sheets. Two times the length of the Main yard.

The Main-Top Mast Rigging.

Pennants ½ Of the Shroudes.
Shroudes One time the length of the Mast.
Stay 1 & ½ times the length of the Mast.
Braces 2 & ½ the length of the Yard.
Burtons ½ Of the Main Yard.
Lifts 2 & ½ of the length of the Main yard.

Bunt-

[7]

Buntlines Two times the length of the Main yard.
Clulines Three times the length of the Main yard.
Tye One time the length of the top mast-Shroud.
Runners One time the length of the Main yard.
Halliards Three times the length of the Main yard.
Leechlines Two times the length of the topsail yard.
Buntlines Two times the length from the Deck to the Hounds.
Top-rope One time the length of the main shrouds
Topropefal Two times the length of the Main Mast.
Pennants ½ of the topsail yard.
for Braces
Backstays 1 & ½ the length of the Main yard.

For the Main-Top-gallant-Mast-Rigging.

Shroudes Once the length of the Mast from the Cross-trees to the heel.
Stay 1 & ½ the length of the Main yard.
Lifts Three times the length of the top gallant Mast.
Braces Two times the length of the Main yard.
Bowlines Two times the length of the main yard.
Tye The length of the mast.
Halliards 2 & ½ times the length of the main yard.
Top-rope Two times the length of the main yard.

Rigging

IV SEAMANSHIP
Details and sources

91 Draught of mast and sail classification, 1831.

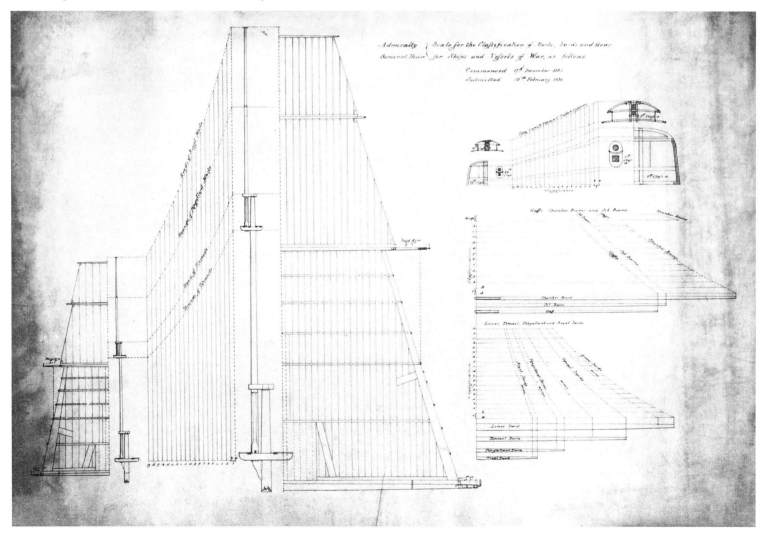

92 Draught of sails of about 1840.

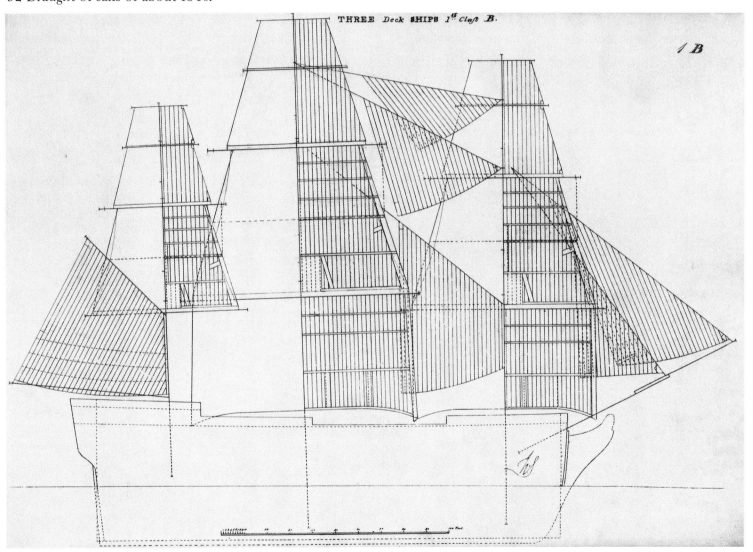

IV SEAMANSHIP
Details and sources

93 HMS *Eurydice*, 1843, a lithograph by Vernon. Nineteenth century etchings and lithographs are a very good source of information.

Appendix I
Proportions of masts, spars and rigging

The following proportions of the masts and spars have either been worked out from contemporary masting tables, or from proportionate tables given in contemporary books and manuscripts. They should be quite suitable for masting any model covered by this book.

LENGTHS OF MASTS

Main mast to ships beam 1627 – 2.4; 1640 – 2.4 .

Main mast to length and beam 1670 – add together the length of the keel, breadth of the ship and depth of the ship then divide the answer by 1.66. If the beam exceeds 27 feet then deduct from the total the amount that the beam is in excess of 27 feet; if the beam is less than 27 feet then add to the total the amount that the beam is short of 27 feet; 1711 – the length of the lower gun deck plus the extreme breadth and divide the total by 2.

Main mast to ships beam 1719 – First, Second and Third Rates of 80 guns 2.28, Third Rates of 70 guns 2.32, Fourth Rates of 60 guns 2.34, Fourth Rates of 50 guns 2.36, Fifth Rates of 40 guns 2.38, Fifth Rates of 30 guns 2.4, Sixth Rates of 20 guns 2.42; 1745 – Fist Rates 2.24, Second Rates 2.26, Third Rates 2.27, Fourth and Fifth Rates 2.22, Sixth Rates 2.28; 1773 – 2.23.

Main mast to lower deck length and beam 1794, 1815, 1836 – add together the lower deck length and the extreme beam of the ship and divide the answer by 2.

Once the length of the main mast has been ascertained it is a simple matter to find the lengths of all other masts and spars as the following proportion tables will show.

Proportionate length of main topmast to the main mast All periods 0.6.

Proportionate length of the main topgallant mast to the main topmast Up to 1719 – 0.42; from 1719 to 1773 – 0.49; after 1773 – 0.5.

Proportionate length of the main royal mast to the main topgallant mast 0.7.

Proportionate length of the fore mast to the main mast 1627 – 0.8; 1640 – 0.87; 1670 – 0.9; 1711 – 0.9; 1719 – 0.9; 1745 – 0.9; 1773 – 0.93; after 1773 – 0.9. The topmasts, topgallant and royal masts of the fore mast followed the same proportions to their respective lower masts as given for the main masts.

Proportionate length of the mizen mast to the main mast All the following gives the length of the mizen mast stepped in the hold, if the mast was stepped on the lower deck the difference between the hold step and the deck should be deducted from the length arrived at. 1627 – 0.5; 1640 – 0.74; 1670 – 0.67; 1711 – 0.86; 1719 – on all except Sixth Rates 0.85, on Sixth Rates 0.8; 1745 – 0.86; 1773 – 0.84; 1794 – 0.85; 1815 – on First Rates 0.87, on Second and Third Rates 0.86, on Fourth Rates and below 0.83; 1836 – as given for 1815 with the addition of 0.75 for sloops.

Proportionate length of the mizen topmast to the main topmast Up to 1719 – 0.5; 1719 to 1794 – 0.7; 1794 – 0.7 on all except sloops, sloops 0.71; 1815 and after – sloops 0.71, other Rates 0.75.

Proportionate length of the mizen topgallant mast to the mizen topmast 1729 – 0.63; 1773 and after – 0.5.

Proportionate length of the mizen royal mast to the mizen topgallant mast 0.7.

PROPORTIONATE DIAMETERS OF THE MASTS

Main Up to 1670 – 1 inch per 3 feet in length. 1670 to 1773 – 15/16 inch per 3 feet in length. 1773 to 1794 – 9/10 inch per 3 feet in length. After 1794 – 1 inch per 3 feet in length.
Fore The same proportions as given for the main.
Mizen 1627 – 1 inch per 3 feet in length; 1670 to 1711 -- 15/16 inch per 3 feet in length; 1711 – 2/3 inch per 3 feet in length; 1719 – on First, Second, Third and Fourth Rates of 60 guns 15/22 inch per 3 feet in length, on Fourth Rates of 50 guns and all Fifth Rates 2/3 inch per 3 feet in length, on Sixth Rates 8/13 inch per 3 feet in length; 1773 – 6/9 inch per 3 feet in length; from 1794 – First to Third Rates 3/5 and Fourth Rates and below 2/3 inch per 3 feet in length.
Main Topmast 1627 to 1719 – 15/16 inch per 3 feet in length; 1719 to 1794 – 9/10 inch per 3 feet in length; 1794 and after – 1 inch per 3 feet in length.
Fore Topmast Up to 1773 – the same diameter as the main topmast; after 1773 – 1 inch per 3 feet in length.
Mizen Topmast Up to 1719 – the same proportionate diameter as on the mizen mast; 1719 – 5/6 inch per 3 feet in length; 1745 – 5/6 inch per 3 feet in length; from 1773 on – 7/10 inch per 3 feet in length.
Main and Fore Topgallant Up to 1719 – 15/16 inch per 3 feet in length; after 1719 – 1 inch per 3 feet in length.
Mizen Topgallant 1 inch per 3 feet in length.
Royal Masts 2/3 the diameter of the appropriate topgallant mast.

BOWSPRIT AND JIBBOOM

Proportionate length of the bowsprit to the main mast 1627 – 0.8; 1640 – 0.83; 1670 to 1719 – 0.66; 1719 – on First and Second Rates 0.6, other Rates 0.59; 1745 – 0.63; 1773 – 0.6; 1794 and later – on ships down to 80 guns 0.64, on 74 gun ships and below 0.6.

Proportionate diameter of the bowsprit per three feet in length 1627 – the diameter of the main mast; 1711 – 9/10 the diameter of the main mast; 1719 – First to Fourth Rates of 60 guns 1 5/9 inch, Fourth Rates of 50 guns 1 3/7, Fifth Rates 1 1/3 and Sixth Rates 1 2/9.

Proportionate length of the sprit topmast to the top masts 1627, 1640 – 0.47 of the fore top mast; 1670 – 0.33 of the main topmast; 1711 – 0.33 of the fore topmast; 1719 – 0.375 of the bowsprit; 1745 – 0.43 of the fore topmast.

Proportionate diameter of the sprit topmast Up to 1719 – 15/16; after 1719 – 1 inch per 3 feet in length.

Proportionate length of the jib boom 1719 – 6 feet less than the breadth of the ship; 1745 – 0.7 of the length of the bowsprit; 1773 – 0.41 the length of the main mast, 1794 and onwards – 0.715 of the length of the bowsprit.

Proportionate diameter of the jib boom 7/8 inch per 3 feet in length.
Proportionate length of the flying jib boom 0.92 of the length of the bowsprit.
Proportionate diameter of the flying jib boom 1/2 inch per 3 feet in length.

LENGTHS OF YARDS

Proportionate length of the main yard 1627 — 5/6 the length of the keel; 1640 — 0.97 of the main mast; 1670 — the same length as the fore mast; 1711 — 7/8 of the main mast; 1719 — 0.571 the length of the gun deck; 1745 — 0.9 of the main mast; 1773 — 0.9 of the main mast, 1794 and after — 8/9 of the main mast.
Proportionate length of the fore yard to the length of the main yard 1627 — 0.8; 1640 — 0.77; 1670 — 0.9; from 1711 — 0.875.
Proportionate length of the crossjack yard 1627 — 16/21 the length of the main yard; 1640 — 0.466; 1670 — the same length as the fore topmast; 1684 — 16/19 the length of the main topmast; 1711 — slightly longer than the main topsail yard; 1719 — the same length as the fore topsail yard; 1745 — the same length as the fore topsail yard; 1773 — 0.72 of the fore yard; 1794 and after — the same length as the fore topsail yard.
Proportionate length of the main topsail yard 1627 — 3/7 the length of the main yard; 1640 — 7/15 of the main yard; 1678 — 1/2 of the main yard; 1711 — 5/9 of the main yard; 1719 — 0.72 of the main yard; 1745 0.72 of the main yard; 1773 — 0.72 of the main yard; 1794 and later — 0.714 of the main yard.
Proportionate length of the fore topsail yard Up to 1711 — 1/2 the length of the fore yard; 1711 — 5/9 of the fore yard; 1719 to 1794 — 0.72 of the fore yard; 1794 and after — 7/8 of the main topsail yard.
Proportionate length of the mizen topsail yard Up to 1711 — 1/2 the length of the crossjack yard; 1711 — 1/3 of the mizen yard; 1719 to 1794 — 3/4 of the crossjack yard; 1794 and after — 2/3 of the main topsail yard.
Proportionate length of the main and fore topgallant yards Up to 1773 — 1/2 the length of their topsail yards;

1773 — 2/3 of their topsail yards; 1794 to 1815 — ships of 74 guns and over 2/3, under 74 guns 3/5 of their topsail yards; 1836 and on — all ships of the line 2/3 of their topsail yards, but frigates' yards varied in the individual classes.
Proportionate length of the mizen topgallant yard The same proportionate length to their topsail yards as given for the main and fore topgallant yards.
Proportionate length of all royal yards 1/2 the length of their topgallant yards.
Proportionate length of the spritsail yard 1627 — 16/21 the length of the main yard; 1640 — 2/3 of the fore yard; 1670 — the same length as the fore yard; 1684 — the same length as the fore topmast; 1711 — 5/7 of the fore yard; from 1719 — the same length as the fore topsail yard.
Proportionate length of the sprit topsail yard Up to 1719 — 1/2 the length of the spritsail yard; from 1719 to 1794 — 2/3 of the spritsail yard; 1794 and after — the same length as the fore topgallant yard.
Proportionate length of the mizen yard 1627 — the same length as the mizen mast; 1640 — 0.9 of the fore yard; 1670 to 1719 — the same length as the fore yard; 1719 and after — 5/6 of the main yard.
Proportionate length of the driver boom The same length as the main topsail yard.
Proportionate length of the gaff 5/8 the length of the driver boom.
Proportionate length of the trysail gaffs 5/8 the length of their appropriate topsail yards.

DIAMETERS OF YARDS

Proportional diameter of the main and fore yards Up to 1794 — 3/4 inch per 3 feet in length; 1794 and later — 7/10 inch per 3 feet in length.
Proportional diameter of the main fore and mizen topsail yards 5/8 inch per 3 feet in length.
Proportional diameter of the main and fore topgallant yards Up to 1719 — 5/8 inch per 3 feet in length; 1719 and later — 3/5 inch per 3 feet in length.
Proportional diameter of the mizen topgallant yard 3/5 inch per 3 feet in length.

Proportional diameter of the crossjack yard Up to 1794 — 8/13 inch per 3 feet in length; 1794 and later — 5/8 of an inch per 3 feet in length.
Proportional diameter of the spritsail yard 5/8 of an inch per 3 feet in length.
Proportional diameter of the sprit topsail yard Up to 1719 — 5/8 inch per 3 feet in length; 1719 and later — 3/5 inch per 3 feet in length.
Proportional diameter of the driver boom 5/8 inch per 3 feet in length.
Proportional diameter of the gaffs The same diameter as the driver boom.
Proportional diameter of the mizen yard Up to 1719 — 1/2 inch per 3 feet in length; 1719 and later — 7/13 inch per 3 feet in length.

STUNSAIL BOOMS AND YARDS

Proportionate length of the lower stunsail booms 5/9 the length of the main yard.
Proportionate length of the topsail yard stunsail booms 1/2 the length of the yard they are carried on.
Proportionate length of the stunsail yards 4/7 the length of their booms.
Proportionate length of the driver yard The same length as the fore topgallant yard.
Proportionate length of the ensign staff 1/3 the length of the main mast above the taffrail.
Proportionate length of the jack staff 1/2 the length of the ensign staff.
Proportional diameter of the stunsail booms and yards 1 inch per 5 feet in length.
Proportional diameter of the driver yard The same diameter as the fore topgallant yard.
Proportional diameter of the ensign staff 1/2 inch per 3 feet in length.
Proportional diameter of the jack staff 3/4 inch per 3 feet in length.

TOPS

When round tops were carried the following were the proportionate widths of the bottom of the tops based on the length of their respective topmasts: Main 0.28, Fore 0.29, Mizen 0.27 and Sprit 0.4.
Once the tops lost their circular design the following proportions came into effect: Up to 1769 the athwartship

breadth on the Main and Fore was 0.33, the Mizen 0.3 and the sprit 0.3, all of their respective topmasts. The fore and after length of all tops were 0.785 of their athwartship breadth. From 1769 all tops were 0.33 the length of their topmasts athwartships and 0.75 the breadth for the fore and aft length.

Information regarding the size of the hole dates back to 1769; I have been unable to find any reference before that date.

From 1769 to 1794 the square hole was 5 inches per foot of the athwartship breadth of the top athwartships, and 0.93 of the athwartship breadth of the hole for the hole's length fore and aft. From 1794 the athwartship breadth of the hole was 0.4 of the breadth of the top, with the same proportionate length of the hole as quoted for the 1769 period.

PROPORTIONATE RIGGING SIZES

With only a very few exceptions the sizes of both standing and running rigging can be worked out in relation to the size of the appropriate mast stay. The sizes of the stays can be ascertained by comparison with the size of the lower stays which in turn are given in ratio size of the lower masts. The exceptions are the ropes where a definite size in inches is required, such as the ratlines, robands, gaskets, brails and fore hatch stay tackle.

The following ratios are applicable to all Rates and all periods except where specifically mentioned.

RIGGING TO THE MASTS

Lower stays 1/2 the diameter of the appropriate lower mast.
Topmast stays 1/2 the size of the lower stays.
Topgallant stays 1/2 the size of the topmast stays.
Royal stays 1/2 the size of the topgallant stays.
Lower stay collars Main, up to 1660 — 0.9; from 1660 to 1680 — 0.8; from 1680 to 1810 — 0.72 of the main stay. Fore, up to 1733 — 0.9; after 1733 and up to 1810 — 0.5 of the fore stay. Mizen, 0.8 of the mizen stay.

Topmast stay collars Main, 0.75 of the main topmast stay. Fore, 0.8 of the fore topmast stay. Mizen, 0.75 of the mizen topmast stay.
Topmast stay collars Main, 0.75 of the main topmast stay. Fore, 0.8 of the fore topmast stay. Mizen, 0.75 of the mizen topmast stay.
Preventer stays Main and fore lower, up to 1810 — 0.7 of the appropriate stay; after 1810 — the same size as the stay. Mizen lower, the same size as the mizen stay. The topmast preventer stays were 0.75 of the topmast stays.
Preventer stay collars These were the same proportionate sizes to the preventer stays as the stay collars were to the stays.
Stay lanyards The lower lanyards were 0.33 the size of the lower stays, the topmast lanyards were 0.5 the size of the topmast stays, the topgallant lanyards were 0.5 of the topgallant stays and the royal lanyards were 0.5 of the royal stay.
Stay tackles These were the same proportions as these given for the stay lanyards.
Shroud lanyards These were always 0.5 of the appropriate shroud.
Bobstays Up to 1719 they were 0.33 of the forestay; after 1719 they were 0.5 the size of the forestay.
Bobstay collars These were the same size as the bobstays.
Gammoning This was 0.44 of the forestay.
Bowsprit shrouds These were the same size as the gammoning.
Shroud collars These were 0.8 of the bowsprit shrouds.
Lanyards These were 0.5 of their respective collars.
Bowsprit horses These were 0.6 of the gammoning.
Wooldings All wooldings were 0.2 the size of the main stay
Worming of the stays This was 0.1 of the appropriate stay.
Shrouds Main and fore lower, 0.6 of the appropriate stay. Mizen, 0.8 of the mizen stay. Fore and main topmast shrouds, 0.66 of the lower shrouds. Mizen topmast shrouds were the same as the mizen topmast stay. All topgallant shrouds were the same size as their appropriate topgallant stays.
Futtock shrouds These were the same

size as the topmast shrouds.
Pendant of tackle These were the same size as the shrouds.
Runners of the tackle These were 0.66 of the pendant.
Falls of the tackle These were 0.66 of the runners.
Pendant of the garnet This was 0.9 of the pendant of the tackle.
Runner of the garnet 0.8 of the pendant.
Falls of the garnet The same size as the falls of the tackle.
Stay tackle pendant This was 0.35 of the mainstay.
Fore hatch stay tackle First to Third Rates the size was 3 1/4 inches, for Fourth Rates and under 3 inches.
Winding tackle pendant This was the same size as the main preventer stay.
Winding tackle fall 0.5 of the pendant.
Burton pendants Mizen lower, 0.66 of the mizen stay; main topmast, 0.75 of the main topmast shrouds; fore topmast, First to Third Rates, 0.8, Fourth and Fifth Rates 0.75, Sixth Rates 0.66 of the fore topmast shrouds.
Burton pendant falls Mizen lower, 0.66 of the pendant; main and fore topmast 0.33 of their appropriate shrouds.
Standing backstays The same size as their appropriate shrouds.
Lanyards 0.5 of the standing backstay.
Breast backstays The same size as the standing backstays.
Running breast backstay 0.7 of their appropriate topmast shrouds.
Running breast backstay falls 0.45 of their appropriate topmast shrouds.
Shifting backstay The same as the running breast backstay.
Top rope pendants These were the same size as their appropriate topmast stays.
Top rope falls 0.5 of the pendants.
Top ropes 0.5 of the appropriate stay.
Mizen stay crowsfeet 0.6 of the mizen stay.
Jib boom guy pendants 0.5 of the bobstay.
Jib boom guy pendant falls 0.66 of the pendants.
Jib boom horses 0.5 of the bobstay.
Dolphin striker stay 0.75 of the fore topmast stay.
Dolphin striker backstay 0.5 of the dolphin striker stay.

Heel lashing The same size as the bowsprit shroud lanyard.
Flying jib guys 0.33 of the dolphin striker stay.
Flying dolphin striker stay The same as the flying jib guys.
Flying jib boom horse The same as the jib boom horse.
Sprit topmast shrouds The same as the mizen topmast shrouds.
Backstay pendants or crane lines The same size as the sprit topmast shrouds.
Crowsfeet or falls 0.8 of the sprit topmast shrouds.
Halliards The same size as the crowsfeet.
Futtock shrouds The same size as the main topmast futtock shrouds.
Upper catharpins Lower, 0.25 of the main shrouds; topmast, 0.25 of the main topmast shrouds.
Lower catharpins The same size as the upper catharpins.
Ropes of a specific size 1 1/2 inches — lower and topmast ratlines, euphroe falls and crowsfeet of all lower masts, snaking between the stays, mizen sail, driver and spanker lacings; 2 inches — mizen stay sail brails; 1 inch — all topgallant ratlines, topmast and topgallant futtock shrouds.
Gaskets, robands and reef pendants These were usually made of flat sennet.

PROPORTIONATE SIZES OF THE MAIN YARD RIGGING TO THE MAIN STAY

Tie 0.5; Tie preventer 0.25; Halliard Halliard 0.375; Jeers First to Fourth Rates 0.45, Fifth and Sixth Rates 0.65; Jeer falls 0.225; Slings 0.4 ; Parrel rope 0.375; Breast rope 0.45; Nave line 0.15; Truss pendants 0.45; Falls 0.18; Lifts 0.33; Span for the cap 0.33; Jigger tackle 0.132; Footropes 0.25; Footrope lanyards 0.1; Stirrups 0.18; Brace pendants First to Third Rates 0.25, Fourth to Sixth Rates 0.33; Brace 0.187; Brace span 0.1; Preventer brace 0.2; Yard tackle pendant 0.4; Falls 0.24; Yard tackle tricing line 0.125; Martnet legs 0.187; Falls 0.168; Leech line legs and falls First and Second Rates 0.165, Third to Sixth Rates 0.2; Leech line long strop 0.198; Slab lines 0.115 Bunt line legs

and falls 0.18; Bowlines and bridles 0.25; Reef pendants 0.25; Reef tackles 0.125; Reefing lines 0.1; Clue garnets 0.2; Sheets 0.4; Tack at widest part up to 1670, 0.6; after 1670, 0.5; Earings 0.158; Quarter pendants First to Third Rates 0.33, Fourth to Sixth Rates 0.45; Quarter tackles 0.2; Stay sail stay 0.25; Staysail collar 0.2 on First to Third rates and 0.25 on other Rates; Lanyard 0.33 of the collar; Staysail halliard 0.12 up to 1745 and 0.2 after that date; Halliard fall 0.1; Staysail sheets, tacks and downhauler 0.21; Outer stunsail halliards First and Second Rates 0.2; other Rates 0.25; Inner halliards First and Second Rates 0.16, other Rates 0.2; Swinging boom topping lift and guys 0.2; bowsing down tackle 0.1; Loose footed stunsail span and guys 0.2.

PROPORTIONATE SIZES OF THE MAIN TOPSAIL YARD RIGGING TO THE MAIN TOPMAST STAY

Ties Up to 1685 the same size, on First and Second Rates 0.66 and on other Rates 0.8 after 1685; Runner of the tie 0.85 of the tie; Halliard of the tie Up to 1685 0.5 and after 1685 0.66 of the tie; Parrel rope 0.5 on First and Second Rates, 0.66 on other Rates up to 1719, after 1719 0.45 on all Rates; Truss parrels 0.6; Lifts The same size as the topsail halliards; Footropes 0.55; Lanyards 0.22; Stirrups 0.36; Flemish horses 0.4; Brace pendants 0.45 up to 1706, 0.55 after that date; Braces 0.3 up to 1706 and 0.36 after then; Leech lines 0.33; Bunt lines 0.43; Bowlines and bridles 0.45; Reef tackle pendants 0.5; Falls 0.3; Clue lines 0.45; Sheets First and Second Rates the same size as the stay, other Rates 0.9; Earings 0.165; Staysail stay 0.5, Staysail sheet pendants 0.5; Staysail sheets 0.5; Staysail sheet whips 0.36; Staysail halliards 0.5; Staysail tacks 0.45; Downhauler 0.237; Brails 0.18; Middle staysail stay 0.5; Middle staysail fall 0.25; Jack stay 0.5; Lanyard 0.25, Halliard 0.4; Sheets and tacks 0.36; Downhauler and tricing line 0.237; Stunsail halliards sheets and tacks 0.36; Downhauler and boom tackle 0.237.

PROPORTIONATE SIZES OF THE MAIN TOPGALLANT YARD RIGGING TO THE MAIN TOPGALLANT STAY

Ties Up to 1685 the same isze as the stay, after 1685 0.9; Halliard Up to 1685 0.8, after 1685 0.5; Parrel rope Up to 1745 0.66, after 1745 0.55; Lifts Up to 1685 0.5, after 1685 0.66; Footropes 0.7; Lanyard 0.3; Stirrups 0.5; Brace pendants 0.66; Braces 0.5; Buntlines 0.33; Bowlines and bridles 0.5; Clue lines 0.5; Sheets The same size as the stay; Earings 0.165; Staysail stay 0.75; Halliard 0.6; Sheet pendants 0.6; Whips 0.5; Tacks and downhauler 0.45; Stunsail halliards 0.5; Sheets 0.385; Tacks 0.5; Downhauler 0.45.

PROPORTIONATE SIZES OF THE MAIN ROYAL YARD RIGGING TO THE MAIN ROYAL STAY

Ties The same size as the stay; Truss 0.5; Brace 0.75; Footropes 0.5; Bowlines and bridles 0.5; Lifts 0.75; Clue lines 0.5; Sheets The same size as the stay; Earings 0.2; Staysail halliard 0.6; Sheets 0.6; Tacks 0.5; Downhauler 0.5.
The following rigging on the fore yard is the same size as that on the main yard: Truss pendant; Truss pendant falls; Lifts; Span for the cap; Jigger tackle; Footropes; Lanyard and stirrups Preventer brace; Yard tackle pendant; Falls and tricing line; Leech line legs and falls; Leech line long strop; Bunt line legs and falls; Bowlines and bridle; Reef pendants and tackles; Reefing lines; Stunsail outer and inner halliards sheets and tacks.

PROPORTIONATE SIZES OF THE FORE YARD RIGGING TO THE FORESTAY

Ties 0.5 on First to Fourth Rates, 0.75 on other Rates; Tie preventer 0.25; Halliard 0.375; Jeers 0.5 up to 1745 and the same size as the main jeers after then; Jeer falls 0.25; Slings 0.25; Parrel rope 0.33; Breast rope 0.5; Nave line 0.165; Brace 0.25; Martnet legs and falls 0.2; Slab lines 0.14; Clue garnets 0.25; Sheets 0.4; Tacks Up to 1670 0.6, after 1670 0.5; Earings 0.125; Bumkin shrouds 0.25; Bumkin lashing and lanyards 0.125; Staysail

halliards and sheet pendants 0.25; Staysail sheet whips and tacks 0.19; Downhauler 0.125; Swinging boom topping lift and guys 0.2; Bowsing down tackle 0.1; Loose footed stunsail span and guys 0.2.
The following rigging on the fore topsail yard is the same size as that on the main topsail yard; Footropes, lanyards and stirrups; Flemish horses; Earings.

PROPORTIONATE SIZES OF THE FORE TOPSAIL YARD RIGGING TO THE FORE TOPMAST STAY
Ties Up to 1685 the same size as the stay, after 1685 0.66; **Runner of the ties** On First and Second Rates 0.9 of the ties, on other Rates 0.85 of the ties; **Halliard** Up to 1685 0.5, after 1685 0.66, both of the ties; **Parrel rope** One First to Third Rates 0.5, on other Rates 0.66, both up to 1719, after 1719 on all Rates 0.45; **Truss parrel** 0.6; **Lifts** On First to Third Rates 0.125, on other Rates 0.165; **Brace pendants** Up to 1706 0.5, after 1706 0.66; **Braces** 0.66 of the brace pendants; **Leech lines** Up to 1706 0.4, after 1706 0.33; **Bunt lines** 0.4; **Bowlines and bridles** 0.45; **Reef tackle pendants** 0.5; **Falls** 0.33; **Clue lines** 0.45; **Sheets** 0.9; **Staysail stay** 0.5; **Lanyard** 0.25; **Tackle** 0.33; **Halliard** On First to Fifth Rates 0.33, on Sixth Rates 0.375; **Staysail sheet pendants** 0.5; **Whips** 0.3 up to 1745, after 1745 0.45; **Tacks** 0.45; **Downhauler** 0.25; **Outhauler** 0.33; **Netting** 0.165; **Jib sail stay** 0.5; **Stay fall** 0.33; **Stay tackle** 0.3; **Halliard and outhauler** 0.5; **Outhauler tackle and downhauler** 0.33; **Sheet pendants** 0.5; **Whips and tacks** 0.33; **Stunsail halliards, sheets and tacks** 0.5; **Downhauler** 0.25; **Boom tackle** 0.33.

PROPORTIONATE SIZES OF THE FORE TOPGALLANT YARD RIGGING TO THE FORE TOPGALLANT STAY
Ties Up to 1685 the same size as the stay, after 1685 0.9; **Halliards** 0.66 up to 1685, 0.45 after 1685; **Parrel rope** 0.55; **Lifts** 0.66; **Footropes** 0.75; **Lanyard** 0.3; **Stirrups** 0.5; **Brace pendants** 0.66; **Braces** 0.5; **Bunt lines** 0.33; **Bowlines, bridles and clue lines** 0.5; **Sheets** The same size as the stay; **Earings** 0.165; **Flying jib sail halliards and sheets** 0.66; **Tacks** 0.55; **Downhauler** 0.33; **Stunsail halliards** 0.5; **Sheets** 0.45; **Tacks** 0.4; **Downhauler** 0.33.

PROPORTIONATE SIZES OF THE FORE ROYAL YARD RIGGING TO THE FORE ROYAL STAY
Ties The same as the stay; **Truss** 0.5; **Braces** 0.75; **Bowlines, bridles and clue lines** 0.5; **Lifts** 0.75; **Sheets** The same size as the stay; **Footropes** 0.5; **Earings** 0.2.

PROPORTIONATE SIZES OF THE CROSSJACK YARD RIGGING TO THE MIZEN STAY
Slings 0.75 up to 1719, 0.66 after 1719; **Truss pendant** 0.6; **Truss pendant falls** 0.5; **Lifts** Up to 1685 on First to Third Rates 0.66, on other Rates 0.33, after 1685 on all Rates 0.66; **Lift lanyards** 0.6 of the lifts; **Footropes** 0.4; **Lanyard** 0.25; **Stirrups** 0.33; **Brace pendants** Up to 1719 0.66, from 1719 to 1745 0.5, after 1745 0.4; **Braces** Up to 1670 0.5, from 1670 to 1745 0.375, after 1745 0.33; **Staysail stay** 0.6; **Collar** 0.56; **Lanyard** 0.25; **Halliard, sheets and tacks** 0.44; **Downhauler** 0.25.

PROPORTIONATE SIZES OF THE MIZEN TOPSAIL YARD RIGGING TO THE MIZEN TOPMAST STAY
Ties The same size as the stay up to 1745, after 1745 only the Fourth to Sixth Rates were of these proportions, on First to Third Rates after 1745 they were 0.8; **Runner of the tie** 0.9 of the tie; **Halliards** Up to 1745 0.75, after 1745 0.66; **Parrel rope** Up to 1719 the same size as the stay, from 1719 to 1745 0.66, after 1745 0.5, **Truss parrel** 0.6; **Lifts** Up to 1670 0.75, from 1670 to 1745 0.66 and after 1745 0.5; **Lift falls** 0.75 of the lifts; **Footropes** 0.66; **Lanyards** 0.25; **Stirrups** First to Third Rates 0.4, other Rates 0.5; **Flemish horses** 0.6; **Brace pendants** Up to 1719 0.75, after 1719 0.66; **Braces** Up to 1745 0.66, after 1745 0.5; **Leech lines** 0.4; **Bunt lines** 0.4; **Bowlines** Up to 1719 0.75, from 1719 to 1745 0.4, after 1745 0.5; **Bowline bridles** Up to 1719 0.66, from

1719 to 1745 0.4, after 1745 0.5; **Reef tackle pendants** 0.6; **Falls** 0.3; **Clue lines** 0.66 up to 1745, after 1745 0.5; **Sheets** The same size as the stay; **Earings** 0.3; **Staysail halliards** 0.5; **Sheets** 0.5; **Tacks** 0.4; **Downhauler** 0.3.

PROPORTIONATE SIZES OF THE MIZEN TOPGALLANT YARD RIGGING TO THE MIZEN TOPGALLANT STAY
Ties The same size as the stay; **Halliards** 0.5; **Parrel rope** 0.6, **Lifts** 0.8; **Footropes** 0.8; **Lanyard** 0.5; **Stirrups** 0.5; **Braces** 0.5; **Buntlines** 0.33; **Bowlines and bridles** 0.6; **Clue lines** 0.6; **Sheets** The same size as the stay; **Earings** 0.165; **Staysail halliard and sheets** 0.66; **Tacks** 0.55; **Downhauler** 0.33.

PROPORTIONATE SIZES OF THE MIZEN ROYAL YARD RIGGING TO THE MIZEN ROYAL STAY
Ties The same size as the stay; **Truss** 0.5; **Braces** 0.75; **Footropes** 0.5; **Lanyard** 0.33; **Bowlines and bridles** 0.5; **Lifts** 0.75; **Clue lines** 0.5; **Sheets** The same size as the stay; **Earings** 0.2.

PROPORTIONATE SIZES OF THE MIZEN YARD RIGGING TO THE MIZEN STAY
Parrel rope The same size as the stay up to 1670, from 1670 to 1719 0.75, after 1719 0.55; **Truss parrel** The same size as the stay; **Truss** 0.55; **Sling** The same size as the stay up to 1773 and 0.75 after 1773; **Ties** 0.36 of the mainstay; **Tie falls** 0.27 of the main stay; **Jeers** Up to 1719 the same size as the stay, from 1719 to 1773 0.9, after 1773 0.7; **Lift** 0.33; **Lift span and falls** 0.33; **Bowlines** Up to 1719 0.66, from 1719 to 1745 0.55, after 1745 0.33; **Sheets** Up to 1719 0.66, from 1719 to 1773 0.75, after 1773 0.5; **Martnets and martnet legs** 0.25; **Brails** Up to 1670 0.5, after 1670 0.4; **Peak brails** 0.25; **Throat and foot brails** 0.33; **Peak and throat brails combined** 0.44; **Peak middle and throat brails when sail was laced to the**

mast 0.44; Fancy lines 0.33; Fancy line span 0.33; Vang pendants 0.5; Vang falls 0.33; Smiting lines 0.25; Earings 0.25; Lacing to the yard Up to 1773 0.22, after 1773 0.15; Lacing to the mast 0.3; Tack Up to 1719 0.6, from 1719 to 1773 0.55, after 1773 0.33; Bonnet lacing 0.25.

PROPORTIONATE SIZES OF THE MIZEN BOOM AND GAFF RIGGING TO THE MIZEN STAY

Gaff parrel 0.66; Gaff topping lift 0.5; Vang pendants 0.55; Whips 0.275; Throat halliards 0.5; Boom topping lift 0.6; Topping lift falls 0.33; Boom sheets 0.4; Boom sheet and guys combined 0.4; Boom guy pendants 0.4; Guy falls 0.3; Boom horses 0.4; Driver halliard 0.25; Driver yard halliards 0.25; Driver throat halliards 0.125; Driver downhauler 0.3; Driver tacks 0.25; Driver sheets 0.4; Sheet falls 0.25; Driver earing 0.25; Spanker earing 0.25; Spanker peak, middle and foot brails 0.3; Spanker throat brails 0.33; Spanker earings 0.25; Spanker tacks 0.33; Spanker sheets 0.5;

PROPORTIONATE SIZES OF THE FORE AND MAIN TRYSAIL RIGGING

FORE TRYSAIL Parrel The same size as the mizen gaff parrel, Throat halliard The same size as the mizen throat halliards; Peak span 0.25 of the fore stay; Peak span pendant The same size as the peak span; Vangs 0.2 of the forestay; Throat, peak and foot brails The same size as the spanker brails; Tacks and sheets The same size as on the spanker.

MAIN TRYSAIL Parrel, throat halliards, brails, tacks and sheets The same as for the fore trysail; Peak span and pendant 0.25 of the mainstay; Vangs 0.2 of the mainstay.

PROPORTIONATE SIZES OF THE SPRITSAIL YARD RIGGING TO THE FORESTAY

Parrel rope 0.3; Slings —
Up to 1745 0.4, after 1745 0.33; Halliard 0.4 up to 1745 and 0.2 after 1745; Lanyard 0.1; Garnet 0.23; Garnet span 0.23; Standing lifts Up to 1745 0.2, after 1745 0.25; Lanyard 0.1; Brace pendant 0.3; Braces 0.25;

Running lifts 0.2; Sheet pendants Up to 1670 0.4, after 1670 0.33; Sheet strop 0.25; Tricing line 0.1; Clue lines Up to 1745 0.2, after 1745 0.15, Footropes 0.25; Stirrups 0.25; Reef points 0.1; Bunt lines 0.2 up to 1745 and 0.125 after 1745; Earings 0.1.

PROPORTIONATE SIZES OF THE SPRIT TOPSAIL RIGGING TO THE FORE TOPMAST STAY

Parrel Up to 1719 —
0.4, after 1719 0.33; Ties Up to 1670 0.6, after 1670 0.5; Halliards Up to 1670 0.4, after 1670 0.33; Lifts Up to 1670 0.4, after 1670 0.33; Brace pendants Up to 1670 0.5, after 1670 0.33; Braces Up to 1670 0.4, after 1670 0.33; Clue lines Up to 1670 0.5, from 1670 to 1745 0.33, from 1745 on First to Third Rates 0.25, and on other Rates 0.3; Footropes First and Second Rates 0.33, other Rates 0.4; Earings 0.125.

PROPORTIONATE SIZES OF THE SPREADER RIGGING TO THE FORESTAY

Jaw ropes 0.3; Fore, lower and after guys 0.25; Lanyards 0.125; Braces double 0.25; Braces single 0.3, Brace fall 0.125.

PROPORTIONATE SIZES OF THE MISCELLANEOUS ROPES TO THE MAINSTAY (EXCEPT WHERE STIPULATED)

Jack stays Lower yards 0.2 of their appropriate lower stay, topsail yards 0.4 of the topmast stays, topgallant yards 0.45 of the topgallant stays, royal yards 0.3 of the royal stays; Jackstay lanyards 0.4 of the jackstay; Bunt gaskets 0.1; Bonnet and drabler lacings The same size as the course earings; Cat falls 0.33; Back rope usually 2 inches; Cat head stopper 0.33; Shank painter tail 0.4; Fish pendant 0.5; Fish pendant tackle 0.25; Fish pendant fore guy 0.5; Fish pendant after guy 0.33; Anchor cable 0.62 the diameter of the main mast. (This proportion is applicable to the sheet and bower cables; spare cables were carried an inch or so smaller. The kedge anchor cable was usually 0.6 the size of the sheet anchor cable.) Cable messenger 0.75; Swifter 0.125; Nippers, hook

ropes and ring stoppers 0.125; Bitt stoppers 0.5; Deck stoppers 0.9; Tack and sheet stoppers 0.25; Anchor buoy ropes 0.45; Anchor buoy slings 0.2; Rudder pendants 0.4; Rudder pendant falls 0.2; Tiller rope 0.25; Quarter davit span 0.3; Span lanyard 0.6; Quarter davit guys 0.3; Lanyard 0.6; Topping lift 0.4; Boat falls 0.22; Man ropes 0.22; Stern davit span 0.3; Stern davit guys 0.3; Stern davit falls 0.2; Gun port tackles Usually 2 inches; Gun tackles Lower deck on First to Fourth rates usually 2 1/2 inches, other decks and Fifth and Sixth Rates 2 inches; Breech ropes 0.95 of the bore of the gun; Muzzle lashing Usually 2 inches; Entering ropes 0.125.

PROPORTIONATE LENGTHS OF PENDANTS AND STROPS

Main and foremast pendants of tackles 0.5 the length of the lower mast from the cap to the upper deck up to 1706, after 1706 the length was the same as the doubling on the lower mast; Mainstay tackle pendant 0.2 the length of the mainstay; Fore hatch stay tackle pendant 0.5 the length of the mainstay tackle pendant; Main pendant of the garnet 0.25 of the mainstay; Mizen burton pendants 0.5 the length of the mizenmast from the cap to the upper deck; Main and fore top rope pendants The same length as the lower yard; Main and fore top burton pendants The same length as the pendants of tackles; Main and fore topmast shifting back stay pendants 1.5 the length of the burton pendants; Mizen topmast burton pendants The same length as the mizen burton pendants; Mizen topmast shifting backstay pendant 1.5 the length of the mizen burton pendants; Brace pendants 0.3 of their respective yards (this varied on some ships between the ratio of 0.25 and 0.33); Main and fore yard tackle pendants Up to 1706 0.25, after 1706 0.2 the length of the lower yards; Quarter pendants The same length as the yard tackle pendants; Mizen yard vang pendant 0.25 the length of the mizen yard; Gaff vang pendant 0.5 the length of the gaff; Boom guy pendant 0.2 the length of the boom; Spritsail sheet pendant 0.7 the length of the spritsail yard, Spritsail sheet strop 0.2 the length of the spritsail yard (this is the doubled strop); **Fish pendant** 0.33 the length of the ship's gun deck; **Winding tackle pendant** 0.33 the length of the mainstay. NOTE When two pairs of mast pendants were carried, the lengths given refer to the foremost one; the aftermost pendants were usually about 1 foot longer. All the lengths given do not include the extra amount needed for splicing or taking round the mast etc. The lengths given for pendants round the mast are from the throat of the pendant to the lower end of the block or thimble; other pendant lengths are measured as after the blocks, thimbles, eyes, etc, are spliced or seized in. The sizes of the ropes mentioned in this book are of the circumference of the rope and not the diameter.

SIZES OF BLOCKS AND DEADEYES ETC

To obviate the need to display masses of individual tables I have worked out the average proportionate sizes of the various blocks, deadeyes, hearts, etc. The block, thimble, euphroe, truck, or rib sizes are based on the size of

the rope reeving through them, and the deadeye and heart sizes are based on the size of the rope that they were seized in.

Common blocks 4 times the size of the rope; **Long double blocks** 8 times the size of the rope; **Fiddle blocks** 10 times the size of the rope; **Shoe blocks** 9 times the size of the rope; **Flat thin blocks** 6.5 times the size of the rope, **Rams head block** 4 times the size of the rope (halliard); **Parrel trucks** 1.5 times the size of the rope; **Parrel ribs lower** 8 times the size of the rope; **Parrel ribs upper** 5.5 times the size of the rope; **Thimbles** 1.25 times the size of the rope; **Shoulder blocks** 4 times the size of the rope; **Deadeyes** 1.6 times the size of the rope; **Hearts** 1.45 times the size of the rope.

NOTE The shoulder blocks used for the fore tacks are based on the tack size at its widest part, and consequently the ratio of this block to the rope should be 2.5 times. Other blocks not specifically mentioned should follow the same proportions as the common blocks.

IMPERIAL CONVERSIONS TO METRIC

To assist any reader who prefers to work on the metric system the following conversions may be of help.

Imperial (inches)		Metric (centimetres)
1/16	=	0.15875
1/8	=	0.3175
1/4	=	0.635
1/2	=	1.27
1	=	2.54
12 (1 foot)	=	30.48
36 (3 feet or 1 yard)	=	91.44

Appendix II
Tables of mast and spar dimensions

The following tables of exact dimensions have been selected from originals dating from between 1600 and 1838. Most of these are in manuscript and have never been published, the exceptions being the 1815 *Falconer's Marine Dictionary* revised by Burney, and the 1832 book on *Equipment and Displacement* by John Edye.

The manuscripts used are as follows:

1600 Admiralty instructions (in the Pepysian Library)

1640 Manuscript made for the Lord High Admiral (in the Science Museum)

1665 Anonymous (in the Admiralty Library)

1716 Anonymous (in the National Maritime Museum)

1719 Establishment Book (in the National Maritime Museum)

1745 Establishment Book (in the National Maritime Museum)

1754 Navy Office to Plymouth Yard dated 1759 (in the National Maritime Museum)

1773 Admiral Penrose's Manuscript *circa* 1780–95 (in the National Maritime Museum)

1838 Admiralty Order dated September 1838 (in the National Maritime Museum) This last manuscript is so complex that I have had to select a few samples only from the total of twenty-four classes given, this period being when the topmasts and spars and the topgallant masts and spars were interchangeable between different classes: for example, the fore topmast of a 1st Class three-decker would serve as a main topmast for a 4th Class two-decker, etc.

TABLE 1: 1600 Admiralty Instructions

Mast or Spar	68 guns TRIUMPH			56 guns ELIZABETH JONAS			50 guns REPULSE			46 guns DEFIANCE		
	Length Ft	Ins	Diam Ins	Length Ft	Ins	Diam Ins	Length Ft	Ins	Diam Ins	Length Ft	Ins	Diam Ins
Bowsprit	87	0	29	86	3	29	73	0	27	72	0	25
Fore Mast	87	0	29	86	10	29	80	11	27	75	0	25
Fore Topmast	41	2	13⅔	37	6	12½	40	8	13½	34	10	11⅔
Fore Topgallant Mast	21	6	7	20	2	6⅔	22	0	7⅓	21	6	7
Main Mast	99	0	33	99	11	33⅓	88	10	29½	85	10	28½
Main Topmast	46	3	15½	44	10	15	46	2	15⅓	43	6	14½
Main Topgallant Mast	24	11	8⅓	26	0	8⅔	27	8	9	23	8	8
Main Mizen Mast	80	0	26⅔	74	2	24⅔	64	10	21½	63	0	21
Main Mizen Topmast	29	0	9⅔	26	10	9	25	0	8⅓	25	0	8⅓
Bonaventure Mizen Mast	60	0	20	67	0	22⅓						
Bonaventure Mizen Topm.	25	2	8	20	8	7						
Spritsail Yard	51	0	12¾	51	0	12¾	48	0	12	43	10	11
Fore Yard	76	3	19	71	0	18	67	0	16¾	63	1	15¾
Fore Topsail Yard	31	10	8	30	0	7½	27	3	6¾	24	3	6
Fore Topgallant Yard	15	0	3¾	12	4	3	12	0	3	12	5	3
Main Yard	98	8	24½	91	0	23	87	0	21¾	81	0	20¼
Main Topsail Yard	40	5	10	36	0	9	38	2	9½	30	10	7½
Main Topgallant Yard	16	0	4	15	0	3¾	16	0	4	14	0	3½
Main Mizen Yard	75	9	12½	64	0	10⅔	63	0	10½	56	7	9⅓
Bonaventure Mizen Yard	58	5	9¾	54	0	9						

Note: The terms Main Mizen and Bonaventure Mizen are those used in the original manuscript. No diameters are given in the original manuscript and the diameters shown in this table are derived from proportionate diameters given in *A Sea Grammar* by Smith, dated 1627.

TABLE 2: 1640 Lord High Admiral's Manuscript

Mast or Spar	100 guns SOVEREIGN			60 guns ST. GEORGE			42 guns VICTORY			34 guns DEFIANCE		
	Length Ft	Ins	Diam Ins	Length Ft	Ins	Diam Ins	Length Ft	Ins	Diam Ins	Length Ft	Ins	Diam Ins
Bowsprit	93	0	32	81	0	27	75	0	26½	72	0	26
Sprit Topmast	27	0	9	18	0	6	19	6	6½	19	6	6½
Fore Mast	95	6	32	81	0	27	79	4	26½	79	0	26
Fore Topmast	51	0	17	41	0	14	40	6	13½	42	0	14
Fore Topgallant Mast	28	0	9⅓	20	6	7	20	6	7	20	6	7
Main Mast	113	0	38	93	0	31	89	8	30	89	6	30
Main Topmast	58	6	19½	46	6	15½	46	6	15½	46	6	15½
Main Topgallant Mast	31	6	10½	23	6	8	23	6	8	23	6	8
Mizen Mast	87	6	29	75	0	25	63	0	21	63	0	21
Mizen Topmast	39	0	13	30	0	10	28	6	9½	28	6	9½
Spritsail Yard	63	0	15¾	48	0	12	48	0	12	48	0	12
Sprit Topsail Yard	30	0	7½	24	0	6	24	0	6	24	0	6
Fore Yard	86	0	21½	72	0	18	65	0	16¼	66	0	16½
Fore Topsail Yard	43	0	11	33	0	8¼	33	0	8¼	33	0	8¼
Fore Topgallant Yard	21	6	5¼	16	6	4	16	6	4	16	6	4
Main Yard	113	6	28¼	90	0	22½	82	6	20½	82	6	20½
Main Topsail Yard	51	9	13	42	0	10½	41	3	10½	41	3	10½
Main Topgallant Yard	25	6	6½	21	0	5¼	20	7½	5	20	7½	5
Mizen Yard	81	0	13½	66	0	11	65	0	11	63	0	10½
Mizen Topsail Yard	25	10½	6½	21	0	5¼	20	7½	5	20	7½	5
Crossjack	52	6	8⅔	42	0	7	41	3	7	41	3	7

Note: No diameters are given in the original manuscript. The diameters shown in this table are derived from proportionate diameters given in *A Sea Grammar* by Smith, dated 1627.

39 Guns			29 Guns			26 Guns			24 Guns			18 Guns		
MARY ROSE			WARSPITE			ADVENTURE			CRANE			ADVANTAGE		
Length		Diam	Length		Diam	Length		Diam	Length		Diam	Length		Diam
Ft	Ins	Ins	Ft	Ins	Ins	Ft	Ins	Ins	Ft	Ins	Ins	Ft	Ins	Ins
73	0	26	73	2	25½	57	0	20	58	2	20¾	58	0	20
78	0	26	76	4	25½	59	10	20	62	4	20¾	60	0	20
38	0	13	37	3	12½	24	6	8	31	2	10¼	30	0	10
21	0	7	22	0	7⅓									
87	4	29	87	9	29	72	0	24	71	6	24	71	0	23½
42	1	14	46	4	15½	31	4	10½	37	0	12⅓	38	0	12⅔
22	6	7½	24	8	8¼									
57	0	19	64	2	21½	48	0	16	43	4	14½	42	0	14
23	3	7⅔	25	4	8½									
46	2	11½	44	0	11	34	0	8½	35	3	8½	31	6	8
59	6	15	64	2	16	51	8	13	47	0	11¾	45	0	11¼
23	6	6	25	3	6¼	21	0	5¼	20	4	5	18	6	4½
10	9	2½	12	5	3									
83	4	21	85	6	21⅓	70	2	17⅔	62	3	15½	60	0	15
35	0	9	31	10	7¾	27	0	6¾	24	2	6	22	2	5½
12	6	3	15	0	3¾									
58	4	9¾	59	4	10	51	0	8½	46	6	7¾	46	0	7¾

32 guns			26 guns			14 guns			10 guns			6 gun Privateer		
BONAVENTURE			ADVENTURE			THE WHELPS			ROEBUCK			NICHODEMUS		
Length		Diam	Length		Diam	Length		Diam	Length		Diam	Length		Diam
Ft	Ins	Ins	Ft	Ins	Ins	Ft	Ins	Ins	Ft	Ins	Ins	Ft	Ins	Ins
67	6	23½	60	6	20½	50	2	20	37	6	15	31	0	16
16	0	5½	15	6	5	10	6	3½	9	0	3			
71	0	23½	62	6	20½	59	10	20	45	0	15	48	0	16
37	6	12½	31	6	10½	28	6	9½	26	0	8½	19	0	6¼
18	9	6¼	15	9	5	13	0	4⅓	13	0	4⅓			
82	6	27⅓	72	3	24	71	8	24	57	0	19	60	0	20
43	6	14½	36	0	12	35	0	12	30	6	10	25	0	8⅓
21	9	7¼	18	0	6	16	6	5½	14	6	5			
57	0	19	48	0	16	46	6	15½	30	0	10	33	0	11
23	0	7¾	22	6	7½	19	6	6½	13	6	4½			
43	6	11	36	0	9	27	0	6¾	22	0	5½	22	6	5½
21	9	5¼	18	0	4½	12	0	3	11	0	3			
58	6	14½	47	6	12	39	0	10	32	3	8	31	6	8
29	3	7½	24	0	6	19	6	5	16	5	4	15	0	3¾
14	7½	3⅔	12	0	3	9	9	2½	8	0	2			
76	6	19	63	0	15¾	48	0	12	40	6	10	39	0	10
36	9	9	31	0	8	24	0	6	19	10½	5	19	6	5
18	4½	4½	15	6	4	12	0	3	9	4½	2½			
56	3	9½	45	0	7½	37	6	6¼	33	9	5½	33	0	5½
18	4½	4½	15	6	4	12	0	3	9	4½	2½			
36	9	6	31	0	5	24	0	4	19	10½	3⅓			

TABLE 3: 1685 Anonymous Manuscript

Mast or Spar	1st rate ROYAL SOVEREIGN			1st rate ST. MICHAEL			All new 2nd rates BUILT 1678–1684			All new 3rd rates BUILT 1678–1683		
	Length Ft	Ins	Diam Ins	Length Ft	Ins	Diam Ins	Length Ft	Ins	Diam Ins	Length Ft	Ins	Diam Ins
Bowsprit	87	0	34	70	6	29½	73	6	34	64	6	30
Sprit Topmast	27	0	8½	19	6	7	22	6	7½	18	9	6
Fore Mast	97	6	34	88	6	29	93	9	31¼	85	6	27⅓
Fore Topmast	54	0	17½	51	0	16	54	9	16½	52	6	15
Fore Topgallant Mast	28	0	9	21	9	6½	24	0	7¼	21	0	6¾
Main Mast	115	6	40½	97	0	32½	105	0	35	95	0	30¼
Main Topmast	61	0	20½	59	0	17½	63	0	19¼	60	0	17½
Main Topgallant Mast	37	6	10	25	6	8	27	9	8¼	24	0	7½
Mizen Mast	100	6	22	88	0	19¼	88	6	21	84	9	18½
Mizen Topmast	39	0	11½	32	0	9¼	36	9	10½	31	6	9
Spritsail Yard	63	0	17¼	54	0	12⅔	57	0	13½	54	0	12¼
Sprit Topsail Yard	30	0	7	28	6	7½	31	6	7½	27	9	6
Fore Yard	56	0	21½	81	0	19¼	90	0	20⅙	78	0	18
Fore Topsail Yard	43	0	12	44	0	11	49	6	12	42	9	10½
Fore Topgallant Yard	21	6	5⅜	21	9	5¼	24	0	6	21	0	5
Main Yard	102	0	23	94	6	21¼	100	6	22½	90	0	20½
Main Topsail Yard	55	6	15¼	51	0	12	56	5	13	48	0	11¾
Main Topgallant Yard	24	0	6	24	9	5⅞	28	6	6½	25	0	6
Mizen Yard	81	0	15	76	0	12⅝	93	0	14	79	6	12½
Mizen Topsail Yard	25	10½	6⅞	26	3	6	30	0	6½	25	6	6
Crossjack	42	9	8½	51	0	8½	55	6	9⅓	54	0	9¼

TABLE 4: 1716 Anonymous Manuscript

Mast or Spar	100 guns			90 guns			80 guns			70 guns		
	Length Ft	Ins	Diam Ins	Length Ft	Ins	Diam Ins	Length Ft	Ins	Diam Ins	Length Ft	Ins	Diam Ins
Bowsprit	75	0	36	73	6	34¼	72	0	30	67	6	29
Sprit Topmast	28	6	9	22	6	7½	19	0	6½	18	0	6¼
Foremast	100	6	34	93	9	31¼	87	0	28	87	0	27
Fore Topmast	60	9	18½	55	6	16½	54	6	16¼	52	0	15¼
Fore Topgallant Mast	28	6	8½	24	0	7¼	22	6	7	21	0	6½
Main Mast	114	0	39	105	0	35	96	0	31	93	0	29½
Main Topmast	67	6	20¼	64	0	19½	60	0	18	58	6	17½
Main Topgallant Mast	33	0	9¼	28	6	8½	25	0	7¾	24	0	7½
Mizen Mast	96	0	22½	88	0	21	87	0	18	84	0	18
Mizen Topmast	31	6	11¾	28	6	12¼	27	0	11	27	0	10½
Spritsail Yard	63	0	15½	57	0	13½	54	0	12½	52	6	11¾
Sprit Topsail Yard	36	0	8	31	6	7½	28	0	6½	26	6	6¼
Fore Yard	93	0	23	90	0	20½	79	0	18	77	0	17½
Fore Topsail Yard	51	0	12½	49	6	12	48	0	10¾	46	0	10½
Fore Topgallant Yard	27	9	6½	24	0	6	24	0	6	23	0	5½
Main Yard	106	6	25	101	6	22½	90	0	20	87	0	19½
Main Topsail Yard	59	0	15	57	0	13	54	0	12	51	0	11½
Main Topgallant Yard	32	3	7¾	28	6	6½	27	0	6¼	25	6	6½
Mizen Yard	90	0	15½	90	0	15	79	0	13½	77	0	13¼
Mizen Topsail Yard	35	3	8	30	0	6½	28	6	6½	29	6	6¼
Crossjack	58	6	11¼	56	3	9¾	52	6	9	51	9	9½
Main Stunsail Boom	59	0	10½	57	6	10				49	6	8¾
Main Topsail Yard Stunsail Boom	38	0	8	37	0	7¾				32	0	6¾
Fore Stunsail Boom	55	0	9½	53	3	9¼				46	0	8
Ensign Staff	43	6	8¼	41	9	9	36	0	7¾	33	0	7¼
Jack Staff	17	3	4½	16	0	4¾				13	6	3¾

Note: Some of the fractions of the diameters given in the original manuscript were unusual: eg ⁹⁄₁₄, ⁵⁄₇ etc. I have converted them to the nearest common fractions.

3rd rate ROYAL OAK			4th rate MARY ROSE			5th rate EAGLE			6th rate GREYHOUND			6th rate DEPTFORD KETCH		
Length Ft	Ins	Diam Ins	Length Ft	Ins	Diam Ins	Length Ft	Ins	Diam Ins	Length Ft	Ins	Diam Ins	Length Ft	Ins	Diam Ins
66	0	29½	55	6	23	43	0	17½	39	0	14½	45	0	15
19	0	6½	19	6	5¾	13	0	4½	9	0	3¼			
88	0	29	72	5	21	64	6	16	52	6	14			
54	0	15½	47	0	13	36	0	10	32	3	8½			
21	0	7	18	0	5¼	15	0	4	13	6	3½			
97	6	32	84	0	24½	72	0	18½	61	6	15½	67	6	17½
62	0	18½	54	0	14	40	6	11	35	0	9½	26	0	8
24	9	8	21	0	5⅔	18	0	4½	15	0	4½	13	0	4
85	0	19	67	0	15	61	6	12	51	0	9½	42	0	8¾
33	0	9	24	0	6	20	0	5	17	0	5¼	12	0	3¾
55	0	13	45	0	10	36	0	8⅓	27	9	6	26	0	6½
29	0	6½	21	0	5	19	0	4½	15	0	3½	13	0	3
82	6	20	62	0	14	48	0	12	43	6	10			
45	0	11	36	0	8½	15	0	3½	21	9	5¼			
22	6	5	18	0	4	9	9	3	12	0	2¾			
93	0	22	72	0	16½	56	0	12½	49	6	11	44	0	11
52	0	12½	39	0	10	34	6	8	25	6	6	24	0	5½
25	6	5½	20	0	4½	14	3	4¼	12	9	3	12	0	3
82	0	13	64	6	10½	55	0	9	42	0	7	31	0	5
26	0	6	19	6	4½	19	6	4½	15	0	3½	12	0	3
55	6	9	38	0	6	34	0	6	26	0	4¼	24	0	4

60 guns			40 guns			32 guns			24 guns			14 guns		
Length Ft	Ins	Diam Ins	Length Ft	Ins	Diam Ins	Length Ft	Ins	Diam Ins	Length Ft	Ins	Diam Ins	Length Ft	Ins	Diam Ins
55	0	27	46	6	20	43	0	18¼	39	9	15½	30	0	13⅛
16	6	6	15	7	5¼	12	7	4¼	12	0	4¼	9	0	3
75	9	26⅓	67	0	20½	63	0	17¾	57	0	15⅚	46	6	13½
49	0	14¼	40	6	12¼	38	7½	10½	35	0	6¾	24	0	5¾
21	6	6	20	3	5⅔	15	0	4½	13	6	3½	11	4	3⅙
88	0	28¼	75	0	22	71	0	20	64	0	17½	52	6	15¼
55	6	16½	45	6	13½	44	4	12	39	0	10⅚	31	6	8¾
24	0	7	21	0	6¼	17	9	5	15	0	4⅙	12	0	3½
77	0	17	66	0	14	59	0	12½	54	0	11½	43	6	9
27	0	10½	15	9	8	16	6	7½	16	2	5⅚	17	0	4½
49	6	11	39	6	9½	36	0	9	34	6	8	27	0	6
25	0	6	21	0	4¾	18	0	4½	17	0	4	13	6	3¾
72	6	16¼	60	0	13¾	54	0	13½	51	0	12	40	6	9¾
45	0	10	36	0	8¾	30	0	7½	32	0	6¾	24	0	5¾
22	6	5¼	18	0	4½	15	0	4	15	0	3½	12	0	3
82	6	18¼	76	6	13½	74	4	12	69	0	10½	61	6	8⅜
49	6	10¾	41	0	10	36	0	9	35	0	8¼	27	9	6¾
25	0	6	21	0	5	18	0	4½	16	6	4	13	10	3½
72	0	12¼	60	0	10¼	54	0	9	51	0	9	40	6	6¾
25	6	6	23	0	5¼	19	6	4½	18	9	4½	13	6	3¼
49	6	8¼	39	9	7	36	0	6½	32	0	6	27	9	4¾
						36	0	6⅓	30	0	5¼			
						24	0	4½	19	0	3¾			
						33	6	5¾	28	0	4¾			
31	6	7	30	0	6¼	27	0	5	22	6	4⅙	19	6	3½
						10	6	2¾	9	0	2½			

TABLE 5: 1719 Establishment

Mast or Spar	100 guns			90 guns			80 guns			70 guns		
	Length Ft	Length Ins	Diam Ins	Length Ft	Length Ins	Diam Ins	Length Ft	Length Ins	Diam Ins	Length Ft	Length Ins	Diam Ins
Bowsprit	69	8	36⅛	65	8	34	60	0	31⅛	57	0	29½
Sprit Topmast	26	11	9	24	8	8¼	22	6	7½			
Jibboom	44	0	12¾	41	2	12	38	6	11¼	35	6	10¼
Foremast	102	7	34¼	96	9	32¼	91	6	30½	86	7½	28
Fore Topmast	62	3	19⅞	58	7	18¾	54	5	17¾	52	4	16¾
Fore Topgallant Mast	30	6	10¼	28	10	9⅝	29	0	9⅛	25	10	8⅝
Main Mast	114	0	38	107	6	35⅞	101	6	33⅞	96	3	31¼
Main Topmast	66	2	19⅞	62	6	18¾	59	0	17¾	55	10½	16¾
Main Topgallant Mast	32	8	10⅞	30	9	10¼	29	0	9⅝	27	6	9¼
Mizen Mast	96	6	22	91	0	20¾	85	11	19½	81	5	18½
Mizen Topmast	46	4	12⅞	43	9	12⅛	41	3	11½	39	0	10⅞
Spritsail Yard	63	2	13⅛	59	7	12⅜	57	5	12	54	10	11⅜
Sprit Topsail Yard	42	2	8⅜	39	9	8	38	3	7⅝	36	7	7¼
Fore Yard	89	11	20	81	11	19	78	11	18¼	75	6	17⅜
Fore Topsail Yard	63	2	13⅛	59	7	12⅜	57	5	12	54	10	11⅜
Fore Topgallant Yard	36	10	7⅜	34	9	7	33	6	6⅝	32	0	6⅜
Main Yard	99	4	23	93	7	21⅝	90	2	20¾	86	3	20
Main Topsail Yard	72	3	15	68	1	14⅛	65	7½	13⅝	62	8	13
Main Topgallant Yard	42	0	8¾	39	9	8	38	3	7⅝	36	7	7¼
Mizen Yard	82	9	14⅞	78	0	14	75	2	13½	71	10	13
Mizen Topsail Yard	47	4	9½	44	8	9	43	0	8⅝	41	1	8¼
Crossjack	63	2	13	59	7	12¼	57	5	11⅞	54	10	11¼
Bowsprit*	48	10		46	0		43	6		41	3	

* Bowsprit to be before the Stem

TABLE 6: 1745 Establishment

Mast or Spar	100 guns			90 guns			80 guns			70 guns		
	Length Ft	Length Ins	Diam Ins	Length Ft	Length Ins	Diam Ins	Length Ft	Length Ins	Diam Ins	Length Ft	Length Ins	Diam Ins
Bowsprit	73	3	26⅝	70	5	35¼	68	5	34¼	61	5	30¾
Sprit Topmast	26	4	8¾	25	4	8½	24	8	8¼			
Jibboom	51	0	14⅞	48	6	14⅛	47	0	13¾	45	0	13⅛
Fore Mast	102	5	34⅛	98	5	32¾	95	9	31⅞	90	3	30⅛
Fore Topmast	61	9	20½	59	5	19¾	57	9	19¼	55	2	18¼
Fore Topgallant Mast	29	8	9⅞	28	6	9½	27	9	9¼	27	9	9¼
Main Mast	114	5	38⅛	110	0	36⅝	106	11	35⅝	100	2	33⅜
Main Topmast	68	10	20½	66	0	19¾	64	2	19¼	60	7	18¼
Main Topgallant Mast	33	0	11	31	8	10½	30	9	10¼	30	9	10¼
Mizen Mast	99	7	22⅝	95	9	21¾	93	0	21⅛	86	9	19¾
Mizen Topmast	48	9	13½	46	10	13	45	7	12⅝	43	6	12⅛
Spritsail Yard	62	8	13⅝	59	10	12¾	58	1	12⅜	57	6	12⅜
Sprit Topsail Yard	43	3	8⅞	41	3	8⅜	40	1	8¼	40	0	8¼
Fore Yard	88	4	20⅞	83	8	20	81	4	19⅜	79	11	19
Fore Topsail Yard	62	8	13⅝	59	10	12¾	58	1	12⅜	57	6	12⅜
Fore Topgallant Yard	46	3	8⅞	41	3	8⅜	40	1	8¼	40	1	8¼
Main Yard	99	8	22⅜	95	0	22⅝	92	5	22	91	3	21¾
Main Topsail Yard	71	9	15¼	68	6	14⅝	66	6	14⅛	65	8	14⅛
Main Topgallant Yard	49	6	10	47	3	9⅝	45	11	9⅜	45	4	9¼
Mizen Yard	81	9	15⅜	78	1	14½	75	9	14	77	6	14⅜
Mizen Topsail Yard	47	0	9⅝	44	11	9¼	43	7	8⅞	43	9	9
Crossjack	62	8	13⅜	59	10	12¾	58	1	12⅜	57	6	12⅜
Bowsprit*	51	4		49	5		49	7		44	5	

* Bowsprit to be before the Stem

60 guns			50 guns			40 guns			30 guns			20 guns		
Length Ft	Ins	Diam Ins	Length Ft	Ins	Diam Ins	Length Ft	Ins	Diam Ins	Length Ft	Ins	Diam Ins	Length Ft	Ins	Diam Ins
54	2	28	50	5	24	46	10	20⅞	43	5	19¼	40	8	16½
33	0	9⅝	30	0	8¾	27	2	8	24	6	7¼	22	4	6½
82	1½	26⅝	76	6	22⅞	70	10½	21¼	65	10	19¾	61	8	18½
49	8	15⅞	46	1	14⅝	42	11	13¾	39	10	12¾	37	3	11⅞
24	5	8⅛	23	2	7⅝	21	0	7	18	9	6½	18	4	6⅛
91	3	29⅓	85	0	25½	78	11	23⅝	73	2	22	68	6	20½
53	0	15⅞	49	3	14⅜	45	9	13¾	42	6	12¾	39	9	11⅞
26	0	8⅝	24	2	8⅛	22	6	7½	20	10	7	19	6	6½
77	3	17⅝	71	10	16	66	3	14⅞	61	11	13¾	54	10	11¼
37	1	10¼	34	6	9⅝	32	0	8⅞	29	9	8¼	27	10	7¾
52	3	10⅞	48	8	10⅛	45	0	9⅜	41	5	8⅝	38	6	8
34	10	7	32	5	6⅜	30	0	6	27	7	5⅜	25	8	5⅛
71	11	16⅝	66	11	15⅜	61	11	14¼	56	11	13⅛	52	11	12¼
52	3	10⅞	48	8	10⅛	45	0	9⅜	41	5	8⅝	38	6	8
30	6	6	28	4	5⅝	26	3	5¼	24	2	4⅞	22	6	4½
82	2	19	76	6	17⅞	70	9	16¾	65	1	15	60	6	14
59	9	12⅜	55	7	11⅝	51	6	10¾	47	4	9⅞	44	0	9⅛
34	10½	7	32	6	6½	30	0	6	27	7	5¾	25	8	5¼
68	6	12¼	63	5	11⅜	59	0	10½	54	3	9⅜	50	5	9
39	2	7¾	36	6	7¼	33	9	6¾	31	1	6¼	28	10	5¾
52	3	10¾	48	8	10	45	0	9¼	41	5	8½	36	5	7⅞
39	0		39	5		33	9		31	4		29	2	

60 guns			50 guns			44 guns			24 guns					
Length Ft	Ins	Diam Ins	Length Ft	Ins	Diam Ins	Length Ft	Ins	Diam Ins	Length Ft	Ins	Diam Ins	Length Ft	Ins	Diam Ins
58	2	29⅛	55	9	27⅞	51	6	25¾	44	6	22¼			
42	8	12½	41	0	12	37	6	11	32	0	9⅜			
85	6	28½	82	0	26⅜	75	8	24⅜	64	11	20			
52	2	17¼	50	2	16½	46	3	15¼	39	9	13⅛			
26	4	8¾	25	4	8½	23	4	7¾	18	11	6¼			
94	10	31⅝	91	0	29¼	84	0	27	73	0	22½			
57	4	17¼	55	1	16½	50	10	15¼	43	10	13⅛			
29	1	9¾	28	0	9¼	25	10	8⅝	21	0	7			
82	2	18¾	78	10	17⅞	72	9	16½	63	6	14½			
41	2	11½	39	6	11	36	5	10⅛	30	8	8½			
54	4	11⅝	52	1	11	47	8	10	41	11	8⅞			
37	6	7¾	35	11	7⅜	32	10	6⅝	28	11	5⅞			
76	1	18⅛	72	10	17¼	66	8	16	57	8	13¾			
54	4	11⅝	52	1	11	47	8	10	41	11	8⅞			
37	6	7¾	35	11	7⅜	32	10	6⅝	28	11	5⅞			
86	5	20⅝	82	10	19⅝	75	9	18	65	6	15½			
62	3	13¼	59	7	12¾	54	7	11⅝	47	7	10			
42	11	8¾	41	4	8½	37	8	7¾	32	10	6⅝			
70	10	13⅛	67	9	12½	62	4	11¾	55	0	10⅞			
40	9	8⅜	39	1	8	35	9	7⅛	31	5	6¼			
54	4	11⅝	52	1	11	47	8	10	41	11	8⅞			
41	11		40	3		37	2		32	2				

TABLE 7: 1754 dimensions, Plymouth Yard manuscript

	100 guns			90 guns			80 guns			70 guns		
	Length		Diam	Length		Diam	Length		Diam	Length		Diam
Mast or Spar	Ft	Ins	Ins	Ft	Ins	Ins	Ft	Ins	Ins	Ft	Ins	Ins
Bowsprit	73	3	36⅝	70	5	35¼	68	5	34¼	61	5	30¾
Jibboom	51	0	14⅞	48	6	14⅛	47	0	13¾	45	0	13⅛
Fore Mast	102	5	34⅛	98	5	32¾	95	9	31⅞	90	3	30⅛
Fore Topmast	61	9	20½	59	5	19¾	57	9	19¼	55	2	18¼
Fore Topgallant Mast	29	8	9⅛	28	6	9½	27	9	9¼	27	9	9¼
Main Mast	114	5	38⅛	110	0	36⅝	106	11	35⅝	106	2	33⅜
Main Topmast	68	8	20½	66	0	19¾	64	2	19¼	60	7	18¼
Main Topgallant Mast	33	0	11	31	8	10½	30	9	10¼	30	9	10¼
Mizen Mast	99	7	22⅝	95	9	21¾	93	0	21⅛	86	9	19¾
Mizen Topmast	48	9	13½	46	10	13	45	7	12⅝	43	6	12⅛
Spritsail Yard	62	8	13⅜	59	10	12¾	58	1	12⅜	57	6	12⅜
Fore Yard	88	4	20⅞	83	8	20	81	4	19⅝	79	9	19
Fore Topsail Yard	62	8	13⅜	59	10	12¾	58	1	12⅜	57	6	12⅜
Fore Topgallant Yard	43	3	8⅞	41	3	8¾	40	1	8¼	40	1	8¼
Main Yard	99	8	22⅜	95	0	22⅝	92	5	22	91	3	21¾
Main Topsail Yard	71	9	15¼	68	6	14⅝	66	6	14⅛	65	8	14⅛
Main Topgallant Yard	49	6	10	47	3	9⅝	45	11	9⅜	45	4	9¼
Mizen Yard	81	9	15⅜	78	1	14½	75	9	14	77	6	14⅜
Mizen Topsail Yard	47	0	9⅝	44	11	9¼	43	7	8⅞	43	9	9
Crossjack	68	8	13⅝	59	3	12¾	58	1	12⅜	57	6	12⅜

TABLE 8: 1773 Establishment, Admiral Penrose's manuscript

	100 guns 1st rate			90 guns 2nd rate			80 guns 3rd rate			74 guns 3rd rate		
	VICTORY			PRINCESS ROYAL			CAMBRIDGE			VALIANT		
	Length		Diam	Length		Diam	Length		Diam	Length		Diam
Mast or Spar	Ft	Ins	Ins	Ft	Ins	Ins	Ft	Ins	Ins	Ft	Ins	Ins
Bowsprit	73	6	36⅛	70	10	35⅝	68	5	30¼	69	5	36
Jibboom	52	6	15¼	50	0	14½	47	0	13¾	46	6	12⅞
Foremast	103	6	34½	100	6	33½	95	9	31⅞	102	0	34
Fore Topmast	62	10	20⅝	59	0	19¾	57	9	19¼	63	0	21½
Fore Topgallant Mast	31	0	10¾	28	6	9½	27	9	9¼	29	2	10½
Main Mast	115	10	38⅞	112	0	37¼	106	11	35⅞	115	4	38¼
Main Topmast	68	10	20⅝	66	0	19¾	64	2	19½	67	4	24½
Main Topgallant Mast	34	5	11⅝	33	0	11	30	9	10¼	32	7	10½
Mizen Mast	101	4	23	96	8	22¼	93	0	21⅛	98	0	23¼
If stepped in the Hold												
Mizen Topmast	49	5	13¾	47	6	13¼	45	7	12⅝	47	7	13¼
Spritsail Yard	64	6	13¾	60	6	12⅛	58	1	12⅜	66	0	12⅛
Sprit Topsail Yard	43	6	8⅝	39	8	8¼	40	1	8¼	42	0	8½
Fore Yard	89	1	20⅞	84	0	20	81	4	19⅝	85	6	20⅞
Fore Topsail Yard	64	6	13¾	60	6	12⅜	58	1	12⅜	64	1	13⅝
Fore Topgallant Yard	43	6	8⅜	40	6	8¼	40	1	8¼	37	0	8
Main Yard	102	4	24	97	0	22	92	5	22	98	5	24
Main Topsail Yard	73	8	15½	69	6	14¾	66	6	14⅛	69	5	15¼
Main Topgallant Yard	48	9	10	46	6	9⅜	45	11	9¾	42	0	8½
Mizen Yard	87	8	15⅞	82	7	15	75	9	14	81	7	16¼
Mizen Gaff												
Mizen Topsail Yard	49	0	10⅛	47	0	9¾	43	7	8⅞	47	8	9¾
Crossjack	64	6	13¾	60	6	12⅛	58	1	12⅜	66	0	12⅛

60 guns			50 guns			44 guns			24 guns			Sloop of 264 tons		
Length		Diam	Length		Diam	Length		Diam	Length		Diam	Length		Diam
Ft	Ins	Ins	Ft	Ins	Ins	Ft	Ins	Ins	Ft	Ins	Ins	Ft	Ins	Ins
58	2	28	55	9	27⅞	51	6	25¾	44	6	22¼	37	6	16
42	8	12½	41	0	12	37	6	11	32	0	9⅜	27	0	8½
85	6	28½	82	0	26⅜	75	8	24⅜	64	11	20	56	2	16
52	2	17¼	50	2	16½	46	3	15¼	39	9	13⅛	36	6	11
26	4	8¾	25	4	8¼	23	4	7¾	18	11	6½	17	0	5½
95	8	31⅝	91	0	29¼	84	0	27	73	0	22½	68	1	19
57	4	17¼	55	1	16½	50	10	15¼	43	10	13⅛	39	6	11
29	1	9¾	28	0	9¼	25	10	8⅛	21	0	7	16	7	5½
82	2	18¾	78	10	17⅞	72	9	16½	63	6	14½			
41	2	11½	39	6	11	36	5	10⅛	30	8	8½			
54	4	11⅝	52	1	11	47	8	10	41	7	8⅞			
76	1	18⅛	72	10	17¼	66	8	16	57	8	13¾	49	3	11½
54	4	11⅝	52	1	11	47	8	10	41	11	8⅞	34	0	7
37	6	7¾	35	11	7⅜	32	10	6⅝	28	11	5⅞			
86	5	20⅝	82	10	19⅝	75	9	18	65	6	15½	51	4	12
62	3	13¼	59	7	12¾	54	7	11⅝	47	7	10	34	0	7
42	11	8¾	41	2	8½	37	8	7¾	32	10	6⅝	24	0	5
70	10	13⅛	67	11	12½	62	2	11¾	55	0	10⅛			
40	9	8⅜	39	1	8	35	9	7⅛	31	5	6¼			
54	4	11⅝	52	1	11	47	8	10	41	11	8⅞			

60 guns 4th rate			44 guns 5th rate			28 guns 6th rate			20 guns 6th rate			14 gun Sloop 6th rate		
RIPPON			ROEBUCK			ACTEON			(No name given)			SWAN		
Length		Diam	Length		Diam	Length		Diam	Length		Diam	Length		Diam
Ft	Ins	Ins	Ft	Ins	Ins	Ft	Ins	Ins	Ft	Ins	Ins	Ft	Ins	Ins
58	2	29⅛	52	6	26	50	5	23⅞	42	5	21⅛	37	6	17⅞
42	8	12½	38	10	11¼	35	3	14¼	30	6	8⅞	27	0	8⅛
85	6	28½	78	0	23¼	71	9	20⅞	60	10	19⅝	62	9	16⅜
52	2	17¼	46	10	15¾	43	0	14⅜	45	5	13⅛	33	9	11¼
26	4	8¾	23	4	7¾	21	6	7	18	11	6¼	16	10	5⅝
94	10	31⅝	88	0	26¼	81	4	23⅝	67	11	22	63	0	18⅞
57	4	17¼	53	0	15¾	48	9	14⅜	43	10	13⅛	37	6	11¼
29	1	9¾	26	6	8¾	24	4	8	21	0	7	18	9	6¼
82	2	18¾	74	4	16⅞	68	0	15¼	61	1	13⅞	48	0	12
												52	6	
41	2	11⅓	40	2	11¾	30	7	10⅛	30	8	8½	26	7	7⅜
54	4	11⅝	51	4	10¾	46	4	9¾	38	6	8⅛	35	0	7⅜
37	6	7¾	36	6	7½	28	4	5⅝	26	7	5⅛	22	0	4⅝
76	1	18⅛	69	10	16¼	62	2	14¼	52	11	12½	48	5	11¼
54	4	11⅝	52	2	10¾	46	4	9¾	38	6	8⅛	35	0	7¼
37	6	7¾	32	2	6¼	28	4	5⅝	26	7	5⅝	22	0	4⅝
86	5	20⅝	78	6	18½	71	3	16⅜	60	6	14⅜	55	0	12¾
62	3	13¼	57	6	11⅞	52	9	11	44	0	9⅜	39	6	8¼
42	11	8¾	36	6	7⅜	32	1	6⅜	30	4	6⅛	25	0	5
70	10	13⅛	71	0	12⅞	63	4	11½	50	5	9¼			
												23	10	6⅝
40	9	8⅝	39	6	8	35	2	6⅝	28	10	5⅛	26	3	5⅜
54	4	11⅝	51	4	10¾	46	4	9¾	38	6	8⅛	35	0	7⅜

TABLE 9: 1815 Burney edition of Falconer

Mast or Spar	110 guns Length Ft	Ins	Diam Ins	90 guns Length Ft	Ins	Diam Ins	80 guns Length Ft	Ins	Diam Ins	74 guns Length Ft	Ins	Diam Ins
Bowsprit	74	0	37	71	0	35½	68	0	34	67	6	35
Jibboom	53	0	15½	50	0	14½	48	6	14	48	6	14
Fore Mast	103	6	34½	100	0	33½	95	9	31⅞	98	6	32¾
Fore Topmast	62	10	20¾	59	0	19¾	59	9	19¼	58	8	19¾
Fore Topgallant Mast	31	0	10¾	29	0	9⅝	28	6	9¼	29	4	9¾
Main Mast	117	0	39	112	0	37¼	107	0	35⅝	110	0	37
Main Topmast	70	0	20¾	66	0	19¾	64	0	19¼	66	0	19¾
Main Topgallant Mast	35	0	11⅝	33	0	11	32	0	10¼	33	0	11¼
Mizen Mast	101	4	23	96	6	22¼	93	0	21⅛	95	0	22¼
Mizen Topmast	52	0	14	49	0	13½	46	0	13¼	49	0	13½
Mizen Topgallant Mast	26	0	8⅝	24	0	8	23	0	7⅝	24	6	8¼
Spritsail Yard	64	6	13¾	61	0	12⅞	58	0	12¼	62	0	13
Sprit Topsail Yard	43	0	8⅝	40	6	8¼	40	0	8¼	40	6	8¼
Fore Yard	89	1	21	85	9	20	81	4	19⅜	85	0	20
Fore Topsail Yard	64	6	13⅜	61	0	12⅞	58	0	12¼	63	0	13
Fore Topgallant Yard	43	0	8⅝	40	6	8¼	40	0	8⅛	40	6	8¼
Fore Royal Yard	27	0	6⅞	25	0	6⅜	24	0	6⅛	25	0	6½
Main Yard	102	4	24	98	0	22½	93	0	22	99	0	23
Main Topsail Yard	73	0	15½	70	0	14¾	66	6	14⅛	72	0	15
Main Topgallant Yard	48	9	10	46	6	9⅜	46	0	9¼	46	6	9½
Main Royal Yard	32	0	7¾	30	0	7⅜	28	0	7	28	0	7½
Mizen Yard	87	0	16	84	0	15	76	0	14½	84	0	15½
Mizen Boom												
Mizen Gaff												
Crossjack	64	6	13¾	61	0	12⅞	58	0	12¼	62	0	13
Mizen Topsail Yard	49	0	10⅛	47	0	9¾	43	0	8⅞	47	0	9¾
Mizen Topgallant Yard	32	9	6½	31	0	6¼	29	0	5¾	31	6	6⅜
Mizen Royal Yard	24	0	5	23	0	4⅞	21	0	4⅜	23	0	4⅞
Stunsail Yards												
Fore Topsail	25	6	5⅛	24	6	5	23	4	4¾	24	6	5
Fore Topgallant	18	6	3¾	17	6	3½	16	6	3¼	17	9	3½
Main Lower	33	0	6¾	31	0	6¼	29	6	6	31	0	6¼
Main Topsail	29	6	6	28	0	5¾	26	6	5¼	27	3	5½
Main Topgallant	21	0	4¼	20	0	4	19	0	3¾	20	0	4

64 guns			50 guns			44 guns			38 guns		
Length		Diam	Length		Diam	Length		Diam	Length		Diam
Ft	Ins	Ins	Ft	Ins	Ins	Ft	Ins	Ins	Ft	Ins	Ins
60	4	31½	56	0	29	52	6	26¼	55	0	27
43	0	12½	40	0	11½	37	6	11	39	3	11½
89	7	29¾	81	6	26⅜	78	0	23⅝	80	0	23⅝
53	0	17⅝	48	0	16	47	0	15¾	48	0	16⅛
26	6	8¾	24	0	8	23	6	7¾	24	0	8
101	0	33½	92	0	29	88	0	26¼	90	0	27
58	6	17⅝	53	0	16	53	0	15¾	54	0	16⅛
29	3	9¾	26	6	8⅞	26	6	8¾	27	0	9
86	0	19¾	78	9	19⅜	74	6	17⅞	75	7	18⅛
43	6	12¼	40	0	11⅛	40	0	11	41	0	11¼
21	9	7¼	20	0	6⅝	20	0	6⅝	20	6	6¾
57	6	12⅛	52	6	11	52	0	10¾	53	0	11½
34	6	7	31	6	6¼	32	0	6⅝	32	9	6½
79	6	18½	72	0	17	70	0	16¼	71	6	16⅜
57	6	12⅛	52	6	11	52	0	10¾	53	0	11½
34	6	7	31	6	6¼	32	0	6⅜	32	9	6½
23	0	6	23	0	5½	23	0	5⅜	23	0	5¾
90	4	21	82	0	19¼	80	0	18½	81	9	19
66	0	13⅝	60	9	12½	57	6	11⅞	59	0	12¼
39	0	7⅞	36	0	7⅜	36	0	7⅜	37	0	7½
27	0	6¾	26	0	6¼	25	0	5⅞	25	0	6⅛
77	0	14									
			44	0	11½	36	8	11	38	0	11½
			31	6	6¼	32	0	6⅜	32	9	6½
57	6	12⅛	52	6	11	52	0	10¾	53	0	11½
43	3	9	39	6	8¼	39	6	8	40	0	8¼
29	0	5¾	26	0	5¼	25	9	5⅛	27	9	5½
21	0	4½	19	0	4⅛	19	0	4	20	0	4⅛
22	9	4½	20	6	4⅛	20	0	4	20	6	4⅛
16	6	3¼	15	0	3	15	0	3	15	0	3
29	0	5¾	26	0	5¼	25	6	5⅛	26	0	5¼
25	9	5⅛	23	6	4⅜	23	0	4¾	23	6	4¾
18	9	3¾	17	6	3½	16	6	3¼	17	0	3½

TABLE 10: 1832 Edye's Equipment & Displacement

Mast or Spar	120 guns SHIP Length Ft	Ins	Diam Ins	80 guns SHIP Length Ft	Ins	Diam Ins	74 guns SHIP Length Ft	Ins	Diam Ins	50 guns RAZEE Length Ft	Ins	Diam Ins
Bowsprit	75	1	36⅞	71	11	36	66	0	34⅛	66	0	34⅛
Jibboom	52	6	15¼	50	0	14½	48	0	14⅛	48	0	14⅛
Fore Mast	110	4	36¾	108	0	36	98	6	31¼	90	6	31
Fore Topmast	62	10	20⅜	62	2	20¾	57	8	19¼	57	8	19¼
Fore Topgallant Mast	31	0	10¾	30	0	10	28	10	9⅝	28	10	9⅝
Main Mast	112	8	40	118	10	39¾	108	0	36	108	0	36
Main Topmast	68	10	20⅝	69	0	20¾	64	10	19¼	64	10	19¼
Main Topgallant Mast	34	5	11⅝	34	6	11⅜	33	0	11	33	0	11
Mizen Mast	81	8	24½	81	8	24¾	73	11	21⅝	79	4½	24
Mizen Topmast	49	5	13¾	50	4	14	47	8	13	47	8	13
Mizen Topgallant Mast	24	8	8⅝	24	8	8½	24	0	8	24	0	8
Spritsail Yard	64	6	13¾	64	8	13⅞	61	6	12¾	61	6	12¾
Fore Yard	91	1	21½	89	9	21½	84	4	19⅝	84	4	19⅝
Fore Topsail Yard	64	6	13¾	64	8	13⅞	61	6	12¾	61	6	12¾
Fore Topgallant Yard	42	8	8⅝	38	10	8	40	0	8½	40	0	8½
Main Yard	104	4	24⅝	103	3	24¾	96	8	22⅝	96	8	22⅝
Main Topsail Yard	73	8	15½	74	3	16	70	6	14⅝	70	6	14⅝
Main Topgallant Yard	48	9	10	46	0	9⅜	45	10	9¼	45	10	9¼
Mizen Boom	69	7	13¾	70	1½	13⅞	68	3	12¾	68	3	12¾
Mizen Gaff	51	6	12⅝	52	1	12	49	11	11⅝	49	11	11⅝
Mizen Topsail Yard	49	0	10⅛	49	0	10⅛	46	1	9⅝	46	1	9⅝
Mizen Topgallant Yard	36	3	6½	34	0	7	31	9	6⅛	31	9	6⅛
Mizen Crossjack	73	8	15½	74	3	16	70	6	14⅝	70	6	14⅝

52 guns			46 guns			26 guns			28 guns/18 guns			18 guns		
FRIGATE			FRIGATE			RAZEE CORVETTE			SHIP/CORVETTE			BRIG		
Length		Diam	Length		Diam	Length		Diam	Length		Diam	Length		Diam
Ft	Ins	Ins	Ft	Ins	Ins	Ft	Ins	Ins	Ft	Ins	Ins	Ft	Ins	Ins
64	6	31½	54	6	26½	54	4	26½	44	7	21⅛	43	4	20
48	0	14⅛	39	5	11¾	39	1	11⅝	33	0	8⅞	27	0	8½
90	6	31	82	6	25	80	10	25⅝	64	6	19	59	9	20
57	8	19¼	47	10	16⅛	45	10	16⅛	38	2	12¾	36	6	12¼
28	10	9⅝	23	5	7¾	23	9	7⅞	19	1	6⅜	25	10	7⅛
99	6	34½	90	0	28	88	0	28	71	0	20½	68	3	21⅜
64	10	19¼	54	0	16⅛	54	0	16⅛	43	2	12¾	38	11	12¼
33	0	11	27	0	9	27	0	9	21	7	7⅛	25	10	7⅛
72	0	22½	65	1	19	62	1	19½	54	0	16¼			
47	8	13	41	0	11⅞	40	6	11¼	32	5	9			
24	0	8	20	6	6⅞	20	3	6¾	16	4	5½			
61	6	12¾	53	4	11½	52	8	11	41	0	8½	42	0	8½
84	4	19⅝	71	5	16⅜	70	7	16¼	55	0	12⅝	54	6	11⅜
61	6	12¾	53	4	11¼	52	8	11	41	0	8½	42	0	8½
40	0	8½	32	11	6¾	32	0	6⅜	25	0	5½	27	6	6
98	4	22⅝	81	9	18⅞	80	10	18⅝	63	0	14½	54	7	11⅜
70	6	14⅝	59	0	12¼	59	0	12¼	46	6	9¾	42	0	8½
45	10	9¼	37	6	7¼	37	6	7½	28	4	6	27	6	6
66	7	12¾	55	9	11½	58	0	13⅛	43	11	8½	58	0	13½
49	11	11⅝	39	0	9⅜	40	10	9¾	32	6	7¾	34	0	9⅜
46	1	9⅝	41	6	8¼	40	0	8	31	0	5⅞			
31	9	6⅛	28	0	5½	28	0	5¼	21	4	4½			
70	6	14⅝	59	0	12¼	59	0	12¼	46	6	9¾			

TABLE 11: 1838 Admiralty Order

Mast or Spar	1st Class THREE DECK SHIP			2nd Class TWO DECK SHIP			3rd Class TWO DECK SHIP			1st Class FRIGATE		
	Length Ft	Ins	Diam Ins	Length Ft	Ins	Diam Ins	Length Ft	Ins	Diam Ins	Length Ft	Ins	Diam Ins
Bowsprit (withoutboard)	52	6	41	51	0	40	48	6	38	45	6	36
Jibboom	53	0	16½	49	0	16	49	0	16	47	0	15½
Flying Jibboom				Length beyond the Jibboom to be ⅔ of the Jibboom								
Fore Mast*	75	0	38	79	3	37	72	9	35	77	0	35
Fore Topmast	65	0	22	62	6	22	59	6	21½	57	6	21½
Fore Topgallant Mast	29	6	12	28	0	11½	27	0	11	26	0	10½
Fore Topgallant Pole	19	6		19	0		18	0		17	6	
Main Mast*	84	0	42	86	3	40	81	0	38	73	6	37
Main Topmast	73	6	22	70	6	22	67	6	21½	65	0	21½
Main Topgallant Mast	33	0	13	31	6	12½	30	6	12	29	6	12
Main Topgallant Pole	22	0		21	0		20	6		19	6	
Mizen Mast*	59	0	26	63	2	26	57	5	24	67	6	24
Mizen Topmast	52	6	17	50	6	16	48	6	15½	46	6	14½
Mizen Topgallant Mast	24	0	9½	23	6	9	22	6	9	21	6	8½
Mizen Topgallant Pole	16	6		16	0		15	0		14	6	
Fore Yard	96	0	23	91	0	22	86	6	21	82	6	20
Fore Topsail Yard**	68	0	15	65	0	14½	62	0	13½	59	0	13
Fore Topgallant Yard	43	0	10	41	6	10	40	0	9½	38	0	9
Fore Royal Yard	30	6	6	29	6	6	28	6	6	27	6	5½
Main Yard	110	0	26½	105	0	25	100	6	24	96	0	23
Main Topsail Yard	78	0	16½	74	0	16	71	0	15½	68	0	15
Main Topgallant Yard	49	0	11½	46	0	11	45	0	11	43	0	10
Main Royal Yard	34	0	7	32	6	6½	31	6	6½	30	6	6
Mizen Boom	72	0	16½	70	0	16	66	6	15½	64	0	15
Mizen Gaff	51	0	11½	49	0	11	47	0	11	45	0	10½
Crossjack	74	6	18	71	0	17	67	6	16	64	0	15½
Mizen Topsail Yard	54	0	12	51	6	11½	49	0	11	47	0	10½
Mizen Topgallant Yard	35	0	8½	33	6	8	32	0	8	31	0	7½
Mizen Royal Yard	25	6	5	24	6	5	23	6	5	23	0	4½
Stunsail Booms												
Fore and Main Lower	63	6	12½	60	0	12	58	0	11½	55	0	11
Fore Topsail	48	0	9½	45	6	9	43	3	8½	41	3	8½
Fore Topgallant	34	0	7	32	3	6½	30	6	6	29	6	6
Main Topsail	55	6	11	52	6	10½	50	3	10	48	0	9½
Main Topgallant	39	0	8	37	0	7½	35	6	7	34	0	7
Stunsail Yards												
Fore and Main Lower	41	0	8	41	0	8	41	0	8	41	0	8
Fore Topsail (Large)	33	3	6½	33	3	6½	33	3	6½	33	3	6½
Fore Topsail (Small)	29	6	6	29	6	6	29	6	6	29	6	6
Fore Topgallant	21	9	4½	21	9	4½	21	9	4½	21	9	4½
Main Topsail	33	3	6½	33	3	6½	33	3	6½	33	3	6½
Main Topgallant	25	6	5	25	6	5	25	6	5	25	6	5

* Deck to Head   **and Spritsail Yard

4th Class FRIGATE			7th Class FRIGATE			10th Class FRIGATE			1st Class CORVETTE			1st Class BRIG		
Length Ft	Ins	Diam Ins	Length Ft	Ins	Diam Ins	Length Ft	Ins	Diam Ins	Length Ft	Ins	Diam Ins	Length Ft	Ins	Diam Ins
40	0	30	34	0	26	29	0	22½	32	0	24	31	0	24
42	0	13½	37	0	12	33	0	10½	36	0	11½	34	6	11
Length beyond the Jibboom to be ⅔ of the Jibboom														
65	0	30	60	0	26	48	6	22½	58	0	24	59	8½	24
52	6	19½	44	6	16	39	6	14	42	6	15½	41	0	14½
23	6	9	21	0	8	18	6	7	20	0	8	19	6	7½
16	0		14	0		12	6		13	6		13	0	
71	6	32	66	0	28	53	6	24	63	0	26	64	10	26
57	6	18½	50	6	16	44	6	14	48	6	15½	46	6	14½
26	0	10½	23	6	9	21	0	8	22	6	9	21	6	8½
17	6		16	0		14	0		15	0		14	6	
57	0	22½	53	6	20	43	6	18	51	6	18			
42	6	13½	37	6	11½	33	0	10	36	0	11			
20	0	8	18	0	7	16	0	6	17	0	6½			
13	6		12	6		11	0		12	0				
71	0	17	61	0	14½	52	6	12½	61	0	14½	55	0	13
51	6	11½	45	0	10	39	0	8½	45	0	10	41	0	9
33	6	8	29	6	7½	26	0	6½	29	6	7½	27	0	6½
24	6	5	22	0	4½	19	6	4	22	0	4½	20	6	4
82	6	20	71	0	17	61	0	14½	67	6	16	64	0	15½
59	0	13	51	6	11½	45	0	10	49	0	11	47	0	10½
38	0	9	33	6	8	29	6	7½	32	0	8	31	0	7½
27	6	5½	24	6	5	22	0	4½	23	6	5	23	0	4½
55	6	13	48	6	11½	42	0	10	46	0	11	59	0	13½
39	0	8½	34	0	8	29	0	6½	32	0	7½	39	0	8½
58	0	13½	50	0	12	43	0	10	47	6	11½			
43	0	9½	37	6	8	33	0	7	36	0	8			
28	6	7	25	0	6	22	0	5½	24	0	6			
21	0	4½	19	0	4	17	0	3½	18	0	3½			
47	0	9½	40	6	8	35	0	7	38	6	8	36	6	7½
35	6	7	30	6	6	26	6	5½	29	0	6	27	6	5½
25	9	5	22	3	4½	19	6	4	21	3	4½	20	6	4
41	3	8	35	6	7	30	6	6	33	9	7	32	0	6½
29	6	6	25	9	5	22	3	4½	24	6	5	23	6	4½
37	0	7½	29	6	6	29	6	6	27	6	5½	27	6	5½
27	6	5½	21	9	4½	19	9	4	19	9	4	21	9	4½
23	9	5	18	0	3½	16	0	3	16	0	3	18	0	3½
18	0	3½	12	0	2½	10	0	2	10	0	2	14	0	3
27	6	5½	21	9	4½	19	9	4	19	9	4	23	9	4½
21	9	4½	16	0	3	14	0	3	14	0	3	14	0	3

Index

Part I

Part II

Part III

Part IV